RESEARCH METHODS
in ACCOUNTING

Sara Miller McCune founded SAGE Publishing in 1965 to support the dissemination of usable knowledge and educate a global community. SAGE publishes more than 1000 journals and over 800 new books each year, spanning a wide range of subject areas. Our growing selection of library products includes archives, data, case studies and video. SAGE remains majority owned by our founder and after her lifetime will become owned by a charitable trust that secures the company's continued independence.

Los Angeles | London | New Delhi | Singapore | Washington DC | Melbourne

Malcolm Smith

RESEARCH METHODS
in ACCOUNTING

FOURTH
EDITION

Los Angeles | London | New Delhi
Singapore | Washington DC | Melbourne

Los Angeles | London | New Delhi
Singapore | Washington DC | Melbourne

SAGE Publications Ltd
1 Oliver's Yard
55 City Road
London EC1Y 1SP

SAGE Publications Inc.
2455 Teller Road
Thousand Oaks, California 91320

SAGE Publications India Pvt Ltd
B 1/I 1 Mohan Cooperative Industrial Area
Mathura Road
New Delhi 110 044

SAGE Publications Asia-Pacific Pte Ltd
3 Church Street
#10-04 Samsung Hub
Singapore 049483

Editor: Matthew Waters
Editorial assistant: Lyndsay Aitken
Production editor: Victoria Nicholas
Copyeditor: Jen Hinchliffe
Proofreader: Camille Bramall
Marketing manager: Alison Borg
Cover design: Francis Kenney
Typeset by: C&M Digitals (P) Ltd, Chennai, India
Printed in the UK

First edition published 2003. Reprinted 2004, 2005, 2006,
2007 (twice), 2009 (twice). Second edition published 2011.
Third edition published 2014.

Library of Congress Control Number: 2016956225

British Library Cataloguing in Publication data

A catalogue record for this book is available from
the British Library

ISBN 978-1-52640-106-9
ISBN 978-1-52640-107-6 (pbk)

This book is dedicated to Beth, Roy and Gracie

Contents

List of Figures   x
List of Tables   xi
Preface   xii
Acknowledgements   xv

1 **Introduction and Overview**   1

    Theory as testable explanation   6
    A critical approach to accounting research   8

2 **Developing the Research Idea**   15

    The research sequence   15
    Emergence of the research topic   19
    The research proposal   21
    Conceptual frameworks   22
    The structure of DNA: the development of new theory   25
    The Bradman problem: the development of new strategies   26
    The longitude problem: implementing solutions   29
    Searching the family tree: qualitative archival research   31
    The Holy Grail: experiments in the field   32
    Strategic management accounting   34

3 **Theory, Literature and Hypotheses**   37

    Sources of theory   37
    Grounded theory   49
    Searching the literature   51
    Modelling the relationship   54
    Developing the hypotheses   58
    Validity concerns   59

4 Research Ethics in Accounting   **63**

The ethics quiz   64
Informed consent   66
Ethical guidelines   69

5 Data Collection   **72**

Choosing a research method   72
Sample selection   74
Measurement issues   75
Data management   78
Qualitative research   79

6 Quantitative Data Analysis   **82**

Descriptive statistics   82
Differences in sample means   86
Measures of association   91
Analysis of variance   94
Multivariate model-building   98

7 Qualitative Data Analysis   **119**

Data management   119
Validity concerns   121
Content analysis   122
Protocol analysis   125

8 Experimental Research   **127**

The problem statement   128
Theory and context   128
Experimental design   131
The validity trade-off   135
Quasi-experimental research   139

9 Survey Research   **143**

Mail surveys   143
Design and planning issues   148
Pilot testing   150
Data collection   151
Measurement error   155
Interview methods   157

10 **Qualitative Methods**   **162**

   Fieldwork   163
   Case study methods   167
   Mixed Methods Research   170
   The qualitative analysis protocol   172
   Grounded theory   175
   Verbal protocol analysis   176

11 **Archival Research**   **179**

   Cross-section data   180
   Time-series data   182
   The validity trade-off in archival research   183
   Content analysis   184

12 **Supervision and Examination Processes**   **187**

   The role of the supervisor   188
   Examiner profiles   193
   The examination process   194

13 **Turning Research into Publications**   **199**

   Why publish?   199
   Where to publish?   200
   What to publish?   206
   How to publish?   210
   Co-authoring issues   213
   Concluding remarks   213

Appendix 1: Journal Rankings (ABDC–2017)   216
Appendix 2: Sample Paper   220

References   238
Index   266

List of Figures

2.1 The research sequence   16
2.2 The positivist approach   17
2.3 Alternative research methods   18
2.4 Kolb's Learning Cycle   23
2.5 The deductive process   23
2.6 The conceptual schema   24
2.7 Measurement issues   24
2.8 The Harvey-Jones approach to problem-solving   34
2.9 Generalised process-improvement sequence   35

3.1 Searching for construct validity   39
3.2 Voluntary disclosure and reciprocal causality   54
3.3 Intervening variables and causality   55
3.4 Non-financial focus as an intervening variable   55
3.5 Moderated causal relationship   56
3.6 Size, industry and culture moderating performance   56
3.7 Influence of extraneous variables   56
3.8 Economic conditions as extraneous variables   57
3.9 Multiple independent variables   57

6.1 Significance of test of proportion   84
6.2 χ^2-test for difference in frequencies   85
6.3 Test of significance of correlation coefficient   86
6.4 t-test for difference in means   87
6.5 t-test for paired-case difference in means   88
6.6 Mann–Whitney U-test for difference in means   90
6.7 Product–moment correlation coefficient (Pearson's r)   92
6.8 Coefficient of rank correlation (Spearman's rho)   93
6.9 Measure of association within contingency tables   94
6.10 One-way analysis of variance (ANOVA)   95
6.11 The Kruskal–Wallis multiple sample test   97
6.12 Summary of regression results for charity shops case study   103

List of Tables

1.1 summary of the differences in research assumptions, process and
     outcomes associated with each of the three major approaches   4

6.1 Summary of significance tests by measurement level   83
6.2 Measures of association by measurement level   91
6.3 ANOVA summary table   96
6.4 Summary of multivariate model-building methods by measurement level   98
6.5 PLS measurement model assessment criteria   107
6.6 PLS Structural model criteria   108

12.1 Expectations of supervisor and candidate   190

Preface

This fourth edition builds on those features that proved to be so successful in the three previous editions. The aim remains to provide an insider's view of the research process, by focusing on the actual choices made in the conduct of accounting research projects. In doing so we emphasise the importance of planning and preparation, in order to have a realistic perception of what might go wrong, so that appropriate corrective action can be taken. We must, however, acknowledge that no single author can be an expert in all research methods; this author is no exception. My own publications will readily reveal a preponderance of studies concerning experimental methods and the use of archival data; there are fewer instances of studies using survey and field study methods. It would be unwise of me to claim expertise in the implementation of all such methods, so this book must necessarily lean heavily on the work of others. For the same reasons, and because of pressure of space, this book does not address issues of finance, capital markets research or stock-price-related accounting research on the fringes of finance. The reactions of readers to the first three editions of the book have been most encouraging, but they have highlighted the acknowledged weaknesses of earlier editions, most notably with regard to 'theoretical foundations' and 'qualitative methods'; new sections have been added to this text to address these weaknesses.

Most other texts in this area remain long, over-theoretical and not particularly user-friendly. This book deliberately plays down both historical and philosophical considerations to adopt a practical approach that takes the reader from the initiation of the research idea right through to the publication of the research findings. The intended readership is wide, embracing instructors, doctoral candidates and academics starting, or re-starting, their research careers, but the focus is firmly on research students. Although the examples are mainly accounting based, much of the material will also be relevant to more general business applications. The practical examples employed are usually UK- or Australia-based, these being the two countries in which I have extensive experience of teaching, research, supervision and examining, but the principles should normally adapt easily to alternative environments.

An early distinction between 'methods' and 'methodologies' in research is essential because the two are so often confused, or else used interchangeably. Research methods are concerned with the technical issues associated with the conduct of research; research methodology is concerned with the philosophies associated with the choice of research method. After Chapter 1 this book is almost exclusively concerned with the former.

Chapter 2 examines the research idea, and the documentary sources that might aid their development. A number of examples, many from non-accounting environments, are used to illustrate the research sequence, and to examine research that is seeking either to improve outcomes, to explain improved outcomes through new theory or to examine the improvement process itself. Theoretical frameworks and research models are used extensively here to help the reader to picture the key variables and relationships underlying their research, and to facilitate their generating a respectable research proposal.

Theory is the focus of Chapter 3, on the basis that 'good research is founded on good theory'. The chapter addresses the sources of the theory widely applied in accounting research, but drawn from other disciplines. In the space available it cannot hope to be all-embracing, but does give an indication of the diversity of what is available, as well as directions for likely future developments. This chapter is expanded to provide increased recognition to non-economic theories, and to reflect the growing importance in accounting of diffusion theory and grounded theory, among others. Recognition of the importance of theory, reliability and validity as desirable characteristics of accounting research, lead, in Chapter 5, to a consideration of the issues of data collection and management. This is followed in Chapter 6 by a discussion of data analysis and hypothesis testing; this chapter remains unashamedly quantitative in nature, and considers panel data analysis, partial least squares and structural equation modelling. Chapter 7 has also been expanded to address further aspects of the analysis of qualitative data and to reflect the importance of mixed methods research in accounting.

Chapter 4 addresses the increasingly important ethical considerations that underpin the conduct of accounting research, and the subsequent publication of research findings. It highlights the confusion that is still apparent among many academics as to what constitutes unethical conduct, and specifies the necessary guidelines for good practice. The importance of ethical research practices is reflected in the early positioning of this chapter, so that it still precedes both **data collection** and **data analysis** in this new edition.

Chapters 8 to 11 are devoted, respectively, to the core forms of accounting research: experimental, survey-based, qualitative and archival. Numerous examples are used to demonstrate the relative advantages of alternative methods so that researchers can both make an informed choice and justify their preferred approach. Research can be based on quantitative or qualitative methods, and both should be equally acceptable as long as the most appropriate method has been chosen. The majority of the readers of this text will likely be higher-degree by research candidates (Masters or PhD) so Chapter 12 is devoted to supervisor–candidate relationships, highlighting the mutual responsibilities of all parties to the supervision process, from the outset right up to the outcome of the examination itself.

Publication is the natural target output of the research process, and Chapter 13 addresses the complexity of the publication process. In doing so it recognises that we are working in a dynamic environment; what was once acceptable in accounting research is no longer so because of a more appropriate emphasis on research ethics; what is publishable, at all or in specific journals, changes too, both with the passage of time and the retirement of particular journal editors. Many journals remain very conservative in the type of research they will publish, often on the grounds that it is difficult to demonstrate that 'new' methods constitute 'good' research in the same way as the traditional methods; this situation is changing but all too slowly! However, the emphasis on journal and university rankings, and associated funding systems based on the quality of publications, provide fresh difficulties. The provision of 'acceptable journals' listings by many universities, and the prohibition of publication elsewhere, perpetuate the position of the well-established journals, while making it extremely difficult for the editors of other journals to attract quality submissions. The opportunities for innovative new journals are also severely diminished in such circumstances.

Contributions to the profession by academic accountants are generally not well regarded, either by one's colleagues or by government bodies providing funding based on publications-performance, even though, arguably, the education of the potential employers of our students might be seen as an important part of our jobs. So journalistic pieces in practitioner magazines and workshops to professional audiences count for close to nought – even though the individuals concerned would never read a refereed journal or attend an academic conference. We need to exploit the available media to get our message, and the power of research findings, over to those implementing change in an unbiased way, before the consultants prevail. This process must be of mutual benefit to all parties, but if the practitioners feel they are being short-changed, or even used, then future collaborative efforts will be threatened. It is just such attitudes that generate the 'them and us' cultures leading to accusations of academics being out of touch with reality. In this context it is no coincidence that we continue to witness a widening of the relevance gap between 'research' and 'practice' during the period when positive accounting research has all but supplanted normative research. Where the emphasis among academics, and top journals, is on producing research that informs theory, rather than practice, then that gap will continue to widen. Since they are based on real-world situations, field studies in particular might be expected to provide the opportunity for bridging the gap between academic researchers and accounting practitioners.

Communication problems also remain. The timeliness and relevance of much of the content of the refereed literature does little more than suggest that it is written by academics, only for the consumption of other academics! Most practitioners do not have an appreciation of research methods, nor do they have easy access to refereed journals, so important findings and recommendations often do not reach the individuals who can make sure it has the greatest impact. A number of journals have emerged with the express intention of providing readable research for practitioner audiences, but even these have tended to become more academic and less readable over relatively short time periods. This book aims to provide a treatment of research methods that will be of use to both accounting practitioners and those contemplating the conduct of research projects. The continued growth of the importance of online sources and methods to accounting research is further reflected in this volume, and students will find a number of online blogs helpful as they progress on their research journey.

Space restrictions mean that this slim volume cannot hope to tackle all of the detail of the application of different research methods, or the associated intricacies of complex quantitative methods. But it should encourage candidates to become more reflective, and to keep asking themselves 'why?' when they make a specific research choice. If the use of this book causes one paper to be published that would otherwise have gone unpublished, then all will have been worthwhile.

Acknowledgements

This fourth edition could not have been completed without the help of numerous colleagues, most notably Zubaidah Ismail of Edith Cowan University, Basil Tucker of the University of South Australia and Saiyidi Matroni of Universiti Teknologi MARA Malaysia. However, as is normal, all errors and omissions remain the responsibility of the author.

Introduction and Overview

ONE

Chapter Contents

- Theory as testable explanation
- A critical approach to accounting research

A number of authors (e.g., Brownell, 1995: 2) describe accounting researchers as 'parasites' who prey on the work of others to generate their findings. The term may be an overstatement, but as with most rash generalisations it contains more than a germ of truth: accounting researchers have little theory of their own (they rely on economics, finance, psychology, sociology and organisational behaviour as their major sources); they have no methods of their own (they are all adapted from the natural and social sciences); and they have few instruments of their own (with many of these originating in, or adapted from, the organisational behaviour literature). Malmi and Granlund (2009) note that theories recognised as being 'real theories' by accounting researchers are generally those that have been adapted from other disciplines. Merchant (quoted in Brownell, 1995: 140) even suggests that organisational behaviourists are much better at developing survey instruments than their accounting counterparts.

The overall aim of this book is to facilitate the conduct of applied research studies in accounting, and to do this we must recognise our reliance on work in other disciplines. To accomplish this aim, a number of subordinate objectives may be identified, all of which will contribute to the overall goal:

- an understanding of contemporary research ideas in accounting, so that readers can identify and define research problems and prepare strategies for their solution;
- an awareness of alternative research methods, to facilitate the selection of the most appropriate method for addressing particular research questions;
- an ability to review existing research and to offer critiques of articles published in refereed journals; and
- an appreciation of the ethical constraints on the conduct of accounting research.

Research in accounting is concerned with solving problems, investigating relationships and building a body of knowledge. Because we rely to such a great extent on prior research in the natural and social sciences to do so, this volume will take a similar approach in leaning on work in other disciplines where it helps to inform accounting research.

Bennett (1991) identifies four basic levels of research:

- Description – concerned with the collection and reporting of data related to what is, or was, the case. This would include means and standard deviations of individual variables, and correlations between pairs of variables.
- Classification – still descriptive, but easing the reporting process, and highlighting similarities and clustering through grouping and classifying (e.g., through the familiar cross-tabulation facility in most basic statistical packages).
- Explanation – an attempt to make sense of observations by explaining the relationships observed and attributing causality based on some appropriate theory.
- Prediction – going beyond the understanding and explaining of the prior stage, to model observations in a way that allows testable predictions to be made of unknown events.

We return to this structure in Chapter 6 when discussing alternative quantitative methods, but an early distinction between 'explanation' and 'prediction' is appropriate here, because, as in the natural sciences, we are able to make excellent predictions of accounting behaviour without the backing of a sound underpinning theory. Bankruptcy prediction modelling provides an excellent example. A number of researchers (e.g., Altman, 1968; Taffler, 1983; Agarwal and Taffler, 2007) have developed models that have proved very successful in identifying 'distressed' companies – those companies that will fail in the short term. These models are statistically excellent but the theory underpinning their content, in terms of the ratios to be used and the variables they represent, is extremely weak; the essential problem is that such theories as we have (e.g., Wilcox, 1971; Blum, 1974; Myers, 1977; Scott, 1981) do not generate very good predictive models!

Good research generates the sound evidence needed to overturn or revise existing theories. These assertions will, in turn, yield to revised theories based on better evidence, so that healthy competition between rival ideas will lead to better explanations and more reliable predictions. Two major processes of reasoning, 'deductive' (theory to observation) and 'inductive' (observation to theory), are important for theory construction and observation testing. Inductive reasoning starts with specific observations (data) from which theories can be generated; a generalisable pattern may emerge from further observations and repeated testing for compliance. The natural sciences, for example astronomy, provide numerous examples of inductive reasoning, thus Hawking (1998) provides a number of fascinating examples of theories revised, or still in question, with implications for the progress of accounting research. However, he notes that generalisations made on the basis of induction can never be regarded as 'certain', since just one contrary instance can cause them to be overturned:

- **Big Bang versus Steady State.** From the late 1940s to the mid-1960s two competing theories were prominent in offering alternative explanations of the origins of the universe. The 'Big Bang' theory recognised a singular event as causing an ever-expanding universe in which matter (notably galaxies) becomes continuously more widely dispersed. The 'Steady State' theory, attributed to Bondi, Gold and Hoyle, on the other hand, suggested that matter was continuously being created to fill the gaps between existing galaxies. They argued that the universe had no beginning, and had been forever expanding, with new matter being created out of apparently empty space. The Steady State theory importantly provided testable hypotheses in suggesting that the universe should look the same at all times and from wherever it was viewed. But surveys of radio waves in the early 1960s showed that sources were more numerous in the past, and that there were many more weak (distant) sources than strong (close) ones. Further, microwave radiation studies in 1965 demonstrated that the universe did not have a common density – it had been much denser in the past. These observations provided disconfirmations of the Steady State theory, causing its abandonment.

- **Newton's Laws of Physics.** New theory emerges when a new observation arises which does not correspond with existing theory. Once the technology permitted accurate observations of the planet Mercury to be made, it was clear that there were small differences between its observed motion and that expected under Newton's Theory of Gravity. Einstein's general theory of relativity matched the observed motions of the planet in a manner that Newton's theory did not, providing confirmation for the new theory.

- **The Wave Theory of Light.** We can attempt to explain the behaviour of light in terms of its being composed of either 'waves' or 'particles'. Each view – both of which are needed to affirm existing properties – produces a plausible explanation of behaviour, but they are incompatible explanations which cannot exist simultaneously. New theories are required (possibly those associated with parallel universes) for a complete understanding of the incompatibility.

Deductive reasoning, on the other hand, starts with the theory and proceeds to generate specific predictions, which follow from its application. The predictions can be verified, or otherwise, from subsequent observation. For example, in his seminal paper, Healy (1985) used agency theory to develop a bonus hypothesis which could be substantially verified through observations of how managers manipulated their accounting earnings to optimise their short-term bonus performance.

However, such a strict division of reasoning processes is not always helpful because interdependencies almost always exist: induction will usually imply some knowledge of theory in order to select the data to be observed (a common criticism of grounded theory advanced in Chapters 3 and 10); deduction will be dependent on the selection of the initial hypotheses for testing.

Even without such problems, the scientific position of 'objective measurement' has come under repeated attack, in both natural and social sciences, because the act of observation is itself 'theory-laden' and influenced by the motives and preferences of the observer. For example, Hopwood (1987), in management accounting, Hines (1988), in financial accounting, and Parker (2012) argue that accounting helps to create the 'facts' that it is supposedly reporting. More radical approaches (e.g., Tinker and Niemark, 1987) suggest that accounting distorts practice in a systematic manner. Such concerns have aided the development of new approaches: an interpretive perspective and a critical perspective.

- **An interpretive perspective** – From an interpretive perspective, human actions are the result of external influences. These actions have both intentions and reflections and take place within a structure of rules, which binds the participants. The task of the researcher goes beyond measurement to developing an understanding of the situation. To do this effectively, active participation, rather than detached observation, may be required. Since the 'action' may be interpreted ambiguously when taken out of context, this perspective places the fundamental emphasis on the understanding of the process. In an accounting context, Arrington and Francis (1989) provide an example of this approach.
- **A critical perspective** – The critical approach expands on the scope of the interpretive approach by focusing on the ownership of knowledge and the associated social, economic and political implications. An empirical approach is criticised on the grounds that the research process is value-laden, and that the acquisition of knowledge provides the opportunity to oppress those being researched. In an accounting context, Tinker (1980) provides an example of this approach.

Table 1.1 summarises the differences in research assumptions, process and outcomes associated with each of these three major approaches.

Table 1.1 summary of the differences in research assumptions, process and outcomes associated with each of the three major approaches

	Positivist	Interpretive	Critical
1. *What is the approach modelled on?*	Classical investigation founded in the physical sciences.	Historical, literary and existential studies in which the subjective understandings of subjects are significant.	Marxist and interpretive studies which focus on the insights and judgements of the subjects.
2. *What does it assume about reality?*	Reality is unitary and it can only be understood by empirical and analytic methods, i.e., the scientific approach.	There are multiple realities which require multiple methods for understanding them.	There are multiple realities which are made problematic through distorted communication.
3. *What is the foundation of data?*	Disciplined rules for observation.	Meanings are the basis of data: meaning precedes logic and fact.	Meanings are found in language and social behaviour and they precede logic and fact.
4. *How is observation done?*	Through clear and unambiguous rules which are not modified by the setting and are totally independent of it.	Through the social, linguistic and cognitive skills of the researcher.	Interpretive methods, plus critical self-reflection concerning the grounds of observation.

	Positivist	Interpretive	Critical
5. What is generated?	Evidence and generalisable laws which are not affected by contexts and have nothing to do with the way in which they were discovered in the first place. Objectivity depends upon the removal of error and bias which is related specifically to the logic of observation and measurement.	Knowledge which is dependent on the process of discovery. The integrity of the findings depends upon the quality of the social, linguistic and cognitive skills of the researcher in the production of data analyses and conclusions.	Knowledge which falls within the interpretive framework, but which also serves the purposes of assisting personal liberation and understanding, and emancipation from forces constraining the rational independence of individuals.
6. What interests are inherent?	Prediction and control, technically exploitable knowledge, and explanation.	Understanding at the level of ordinary language and action. Discovering the meanings and beliefs underlying the actions of others.	Interpretive interests and those which underlie other forms of inquiry. Radically improving human existence. Practical and public involvement in knowledge formation and use.
7. What values are inherent?	Science and scientific knowledge are inherently value-neutral.	Science and scientific knowledge both have to be interpreted in terms of values they represent.	Science and knowledge are never value-neutral: they always represent certain interests.

Three alternative approaches (adapted from Connole, 1993: 37)

In a similar vein Malsch and Salterio (2016: 5) modify the Power and Gendron (2015) structure which highlights the distinguishing characteristics of positivist and interpretive approaches to fieldwork, as follows:

	Positivist	Interpretive
Research aims	Empirical generalisation	Empirical examination of of cause-and-effect global concerns
Focus	Breadth	Depth
Analytical emphasis	Cause-and-effect	Complexity of human behaviour
Explanation	Prediction	In-depth understanding
Viewpoint	Reality is external	Reality is socially constructed
Objectivity	Researcher and research	Subjective interpretation process objective throughout
Flexibility	Flexibility constrained	Flexibility paramount by objectivity
Writing style	Concise	Reflects real-world complexity

Kuhn (1970) suggests that researchers are concerned with problem-solving within a single framework of widely accepted beliefs, values, assumptions and techniques. This shared framework, or view of the world, he termed a paradigm, so that a 'paradigm shift' corresponds with some revolution where the existing framework and theories can no longer cope with the volume of disconfirming evidence. Kuhn (1970: 64) neatly illustrates such a shift by reference to a simple psychology experiment:

Subjects viewed cards from a deck. The deck included some unusual cards, including black hearts and red spades, but the subjects were not informed in advance about their presence. Initially the subjects saw only 'hearts' and 'spades', because they believed that only 'red hearts' and 'black spades' existed; only with repeated viewing did they grasp that these cards were not typical of a normal deck. Then they could recognise the cards that existed rather than the ones they were expecting.

In accounting research the parallels might be the paradigm shifts associated with the ideas introduced by Ball and Brown (1968) (as reported in Ball and Brown, 2014) and the difficulty they had in getting a paper published which questioned the existing paradigm by showing a link between stock prices and accounting earnings, through the abnormal performance index. A similar, though perhaps less radical, movement is associated with Watts and Zimmerman (1978) and their popularisation of agency theory in an accounting environment.

What is inescapable is that we are dealing with people, and in the research community that means individuals with their own agenda and with reputations to build and protect. The natural sciences are littered with character assassinations of individuals and their work, by others who have been less than willing to accept the impact of new findings on their own fiefdoms.

Sir Humphrey Appleby, in Lynn and Jay (1987: 258), outlines the four stages of the process necessary to discredit an unwelcome report. The parallels between the fictitious Department of Administrative Affairs and academia are uncomfortable, where unwelcome findings might arise from academic competitors:

1. **Refuse to accept the findings** on the basis that they could be misinterpreted, and that a wider and more detailed study is required.
2. **Discredit the evidence** on the basis that it is inconclusive and the figures are open to other interpretations, or that the findings are contradictory and leave important questions unanswered.
3. **Undermine the recommendations** because they say nothing new, and provide insufficient information on which to draw valid conclusions.
4. **Discredit the researcher** by questioning his or her integrity, competence and methods employed.

We thus have doubts about the researchers, their research questions, their research methods, the means of data collection and analysis, and the validity of the interpretation and recommendations – all issues to which we will return.

Theory as testable explanation

Faced with a set of diverse observations, we can establish a set of tentative explanations, which help to make sense of the diversity. Such explanations constitute theory. In any set of circumstances there will usually be multiple theories available to explain the observations. The systematic collection of further data allows for the testing of the alternative theories so that we can establish which of the existing theories best explains the facts. A layman's perspective of 'theory' is cynically expressed in Michael Crichton's *The Lost World* as: 'A theory is nothing more than a substitute for experience put forward by someone who does not know what they are talking about' (1995: 67).

The data collection itself allows only a descriptive approach (e.g., means, standard deviations, ranges, correlations); we cannot attempt to attribute causation in any meaningful way without recourse to an explanatory theory. We are always looking for another theory which may fit better, so that, as Popper (1959: 104) suggests, a 'genuine test of a theory is an attempt to falsify it or refute it'. We look for disconfirmations rather than confirmations.

In the short term this may not be successful. In accounting, we witness the frequent and numerous 'anomalies' to which the Efficient Markets Hypothesis is subject, but we have no other widely accepted theory of the manner in which stock prices react to the availability of relevant information.

Popper's suggestions are very attractive in providing a powerful empirical methodology for subjecting theories to attempts to refute them. However, this position is not always ideal because the process of 'observation' in itself may be fallible. Thus, Hawking (1998: 59) reports **Heisenberg's Uncertainty Principle**:

> If we are to predict the future position and speed of any particle, then we require accurate measurement of both its present position and current speed. Heisenberg did this in 1926 by shining light on a particle, and observing the resultant scattering of light in order to reveal its position. However, to determine the position of the particle accurately an amount of light needed to be used which changed the speed of the particle in an unpredictable way: the more accurately he tried to measure position, the less accurate was the measurement of speed!

The Uncertainty Principle has wide implications for research conducted in any environment, where it is impossible to measure the size and speed of a particle without altering all other characteristics in the process of measurement. We have a parallel situation in accounting research where the actions of the participants in ethnographic, experimental, survey or fieldwork impact on the outcomes of the measurement process.

Three fundamental criteria exist to judge whether theory fits observation:

1. **Co-variation** – even where no causality exists we would expect the two variables to move together so that a high degree of correlation exists between the two variables. Where there is no co-variation it will be difficult to establish a causal link.
2. **Cause prior to effect** – if a causal link is to be established then the 'causal event' should occur before the 'effect event'. The sequence of events can therefore help to establish an explanatory direction.
3. **Absence of plausible rival hypotheses** – the third rule seeks to eliminate alternative explanations of the events as being implausible. This may only be possible in the present, because future researchers may develop competing explanations of the events from a re-analysis of the data.

Consider, for example, the voluntary disclosure of information in corporate reports and analyst following (i.e., the number of analysts examining the performance and reporting on the disclosures of large companies). There is a relationship between these two variables – they co-vary: the volume of voluntary disclosures and the number of analysts reporting move together. But which is causing which? Rival hypotheses suggest:

a. companies are supplying more information voluntarily to the market to signal their intentions and reputation, attracting the attention of more investment analysis;
b. investment analysts are focusing their attention on particular companies and demanding more information and more detailed disclosures.

The existing empirical evidence is less than convincing: Lang and Lundholm (1996) find (a); but Walker and Tsalta (2001) provide only weak evidence for (a) but stronger evidence to support (b). Kent and Ung (2003) find support for the Walker/Tsalta position finding no correlation, while Aljifri and Hussainey (2007) observe a negative correlation. Clearly more empirical work is required to clarify the nature and direction of causation.

A critical approach to accounting research

Researchers must demonstrate a healthy scepticism towards both their own findings and those of other researchers. They must adopt a critical posture, questioning everything that they read until sufficient evidence has been provided for them to be satisfied with the quality of the outcomes. The development of critical appraisal skills is a fundamental requirement in researchers, so that they can distinguish between good and bad research, and clearly identify flaws of argument, methodology and analysis.

Honest and transparent reporting of research practice is an ethical duty of those participating. Researchers should report everything that they did, why they did it and how they did it. If they have doubts about any stage of the procedure, then these should be stated, along with their likely implications and what, if anything, has been done to overcome these doubts. Where researchers have been 'economical with the truth', this is usually apparent in their papers and is often an indicator of bad research.

Students frequently struggle initially when they are asked to critique published articles. They are often in awe of the reputation of the authors, or doubt whether they are able to offer sensible criticism of papers which, after all, have already undergone editorial scrutiny and double-blind review. Despite the above, some flawed papers do get published, and these are not always in lower-tier journals (see Hartmann and Moers, 1999, for their critique of 28 papers on contingency analysis in three top accounting journals – *Accounting Organizations and Society* (AOS), *The Accounting Review* and *Journal of Accounting Research* (JAR) – in which they identify problems in the design and analysis of 27 of the studies!). Similarly, Dowd (2004: 510) notes the publication in the respected tier of economics literature of papers with nonsensical assumptions. With appropriate guidelines as to the right questions to ask, students can quickly develop some confidence in their ability to spot flaws and omissions. For example,

Abernethy et al. (1999) provide a stimulating critique of the three subsequent papers in the same, outstanding, edition of the journal *Accounting and Finance*.

We would usually want to address the following:

1. **Why is this article interesting/important?** The paper must offer some new insights which constitute a contribution to knowledge. These insights should be non-trivial, so that they can be embraced in either further theory development or recommendations for improvement.

2. **Are the outcomes important?** Effectively, does the paper pass the 'so what' test? Will anyone be interested in the outcomes of this research, or will it have any implications for future practice? Would the scope of the research be well regarded by competitive grant authorities? This has important implications for those papers which produce 'negative' findings; that is, they test reasonable hypotheses based on the research literature, but their data sets fail to support any of the expectations. These findings still make a contribution in that they demonstrate that findings from elsewhere (often other disciplines) do not hold in accounting, but their negativity may restrict their publication opportunities.

3. **What motivates the authors to write this article now?** The paper may be clearly addressing issues of contemporary concern; on the other hand, it may be addressing more historical issues and/or be using 'old' data. If we have the latter, we may be dealing with an old paper recently recycled, or a paper which has been through multiple iterations at several different journals before being deemed 'publishable'.

4. **What is the research problem/question?** We are looking for a clear statement of the problem very early on in the paper, so that its objectives are readily apparent. If we reach page 11, say, of the paper without a clear idea of its direction, or any sort of research model, then perhaps the authors need to readdress the fundamental purpose of the research.

5. **What theory or theoretical framework underpins the research?** Without some theoretical foundations we have a problem-solving exercise or a consultancy project, neither of which should be gracing the pages of a refereed journal. There must be some theoretical justification for the question being addressed and the research approach adopted. Theory will often not come first in the research process – it will frequently be preceded by an interesting idea or a perplexing observation. But we require some theoretical explanation for the relationships under investigation before we have the basics for a refereed journal article. Observed deficiencies in this area usually fall into one of four categories:

   - the underlying theory is either non-existent or extremely thin;
   - the theoretical context is there but appears to have been tacked on as an afterthought – usually at the beginning of the paper and often written by a co-author. Examination of writing styles suggests that we frequently do not have a seamless divide between 'theory' and 'conduct of research';
   - the theoretical arguments are unconvincing, so that there are competing theories that may reasonably have been adopted in the paper but have been overlooked; and
   - a sound theoretical framework but findings which are totally at odds with theory. Apparently, a competing theory may be more appropriate, although this is unknown to the authors at the time.

6. **What are the key motivating literatures on which the study depends?** There will normally be a small number of seminal pieces of literature that are driving the research. If any of these are themselves unreliable, it may cast doubt on the state of the foundations on which the paper is based. If one of the papers is an unpublished conference or working paper from several years before, then alarm bells ring to question why that piece has not itself been published in the refereed literature. If key seminal pieces of literature have been overlooked, then again the integrity of the findings is reduced.

7. **Which research method has been chosen?** There should be a justification for the chosen method, and a clear preference over alternatives. The method should be consistent with both theory and literature and, ideally, prior empirical studies in the field will have adopted similar methods. Most importantly, we want to see a research method that has evolved rather than one that has been selected first, even before the research question has been fully developed. The use of survey methods should always be questioned in this way since frequently they seem to have been selected without explanation of the elimination of alternatives. Ideally, we should be able to trace through the emergence of abstract concepts, from theory, through their operationalisation and measurement, so that any hypotheses are entirely consistent with both theory and literature.

8. **How has the sample been selected?** Details on sample selection are often sketchy in many articles, perhaps because the authors feel vulnerable about the procedures adopted. Sometimes (see, for example, Young, 1996 and Van der Stede et al., 2005) the actual sample size employed is omitted, as is the response rate. Both omissions should be regarded as bad news. It is usually clear that scientific methods have not been adopted (unfortunately far too commonly in accounting research) where there is an over-reliance on convenience samples. What may be apparent is an attempt by the authors to obfuscate in this regard, to overlook detail and try to create an impression that the sample selection is more systematic than it has actually been.

9. **How have questions of validity been addressed?** Choice of research method should address issues of validity. Where experimental methods have been employed we would anticipate questions of internal validity to be paramount; where field studies are involved we would expect issues of external validity to be addressed. For survey methods we would anticipate the focus to be more on the reliability of the test instrument and the rigour of the subsequent statistical analysis, rather than on validity issues.

10. **How have the results been analysed?** We want to see the simplest analysis of the results consistent with the relationships being explored. We do not wish to see unnecessary complexity; this will make the paper less readable and tend to mask the findings and their significance. On the other hand, most academic accountants are only 'amateur' statisticians; if the level of their analysis is inadequate, then they may need to bring in a statistician as co-author (evidenced by the number of 'quant jocks' appearing as third or fourth authors on accounting papers to satisfy the reviewers). Importantly, we do not wish to see the method of analysis driving the study. In just the same way as the research method should not precede the research question, then neither should the method of analysis. For example, I recall a paper of my own (M. Smith, 1992) presented

at a conference but never published. It attempted to show the advantages of using multi-dimensional scaling (MDS, then a little-used technique in the accounting literature) for problem-solving, but the journal referees rightly observed that the method was inappropriately sophisticated for a relatively simple research question. MDS was abandoned, simpler methods instituted and the revised paper eventually published as Smith (1996).

11. **Are the conclusions and recommendations consistent with the findings?** Effectively, does the paper hold together? Is the title appropriate? Do the abstract and introduction lead us to expect what we find at the end of the paper? In many papers the final sections are the weakest and may not do justice to the breadth of the research conducted. We look for explanations, limitations and a future research agenda.

Let us now consider how this framework may be applied to a critique of a published piece. Naturally, I chose one of my own publications (Smith et al., 2001) for the treatment because a knowledge of the history of the development of the paper, from an insider's perspective, can be most instructive. Readers will be able to make the most of the subsequent discussion if they are first able to read a copy of the paper, and for this purpose the complete paper is reproduced as Appendix 2 of this volume.

1. **Interesting new insights:** The paper posits an interesting connection between (1) audit firm; (2) manner of conduct of the audit; and (3) classification of audit firms based on their procedures and culture. The paper also attempts to impose a global perspective by employing findings from the USA, the UK and Australia. But neither the data nor the supporting literature is new, and it compromises the originality of the paper.

2. **Importance:** The paper is important if it makes a contribution to knowledge. This may be a contribution to theory development or implications for business practice. If the paper can demonstrate a relationship between 'auditor' and the manner in which the audit has been conducted, then this makes a contribution, even though it may only be of historical relevance. Such a relationship is shown for 1987/88 data, but evidence is also presented to suggest that this relationship no longer holds. The absence of a current relationship suggests that the paper has no implications for current auditing practice. The reasons for a relationship between the audit firm and its propensity towards tolerance of particular accounting policies among its clients is by no means clear.

3. **Motivation:** The timing of the paper is problematic. It is published in 2001 but uses data predominantly from 1987/88. There is a danger of its being regarded as a historical piece with little relevance to current practice. The authors justify the use of this data set in that the Kinney classification, the target test of the paper, is based on data relating to the Big 8 group of accountants, with 1988 being the last year of existence of the Big 8 in Australia, prior to extensive merger activity in the sector. There is the suggestion, though, both from the paper itself and the references cited, that the data have been used primarily to generate failure prediction models for the Western Australian government (i.e., Houghton and Smith, 1991) and that the further use of this data in this paper may be incidental and opportunistic.

4. **Problem statement:** The problem statement is quite clearly stated as: Accounting Policy Changes = f {auditing firm}, where both sides of this equation are elaborated and measured for a large number of companies:

    - Accounting policy changes: discretionary/mandatory, income increasing, income reducing, neutral.
    - Auditing firm: by individual name, and by grouping according to classifications developed by Kinney (1986) and Moizer (1998).
    - A number of extraneous variables (notably firm size, financial performance and industry) are also examined to determine their impact.

5. **Theoretical framework:** This remains something of a problem with this paper, despite strenuous efforts to overcome omissions. The literature demonstrates that there are differences between auditors, and in the procedures that they adopted for audit in 1988 (i.e., Sullivan, 1984; Cushing and Loebekke, 1986). However, why these procedural differences between auditors translate into differing tolerances towards income-impacting accounting policy changes is unclear, and is largely attributable to unpublished anecdotes from practising auditors and the discussion arising in a single paper (Dirsmith and Haskins, 1991).

6. **Motivating literatures:** Relatively few articles, noted above (i.e., Sullivan, Kinney, Cushing and Loebekke, Dirsmith and Haskins) motivate this paper, while Terry Smith (1992) and Peter Moizer (1998) provide the opportunity for UK comparisons. The pivotal paper is Dirsmith and Haskins (1991), published after the conduct of the data collection; there is thus a strong suspicion that interesting findings have arisen from data mining operations in 1988, for which Kinney (1986) provides a conceptual framework, but that publication must wait for a suitable theory. There is very little other supporting literature, though self-citation by the authors is also revealing:

    - Houghton and Smith (1991) relates to failure prediction models constructed with the same data and is employed here to provide a measure of overall financial performance;
    - Smith (1998a) reports current UK findings linking auditor with attitude to accounting policy change;
    - Smith and Kestel (1999) update the present study with a time-series analysis, but the results are apparently insufficiently interesting to constitute publication in a refereed journal;
    - Brown (1988) reports on the most appropriate means of conducting statistical tests with contingency tables.

7. **Research method:** Archival methods are employed, since they are the only realistic alternative given the nature of the data: namely, historical, documentary and covering many companies that are no longer in existence. The authors' access to a data set comprising the population of Western Australian public companies is a considerable strength of the paper. Data collection is meticulous and involves checks for consistency both between individual researchers and for temporal validity.

8. **Sample selection:** The paper accesses the annual reports of all 463 publicly quoted companies in Western Australian (WA), so does not encounter any sampling issues other than a restriction on the nature of statistical tests that may be employed because of using a population rather than a sample from a normal distribution.

9. **Validity issues:** There are potential internal validity threats consequent upon the failure to consider competing theoretical explanations for the observations. The incidence of accounting policy change is apparently associated with the auditing firm, but both the direction of causation for the relationship and alternative auditor motivations might be considered. The authors acknowledge the lack of external validity in the study – the applicability of the findings to other time periods and other data sets – in that conditions have changed so substantially since the data collection period that the procedures adopted by all auditors are now very similar.

10. **Analysis:** The fundamental analysis is relatively unsophisticated, involving the comparison of 'observed' and 'expected' frequencies through a chi-squared test. A variation on the traditional approach is introduced to take account of an ordering effect in the contingency tables, the power of the tests being increased with the use of Kendall's-tau. (A co-author with specialist statistical publications has been included to address testing issues, potentially in response to reviewer concerns on previous versions.) A comparative fundamental analysis for UK data (alluded to in Smith, 1998a) is apparently not possible, and further analysis is restricted to tertiary sources.

11. **Conclusions:** There are no formal conclusions or recommendations, rather a discussion of other interesting findings in related fields which may impact on the integrity of the outcomes. The findings of this study are linked to merger activity in the Big 8, showing a pattern with considerable similarities to past successes. The paper suggests that future merger activity in the sector may be influenced by the organisational culture aspects of the Kinney classification and the clustering of companies generated by Moizer (1998); thus if we were looking at potential suitors for Arthur Andersen, say, then the analysis suggests that Ernst & Young would provide potentially the most successful alternative.

Such a critique is revealing, giving glimpses of a less-than-optimum approach adopted in the development of this particular paper. Data were collected for the specific purpose of generating failure prediction models for the WA government, and corporate monitoring of distressed enterprises (i.e., Houghton and Smith, 1991). The interesting auditor findings were generated at the same time, but there was no substantive theory to justify the observed relationship – and consequently no research paper. Only with the emergence of new theories (e.g., Dirsmith and Haskins, 1991), which might motivate the study, could further development towards a publishable paper proceed.

Clearly research is not always simple, systematic and clean – despite the sanitised versions that we read in the published journals. The research process can be both chaotic and exciting, and very rarely proceeds exactly according to plan. Unfortunately, this impression is rarely created by what we read because published pieces usually have happy endings – positive findings and cooperative participants. For a more realistic version of events we must rely on books like this, conference presentations and research workshops.

Armed with a critical and sceptical approach to the research of others, we can now start to develop the skills required to conduct competent research of our own, and commence a sequence that will eventually result in the publication of our research findings.

Further reading

Abernethy, M.A., Chua, W.F., Luckett, P.F. and Selto, F.H. (1999) 'Research in Managerial Accounting: Learning from Others' Experiences', *Accounting and Finance*, 39 (1): 1–28.

Aljifri, K. and Hussainey, K. (2007) 'The Determinants of Forward-looking Information in Annual Reports of UAE Companies', *Managerial Auditing Journal*, 21 (5): 476–96.

Ball, R. and Brown, P. (1968) 'An Empirical Evaluation of Accounting Income Numbers', *Journal of Accounting Research*, 6 (2): 159–78.

Ball, R. and Brown, P. (2014) 'Ball and Brown (1968): A Retrospective', *The Accounting Review*, 89 (1): 1–26.

Brownell, P. (1995) *Research Methods in Management Accounting*. Melbourne: Coopers & Lybrand.

Dowd, K. (2004) 'Qualitative Dimensions in Finance and Risk Management Research', in C. Humphrey and B. Lee (eds), *The Real Life Guide to Accounting Research*. London: Elsevier. pp. 509–24.

Kent, P. and Ung, K. (2003) 'Voluntary Disclosure of Forward-looking Earnings Information in Australia', *Australian Journal of Management*, 28 (3): 273–85.

Malmi, T. and Granlund, M. (2009) 'In Search of Management Accounting Theory', *European Accounting Review*, 18 (3): 597–620.

Malsch, B. and Salterio, S.E. (2016) 'Doing Good Field Research: Assessing the Quality of Audit Field Research', *Auditing: A Journal of Practice and Theory*, 35 (91): 1–22.

Parker, L.D. (2012) 'Qualitative Management Accounting Research: Assessing Deliverables and Relevance', *Critical Perspectives on Accounting*, 23: 54–70.

Power, M. and Gendron, Y. (2015) 'Qualitative Research in Auditing: A Methodological Roadmap', *Auditing: A Journal of Practice and Theory*, 34 (2): 147–65.

Smith, M., Fiedler, B., Brown, B. and Kestel, J. (2001) 'Structure versus Judgement in the Audit Process: A Test of Kinney's Classification', *Managerial Auditing Journal*, 16 (1): 40–49.

Smith, T. (1992) *Accounting for Growth: Stripping the Camouflage from Company Accounts*. London: Random House.

Van der Stede, W., Young, S.M. and Chen, C.X. (2005) 'Assessing the Quality of Evidence in Empirical Management Accounting Research: The Case of Survey Studies', *Accounting, Organizations and Society*, 30 (5): 655–84.

Wilmott, H. (2008) 'Listening, Interpreting, Commending: A Commentary on the Future of Interpretive Accounting Research', *Critical Perspectives on Accounting*, 19 (6): 920–5.

Young, S.M. (1996) 'Survey Research in Management Accounting: A Critical Assessment', in A.J. Richardson (ed.), *Research Methods in Accounting: Issues and Debates*. Vancouver: The Canadian General Accountants Research Foundation. pp. 55–68.

Developing the
Research Idea

TWO

Chapter Contents

- The research sequence
- Emergence of the research topic
- The research proposal
- Conceptual frameworks
- The structure of DNA: the development of new theory
- The Bradman problem: the development of new strategies
- The longitude problem: implementing solutions
- Searching the family tree: qualitative archival research
- The Holy Grail: experiments in the field
- Strategic management accounting

We recognise in Chapter 1 that research processes are usually not simple, systematic or clean, because research rarely proceeds exactly to plan. However, this should not deter us from planning thoroughly in the first place to specify how, in an ideal world, we would like the research to be conducted.

The research sequence

Figure 2.1 specifies the typical research sequence described by Howard and Sharp (1983) as a series of stages we would expect to progress through in most forms of accounting research, while moving from original idea to eventual publication.

The following chapters of this book address each of these stages, and detail the constraints we might anticipate.

Figure 2.1 The research sequence

1. **Identify broad area:** Narrow the focus from accounting in general to a stream associated with financial accounting, management accounting, auditing, accounting education or accounting information systems.
2. **Select topic:** Specification of a sub-area to provide a tighter focus, and one for which supervision capacity is available, but one which may be modified in light of the subsequent developments.
3. **Decide approach:** Early thoughts regarding the approach to be adopted will revolve around the resources available, and in particular, access to the necessary data sources. A detailed specification of research methods to be adopted must wait until the literature review has been conducted and theoretical foundations and outline hypotheses have been established.
4. **Formulate plan:** Milestones and targets should be established at the outset so that it is clear how the research will progress over an extended period. This is particularly important for part-time researchers who may be contemplating study over six or seven years. A Gantt chart, or similar, is very helpful in clarifying the extent of the programme of work and the mutual expectations of those involved, especially if this concerns the relationship between candidate and supervisor in doctoral work. This plan should include target conferences where preliminary findings may be presented, especially where deadlines are important to the candidate. The commencement period can often cause anxiety because of the perceived need to make swift progress. It cannot be emphasised enough how important an extended period of reading is to ensure that effort is not wasted performing experiments or surveys which subsequently emerge as being unnecessary or fatally flawed.

5. **Collect information:** Data collection can safely proceed only when we recognise exactly what we want to know, and for what purpose. The planning stage should highlight the period over which we want to collect data; this usually effectively precludes most longitudinal studies, partly because it takes too long to collect data and partly because of the increased vulnerability associated with extended site access. We may require access to commercial databases; if these are an essential requirement then permissions should be sought immediately.

6. **Analyse data:** Methods of data analysis and software requirements should be apparent early in the research process.

7. **Present findings:** Preliminary findings will normally be presented at university workshops and seminars, and then at specialist conferences. These provide the precursor to publication in the refereed literature, which may take place before completion of any associated doctoral dissertation. Publication in the professional literature will bring important findings to the attention of interested practitioners.

The research sequence above can easily be squeezed to provide the elements of the traditional positivist approach as devised by House (1970), and illustrated in Figure 2.2. Again this approach assumes the presence of specific conditions:

- the specification of a priori hypotheses: formulated on the basis of theory and literature before any data are collected or fieldwork contemplated;
- the specification of a priori criteria: to measure the acceptability of the hypotheses, most commonly in the form of standard statistical tests;
- the isolation and control of the variables to be investigated: determination of which variable(s) will be treated as dependent, which will be independent (explanatory) and which will be held constant, matched or ignored; and
- the verification of the methods for measuring and the variables: specification of which variables can be measured directly, and how, and those which will require the use of proxy variables, or measurement instruments, of some form.

Figure 2.2 The positivist approach

However, we have to acknowledge that there is no single method that necessarily applies to research in all situations. Thus, while the positivist tradition remains the most prominent in the accounting literature, non-positivist approaches have become increasingly acceptable. (Even so, some of the top US journals are still unmoved in their attitude to non-positivist approaches. Baker and Bettner (1997), Lee (2004: 69) and Parker (2012) among others, observe that most of the top journals are devoid of interpretive and critical research studies.) However, management-oriented investigations of change (e.g., the implementation of accounting innovations) may be particularly unsuited to a scientific approach. Where people are involved and multiple variables are beyond the control of the researchers, including management's own motivation and agenda, scientific approaches are of questionable validity. Checkland (1981: 316) observes: 'attempts to apply scientific methodology to real world, essentially social problems, have been responsible for the limited success of management science'.

Thus, we can stay within our original 'research sequence' framework but extend out beyond the positivist approach. Figure 2.3 illustrates the range of possibilities. As we move from top to bottom in the figure, we move from the traditional positivist approaches (archival and experimental studies) through field studies towards a case-based approach typically associated with ethnographic studies. This movement corresponds with an increase in the number of uncontrolled variables, with our increasing inability to formulate testable hypotheses, and with the increasing prominence of the 'human' element.

Figure 2.3 Alternative research methods

Emergence of the research topic

We should begin by choosing a research topic which is of interest both to the researcher and the supervisor, where the project is contributing to a doctoral qualification. The topic should generate enthusiasm in the researcher at the outset, otherwise he or she is unlikely to last the course of a protracted period of study in which motivation is bound to wane, even temporarily. The source of the topic can be from anywhere, but most commonly:

- a problem at work with potentially wider implications;
- a problem or application spotted in the newspaper, from television or during a web-search;
- a conference presentation revealing the directions being explored by other researchers;
- working papers and completed theses elsewhere – the contents of which are usually at least two years away from publication;
- textbooks – particularly in management-related areas – which are a constant source of untested theories;
- review articles, analysis of the literature in a particular area, to reveal the current boundaries of knowledge and a potential research agenda. The *Journal of Accounting Literature* is a particularly useful source in this regard (e.g., Jones and Shoemaker, 1994; Bauman, 1996; Dunk and Nouri, 1998; Gramling and Stone, 2001; Searcy and Mentzer, 2003; Cole and Jones, 2005; Henri, 2007; Khlif and Chalmers, 2015). Also good is *Accounting Organizations and Society* (e.g., Libby and Luft, 1993; Langfield-Smith, 1997; Hartmann and Moers, 1999; Ahrens and Chapman, 2006; Gerdin and Greve, 2008). The underrated *Journal of Accounting, Accountability and Performance* (e.g., McGowan et al., 2000; Liou and Smith, 2007; Smith and Chang, 2009) also provides a useful source;
- review monographs (e.g., Ashton and Ashton, 1995, information processing; Brownell, 1995, management accounting; Smith and Gurd, 2000, behavioural issues; Trotman, 1996, auditing) are also helpful, as is Foster's (1986) excellent book, which unfortunately has never been updated beyond this second edition; and
- refereed journal articles, particularly the final sections, revealing flaws in existing research, gaps in our knowledge and research opportunities. This may, directly or indirectly, establish a future research agenda in the topic area, which the current authors may not be pursuing.

The ideas will rarely emerge, therefore, from a 'spark' of original thought. More likely, the thought development will have emerged elsewhere, with the originator having either discarded his or her ideas or not seen their full value. It may fit an 'added-value' concept in the same way as a successful innovation may be remote from the inventor. This may be in the form of relating two concepts from different disciplines, in a manner that provides an application opportunity in the accounting environment. Here the 'success' is in the publishing of research findings in a respectable journal. To do so we will inevitably be building on the work of others.

The common element in each of the above approaches is 'reading' – hence the common advice given to doctoral candidates of 'reading, reading and yet more reading' to know an area and spot the opportunities. Candidates usually have a much greater commitment to a topic if they have developed it themselves, yet many find idea-generation an extremely difficult process. Thus, it is not uncommon for the supervisor to be the source of the research idea, because active and experienced researchers usually have far more ideas than they are capable of exploring by themselves. As Gill and Johnson (1997, 2002, 2010) observe, topic selection can be risky if left entirely in the hands of the candidate; the chosen topic may prove to be too small, too large, or simply not feasible in the time frame (especially for longitudinal studies). There may need to be a trade-off between the ownership/commitment associated with a student-selected topic and the practicability/timeliness expected of a supervisor-directed preference. Commonly, candidates will contemplate studies that involve the implementation of an accounting change, in order to monitor the change process and the resulting impact on financial outcomes. Such a model is rarely feasible because, apart from the access problems, involvement and data collection will be necessary over a period usually extending beyond that permitted within a standard candidature.

Once the germ of an idea is forthcoming it must be worked over to see if it really constitutes 'research'. For example, are we sure that it is more than a consultancy project? Is it more than a trivial problem with no wider implications? Is it more than a replication of something someone else has done before, or done in a different industry or different country? If we are happy in this regard then several other questions emerge:

- Is the project 'doable' in a reasonable time frame (e.g., the period of candidature)?
- Will the project fit the NIRD acronym (usually attributed to Rashad Abdel-Khalik during his tenure as editor of *The Accounting Review*) in that it is New, Interesting, Replicable and Defendable? Unsurprisingly, the acronym fits a positivist outlook since replicability may be impossible to guarantee in field study settings.
- Will the data required be readily available? If site visits are required, will access be available over a sufficient time period and to a sufficient depth? This last scenario is of great practical concern and difficult to control. Young and Selto (1993) and Lapsley (2004: 184) each report on studies whose depth was seriously curtailed because management changed its mind and restricted the access to personnel due to be interviewed. Worse than that, there are numerous cases of change of company ownership during the data collection period, resulting in further site access being permanently denied. Thorough examination of a small sample of firms over an extended period also constitutes a high-risk project, since the host firms can withdraw their collaboration at any time.

Once the general topic area has been determined, it may be refined by formal methods (e.g., brainstorming, attribute listing etc.) to identify possible fruitful directions and potentially interesting relationships, and to eliminate blind alleys. Diagrammatic aids, particularly whiteboards, are very helpful at this stage for mapping ideas, variables, relationships and processes.

The research proposal

Attention to the fundamental requirements of the refereed literature will allow the researcher to produce an outline research proposal, one that is continually revised during the reading period and may nevertheless have to be revised further during the conduct of the research itself, due to unforeseen circumstances. A typical research proposal will include the following elements:

- **Title** – what you are tyring to do.
- **Abstract** – the problem, objectives and expected outcomes.
- **Issues** – why they are interesting and important.
- **Objectives** – how the study relates to the problem.
- **Literature** – review of relevant, themed publications.
- **Method** – the how and why of the process.
- **Benefits** – the anticipated outcomes that make this study worthwhile.

A working **title** is important to clarify the topic, especially if external grant income is being sought to support the project. However, the final title is rarely the original one and there are plenty of opportunities to make changes.

The **abstract** is an important departure at this stage, because it allows the researcher to speculate on what the outcomes of the research might be, should everything go according to plan. The abstract can be ambitious initially, but will require revision (perhaps radical revision) as problems and constraints emerge in the research process.

The contribution of the paper and the way that it aims to address important **issues** in a systematic manner are fundamental to its success. Internal consistency and overall coherence should ensure that the **objectives** and the intended approach are appropriate.

The outline **literature** review may be incomplete but it must none the less identify the key motivating literatures and theories. Research candidates must recognise that the literature review is a constantly moveable feast and something that will be added to right up to the final presentation of the research findings. One of the major deficiencies of both papers and dissertations is that they frequently overlook the most recent relevant publications: it can be a heart-stopping moment when one is about to submit the thesis, and the latest issue of a journal appears to report the outcomes of a research project very similar to one's own! At the very least this new paper must be cited. A common complaint from inexperienced researchers is that there is 'no literature' available. If this is true, it may mean that the projected topic may be too trivial to consider. More likely, however, is that the literature review should drill down further and search on different keywords. That there is a dearth of recent literature on a topic may foreshadow problems. For example, papers on 'decision-making heuristics' were common in the late 1970s and early 1980s, and papers on 'group decision-making' common in the mid-1980s, but progress in both of these research areas has slowed, and publications are relatively rare because the psychological theories underlying the research have not developed sufficiently to facilitate new approaches. In a similar manner, we have witnessed the demise of normative accounting research since the early 1970s, it being increasingly supplanted by research based on positive accounting theory. With respect to apparently new projects, for example, research into 'e-commerce'-type topics, students must recognise that e-commerce is just a new way of doing business, and that their review must address the implementation of prior business innovations. Rogers' (1995, 2003) diffusion of innovations theory would normally provide an excellent starting point for theorising such projects.

Discussion of **method** and **theory** should address the alternatives available in order to demonstrate that the preferred choice is the most appropriate. The proposal should also echo the **benefits** of the research, in particular its contribution to knowledge and the potential implications for business practice.

The research proposal would normally form a central feature of any application for ethics approval, and must therefore demonstrate the value of the research, the integrity of the methods employed and the extent of the involvement of human participants. Students are often unsure as to the length and detail required in a research proposal, and there may be restrictions imposed by the academic institution as to length. But focus is the essential element – it should be clear what the objective of the research is, and what theories and literatures are driving it. Where longer proposals are permitted students may also see the proposal as providing a much-abridged first draft of chapters 1, 2 and 3 of a subsequent thesis!

Conceptual frameworks

A valuable part of the initial planning process is the development of a conceptual representation of the research project. This can help to clarify the important relationships (and the need for supporting theory), the explanatory and intervening variables, as well as the demonstration of causation.

The inductive and deductive approaches identified in Chapter 1 provide an objective alternative to the conduct of research, but neither allows the opportunity for human interaction: the inductive approach is where new theory is developed on the basis of fresh observations (as is most commonly the case in hard sciences, like astronomy); and the deductive approach is where theory provides the basis for the testing of empirical observations (and which is the most common form of positivist accounting research). The deductive approach is suitable in a highly structured environment, involving the empirical testing of theoretical models, so that its reliability is dependent on the integrity of quantitative and statistical methods. However, the causal relationships explored rely on an internal logic and take no account of the human relationships present. The application of the inductive approach in the accounting environment necessitates a variation to the traditional model, such as that provided by Kolb's Experiential Learning Cycle (Kolb et al., 1979: 38), which is illustrated in Figure 2.4. Recognition of the importance of internal processes and human relationships to the inductive approach allows for the existence of human subjectivity without distorting research findings, even though they may be qualitative and not replicable. Where human relationships are central to an understanding of accounting behaviour the approach exploits the subjective environment.

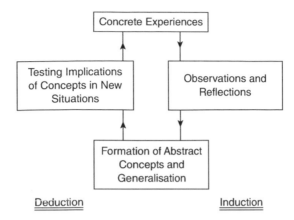

Figure 2.4 Kolb's Learning Cycle

Although both models provide opportunities in accounting research, the deductive approach offers greater possibilities for the implementation of scientific methods, since it facilitates arguably more reliable measurement and control. Grounded theory (discussed in more detail in Chapters 3 and 10) illustrates the potential for inductive methods in accounting research.

We can therefore develop the model of the deductive process (see Figure 2.5) so that it corresponds with Popper's (1959) defining characteristics of scientific theory:

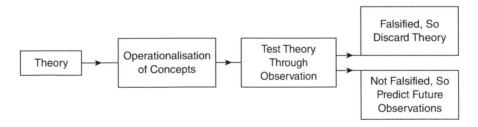

Figure 2.5 The deductive process

- the theory is capable of empirical testing;
- scientists (and researchers) should make rigorous attempts at falsifying theory;
- science advances as falsified propositions are left behind, leaving a core of theory still to be disproved.

Figure 2.6 The conceptual schema

The basic conceptual schema (see Figure 2.6) provides a powerful tool for the examination of causal relationships in a positivist environment. By establishing the key variables of interest, and the other potentially influential factors, we can form a better impression of the breadth of the problem.

The design problems associated with the identification and measurement of variables may mean that the basic schema needs to be modified according to Figure 2.7.

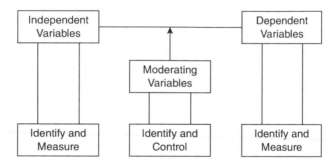

Figure 2.7 Measurement issues

What is also apparent is that the simple conceptual schema of Figure 2.6 must be regarded very much as a preliminary picture which will quickly outlive its usefulness. While helpful to begin with it must now be modified, and further detail added, to allow the further development of hypotheses and data collection methods. Chapter 3 focuses on these issues in the development of the important links between theory, literature, hypotheses and methods.

In Chapter 1 we acknowledged our debt to researchers in the natural and social sciences. It is now helpful to turn to popular literature, which provides highly readable explanations of complex situations, for an insight into the emergence of research ideas, the development of research questions and the airing of potential solutions for testing, to illustrate the research sequence in practice. It is instructive to consider the different scope of original research in solving practical problems by examining the particular aspects of well-documented stories from non-accounting environments. Thus, we explore the development of new theory in a chemical environment in 'The Structure of DNA'; the development and testing of alternative strategies to address a sporting issue in 'The Bradman Problem'; the solution of apparently insuperable implementation issues to a problem where the 'answer' was well known in 'The Longitude Problem'; and problems associated with qualitative archival research, as illustrated by reference to 'Family Tree' searches.

The structure of DNA: the development of new theory

James D. Watson's (1968) *The Double Helix* (subsequently filmed as *Life Story*) provides a brilliant description of the exciting process of discovery in scientific research, even if the approach adopted is rather unorthodox. The development of theory and conceptual modelling, from systematic deductions based on the empirical findings of others, is conducted in a competitive environment where the ultimate prize for winning the 'race' is the Nobel Prize. (Watson, together with Francis Crick, both of Cambridge University, and Maurice Wilkins, of King's College, London, were awarded the 1962 Nobel Prize for Physiology of Medicine for their pioneering work during 1951–52.)

Sir Lawrence Bragg reflects on these achievements by researchers in his Cavendish Laboratory through a revealing preface to Watson's book, with implications for research ethics:

> He knows that a colleague has been working for years on a problem and has accumulated a mass of hard-won evidence, which has not yet been published because it is anticipated that success is just around the corner. He has seen this evidence and has good reason to believe that a method of attack which he can envisage, perhaps merely a new point of view, will lead straight to the solution. An offer of collaboration at this stage might well be regarded as trespass. Should he go ahead on his own? (Bragg, in Watson, 1968: vii)

That Watson and Crick, at the Cavendish, did proceed with a belated relationship – though collaboration is too strong a word – with Wilkins and Rosalind Franklin is a matter of history. The course of their investigations, and the factors leading to their success in developing a new theoretical model, have implications for all research. Essentially, they proceed to develop a model that fits all of the evidence currently available to them, and they await confirmation or disconfirmation of their framework from the empirical findings of others:

- The work of Linus Pauling in the US on a helix formation for polypeptide chains suggested that DNA (deoxyribose nucleic acid) too had a helical structure. Pauling's early attempts at modelling though, without crystallographic evidence, had produced stereochemically impossible components. Early evidence from X-ray crystallographic diffraction presented by Wilkins also seemed to suggest a helical structure, but there was no evidence of whether a single, double or triple strand helical configuration was most appropriate. Crick and Watson apparently proceeded on the basis of an educated guess favouring the double helix because most things biological come in twos!

- Ernst Chargaff had produced vital evidence on the ratios of constituent bases, and particularly the equalities existing between adenine (A) = thymine (T), and guanine (G) = cytosine (C). The A–T, G–C flat hydrogen-bonded base pairs formed the core of the Crick and Watson structure, rather like a spiral staircase in which the bases form the steps.
- Important advice from a structural chemist colleague (who just happened to be sharing the same office with Crick and Watson) suggested that the normal textbook formulation of the A–T, G–C bases was incorrect and that they should work with an alternative 'keto' form. Without this important questioning of textbook content, and accepted knowledge, their structure would not have held together. The impact of this finding was that a given chain could contain both purines and pyrimidines (with the capacity to carry the genetic material for self-replication) and that the backbones of the chains should run in opposite directions.

Thus, Crick and Watson were able to construct a physical model comprising two intertwining helically coiled chains of nucleotides, right-handed and running in opposite directions, with complementary sequences of hydrogen-bonded bases. The resulting structure was stereochemically possible, and subsequent X-ray evidence from Franklin confirmed that the sugar-phosphate backbone was indeed on the outside of the molecule.

The more general implications for researchers are constant vigilance and a questioning attitude to the work of others and existing publications.

The Bradman problem: the development of new strategies

Test match cricket in the 1930s was dominated by a single, outstanding individual whose unique gifts of batsmanship threatened to change the way the game was played. Donald Bradman scored so many runs, and scored them so quickly, that he was likely to win a game almost single-handedly. Ashes test series, once so closely contested, threatened to be one-sided affairs, with Australia the perennial victor. In the 1930 England v. Australia test matches Bradman totalled a record 974 runs at an average of 139.14 per innings, and recorded separate scores of 334, 254 and 232. At the commencement of the 1932/33 series he averaged 112.29 in all test matches, and had already posted six scores in excess of 200 in only 24 completed innings.

Bradman was a phenomenon, some would say a 'freak', and curtailing his dominance became a pressing question for successive England captains. 'The Bradman Problem' is capably detailed by Lawrence Le Quesne in his book *The Bodyline Controversy* (1983), and presents an intriguing research question, investigating a number of alternatives that might provide successful solutions.

1. Changing the playing conditions

Cricket was played on hard, fast wickets, largely true, though with the occasional unpredictable bounce. If bowlers did not take wickets in the first few overs, when the ball was still shiny and swinging, then they might have a lot of overs to bowl before they got a replacement ball, by which time 200 runs had been scored. Wickets were uncovered and exposed to the elements once a game had started and could become unplayable as a hot sun dried out a wet pitch; these 'sticky' wickets provided a possible solution to the problem because Bradman was nowhere near as prolific on bad wickets as many of his contemporaries were. However, captains could hardly rely on this occurrence to blunt Bradman's genius on a regular basis.

2. Changing the rules of the game

Test matches were timeless in the 1930s and played to a finish. Declarations were rare and slow play very common. Further, the leg-before-wicket (LBW) rule made it difficult for the batsman to get out in that way – he had to be caught in front of the stumps by a ball pitching in line, wicket-to-wicket. Life was difficult for bowlers, and a number of other batsmen (notably Ponsford for Australia and Hammond for England) regularly completed double and triple centuries, although none with the regularity, reliability or speed of Bradman.

Reduction of the specified playing time to five (or four) days would mitigate slow play and dull the impact of less talented batsmen content to occupy the crease, but would not affect Bradman – witness his 309 in a day against England at Leeds in 1930. However, timeless tests were outlawed before the end of the inter-war period. Similarly, the LBW law was changed so that batsmen could be given out to a ball breaking back from outside the off stump and striking the pads in front of the wicket.

3. Changing the bowling

Bowlers had often sought to restrict the batsman by bowling outside of the leg stump (e.g., Hirst and Foster in the early 1900s), ostensibly to cut out off-side shots but also to restrict the on-drive through bowling just short of a length. An accurate bowler could therefore depress the scoring rate by keeping the batsman to deflected singles in the arc between the wicketkeeper and square leg. As a consequence the whole game is slowed to a snail's pace – a strategy still used today to curb an aggressive batsman's dominance. But Bradman was too good to fall for such tricks and used his agility, quick reflexes and nimble footwork to move to leg, outside the line of the ball, so giving himself room to hit through the off-side field. Such a strategy would have made less gifted batsmen vulnerable because it entailed the exposure of all three stumps to the bowler, but Bradman could execute the manoeuvre without undue risk.

4. Changing the field placings

An orthodox field will involve the placing of fieldsmen on both sides of the wicket, with a majority coincident with the bowler's planned line of attack. This means plenty of gaps in the field and, for inaccurate bowlers, plenty of scoring opportunities. Clearly, a preferred strategy would be to place all the fielders in a tightly confined space and have the bowler deliver a line and length that forces the batsman to play the ball there. This is a sound strategy for an accurate bowler – witness Laker's devastating use of a packed leg-trap to a turning ball in 1956 – but for a batsman of Bradman's ingenuity we now have a vacant off-side to be penetrated by inventive, unorthodox shots.

5. Introducing a 'bodyline' attack

While a combination of numbers (3) and (4) above provides a partial solution in restricting scoring opportunities, only impatience will induce eventual dismissal. For Bradman it may do neither. However, together they provide the basis for a potentially successful solution: 'leg theory' will dictate the line of delivery, but we need also to control the height of the delivery to induce the batsman to give chances from playing the ball in the air. Herein lies the Jardine–Larwood proposition, initiated by Douglas Jardine, England's captain in 1932 and executed brilliantly by Harold Larwood, the fastest and most accurate bowler of his time.

Extreme fast bowling does not provide even Bradman with the time to move outside the line consistently without risk. The introduction of a high proportion of short-pitched balls rearing towards the throat or the rib-cage of the batsman makes scoring without risk extremely difficult. Batsmen are likely to fend off the ball defensively – to be caught in the leg-trap ring of close catchers. If they try to attack by hooking the ball over the in-field, they fall prey to a number of deep-set fielders on the leg-side and behind the wicket. Concentrating almost all the fielders in the arc between wicketkeeper and mid-wicket, five close to the bat and three close to the boundary, covers almost all the options. Scoring is restricted to risky options and bad balls.

This form of attack was 'successful' in that it resulted in a 4–1 series victory for England and also provided an appropriate solution to 'the Bradman problem' in that he scored only one century in the series, a total of only 396 runs at an average of just 56.57. He still tried to play in a cavalier fashion, moving outside the line to play tennis-like shots; the result was brilliant, hectic cameos that were over all too soon for his team's requirements.

However, the risks of bodily injury to the batsman from the bodyline solution were high, and its introduction was seen to be ungentlemanly and against the spirit of the game. Jardine and Larwood were never chosen to play against Australia again. The subsequent 1934 test series was very much a fence-building exercise, with the England bowling friendly and 'bouncer' free. Bradman was again unconstrained and scored 758 runs at an average of 94.75. The success of the leg theory solution generated further changes to the rules of the game, with a restriction on the number of fielders permitted on the leg-side behind the wicket and the number of short-pitched balls that were allowed to be bowled per over.

The more general implications for research are that there may be legal, moral, ethical or professional circumstances, which prevent either the conduct of the research or the implementation of recommendations from the research findings.

The longitude problem: implementing solutions

The measurement of longitude at sea requires the accurate measurement of both the time at the current location and that at the Greenwich meridian, or some other similar base point. The time difference allows the calculation of geographical separation – since the 24-hour revolution of the Earth constitutes a 360 degree spin – so that a one-hour time difference constitutes 15 degrees of longitude, where one degree of longitude is equivalent to 68 miles on the Equator. The measurement of local time is not a problem, especially during hours of daylight, but in the absence of accurate timepieces knowledge of the corresponding time at the base point remains a considerable problem.

The consequences of being unable to measure longitude were serious and have been detailed by Dava Sobel in her book *Longitude* (1995). Shipwrecks and lost vessels were common, and piracy was facilitated by the need for ships to track across common lines of latitude on the 'trade routes' to maintain their position. The pendulum clocks of the 1660s, due to the work of Christiaan Huygens, had been used to demonstrate the possibility of measuring longitude at sea with timepieces, but they were only helpful in favourable weather. So much so that Sir Isaac Newton (cited in Sobel, 1995: 52) was forced to admit in 1714:

> One [method] is by a watch to keep the time exactly. But by reason of the motion of the ship, the variation of heat and cold, wet and dry, and the difference of gravity in different latitudes, such a watch hath not been made.

Newton clearly had astronomical, or at least scientific, solutions in mind rather than mechanical ones, necessitating the consideration of alternative solutions.

1. Existing methods

These were largely confined to 'dead reckoning' and 'compass method' approaches. Dead reckoning required estimates to be made of the speed of the ship, in conjunction with the calculation of the effects of wind speed and currents. Its success relied on good seamanship, reliable maps and luck! Compass methods were concerned with comparisons between magnetic north and 'true' north as shown by the pole star. Relative positions allowed the estimation of longitude without the necessity of measuring time. However, compass needles were notoriously unreliable, with a great deal of variation for the same compass on successive voyages. This, coupled with variations in terrestrial magnetism, made readings highly dependent on the particular seas being traversed.

2. Eclipse data

Eclipse data were thought to be potentially useful. Sonar and lunar eclipses provided opportunities if it was known when they were expected to be observed in other locations, but such occurrences were far too rare to provide a realistic navigational aid. Galileo had established that eclipses of the moons of Jupiter were extremely common and predictable, making them an accurate means of specifying longitude at specific land-based locations. However, movement aboard ship made this an impossible strategy for navigation, even when the night skies were clear.

3. Lunar distances methods

These involved measuring the distance between the moon and the sun, by day, and between the moon and stars at night. Such methods required detailed data on the track of the moon and the positions of individual stars so that the disappearance of particular stars behind the moon could be predicted. The complexities of the moon's orbit impeded progress in the prediction of the required measurements at different locations, and it was not until 1725 that Flamsteed's posthumous almanac of star positions was published. Even so, the available tables still meant it took four hours to calculate longitude (subsequently reduced to 30 minutes by Maskelyne's 1766 almanac).

The lunar distance method was therefore shown to be a theoretically possible means of accurately computing longitude, made more practicable by the invention of the quadrant (later sextant) in 1731 to measure elevations of, and distance between, moon and sun by day, and moon and stars by night. This permitted an estimate of time differences between a ship and known, fixed land locations. Even so, actual measurement proved impossible at times for a variety of reasons:

- weather conditions occasioning fog or thick cloud cover;
- the moon is so close to the sun for about six days per month that it disappears from view; and
- the moon is on the opposite side of the Earth from the sun for about 13 days per month.

John Harrison adopted a more direct solution to the problem, questioning the position of Newton and proceeding to build a succession of clocks that were shown to be accurate to fractions of a second per day. By eliminating problems of friction, he developed clocks that required no lubrication or cleaning. This, combined with the use of bi-metal strips of non-corrosive materials, overcame the problems of temperature change and rust. The choice of innovative balancing mechanisms also meant that the clocks were virtually unaffected by the most severe weather conditions.

By the time Harrison died in 1776 copies of his watch were still rare and expensive (in excess of £200) whereas a good sextant and set of lunar tables could be purchased for as little as £20. This considerable price difference meant that the 'lunar distance method' of calculation remained prominent until more affordable watches became available in the early 1800s through the sale of the mass-produced Arnold/Earnshaw pocket 'chronometers'.

Both timeliness and resource cost remain fundamental elements in the conduct of research projects and the implementation of their findings.

The scope of these three examples is very different, concerned respectively with the development of new theory, the development of workable solutions and the implementation of workable solutions. As we suspected, the research process is not simple, systematic or clean in any of the cases. What is common throughout are the pivotal roles played by 'theory' and 'validity': good theory produces good findings, and we are able to evaluate both the reliability and the validity of these findings through external reference. The following chapter examines theory in more detail, and expands the consideration of reliability and validity as desirable characteristics of accounting research.

Searching the family tree: qualitative archival research

One area of archival research available to all of us is the genealogical research necessary to establish reliable family trees. The elements of the search will provide examples of the most problematic issues that can arise in archival research – particularly in qualitative accounting research: missing data, errors, deliberate obfuscation, inconsistencies, ambiguities and alternative explanations. Triangulation of data sources may be necessary where problems persist in validating suspected relationships – in this case familial relationships.

Initial primary sources will usually be readily available in the form of documentary evidence: birth, marriage and death certificates. Where originals are not available then copies can be sourced (at a cost) from government sources – in the UK from the General Register Office of HM Passport Office at www.gro.gov.uk. Despite their pivotal nature the contents of these basic certificates might be misleading the further back we go – registration and certification only became mandatory in UK in 1837. Thus, age at death reported by a 'next of kin' on a death certificate may be unreliable, as could the ages reported on wedding certificates, especially where minors were seeking to marry without parental consent. But the calendar dates on certificates will be reliable and vital to future research, providing additional data with respect to addresses, names of parents and occupations. Before 1837 we must rely on parish records of baptisms, weddings and burials; accessible records of these may be incomplete since they rely on local transcription. While wedding dates are reliable, the dates of baptisms and burials will necessarily not correspond precisely with those of births and deaths, with differences of several weeks not uncommon. Indeed many families chose to have several children baptised at the same time, meaning in some cases gaps of several years between birth and baptism. The Church of Latterday Saints provides the most comprehensive coverage of UK parish records.

Secondary data sources are available from a number of organisations with efficient search engines capable of tracing relationships back to the 1500s. The cheapest of these is available free through the FamilySearch facility of the Church of Latterday Saints (www.lds.org). Alternative, arguably more sophisticated, sites are available via subscription and include Ancestry, My Heritage and The Genealogist, and these will provide access to both newspaper archives and, most importantly, census records. UK census records are currently accessible between 1841 and 1911, with results from the 1921 available in 2021. While the census provides an essential secondary source of historical information, it also provides examples of the potentially misleading nature of data from archival sources:

- Transcription errors – as we might also anticipate from interview data, since prior to 1911, census data were collected by a third party standing on the doorstep of the residence transcribing verbal responses – since many of the residents could neither read nor write. Names were frequently misspelled and nicknames often recorded as valid forenames.
- Errors of omission – individuals may be left off the census record – particularly children who may be staying elsewhere on census night, and who are omitted there too.
- Errors of accuracy – perhaps deliberate in order to obfuscate age at marriage, or accidental because the respondents may not be sure of the ages of their children, especially for very large families.

Census data must therefore be treated with caution, especially with reference to dates and ages since they are often in error by several years. Repeated checks for the same family over consecutive census declarations may provide explanations. When searching for relatively unusual names the basic primary and secondary sources will generally get you back through several generations easily and reliably. With more common names (e.g., Smith) problems will arise – but these are not insuperable, they just necessitate a wider search of different family strands using 'clues' provided by the persistence of family forenames through generations – and the common incorporation of a grandmother's surname as forename. A major problem arises where brothers give their children identical names (surprisingly common in the 1800s); then a careful tracking of all families through the census will need to be backed up with documentary evidence from primary sources (particularly birth certificates) to ensure that we are indeed in the right place.

The numerous ways in which errors can arise in such research is typical of that in qualitative archival research, making it essential that we take a rigorous approach, following Nisbett and Ross (1980) by ensuring that we do not ignore evidence contrary to our hypotheses, and following Kahneman and Tversky (1972) in ensuring that we do not draw conclusions based on insufficient evidence.

The Holy Grail: experiments in the field

Field studies are noted in Chapter 10 for their real-world emphasis with a focus on external validity, while experimental research (see Chapter 8) focuses on research designs which emphasise internal validity in order to establish reliable cause-and-effect relationships. A combination of the two, where we seek to maximise internal validity in an experiment conducted under field conditions will be challenging at least, and virtually unknown in accounting research. The number of variables involved, most of which cannot be measured and some of which cannot be observed, make experiments very difficult, conditions which are amplified in longitudinal studies. The infamous Hawthorne studies (Mayo, 1933) remain the prime example of experiments conducted in the field in a management environment. Chapter 8 details the problems and flaws in this study, and gives clear indications of why field conditions are so difficult to conquer when searching for success in experimental projects – hence the Holy Grail description! Unsurprisingly, therefore, my own efforts in this respect have not been notably successful, except in further illustrating the problems to be encountered.

In an industrial setting my research efforts were thwarted by the possibility of undesirable effects on participants as a result of taking part. The experiment was designed to examine how the information processing styles of two work-teams impacted on their ability to address a bottleneck issue (reported in Smith and Tucker, 2013: 134). But trade union intervention prevented the experiment from proceeding. The union representatives argued, that the provision of different information might disadvantage some of their members, potentially impacting on their bonuses and future employment security!

Education has proved to be fertile ground for field experiments that have persisted over many years in conditions where performance outcomes have been inconsistent or difficult to measure. Where the outcomes are clear in the short term, ethical considerations may impact the conduct of the experiments (in sharp contrast to the Tuskegee research study reported in Chapter 4). My own efforts at experimenting with different teaching methods for multiple accounting groups were abandoned before the completion of the experimental period when it became clear that one particular method was vastly superior to the alternatives. Continuing with the experiment would have been unethical because some groups of students would have been disadvantaged.

Political objectives in pursuit of equality of opportunity were behind an educational 'experiment' in the UK in the 1970s with the abolition of the 'Eleven+' examination to determine selective streaming based on ability, and with it the grammar schools. All new public secondary schools became 'Comprehensive' in nature as a result. The outcomes of the experiment in terms of improved performance, and any perceived causality, were always going to be difficult to measure, as is typical of experiments conducted longitudinally and with many variables involved. But after 50 years it appears that there is now a renewed clamour for the supposed benefits of selection and streaming with the return of the grammar schools.

UK academics of advancing years may recall the business education 'experiment' thrust upon those teaching business subjects in polytechnics and colleges of higher education in the mid-1980s. Subjects taught at the National Certificate and Diploma levels (OND/HND) were to cease being single subjects, but were rather to be multidisciplined. The logic suggested that since 'business' was multidisciplinary then so should the way it was taught. As a consequence single subjects like statistics, accounting and computing disappeared to be merged into units termed 'Quantitative Methods', while economics, sociology and psychology were merged into units termed 'Understanding Organizations', or similar. The downside was that academics in tertiary institutions were single subject specialists, with incentives to remain so, and to specialise even more narrowly from a career perspective. Team teaching was problematic because academics' knowledge of their partner subjects was limited or non-existent, learning objectives were narrow and the depth of knowledge shallow. As a consequence students were taught less but the evidence of declining student outcomes was difficult to measure or demonstrate. Thus, the 'experiment' persisted for five years before a return to the sanity of individual subjects.

Strategic management accounting

Within an accounting environment we can observe the identification, definition and solution to practical business problems – solutions which require the careful specification of the research question, the development of hypotheses and alternative implementation strategies. Thus, John Harvey-Jones (1992; Harvey-Jones and Massey, 1990), the celebrated 'troubleshooter' of the eponymous television series, and who predates the recent 'reality' television explosion, details his approach to the investigation of practical issues in real business situations. His activities might be considered to correspond to a form of action research in that he is actively collaborating onsite with other individuals, although his practices rarely correspond with accepted 'good practice' in action research. Harvey-Jones appears to develop a systematic model during the first series for application in the second series (*Troubleshooter 2*). Central to this model is the specification of a fundamental research question based on an analysis of the published financial accounts and empirical observation of the site. Interestingly, this specification of the research question rarely coincides with that of the CEO of the organisation concerned. Further observation and benchmarking against the performance of other organisations allows the development of hypotheses and alternative approaches that may yield the desired outcome. Reporting of the recommendations often causes conflict with the senior management of participating organisations, especially in the earlier episodes, where the importance of organisation culture to an acceptable solution appears to have been underestimated or overlooked. The stages of analysis depicted in Figure 2.8 generate the more generalised framework for business solution and improvement opportunities in Figure 2.9.

Figure 2.8 The Harvey-Jones approach to problem-solving

Figure 2.9 Generalised process-improvement sequence

This approach has provided the basis for a number of similar, more recent, consulting ori- ented 'factual entertainment' ventures: thus Gerry Robinson examines the frailties of family business relationships in *I'll Show them Who's Boss* (2000) and in Robinson (2004). Here he highlights the importance of management strength in each of six areas: leadership, strategy formulation, staff relations, implementing redundancies, focus on the key issues and com- munication. Other business analysis and solution cases are explored by the BBC in, for example, *Trouble at the Top* (2004), *The Ferocious Mr Fix It* (2006) and in *Alex Polizzi: The Fixer* (2012). It is apparent in all these ventures that we have here a systematic, almost stra- tegic, approach that owes relatively little to theory. An accepted positivist research sequence offers great similarities, except that a much wider preparatory stage is undertaken, which is rarely restricted to the consideration of a single case. Specification of the individual elements of the research sequence here provides the basis for their detailed discussion in Chapter 3, with the focus on theory and literature sufficient to be able to build testable hypotheses.

Further reading

Ahrens, T. and Chapman, C. (2006) 'Doing Qualitative Field Research in Management Accounting: Positioning Data to Contribute to Theory', *Accounting, Organizations and Society*, 31 (8): 819–41.

Foster, G. (1986) *Financial Statement Analysis*, 2nd edn. Englewood Cliffs, NJ: Prentice Hall.

Gill, J. and Johnson, P. (2010) *Research Methods for Managers*, 4th edn. London: SAGE.

Kahneman, D. and Tversky, A. (1972) Availability: A Heuristic for Judging Frequency and Probability', *Cognitive Psychology*, 5 (2): 677–95.

Khlif, H. and Chalmers, K. (2015) 'A Review of Meta-Analytic Research in Accounting', *Journal of Accounting Literature*, 35: 1–27.

Lapsley, I. (2004) 'Making Sense of Interactions in an Investigation of Organizational Practices and Processes', in C. Humphrey and B. Lee (eds), *The Real Life Guide to Accounting Research*. London: Elsevier. pp. 175–90.

Lee, T.A. (2004) 'Accounting and Auditing Research in the United States', in C. Humphrey and B. Lee (eds), *The Real Life Guide to Accounting Research*. London: Elsevier. pp. 57–62.

Mayo, E. (1933) *The Human Problems of an Industrial Civilisation*. New York: MacMillan.

Nisbett, R. and Ross, L. (1980) *Human Inference: Strategies and Shortcomings of Social Judgment*. Englewood Cliffs, NJ: Prentice Hall.

Parker, L.D. (2012) 'Qualitative Management Accounting Research: Assessing Deliverables and Relevance', *Critical Perspectives on Accounting*, 23: 54–70.

Rogers, E.M. (2003) *The Diffusion of Innovations*, 5th edn. New York: Free Press.

Ryan, R., Scapens, R.W. and Theobald, M. (2002) *Research Method and Methodology in Finance and Accounting*, 2nd edn. London: Thomson.

Smith, M. and Tucker, B. (2013) *Advanced Strategic Management Accounting: Theory and Practice*. Melbourne: Cengage.

Trotman, K.T. (1996) *Research Methods for Judgment and Decision-Making Studies in Auditing*. Melbourne: Coopers & Lybrand.

Watson, J.D. (1968) *The Double Helix*. New York: Penguin Books.

Theory, Literature and Hypotheses

THREE

Chapter Contents

- Sources of theory
- Grounded theory
- Searching the literature
- Modelling the relationship
- Developing the hypotheses
- Validity concerns

We have established theory, reliability and validity as three of the characteristics of accounting research that we wish to achieve. In this chapter we expand this list to five: good theory, reliability, construct validity, internal validity and external validity. We also recognise that because of the inherent trade-offs we can only have some part of each of these characteristics at the same time; choices and compromises are necessary. In this chapter we continue to explore these aspects of good research so that we are in a position, in Chapter 5, to choose between alternative methods in identifying the most appropriate approach to a particular research question.

Sources of theory

We begin with some definitions to overcome potential confusion with terminology, especially where the edges to some concepts appear blurred and the definitions interdependent.

- **Theory** is a network of hypotheses or an all-embracing notion that underpins one or more hypotheses. In Chapter 1 we described theory as 'a set of tentative explanations' with which to justify diverse observations. We need a theory to have some justification for expecting a relationship to exist. Where we have none our *hypotheses* are immediately disputable.

- **Hypotheses** are supposed relationships, possibly causal links, between two or more concepts or variables. A hypothesis should be testable, but it may not be directly so if it comprises a number of abstract *concepts*.
- **Concepts** are abstract ideas, not directly observable or measurable, which must first be 'operationalised' in some way to provide measurable indicators. This will be achieved either by identifying a variable that is an adequate substitute for the concept or by developing a *construct* to provide a new measure of the concept.
- **Constructs** are indirect measures of concepts usually generated in the form of multi-item questions. The sum of a set of valid and reliable responses to the construct provides a measure of the concept.
- **Variables** are observable items which can assume different values. These values can be measured either directly or, if this cannot be done satisfactorily, indirectly through the use of proxy (substitute) variables. Variables are usually independent (i.e., explanatory), dependent (i.e., are explained by the independent variables), moderating (i.e., have a conditional influence) or intervening (i.e., with an influence, potentially spurious, that needs to be controlled).
- **Reliability** establishes the consistency of a research instrument in that the results it achieves should be similar in similar circumstances. Thus, the same survey subjects (participants) using the same instrument should generate the same results under identical conditions.
- **Validity** measures the degree to which our research achieves what it sets out to do. We would usually distinguish between construct validity, internal validity and external validity, each of which will be addressed later in this chapter and in subsequent chapters.

We can illustrate these terms with reference to particular examples in the accounting literature, and many further examples will arise in subsequent chapters. The source of most **theory** in accounting research is not the accounting literature but the economics (and finance), behavioural and sociology literatures. Thus, Smith and Taffler (2000) use signalling theory to examine the nature of corporate disclosures, in the expectation that firms will behave in a manner that 'signals' to the market that they are high achievers and are adopting industry best-practice. They use this as a basis to establish a formal hypothesis, for subsequent testing, that the positive content of corporate narratives will be directly associated with the financial performance of the company. The incentive-signalling literature was originally developed by Spence (1973) and has since been adopted in a number of accounting and finance applications.

Brownell (1982) establishes a **concept**, termed 'budgetary participation' in his study, as one of the desirable attributes of leadership in management. He is unable to measure this concept directly so he uses the Milani (1975) **construct** to operationalise it instead. This multi-item instrument measures influence, involvement and participation in budget-setting but is deemed a satisfactory indicator of budgetary participation.

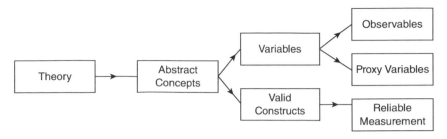

Figure 3.1 Searching for construct validity

Much of the literature examining agency relationships (e.g., Watts and Zimmerman, 1978) uses 'political influence' as one of the variables under examination, but because of the difficulty in observing and measuring this **variable** directly, company size (measured by assets or employees) is often used as a proxy variable. The prominence of unobservable 'latent' variables in much accounting research makes structural equation modelling (SEM) and partial least squares (PLS) approaches particularly appropriate in this context.

The formal **reliability** of the research instruments employed is rarely addressed in the accounting literature; only survey-based research makes a virtue out of the use of measures like the Cronbach alpha to detail the degree of confidence we have in the means of data collection. Questions of validity are best considered in the trade-offs we have to make, usually between reliability and **construct validity** on the one hand, and between **internal validity** and **external validity** on the other. Thus, in the example cited above, Brownell chooses to use the well-accepted Milani instrument. Reliability is not in doubt because this instrument consistently generates high Cronbach alphas, but construct validity is in doubt since Brownell wants to measure 'participation' in budget-setting but the chosen instrument also measures 'influence' and 'involvement'. The construct being used may therefore not be measuring exactly what is required or being specified. Figure 3.1 illustrates the problem we encounter in striving to achieve construct validity.

We start with a theory that establishes a series of relationships between ill-defined concepts. These may be difficult to pin down and impossible to measure directly. We first search for an observable variable, which may act as a proxy for the concept. For example, 'absenteeism' is often used in the management literature to proxy for the concepts 'morale' and 'team spirit'. But if we consider these to be inadequate proxies, then we need to search for an alternative, perhaps by identifying a construct that satisfactorily measures the concept. Ideally, an established construct will already be in existence to measure exactly what we want – this is the best of both worlds: reliability and construct validity. More often we are faced with a dilemma: either use an established construct which does not quite hit the target (threatening construct validity) or develop a new or adapted instrument, by devising a revised set of questions, which does hit the target (threatening reliability). The former trade-off is the one most likely to be encountered in the accounting literature, though we might argue that we would prefer to see more of the latter.

If we have **internal validity** then we are able to eliminate rival hypotheses with confidence because we can specify causal relationships; we know what is causing what because we are controlling for all other influential factors. This scenario only precisely fits experiments under laboratory conditions, conducted under strict control and perhaps based on unrealistic assumptions. The findings may have no **external validity** whatsoever; they cannot be generalised to the 'real world' because they only apply in the laboratory. This is another fundamental trade-off, and one where we may have to compromise loss of internal validity (loosening the confidence we have in the relationships) in order to increase external validity (and realism).

Both construct validity and internal validity are wholly dependent on good theory: establishing a research design with appropriate concepts which are underpinned by theory and which are realistically linked to their means of measurement. It is instructive to turn first to the sources of theory available to accounting researchers and to look at these in more detail.

The fundamental distinction underpinning accounting theory is that between normative theory (of what ought to be) and positive theory (of what is or will be). Much of the pioneering work in financial accounting (e.g., Littleton, 1933; Paton and Littleton, 1940) was an embodiment of current practice to establish what **ought** to be the optimal accounting practices, particularly for income determination purposes. Such research offered little opportunity for empirical testing or for the development of positive theory, concerning, for example, how managers and investors would actually react to the provision of new accounting information in their decision-making. Ryan et al. (2002: 68) identify three distinct research streams emanating from the positivist movement:

- microeconomic theory applied to financial accounting through agency theory, and to management accounting through production economics;
- behavioural accounting research, developed by applying elements of sociology, cognitive psychology and decision theory – predominantly in the audit judgement sphere; and
- organisation theory applied in the form of contingency theory and systems theory.

The pivotal Ball and Brown (1968) paper, linking accounting information to stock market reaction, effectively signalled the demise of normative accounting research and triggered a change in the nature of accounting research. Ryan et al. (2002: 35) note the importance, too, of the Abdel-Khalik and Ajinkya (1979) paper in this regard, which promoted the desirability of a scientific approach to accounting research, despite opposition from, among others, Tomkins and Groves (1983), protesting the greater suitability of alternative methods in particular circumstances. These changes have contributed to a division between practitioners and accounting researchers, which appears to reflect an ever-widening gap (e.g., Jayazeri and Cuthbert, 2004; Tucker et al., 2016). Parker (2012: 57) identifies a variety of theoretical perspectives adopted by qualitative researchers in examining management accounting change, embracing contingency theory, structuration theory, actor-network theory, Foucauldian theory, Habermasian theory, labour process theory, grounded theory and neo-institutional theory.

Scapens and Roberts (1993), Hoque (2006), Lukka (2007) and Stringer (2007) provide authoritative sources for the detailed discussion of alternative theories.

We look particularly at developments in economics, finance, sociology, psychology and organisational behaviour for sources of testable theory that may be applied in an accounting environment; the coverage here is necessarily not comprehensive, but illustrative of the potential sources in other disciplines.

Economics

Early researchers (e.g., Canning, 1929; Edwards, 1938) used economic analysis in a deductive manner to develop alternative approaches to income determination, theorising of which was subsequently combined with normative findings by Bedford (1965) to provide a conceptual framework for income determination. Much earlier still, the neoclassical theory of the firm had established an economic framework with fundamental assumptions: decision-making by rational, profit-maximising individuals, working under conditions of certainty, and with freely available information. These basics have had far-reaching effects, leading, for example, to the development of normative decision-making models of practices, which would yield profit-maximising outcomes under appropriate assumptions (e.g., those associated with linear programming solutions, cost–volume–profit analysis and discounted cash flows). But neoclassical theory is unhelpful in providing guidance on the practical behaviour of individuals without significant modifications to the general theory, and a relaxation of its key assumptions:

- Friedman (1953) established the positivist economics perspective: that the purpose of theory is to enable us to make verifiable predictions. In doing so he suggested that even if theory makes unrealistic assumptions, it does not matter so long as verifiable predictions result. These sentiments provided the impetus for the positivist approach to accounting typified by Watts and Zimmerman (1986).
- Stakeholder theory emerged in response to the perceived failure of the 'shareholder theory' advanced by Friedman (1970), Argenti (1993) and Dunlap (1996), among others, to advance wider claims. Donaldson and Preston (1995) press normative stakeholder interests on the grounds that other groups add value, even if they lack power; they argue that human decency should balance commercial success. The adoption of stakeholder concepts in the accounting literature is illustrated by Gray et al. (1988, 1997); Owens et al. (2000) and Saravanamuthu (2013).
- Simon (1959) developed the concept of 'bounded rationality', which permitted the emergence of 'satisficing' rather than 'maximising' behaviour, as further developed by Cyert and March (1963).
- Nelson and Winter (1982: 482) conceptualise **institutional theory** by identifying the routine nature of business practice, including accounting methods, as being the tacit knowledge that underpins a firm's acknowledged 'know-how'. Williamson (1985) contributes to initial theoretical developments with an emphasis on transaction-cost

economics (e.g., Williamson, 1975) and bounded rationality (e.g., Simon, 1976). Accounting applications include those of Burns and Scapens (2000), Johannson and Baldvinsdottir (2003), Soin et al. (2002), Scapens and Jayazeri (2003), and Major and Hopper (2007).

- Demski and Feltham (1976) explored information economics theories.
- Agency theory is grounded in neoclassical economic principles of utility maximisation (e.g., Watts and Zimmerman, 1978, 1990) and provides an established framework, forming what they termed 'a nexus of contracts' between managers and shareholders, and between managers and subordinates, to discuss principal–agent relations, transaction-cost economics and positivist models. Subramaniam (2006: 65) provides a clear distinction between these three branches of study and their respective assumptions. In the literature Baiman (1990) reviews agency theory applications in management accounting, Watts and Zimmerman (1986) financial accounting applications and Covaleski et al. (2003) applications specific to the budgeting literature.
- Williamson (1979) developed a theory of economic organisation to explain why activities are organised in particular ways and how choices are made, with implications for accounting research on decision processes (e.g., Spicer and Ballew, 1983).
- Rational choice theory (RCT) is an economic theory associated with behaviours consistent with maximising utility. RCT embraces neoclassicism, expected utility theory and rational actor theory. Examples of its use appear in Ansari and Euske (1987), Carruthers and Espeland (1991), Ansari and Bell (1991), Covaleski et al. (1993), Jones and Dugdale (1994), and Rahaman and Lawrence (2001).

Each of these developments has had a wide influence on accounting research, particularly in terms of decision-making processes, the motives of the decision maker and the way in which accounting information is used. They have coincided with the prominence of the decision usefulness approach to financial accounting, especially since the 1970s, prompting empirical developments in the pursuit of a conceptual framework for accounting – a body of knowledge underpinning the discipline.

Finance

Although we might perceive finance as a sub-discipline of economics, the developments in this field have had such a radical influence on accounting research that they deserve separate consideration. Advances in finance theory have had implications particularly for research in financial management, corporate policy and investor behaviour:

- Markowitz (1952), with work on portfolio risk, led to Sharpe (1964) and the capital asset pricing model. This formed the basis for the pioneering work of Ball and Brown (1968), linking stock market reaction to the provision of accounting information.

- Modigliani and Miller (1958) developed a theory regarding the risks associated with capital structure.
- Fama (1970) developed the notions of market efficiency associated with the processing of stock price information.
- Black and Scholes (1973) formulated the option pricing model as a vehicle for handling decision-making under uncertain conditions.
- Jensen and Meckling (1976) first expounded the agency costs argument associated with debt–equity trade-offs, which initiated a stream of research linked to the choice of accounting policy, and subsequently to management accounting (see Baiman, 1982).
- Ross (1977), following Spence (1973), initiated incentive-signalling theories in finance, spawning a research stream concerned with voluntary disclosures in financial reporting.
- Scott (1981), following Myers (1977) and the financial economics tradition, developed a theory of corporate failure based on cash flows, underpinning some of the earlier work in failure prediction (e.g., Beaver, 1966; Altman, 1968; Taffler, 1983).

Psychology

- Locke (1968) leans on Aristotle's 'final causality' concept to develop *goal-setting theory*, suggesting complex goal-performance relationships, in which individual activity is conditioned by the nature and scope of goals. Chong and Johnson (2007) and Lehmann et al. (2009) provide examples of its application in accounting research.
- Bem (1972) developed **self-perception theory** to argue that attitudes are used to rationalise behaviour choices after the event. Such outcomes are evident in the incidence of hindsight bias in interview-based accounting research.
- Kahneman and Tversky (1972) recognised that decision-making under conditions of uncertainty required the development of appropriate behavioural theories, theories which have led to a stream of accounting research concerned with decision-making heuristics and decision processes (e.g., Joyce and Biddle, 1981; Smith, 1993).

Sociology

- Bandura (1977) developed **social learning theory**, suggesting that we learn through both observation and direct experience so that individual perceptions can be influenced by teachers, peers and the media. Hamilton and Troiler (1986) show how social learning theory can impact on the individual's decision-making process, through the influence of socialisation and prior personal experiences. This has impacted research on the development and maintenance of accounting stereotypes and their impact on accounting recruitment (e.g., Friedman and Lyne, 2001; Smith and Briggs, 1999).
- Freeman (1984) develops **stakeholder theory** to identify the interested parties within an organisation, and a modelling of the methods that managers might employ to address the interests of diverse groups. Within accounting research, Magness (2008), Kelly and

Alam (2008), and Van der Laan et al. (2008) provide examples from different spheres of research: financial, management and corporate social reporting, respectively.

- **Legitimacy theory** derives from Plato's 'social contract' and Thomas Hobbes' seventeenth-century treatise on 'self-interested enlightenment'. It is associated with the perception that entities will act in a desirable manner consistent with an acceptable social structure. More recently Rawls (1971) has popularised the theory for application in accounting, and elsewhere, with respect to mutually advantageous agreements sought by members of society. O'Donovan (2002), Campbell (2003), Chen et al. (2008), and Rapkin and Braaten (2009) provide interesting examples applying legitimacy theory. Deegan (2006: 161–177) observes the increasing use of legitimacy theory in accounting research, particularly in social and environmental accounting, but notes that empirical support for legitimacy theory is not universal. Patten (1992) and Deegan et al. (2002) provide examples of organisations making disclosures to advance their legitimacy. But there is still little research to examine whether such disclosures have been successful in changing legitimacy perceptions.

- Berry et al. (1985) adopt a case study approach based in sociological and conflict theories to explore the complexity of organisational processes in the National Coal Board. Campbell (1965) had earlier shown how **realistic conflict theory** could impact on the competition for scarce physical resources; Tajfel and Turner (1985) developed a **social identity theory**, which further modified **conflict theory** to embrace scarce social resources, like status and prestige. Homans (1961) and Blau (1964) promote **social exchange theory** (SET) as the basis for a subjective cost–benefit analysis established by the participants of any relationship to justify their continuing to do so; Tucker et al. (2016) use SET to explain how interpersonal relationships promote collaboration in co-authorship relationships in accounting publishing.

- MacIntosh (1994) details the labour process paradigm devised by Marx and Engels and which was based in the tradition of political economics. This view places the manager in the position of both victim and user of management accounting information and control systems, and provides for a stream of accounting research in the **radical structuralist** tradition (e.g., Tinker, 1980).

- Callon (1986) and Latour (1986) developed **actor-network theory**, to emphasise the interdependencies of human (and non-human) activity within social networks. Actors are linked to all associated influencing factors to produce a network, in order that society can develop according to the scope of human endeavours. The 1998 quotation from Sir Henry Harris, with respect to the 'actors' involved in the development and commercialisation of penicillin, provides a neat illustration of the concept: 'Without Fleming, no Chain or Florey, without Florey, no Heatley, without Heatley no penicillin'; Fleming had identified its existence, but had been unable to separate it; Florey and Chain did so, but not without Heatley's technical wizardry. Alcouffe et al. (2008) provide an example of the application of the theory in the management accounting environment, Gummerson (2007) one in case study-based research.

Organisational behaviour

Robbins (1995) observes three levels of research interest in organisational behaviour, associated respectively with individuals, groups and organisation systems, and he develops a theoretical framework for each. Models at the individual level are heavily influenced by the psychology discipline, while those at the group and organisation level are influenced more by sociology and social psychology. All have been highly influential in the development of accounting research.

The **individual** focus looks at contributions to knowledge from the impact of, for example, learning, motivation, personality, perception, training, leadership, job satisfaction, decision-making, performance appraisal, attitudes and behaviour, together with their relationship to biographical characteristics. A selection of the multitude of theories generated in this area illustrates their potential accounting applications:

- Kelley (1972) developed **attribution theory** to explain how we perceive people differently depending on the meaning that we attribute to a given behaviour. This would have relevance to management accounting research based in the appraisal of subordinate performance by managers (e.g., Mia, 1989).
- Festinger (1957) developed **cognitive dissonance theory** to explain the relationships between attitudes and behaviour, and the potential impact of conflict therein on both individual and organisation. The theory is relevant to studies of accounting research involving conflicting information or where messages conveyed are alien to the user (e.g., Smith and Taffler, 1995; Smith, 1998b).
- Early motivation theorists (e.g., Maslow, 1954; Herzberg, 1966; McClelland, 1967) identified various intrinsic and extrinsic rewards which motivate performance. More recently, **expectancy theory** (Vroom, 1964; Lawler, 1973), leaning heavily on cognitive psychology, has become the most widely accepted explanation of motivation, arguing that behaviour will depend on the likelihood of our attaining an attractive reward. This theory has been used in the accounting literature by Ronen and Livingstone (1974) to suggest that subordinates will only expend effort in the expectation that their actions will provide intrinsic and extrinsic satisfaction. It has subsequently been used to explore the major behavioural variables linked to the motivation effects of budgets (e.g., Ferris, 1977; Rockness, 1977), and more recently with respect to accounting choices (e.g., Watts and McNair, 2008; Clor-Proell, 2009).
- Giddens (1984, 1991) develops **structuration theory** to describe a social process in which individuals interact with structures to generate regulations and behavioural expectation, suggesting that human action takes place within the context of a pre-existing social structure, a structure that can be modified by human action. Scapens and Roberts (1993) identify three layers in the structuration process: signification (the creation of a shared meaning), domination (generating a power structure) and legitimation (providing morally acceptable behaviour). Thus, if accounting changes can simultaneously 'signify,

dominate and legitimate' they will prevail, otherwise they will encounter resistance. Collier (2001) uses structuration theory to examine a system of devolved budgeting in the UK police force, and demonstrates the acceptance of enabling change after initial resistance. More recent examples of the application of structuration theory in the accounting literature are provided by Coad and Glyptis (2014), Conrad (2014), Roberts (2014) and Englund and Gerdin (2014). De Sanctis and Poole (1994) propose an **adaptive structuration theory** in which technology is used in group decision support systems. MacIntosh and Scapens (1990) and Jack and Kholeif (2007) provide examples within an accounting environment.

- Griffith et al. (2015) follow DiMaggio and Powell (1983) in employing **institutional theory** to propose alternative causes for observed auditor behaviour.
- Rogers (1995) used **diffusion theory** to establish a formal process for the acceptance and implementation of management innovations. He posited four distinct stages of change: **discovery** (identification of the innovation); **translation** (recognition of the benefits of the change); **dissemination** (selling the idea to colleagues to secure implementation); and **change** (where we innovate and monitor the effects). Askarany and Smith (2008) use diffusion theory to examine management accounting innovations; Tucker and Lowe (2014) and Tucker and Parker (2014) use diffusion theory to examine how practitioners respond to potential innovations resulting from the consequences of accounting research projects.

In Chapter 1 we distinguished between positivist, interpretive and critical approaches to accounting research. Much of the content of our earlier chapters has been devoted to 'positivist' perspectives, so it is opportune here to return to the other two approaches, especially since much of the associated literature is documentary, historical and archival in nature, and frequently without an empirical base.

Roslender (2006: 247) provides a robust outline of the development of critical theory, and cites the Berry et al. (1985) paper as a seminal work in the sociology of accounting, which has forged the development of critical perspectives on changes in management control systems. He identifies the three Marxist perspectives, which have been influential in the accounting literature: labour process theory (e.g., Hopper et al., 1987), political economy (e.g., Tinker, 1980, 1985) and critical theory (e.g., Laughlin, 1987).

Power et al. (2003) reflect on a decade of accounting research informed by critical theory, which has embraced the use of Habermasian concepts (e.g., Broadbent et al., 1991) to identify the potentially damaging consequences of accounting practices; the need to promote welfare, justice and emancipation (e.g., Dillard, 1991); the extension of the contribution to social philosophy (e.g., Arrington and Puxty, 1991); and encouragement of debate from a feminist perspective (e.g., Broadbent, 1998).

Baker and Bettner (1997) note that this lack of empiricism contributes to the absence of critical and interpretive studies from the top US accounting journals. Jönsson and MacIntosh (1997) question the appropriateness of the 'critical-Marxist' stance adopted by those such as Tinker (1980) and Ezzamel and Willmott (1992), especially where their conclusions are largely determined in advance, and without the necessity for fieldwork of any kind. At the other extreme, 'interpretive' research conducted in the hospital sector (e.g., Preston et al., 1992, 1997; Chua and Degeling, 1993) is highly empirical and dependent on extensive fieldwork assignments. Malsch and Salterio (2016) report that the traditional 'positivist' journals in the US, Europe and Australia (notably *Contemporary Accounting Research, The Accounting Review, European Accounting Review, Accounting and Finance*) have been slow to accept interpretive field studies, while the traditional 'interpretive' journals (like *Accounting, Organizations and Society*) have been slow to accept positivist pieces. They note that field studies, which are little more than descriptions of practice, though arguably valuable, will be virtually unpublishable in leading journals because of their lack of contribution.

Power et al. (2003) criticise the view that accounting represents economic reality. They follow Hopwood (1987) and Hines (1988) in suggesting that accounting is implicated in the creation of that reality. Arrington and Puxty (1991) suggest the need for 'less accounting', but more 'accountability'.

Laughlin (1999) provides an interesting summary of critical research, but it is possible to identify the development of a number of narrower fields of critical/interpretive research, adopting different perspectives on the distorting nature of accounting, notably:

- **Critical-Marxist:** for example, Tinker (1980); Tinker et al. (1991); and Bryer (1999).
- **Critical-radical:** for example, Armstrong (1987); Cooper and Scherer (1984); and Tinker and Niemark (1987), who adopt neo-Marxist perspectives to suggest that accounting distorts reality by representing the interests of capital.
- **Critical-feminist:** for example, Hammond and Oakes (1992); Oakes and Hammond (1995); and Hines (1992), who provide critiques founded in a gendered conception of accounting logic.
- **Interpretive:** for example, Arrington and Francis (1989); Lehman (1999).
- **Critical-interpretive:** for example, Laughlin (1987); Power and Laughlin (1996); and Willmott (2008).
- **Feminist-interpretive:** for example, Broadbent (1998); Gallhofer (1998).
- **Radical:** for example, Sikka (2001); Sikka and Willmott (1997).
- **Radical-feminist:** for example, Hammond (1997); Dwyer and Roberts (2004).

Such labelling is always fraught with danger and likely to raise the ire of the authors concerned. What it does do is demonstrate the breadth of research being conducted in the critical paradigm, despite the restricted nature of the publication opportunities. Indeed, almost all of the works referenced in this section have been published in just three journals: *Accounting Organizations and Society, Critical Perspectives on Accounting* and *Accounting, Auditing and Accountability Journal*.

The group focus looks at the contribution to knowledge of the impact of group dynamics and processes, communication, behavioural and attitude changes, norms, roles, status, power and conflict:

- Argyris (1952) and Becker and Green (1962) use contingency theories to explore the impact of group dynamics on the budgetary process.
- Barrow (1977) developed a contingency theory of leadership in trying to explain successful leadership and consequent group behaviour as a combination of specific leadership styles and situational conditions.
- Vroom and Yetton (1973) developed the **leader–participation** model, a popular contingency variant, to relate leadership behaviour to participation in decision-making, while emphasising the importance of task structure. This theory has clear implications for accounting research in areas such as budget-setting.

The **organisation systems** focus looks at the contribution to knowledge of the impact of organisation culture and change, structure and hierarchy, conflict and power structures, together with their relationship to human resource policies and job design:

- Organisation theorists (e.g., Burns and Stalker, 1961; Woodward, 1965) explore the relationship between environmental and organisational variables. Accounting researchers have expanded the scope of these variables to include relationships between the environment (e.g., technology, uncertainty), the organisation (e.g., structure, task complexity, decentralisation, supervisory style, job-related tension) and accounting variables (e.g., performance evaluation, budgetary participation). The aim is to produce a contingency theory that 'must identify specific aspects of an accounting system which are associated with certain defined circumstances and demonstrate an appropriate matching' (Otley, 1980: 414). Such studies have established relationships between accounting practices and environmental and organisational factors, and have produced a recognised body of knowledge (see Otley, 1984), which is arguably the most coherent in management accounting. Contingency theory underpins a great deal of the management control systems (MCS) literature with regard to how MCS can be designed to reflect the contextual circumstances. Chenhall and Chapman (2006: 35) emphasise the role of contingency theory in establishing: (a) the fit with the context; (b) the link to context in 'selection fit' studies; and (c), how MCS impact on performance through 'interaction fit' (e.g., Gerdin and Greve, 2004). Simons (1987) and Davila (2000) show how 'selection' studies can exercise novel aspects of 'fit'. Other key literature in the area is provided by Otley (1980); Chapman (1997); Chenhall and Langfield-Smith (1998); Chenhall (2003); Ittner et al. (2003); and Bisbe et al. (2007). Luft and Shields (2003) and Hartmann and Moers (1999) are critical of much of the published work in the area – the former for the implicit assumption of linear relationships, the latter for technical inconsistencies in the implementation of the contingency framework. Chenhall (2005) sees opportunities for advances in the field through improvements in PLS and SEM that should offer new ways of examining how more elements of context impact on MCS.
- Other organisation theorists (e.g., Thompson, 1969; Perrow, 1970, 1972; Ouchi, 1977) have provided alternative frameworks for systems theory that have facilitated the

discussion of the roles of control structures and subordinate behaviour. This has allowed developments in accounting research on budgetary control devoted to the distortion of accounting information systems (e.g., Birnberg et al., 1983). **Human relations theory** is concerned with the impact of motivation, satisfaction, participation and leadership on outcomes and relationships, and forms the basis for psychology-based budgeting research, e.g., Hopwood (1974), Otley (1978), Brownell (1981), Hirst (1983), Shields and Shields (1998) and Covaleski et al. (2003).

Grounded theory

Grounded theory is included here (and also considered separately in Chapter 10) because of its increasing importance in qualitative research. In grounded theory the theory evolves from the empirical data rather than being developed and imposed in advance of data collection. Pre-determined sample sizes are inappropriate to grounded theory, since, as Sandelowski (1986) observes, the level of sampling will be determined by the findings: once the findings start to become repetitive, and nothing new is being learned, then 'saturation of themes' (Glaser and Strauss, 1967) is evident, justifying an end to further sampling.

Glaser and Strauss (1967) observe three distinct stages in the conduct of grounded theory:

- Conceptual specification – which allows relevant theories to emerge from the data.
- Theoretical sensitivity – which provides the tools to facilitate the emergence of connections within the data (comparisons, questioning, coding, memo-writing, theoretical sampling, literature review, sorting).
- Coding – to provide links between data and theory.

They are very strict and protective in their insistence that all of these stages are carried out, thus:

> the core stage is the process of generating theory, the bedrock of theory generation, its true product is the writing of theoretical memos. If the analyst skips this stage by going directly from coding to sorting or to writing, he is not doing grounded theory. (Glaser, 1978: 83).

This almost religious zeal in observing a strictly sequential process is reminiscent of that employed by Deming (1986) in 'total quality management' investigations, and is likely to generate similar researcher frustration.

Ferreira and Merchant (1992) report notable accounting examples of surprising findings emerging from a grounded theory approach.

A parting of the ways between the two major protagonists of grounded theory, Glaser and Strauss, foreshadowed the development of two competing versions of the methodology apparent in Strauss and Corbin (1990) and Glaser (1992). The rift is something of a qualitative/quantitative split in focus, and students need to be careful which version of (the two) grounded theory approaches they are adopting. Lye et al. (2006: 152) highlight the major differences in the two approaches and note that while the processes are different, the objectives of the techniques remain the same. Critically Strauss and Corbin (1990) suggest the initial formulation of a research question, while Glaser (1992) suggests entering the research domain with no predefined problem in mind. The step-by-step approach advocated by Strauss and Corbin (1990) is arguably easier to follow for beginning researchers.

In the accounting literature Gibbins et al. (1990) follow Glaser and Strauss (1967) and Glaser (1978); Lightbody (2000) and Goddard (2004) follow Strauss and Corbin (1990, 1998). Parker (2001, 2002) and Lye et al. (2005) each appear to use a hybrid Glaser/Strauss approach.

Alternative research methods are consistent with these different theoretical approaches for individual, group and organisation focus. Thus, experimental methods (based on behavioural and psychological expectations) will most frequently be used to measure individual behaviour; survey methods can be used to reveal self-reported attitudes and preferences, and case studies used to explore organisational change. However, a note of caution is warranted in that a consistent factor of the studies in the organisational behaviour area is their focus on relatively few dependent variables: productivity, absenteeism, job turnover and job satisfaction predominate to the exclusion of almost anything else. Staw (1984), among others, has argued for more attention to be devoted to new dependent variables, such as job stress, innovation and individual dissent. Briers and Hirst (1990: 374), in their review article, show that the contingency theory literature in accounting has followed a very similar line, in that only four major dependent variables (dysfunctional behaviour, job performance, budgetary performance and unit performance) have been the subject of study. The parallels reveal how dependent we are, as accounting researchers, on the theoretical developments in related disciplines.

There are clearly many potential theories to choose from – even if they are all borrowed or stolen from other disciplines. Disappointing then, that most of my PhD candidates, and most of the doctoral theses I examine, prefer to take the safe option – pursuing contingency theory, agency theory or **market-forces theory** (e.g., Porter 1980, 1985) options. There is rarely any attempt to explore the alternative theories that might explain common events, and even fewer attempts to test different theories. In this respect PhD candidates mirror the accounting literature, because it is rare to find papers that address multiple theories for a single phenomenon, or test the applicability of alternative theories; Ittner, Larcker and Meyer (2003) provide a rare example.

But is there no 'real' accounting theory? Malmi and Granlund (2009) note that theories in accounting are rarely recognised as 'real' theories by accounting researchers; they are much more prepared to accept the adequacy of theories drawn from other disciplines. Perhaps this is just some accounting inferiority complex of a discipline with no theory of its own; or perhaps it is just a hangover from the demise of normative accounting research, and the times when accountants, particularly financial accountants, had their own theories! Indeed, one consequence, according to Inanga and Schneider (2005), is that accounting research has little to offer either accounting practice or the development of accounting theory, perhaps because the findings are usually so general in nature that they are of no use to practitioners. Both Ittner and Larcker (2002) and Luft and Shields (2003) argue that accounting research must address the links between accounting choice and performance if it is to prove useful to practitioners.

Malmi and Granlund (2009) call for new theories that are useful to practice, without necessarily being normative; they suggest that researchers focus on different dependent variables (e.g., social equality, environmental sustainability), or if they want to stay with a 'performance'-based dependent variable, then they focus on specifically management accounting-oriented themes (e.g., organisational incentive schemes).

Luft and Shields (2003) review the literature on the causes and effects of management accounting research, mapping the theories and methods being employed. They note that theory is almost always derived from economics, organisational theory, contingency theory, sociology and psychology. They detail specific preferences for principal–agent theory, information economics theory, structuration theory, actor-network theory, expectancy theory and goal-setting theory in addressing management accounting issues. Malmi and Granlund (2009) see this as a missed opportunity, in that management accountants have the opportunity to apply their own (normative) theories. Thus, they see activity-based costing, the balanced scorecard, total quality management and value-based management as normative theories for, respectively: assigning overheads, designing control systems, reducing quality costs and effective decision-making. They stress that each 'theory' has the potential for development in order to explain and predict, if they can be refined to identify the specific circumstances in which they will apply. This is a challenging agenda, which needs to address the shifting objectives observed in the literature for activity-based costing (e.g., Jones and Dugdale, 2002) and for the balanced scorecard (e.g., between Kaplan and Norton, 1992 and 2004).

Of course it is possible that no single theory can adequately explain observed practice. Thus, Cohen et al. (2008) suggest that a multi-theory approach will be necessary in some circumstances. As an example they cite a series of studies which have consistently revealed that a combination of agency, institutional and resource dependency theories are necessary to explain the impact of corporate governance on the audit process. Indeed Malsch and Salterio (2016) go further in suggesting that the interdisciplinary nature of interpretive research in auditing means that theory development will necessitate the adoption of theories drawn from sociology, psychology, philosophy and politics.

Searching the literature

In conducting a search of the literature there are two fundamental questions that need to be answered: Where do we start? and What do we look for? Analagous to the development of a family tree, we want to be able to locate relevant, interesting and perhaps pivotal works from the past, but we do not know where they are! With genealogy we try to locate worthy ancestors whose characteristics might provide insights into our own skills and personalities. In both instances we need to work backwards, from the known to the unknown. To locate ancestors we examine records of births, marriages and deaths which establish links with relations; to locate the direction of the literature to need to drill down through current references to identify important past works. The initial literature search will start with a topic area, perhaps broad, perhaps a more refined research question. These may suggest both the type of journals likely to be influential, and the identity of some of the key authors who have published in the area. Each of these provides an excellent start point for a more exhaustive search. Thus, if, for example, our research question were concerned with the nature and impact of corporate narrative disclosures, our initial focus would likely be on the works of Adelberg, Courtis, Jones, and Smith and Taffler; *Accounting and Business Research* and *Accounting, Auditing and Accountability Journal* would be the obvious journals to target.

By looking at the works of key authors (at least their relevant papers), the 'references' section of these papers will quickly reveal other important authors in the area, and the seminal works – those which are cited by everyone. The latter must be read, because they will provide the foundation literature for the research topic; and for most topics there will be no more than two or three such pivotal articles.

Once the key references over the past, say 20 years, have been established then we can fast-forward in the direction of the current literature through the use of citation indexes; these will identify other papers which have referenced those same sources. Not all of these papers will be relevant to our search; often the title of the paper alone, sometimes the abstract, will be sufficient to eliminate them from further consideration. Any final doubts will be addressed by reading the introduction – only if that appears relevant should we download and read the whole paper.

This process will help us to avoid potentially embarrassing gaps in our literature search. This is particularly important if we are to locate papers published in other fields (e.g., psychology), which may be relevant to our topic. By complementing a search of the databases with reference to current (and in press) issues of prominent journals and conference proceedings, this will provide some assurance of the comprehensive nature of the search. Online sources have made this process much easier than it once was: thus we can conduct tertiary literature searches for journal articles (e.g., through ABI Inform, EBSCO, Science Direct, Google Scholar and Emerald), for newspaper articles (e.g., through Lexis Nexis) and for published conference papers (through the Index to Conference Proceedings). But there is still no guaranteed easy way to locate everything we need, partly because of gaps in the databases and partly because online databases may still not include very early papers, making continued access to archived hard copy journal articles essential, either through library serial holdings or through inter-library loans.

At this point it is worth reminding ourselves what we are looking for – so that we do not waste a great deal of time. The key questions might be considered as:

- **What has been done already?** We do not wish to reinvent the wheel, nor to conduct a study which makes no original contribution.
- **What has not been done?** Not for the reasons that the topic is either obsolete or too trivial to contemplate, but because the topic is rather interesting but relatively neglected.

- **What has not been done very well?** Perhaps because of theoretical or methodological flaws, certainly because the findings appear contradictory. This may be difficult to judge, but we will want to identify the different circumstances (e.g., theory, industry, country, methods etc.) associated with the studies that may have contributed to counter-intuitive findings.

Knopf (2006) summarises the purpose of the literature review, from the political policy perspective. Adapting his suggestions to the accounting literature highlights seven major concerns that should be addressed:

1. the questions that previous publications have/have not examined;
2. the conclusions of existing research;
3. the areas of consensus and contradiction in the literature;
4. the theories and methods that have been applied;
5. the reliability of the findings, and the validity of the associated interpretation;
6. the overall quality of the literature (i.e., where has it been published? Does it contribute to what might be perceived to be a coherent body of knowledge?); and
7. where are the gaps in the literature that might provide opportunities for further research?

Seminal papers in the *Journal of Accounting Literature* (e.g., Han, 2013; Stuart et al., 2013) provide examples of the application of such a structure. Thus, while evidence of what we know (i.e., the current boundaries of our knowledge) is important, then so is what we do not yet know, because this constitutes future research; the nature of empirical findings will also show what we are not sure of because of inconsistent or contradictory findings.

An indication of the theoretical frameworks adopted in prior relevant research will provide a guide to future research in the area, and have implications for our own research; the theories will indicate the relationships we are able to justify, while the empirical literature will have measured associations to identify those variables that are likely to be influential, and which are therefore the leading candidates to appear in our early conceptual models.

When writing up the results of the literature search it is important to remind ourselves what it is **not**: it is not a summary of all the publications you have read; it is not even a summary of all the **relevant** articles you have read! It **should** be logically ordered, critical and directly relevant to the topic in hand; the implications of each key piece of literature to the research being contemplated should be addressed. Indeed, when candidates are editing their literature review write-up, I encourage them to 'work backwards' again. Given the common reluctance of candidates to delete reference to anything they have read – and in consequence the lengthy, meandering reviews produced – a ruthless approach needs to be adopted! By working backwards from their own hypotheses they should be able to identify all of the literature which impacts, directly or indirectly, on the formation of these hypotheses. The presence of any other literature in the review is, at least, questionable, and needs to be justified. Easterby-Smith et al. (2008) see the literature review as a legitimate research activity, fundamental to both the refining of the research topic and the development of a rationale for a significant study. Lee and Lings (2008) stress that the literature review must be seen to add value, in that it is more than a description of what has gone before, rather it must be both critical and reflective. More detailed aspects of the literature review are considered in Chapter 10 (with respect to archival searches) and Chapter 11 (with respect to thesis writing).

We began to consider variable definition and measurement issues in Chapter 2, but it is opportune at this stage to return to Figure 2.6 to consider alternative, perhaps more appropriate, configurations for our conceptual schema.

Modelling the relationship

Our fundamental relationship is an association between two variables of interest, with the relationship subject to influence by another group of variables. At this stage we have only an 'association'; we cannot postulate a causal direction without some underpinning theory. We potentially begin with a reciprocal causality – where dependent and independent variables are conceivably reversible in their roles – until rival hypotheses can be eliminated. The scenario described earlier in Chapter 1, with respect to levels of voluntary disclosure, and depicted in Figure 3.2, fits this situation.

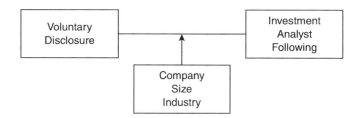

Figure 3.2 Voluntary disclosure and reciprocal causality

There is a relationship between levels of voluntary disclosure by a company and the number of investment analysts who are following (analysing, reporting and issuing recommendations on) that company. A causal link in either direction is feasible, with each supported by a rival explanation:

- firms are 'signalling' their practices, innovativeness and early adoption by choosing to disclose additional information voluntarily; or
- firms are subject to the demand for more information from analysts and are responding to the analysts' and the company's mutual benefit.

It is unlikely (but feasible) that both explanations are correct, and we await theory disconfirmation to establish an appropriate causal direction for the relationship. Co-variation is in evidence, but one of the events likely precedes the other. Evidence from Lang and Lundholm (1996), in the USA, suggests that increases in disclosure quality are followed by higher levels of analyst following. However, Walker and Tsalta (2001), with UK data, report contradictory findings of an increase in page length following an increase in analyst forecasting activity, suggesting that the controversy remains. Subsequent findings (e.g., Lang et al., 2003) appear to support the earlier Lang and Lundholm (1996) study in the USA. Luft and Shields (2014) examine strategies for the development of alternative explanations when seeking to establish a causal relationship.

A further consideration is the nature of the 'influential' variables in a model. A tighter specification of their precise role will be helpful because it will determine both how we manage their control and how we subject the subsequent findings to statistical analysis. Where the influential variables can be thought to be 'intervening', we have the model shown in Figure 3.3.

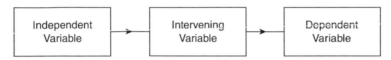

Figure 3.3 Intervening variables and causality

There is no longer a direct relationship between the original independent and dependent variables. Instead, the intervening variable is effectively the dependent variable in one (left-hand) relationship and the independent variable in a second (right-hand) relationship. Figure 3.4 illustrates a possible example of this arrangement in that the introduction of a particular accounting innovation impacts on the adoption and monitoring of non-financial performance measures. It is this new focus, rather than the original innovation itself, that causes improvement in overall financial performance. The implication for statistical analysis of such a model is that we should adopt a partial regression approach.

Figure 3.4 Non-financial focus as an intervening variable

Alternatively, the influential variables may have a 'moderating' effect in that the relationship between dependent and independent variables is conditional on the values assumed by the other variables, in the manner of Figure 3.5.

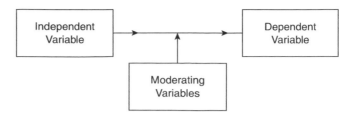

Figure 3.5 Moderated causal relationship

For the situation described above, the impact of accounting innovation may be conditional on the moderating variables of Figure 3.6.

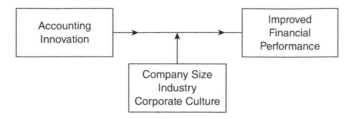

Figure 3.6 Size, industry and culture moderating performance

Thus, the strength of the relationship may depend on the size of the company, for example, so that the association is conditional on companies being larger than a certain level. Where dichotomous variables are being used to reduce measurement error (i.e., large/small companies) then moderated regression analysis (MRA) is the most appropriate form of analysis (see Hartmann and Moers, 1999, for a fascinating description and critique of the technique) and is commonly used within contingency modelling studies (e.g., Dunk, 1993; Mia, 1989). See Chapter 6 for a fuller discussion of MRA in accounting.

The influential variables may be superfluous to the relationship of interest because they impact on each separately by exerting an overriding influence. They are then termed 'extraneous' and are shown in Figure 3.7.

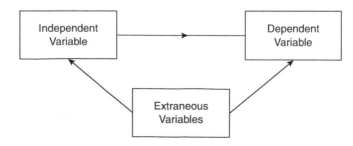

Figure 3.7 Influence of extraneous variables

For example, economic conditions may dictate the nature of the relationship. Both levels of accounting innovation and improved levels of financial performance may be linked to the up-swing of the business cycle. To examine any relationship between the variables of interest, we should either examine partial correlations or we should control for the effects of the business cycle by confining our data collection to a single, specified level of economic conditions, as suggested in Figure 3.8. Naturally, in doing so our findings may threaten external validity considerations because relationships may only hold for the particular economic conditions for which sample data are sought.

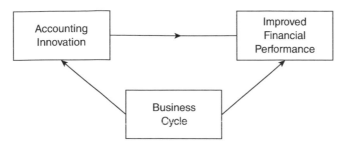

Figure 3.8 Economic conditions as extraneous variables

These simple models may be further complicated by the generation of multiple explanatory variables, whose simultaneous effect needs to be examined. For example, the explanation of business failure (e.g., Taffler, 1983), as illustrated in Figure 3.9, would normally be associated with dependence on at least four financial variables (measuring profitability, risk, liquidity and working capital) with the effect moderated by other company-specific characteristics. Even so, a further model would be needed to explain the 'timing' of failure.

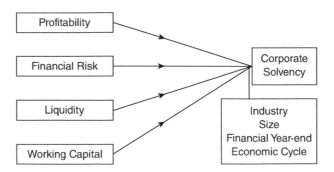

Figure 3.9 Multiple independent variables

Rarely are the 'final' models we work with as simple as the ones specified here. Indeed, in my experience, doctoral candidates are fond of developing highly complex models which start to resemble a 'theory of everything'. These models are usually beyond their capacity to test in the available time and with the sample size at their disposal. Clearly supervisor action is necessary to guide the modification of the model or to advise a focus on just one part of the framework. In all such cases, the precise nature of the analysis that we can perform will be dictated by how we measure the variables of interest. Issues of measurement and testing are discussed in detail in Chapters 5, 6 and 7 as part of the data collection and analysis procedures.

Developing the hypotheses

Hypotheses must be testable. Their content must be measurable in some way even if they are not directly observable. For these purposes, **ratio** (multiplicative) and **interval** (continuous) scales of measurement are preferred because they make possible a wider number of analytic alternatives, but ordinal (i.e., involving ranks) and nominal (in particular dichotomous, yes/no) scales are common in the accounting literature, and methods exist for their analysis. Once a research question consistent with theory has been formulated, and the research design specified, we need to develop one or more hypotheses for testing. Theory and existing literature should drive the formation of hypotheses so that what we postulate is eminently feasible based on the existing evidence. This is always something of a jump because we are venturing from the known (existing empirical findings) to the unknown (what we are investigating). It is easy to feel uncomfortable about this jump because even where all relevant literature has been digested, the move to hypotheses may still seem large and vulnerable. Where authors are particularly sensitive about this jump they may opt to establish 'propositions' of what may be anticipated rather than formal hypotheses in the form of testable expectations.

The hypotheses will normally be stated in null or alternative forms, but which form reviewers prefer may be journal dependent! The Null Hypothesis (H_0) postulates the existence of no relationship between the variables of interest; we then attempt to assemble sufficient evidence to suggest that, statistically, the Null Hypothesis is not a reasonable assumption. If we have no prior evidence to suggest a direction of causality, then we have no realistic alternative but to adopt a Null Hypothesis format.

The Alternative Hypothesis (H_1) postulates the existence of a directed (often causal) relationship, and our assembled evidence must show that findings are inconsistent with no significant relationship (the null position). Examples of hypotheses and associated tests of significance are dealt with in more detail in Chapter 5 while addressing quantitative aspects.

In conducting tests of hypotheses we are faced with the possibility of making two errors:

Type 1 error – the rejection of a true Null Hypothesis

Type 2 error – the acceptance of a false Null Hypothesis

In a legal scenario, the conviction of an innocent man would constitute a Type 1 error, while freeing a guilty man would provide a Type 2 error. In a bankruptcy prediction environment, the misclassification of a failed company as healthy would constitute a Type 1 error, while the classification of a healthy company as a failed one would constitute a Type 2 error. It is generally more important to reduce the probability of Type 1 errors (since they are seen as more serious or more expensive) so that hypothesis testing places more emphasis on Type 1 rather than Type 2 errors. Reducing the level of Type 2 errors would normally involve a trade-off for more Type 1 errors – a trade-off which may be unacceptable. Thus, in the bankruptcy prediction environment, Type 1 errors are virtually unknown, but Type 2 errors are plentiful. It remains a challenge to accounting researchers to reduce the level of Type 2 errors while maintaining current levels of Type 1 error.

If a hypothesis is not supported, we must consider the possibility of competing explanations for the findings. We must also be sceptical of our own findings, question where inconsistencies may have arisen and be prepared to collect more data or replicate the study.

Validity concerns

These concerns are covered in detail with respect to each of the methods examined in Chapters 8–11, but an early impression of the overall problem is helpful prior to the discussion of data collection. The trade-off between reliability and construct validity has been referred to above; that between internal/external validity needs further embellishment. Internal validity threats are confined to what can go wrong during the research. The most fundamental errors are those associated with the development of the model: the misspecification of the functional relationships, and the omission of important influential or explanatory variables. But we must also take great pains to avoid any potential bias in our sample: errors in, or changes to, the measurement instrument may dictate the use of a single version of the instrument to overcome **instrumentation** concerns, but the nature of the manipulation, or ordering concerns, may make this unfeasible. Similarly, **selection** problems in both the attraction of participants and their assignment to groups may be unrepresentative. The passage of time causes particular concerns in longitudinal studies, or in studies where data are collected at more than one time, through drop-outs (**mortality**), fatigue or waning enthusiasm (**maturation**), non-comparability of materials (**history**) and the effects of serial testing where repeated measures are being used (**testing**). These concerns suggest conducting the research over a short time period and at one visit, but this may conflict with the requirements of the research question under study, necessitating more complex remedies. Random selection of subjects is almost unknown in accounting research, so we need to try to introduce randomness at subsequent stages in the process, while performing the supporting measurement of potentially influential demographics (e.g., age, gender, experience).

External validity requires that research findings have implications for other sites (companies and countries) and people at different time periods. Unfortunately, the highest levels of internal validity are associated with artificial conditions (the findings may be restricted to the time, cases, participants and location of the research setting). Relaxing assumptions there to introduce greater external validity will inevitably threaten internal validity, and this remains a challenge to accounting researchers.

Where we have solved our variable definition and control methods, we still have to make an informed choice as to the most appropriate research method to be employed. These fall into five broad categories:

- scientific reasoning and/or model-building;
- historical research using archival data and/or secondary sources;
- case studies requiring extensive exploration in the field;
- surveys, often involving large-scale sampling, though lacking control and richness of outcome; and
- experiments, either in the field or, more usually, in laboratory-type conditions.

Issues of validity (both internal and external) are central to this choice, and they are considered with respect to the alternative methods in each of the succeeding chapters. Some form of trade-off is usually anticipated between control and structure, on the one hand, and real-world application on the other. Whereas the impact of particular variables (internal validity) will be much clearer under highly structured and tightly controlled conditions, the artificiality of laboratory conditions will reduce the opportunity for generalisation (and external validity). Experimental conditions necessitate the use of less complex situations than those encountered in the real world, with fewer variables and lower information content; most experiments would be impossible to conduct otherwise. Thus, research studies in accounting are rarely truly experimental (though Bloomfield and O'Hara, 1999 come close); it would be more appropriate to deem experimental accounting research as quasi-experimental in almost all cases. The key question remains whether a simplistic situation still includes sufficient elements of reality for it to be a realistic predictor of actual decision-making environments.

Further reading

Askarany, D. and Smith. M. (2008) 'The Diffusion of Management Accounting Innovation: A Longitudinal Study of PACIA', *Managerial Auditing Journal*, 23 (9): 900–16.

Ball, R. and Brown, P. (1968) 'An Empirical Evaluation of Accounting Income Numbers', *Journal of Accounting Research*, 6: 159–78.

Berry, A.J., Capps, T., Cooper, D., Ferguson, P., Hopper, T. and Lowe, E.A. (1985) 'Management Control in an Area of the NCB: Rationales of Accounting in a Public Enterprise', *Accounting, Organizations and Society*, 10 (1): 3–28.

Callon, M. (1986) 'The Sociology of an Actor-Network: The Case of the Electric Vehicle', in M. Callon, J. Law and A. Rip (eds), *Mapping the Dynamics of Science and Technology*. London: MacMillan. pp. 19–34.

Campbell, D. (2003) 'Intra- and Intersectoral Effects in Environmental Disclosures: Evidence for Legitimacy Theory?', *Business Strategy and the Environment*, 12 (6): 357–71.

Easterby-Smith, M., Thorpe, R. and Jackson, P.R. (2008) *Management Research*, 3rd edn. London: SAGE.

Foster, G. (1986) *Financial Statement Analysis*, 2nd edn. Englewood Cliffs, NJ: Prentice Hall.

Gummerson, E. (2007) 'Case Study Research and Network Theory: Birds of a Feather', *Qualitative Research in Organizations and Management*, 2 (3): 226–48.

Han, J. (2013) 'A Literature Synthesis of Experimental Studies on Management Earnings Guidance', *Journal of Accounting Literature*, 31 (1): 31–48.

Inanga, E.L. and Schneider, W.B. (2005) 'The Failure of Accounting Research to Improve Accounting Practice: A Problem of Theory and Lack of Communication', *Critical Perspectives on Accounting*, 16 (3): 227–48.

Ittner, C.D. and Larcker, D.F. (2002) 'Empirical Management Accounting Research: Are We Just Describing Management Consulting Practice?' *European Accounting Review*, 11 (4): 787–94.

Jack, L. and Kholeif, A. (2007) 'Introducing Strong Structuration Theory for Informing Qualitative Case Studies in Organization, Management and Accounting Research', *Qualitative Research in Organizations and Management*, 2 (3): 208–25.

Jones, M.J. and Shoemaker, P.A. (1994) 'Accounting Narratives: A Review of Empirical Studies of Content and Readability', *Journal of Accounting Literature*, 13: 142–84.

Jones, T.C. and Dugdale, D.A. (2002) 'The ABC Bandwagon and the Juggernaut of Modernity', *Accounting, Organizations and Society*, 27 (1/2): 121–63.

Joyce, E.J. and Biddle, G.C. (1981) 'Anchoring and Adjustment in Probabilistic Inference in Auditing', *Journal of Accounting Research*, 19 (1): 120–45.

Kahneman, D. and Tversky, A. (1972) 'Subjective Probability: A Judgment of Representativeness', *Cognitive Psychology*, July: 430–54.

Knopf, J.W. (2006) 'Doing a Literature Review', *Political Science and Politics*, 39 (1): 127–32.

Lee, N. and Lings, I. (2008) *Doing Business Research: A Guide to Theory and Practice*. London: SAGE.

Luft. J. and Shields, M.D. (2003) 'Mapping Management Accounting: Graphics and Guidelines for Theory Consistent Empirical Research', *Accounting Organizations and Society*, 28 (2/3): 169–249.

MacIntosh, N.B. and Scapens, R.W. (1990) 'Structuration Theory in Management Accounting', *Accounting, Organizations and Society*, 15 (5): 455–77.

Malmi, T. and Granlund, M. (2009) 'In Search of Management Accounting Theory', *European Accounting Review*, 18 (3): 597–620.

Merkl-Davies, D.M. and Brennan, N.M. (2007) 'Discretionary Disclosure Strategies in Corporate Narratives: Incremental Information or Impression Management', *Journal of Accounting Literature*, 26: 116–94.

O'Donovan, G. (2002) 'Environmental Disclosures in the Annual Report: Extending the Applicability and Predictive Power of Legitimacy Theory', *Accounting, Auditing and Accountability Journal*, 15 (3): 344–71.

Otley, D.T. (1980) 'The Contingency Theory of Management Accounting: Achievement and Prognosis', *Accounting, Organizations and Society*, 5 (4): 423–28.

Rogers, E.M. (1995) *Diffusion of Innovation*. New York: Free Press.

Ryan, R. Scapens, R.W. and Theobald, M. (2002) *Research Method and Methodology in Finance and Accounting*, 2nd edn. London: Thomson.

Smith, M. and Taffler, R.J. (1995) 'The Incremental Effect of Narrative Accounting Information in Corporate Annual Reports', *Journal of Business Finance and Accounting*, 22 (8): 1195–210.

Smith, M. and Taffler, R.J. (2000) 'The Chairman's Statement: A Content Analysis of Discretionary Narrative Disclosures', *Accounting, Auditing and Accountability Journal*, 13 (5): 624–46.

Stuart, I., Shin, Y-.C., Cram, D.P. and Karan, V. (2013) 'Review of Choice-based Matched and Other Stratified Sample Studies in Auditing Research', *Journal of Accounting Literature*, 32 (1), 88–113.

Tucker, B.P. and Lowe, A. (2014) 'Practitioners are from Mars; Academics are from Venus? An Investigation of the Research–Practice Gap in Management Accounting', *Accounting, Auditing and Accountability Journal*, 27 (3): 394–425.

Tucker, B.P. and Parker, L.D. (2014) 'In Our Ivory Towers? The Research–Practice Gap in Management Accounting', *Accounting and Business Research*, 44 (2): 104–43.

Tucker, B.P. Parker, L.D. and Merchant, K.A. (2016) 'With a Little Help From Our Friends: An Empirical Investigation of Co-authoring in Accounting Research', *The British Accounting Review*, 48 (2): 185–205.

Willmott, H. (2008) 'Listening, Interpreting, Commending: A Commentary on the Future of Interpretive Accounting Research', *Critical Perspectives on Accounting*, 19 (6): 920–25.

Research Ethics in Accounting

FOUR

Chapter Contents

- The ethics quiz
- Informed consent
- Ethical guidelines

Some of the atrocities committed during the Second World War in the name of medical research prompted the development of a generally accepted code of research ethics which has spread from the medical arena to all other research disciplines. Unfortunately, the transfer of such codes to the business discipline has often been seen by researchers to be an imposition, unnecessarily constraining their activities, and something better left in medicine. Such attitudes display an ignorance of the fundamental objectives of ethical guidelines and the benefits that they can convey to all concerned.

The best-documented abuses by misguided researchers remain in the medical field. Thus, Dooley (1995: 24) reports on the Tuskegee syphilis study in the USA, where researchers conducted a 40-year longitudinal study, right up to the 1970s, of an isolated black community with high incidence of the disease. Even though effective treatment through penicillin was widely available, the researchers actively sought to prevent subjects from being treated, and to avoid the disclosure of deaths caused by untreated disease, because of potential distortion to their research findings.

This may be an extreme instance, but the potential for the researcher to act in a manner which is not in the interests of the participants exists in all disciplines, especially where the participant has little control over the events associated with the research. For example, in the accounting education sphere, it may be possible to devise a field experiment where two groups of students are taught in parallel, using very different methods in order to evaluate the relative superiority of techniques. But if this experiment were over an extended period (say ten weeks), and after week two it became clear that one method was vastly superior to the other, could we on ethical grounds continue the experiment, when one group of students was clearly being disadvantaged? The natural focus would therefore be on business scenarios in which participants could be exploited in a manner that endangers their future welfare, but ethical considerations are much wider than this in practice, and concern issues of honesty, trust and subjugation.

Australia's National Health and Medical Research Council specifies the scope of research ethics in terms of three underlying principles: 'the protection of the welfare and the rights of participants in research; to facilitate research that is or will be of benefit to the researcher's community or to humankind; to provide a national reference point for ethical consideration relevant to all research involving humans' (NHMRC, 2000: 3).

The ethics quiz

The following 'ethics quiz', inspired by Agnew and Pyke (1994: 273), aims to explore some of the confusion and misunderstanding that surrounds ethical issues in accounting research. You have to determine whether the key figure in each of the following scenarios has behaved ethically or not:

1. Professor A has sought the collaboration of the CEO of Delta Corp in the conduct of interviews with the workforce. The CEO has agreed, on the condition that no further separate permissions are sought from the workers; he has provided permission and the workforce will participate as part of its job. Professor A agrees to continue on this basis.

2. Candidate B is conducting interviews with accounting managers in Hong Kong. She suggests that the requirement to have interviewees 'sign-off' on completion of the interview is an insult to the participants, which will cause loss of face. Her supervisor, Dr C, agrees that the ethical guidelines need not be observed in this instance because of cultural differences.

3. Associate Professor D is applying for promotion and, in order to strengthen her case, has sought testimonials from graduate students under her control as to the quality of her teaching, research and supervision.

4. Professor E supervises a number of Masters and PhD students. Contact typically involves discussions prior to the commencement of the study (usually not exceeding five hours in total), some discussion concerning analysis of the results and the review of one or two thesis drafts. Professor E insists on co-publication of any research papers, where he is invariably the first-named author.

5. Associate Professor F used deception in her study of the impact of gender and self-esteem on accounting decision-making. Prior to participation, all subjects are informed of the requirements and purpose of the experiment as much as possible, given the deception component, and of their right of withdrawal. Following an initial accounting task, an assessment of gender-role orientation was conducted: all female subjects, irrespective of actual performance, were told they had exhibited a masculine orientation; all masculine subjects that they had revealed a feminine orientation. Measures of self-esteem and a second accounting task were then administered. On completion,

subjects were thanked for their help and promised a detailed report of the outcomes of the study. Two months later subjects received the report, which fully described the deception.

6. Dr G is conducting a field study examining the relationships between performance and management control systems at a number of different locations of the same organisation. There is a friendly rivalry between the locations with each keen to be seen to be outperforming the others. Dr G does not disclose any performance or budgetary information, but he is willing to talk about differences in organisational structure and management style.

7. The Director of an Accounting Research Centre is aware that one of his most consistently successful grant-winners is behaving in a seriously unethical manner. Despite repeated warnings about violation of ethical standards, the colleague's behaviour persists. The Director decides to take no further action.

8. A requirement for Dr H's computer-based accounting course is participation in an extended multiple choice experiment. Minor electric shocks are to be administered to the fingers of students who make an error, in the belief that it will improve their subsequent performance. On learning of the nature of the experiment, one student seeks to withdraw, but his protests are waved aside by Dr H, who insists that participation is a course requirement.

9. Professor J is leading a team of researchers examining the achievement, motivation, creativity, personality and numeracy of Year 10 school students to determine their suitability for enrolment in an accounting undergraduate course. The principals of some of the schools have requested copies of all the test scores for each of their students by name. The researchers provided the information in the interests of preserving the continuing goodwill of participating schools.

10. Dr K has published the results of a large study examining the response of investment analysts to changing levels of accounting information disclosure. She subsequently receives a request from the Stock Exchange for access to her data so that they can re-analyse the data and confirm her conclusions. Dr K refuses the request on the grounds that a computer crash has caused the loss of part of the data set.

Each of these practices is likely to be in breach of typical ethical guidelines for accounting research because they fail, in one way or another, to observe acceptable relationships with human participants.

1. The principle of 'informed consent' is fundamental to the conduct of ethical research. It appears that the employees of DeltaCorp will have no opportunity to withdraw their participation, without threatening their continuing employment. Professor A should not continue to pursue the research project on this basis.

2. The transplanting of 'Western' guidelines to other cultures will inevitably cause difficulties. Where the data collection is being conducted offshore for a research degree in another country, then the ethical guidelines of the host university should be observed, even though their implementation causes practical difficulties.

3. Testimonials should not be solicited from persons who, because of their particular circumstances (in this case as part of a close supervisor–supervisee relationship), are vulnerable to undue influence.
4. Publication credit should reflect the contributions of the parties involved. Unless Professor E made a significant contribution to the final version of the published paper, he should not receive co-authorship. Where a paper is based on a thesis, the author of the thesis would normally expect to be first author.
5. Although Professor F was sensitive to certain ethical issues, there was no attempt to detect and remove any potentially damaging consequences for the individual participants arising from the deception. Any anger or resentment arising from the eventual disclosure of the deception was apparently neither monitored nor evaluated.
6. Dr G has contravened his obligation to safeguard the confidentiality of the information obtained from the different locations of the organisation during the course of the research.
7. The Director has failed in his duty to bring these unethical activities to the attention of the appropriate committees on ethical standards and practices for the accounting profession.
8. The investigator must respect the individual's freedom to decline to participate, or withdraw from, research at any time. The investigator should have provided the student in this case with a choice of alternative activities to fulfil course requirements. The research may also breach requirements associated with protecting the subjects from physical discomfort.
9. This form of reporting is unethical since there is no indication of any limitations on the information provided. There has apparently been no attempt to examine the potential misuse of the information supplied.
10. Once research results are published, the data should not be withheld from other competent professionals as long as the confidentiality of the participants is maintained and protected. The researcher is obligated to keep the data safely so that verifications of this nature can be carried out.

Although the scenarios above are hypothetical, they are close to many of the situations that arise in practice and that will cause concern to researchers, especially where they appear to be faced with a choice which means that they either compromise their ethical principles or sacrifice the outcomes of a research effort.

Informed consent

Strict guidelines, based on the medical research model, are applied, and adherence is monitored in business research too, extending to written consent of respondents and a code of voluntary participation. Thus, any research involving human participants would require approval of a university ethics committee. This would embrace research involving data collection by interviews, questionnaires, focus groups and observation. Indeed, informal professional conversations with practitioners, while not normally requiring ethics approval, would do so if such conversations were systematically employed by the researcher as a means of collecting data. Even if there is no human participation, archival research which leads to accessing medical records, or other sources which are not publicly available, and contain sensitive information (e.g., identifying people by name) still requires ethics approval. Where the agreement of other organisations is necessary for the research to be conducted, then written organisational approval (from the CEO or similar) to access staff members, clients or proprietary information is necessary. This would extend, for example, to written permissions from deans and/or heads of school, as appropriate, to access students for research purposes – even though no harm will result from their participation. Informed consent and anonymity are paramount in the process.

Some of these situations can be extremely problematical. Even gaining access to a site in order to conduct research is becoming increasingly difficult. Firms often need to be convinced that there is 'something in it for them' before granting permission for research to be conducted. While researchers need to be able to demonstrate such benefits, they must also be aware of the potential disadvantages for other participants that can arise. A number of examples from my experience are illustrative:

- A firm employs a research student to conduct a benchmarking exercise as part of a research degree. The student is asked to survey competitors to determine their current practices, but not to reveal their affiliation to the employing firm. This situation is one which could easily be represented as 'industrial espionage', especially where the base firm is unscrupulous in its use of the information gathered covertly.
- A firm grants permission for the conduct of staff interviews, with the view that it becomes 'part of their job'. The boss has given permission and they will accede to his/her wishes. A researcher properly seeking the informed consent of the participants may be faced with both reluctant subjects (who feel they have to take part, even unwillingly) and the wrath of a boss who is not used to having his/her authority questioned (and who may consequently refuse any further collaboration).
- A firm willingly engages in research concerned with the implementation of new business processes, but its participation is part of a wider downsizing agenda. As a result, some of the subjects involved in the research may subsequently indirectly lose their jobs because of the responses they have made as part of the research.
- In order to gain access in the first place, Hammersley and Atkinson (1983) and Lapsley (2004) both highlight the importance of the initial impressions created by researchers and the impact that these may make on the successful completion of research projects. Such impressions may secure comprehensive access, or cause access to be restricted or denied completely. They suggest that 'impression management' with respect to such issues as dress, gender, age, attractiveness, ethnicity, manner of speech and perceived level of expertise may all facilitate the conduct of the project. The creation of a favourable impression therefore contributes to the success of the

process, but at what cost to ethical considerations? Such findings have implications for the use of minorities and for changing acceptable stereotypes, since to secure access we may have to provide 'acceptable' researchers, in a similar manner to the audit client requirements observed by Grey (1996), which restricted the opportunities for young female auditors.

Several of the preceding chapters, detailing the implementation of specific research methods, highlight particular ethical concerns. Those relating to complete honesty, and the disclosure of the whole truth, for example, generate a number of concerns:

- The use of experimental methods identifies instances where completely honest dis- closure is avoided in order to preserve the integrity of research outcomes. Smith and Taffler (1996) report the use of, arguably harmless, untruths in setting the task require- ments in judgement decisions – telling participants that they are evaluating separate companies even where there is considerable replication – in order to induce unique decisions. Trotman (1996) emphasises that the researchers must make the purposes of the research clear to participants, but not in such a way that they might deduce the research hypotheses, since this would impact on the internal validity of the study. However, Gibbins (1992) warns that if research subjects have been deceived by researchers, this will alter the way in which they receive future requests to participate. Without straining the strict 'letter of the law' of ethical guidelines in terms of deception, some research, particularly experimental studies, cannot be contemplated.
- Involvement in field studies offers the possibility of covert research. Where researchers are involved in studies where other participants are unaware of their role and objectives, then both honesty and trust must be jeopardised. However, without stretching the ethical guidelines in this way, it is doubtful whether potentially important findings would emerge.
- The imposition of ethical requirements, and the subsequent interaction between ethics committee and candidate, may strain the traditional supervisor–candidate relationship, especially where this may be construed as interference in the implementation of selected research methods. One particular issue often arises with data collection where candidates wish to use mixed methods – archival (to provide company informa- tion) and surveys (to source opinions from individuals within these companies); they seek to match these pieces of information, and this is not problematic if the survey respondents voluntarily disclose the name of their organisation. But if they do not, the match cannot be made and the information may be lost; under such circumstances candidates may wish to adopt unethical practices (e.g., by using discretely numbered survey documents), which would facilitate the match, but would violate the principle of anonymity of disclosure. While I would countenance the use of research instruments with different coloured paper (e.g., white for manufacturing; cream for retailing etc.) to allow sectoral comparisons, this remains an aggregation; if anonymity is threatened, so that survey responses could potentially be matched to named individuals, then this represents a serious ethical violation.

Ethical guidelines

Ethical issues in business research extend from those concerned with the conduct of the research through to the publications process subsequent to the research. Some of these issues remain hopelessly under-addressed in many universities (those in the UK are a good example) especially compared to what is undertaken in Australian universities. An apparent conflict with the traditional all-embracing role of the supervisor may contribute to the problem, especially where ethics committees are perceived to be interfering unnecessarily.

However, some of the apparently acceptable US practices (e.g., those on co-authorship, see Coppage and Baxendale, 2001) may be construed to constitute academic malpractice in UK and Australia. Typically, co-authorship of a paper would involve substantial participation from all authors in its construction, embracing **all** of the following conditions:

- conception and design, or analysis and interpretation of data;
- drafting the paper or revising it critically for important intellectual content; and
- final approval of the version to be published.

Clearly supervision or funding of the work are not grounds alone for appending one's name to the work of a student!

Any consideration of the ethics of a research proposal would normally address at least the following issues:

- appropriate written permissions from participating organisations;
- eliminating opportunities for personal harm, physical or mental, to research participants, including the researcher;
- informing participants of the motives for the research;
- providing feedback of the results to the participants;
- gaining permission from participating individuals (other than for mail surveys, where return of the questionnaire is taken to imply permission);
- avoiding coercion in management settings;
- guaranteeing and delivering both confidentiality and anonymity to the participants;
- granting the right of withdrawal to participants at any time; and
- guaranteeing the safe storage of research data, usually for a period of up to seven years.

As we will see, it is not always possible to satisfy all these conditions absolutely and still ensure the integrity of the research approach. Hartmann (2000) emphasises three issues which cause the greatest difficulty for researchers in securing ethics approval from their university scrutinising bodies:

- A clear view of how the research results will be used, especially in situations where the research findings will be made available to the management of the host organisation, but which may be of restricted availability to the participants themselves.

- The issue of consent, especially in action research projects. The circumstances of participation require a level of involvement, honesty and openness of communication unusual for both the organisation and the researcher. Hartmann observes that 'guarantees by the researcher of confidentiality may be meaningless in the long term; such research is common and yet current guidelines mean that it cannot occur, or the usual consent procedures are meaningless' (Hartmann, 2000: 6).
- The importance of issues associated with national and organisational culture complicates the behaviour of both individuals and groups, and constrains their actions in a manner that may invalidate the research outcomes. Some flexibility has to be imported to cope with cultural differences. For example, the requirement for written consent of individual interview participants, subsequent to the interview, causes considerable problems associated with 'loss of face' in South East Asia. Frequently, tight guidelines have to be relaxed because a formal 'signing off' is often seen to be insulting to those involved and too great an imposition!

We have a professional duty as academics to inform both our student and practitioner audiences of the outcomes of current research and their implications for practice. Students should be placed in a position where they are able to question the whole research process by providing critical comment on alternative methods. For example, the running of quasi-experiments in class with the express intention of exposing their limitations rather than collecting data can be most rewarding, clarifying exactly what can go wrong while increasing levels of cynicism all round. Similarly, reviewing the survey instruments on which past publications have been based helps to expose both the ambiguity and uncertainty of this particular research process so that nonsensical outcomes become all the more understandable, though no more palatable.

Honest and transparent reporting of research practice is an ethical duty of those participating in accounting research. Researchers should report everything that they did, why they chose that course of action and how the procedures were conducted. Any doubts that are apparent at any stage of the research should be highlighted, along with their implications and the actions taken to overcome deficiencies, in the stated limitations to the research. Where researchers appear to have been 'economical with the truth' in their reporting, this is normally apparent in their papers and is indicative of poor research.

Hartmann and Moers (1999) reported findings that were of ethical concern in respect of the availability of research data to other researchers. Despite published papers advertising the availability of data from a specified author, their attempts to obtain such data for re-analysis were thwarted. Their requests either went unacknowledged or were met with excuses ranging from 'data lost in computer crash' through to 'data lost in move to a new university'. Such responses are hardly consistent with our ethical responsibility to guarantee the safekeeping of research data for at least seven years.

Further reading

Agnew, N.M. and Pike, S.W. (1994) *The Science Game: An Introduction to Research in the Social Sciences*, 6th edn. Englewood Cliffs, NJ: Prentice Hall.

Coppage, R.E. and Baxendale, S. (2001) 'A Synergistic Approach to an Accounting Educator's Primary Responsibilities', *Accounting Education: An International Journal*, 10 (3): 239–46.

Dooley, D. (1995) *Social Research Methods*. Englewood Cliffs, NJ: Prentice Hall.

Gibbins, M. (1992) 'Deception: A Tricky issue for Behavioral Research in Accounting and Auditing', *Auditing: A Journal of Theory and Practice*, Fall: 113–26.

Grey, C. (1996) 'On Being a Professional in a "Big Six" Firm', *Accounting, Organizations and Society*, 23 (5/6): 569–87.

Hammersley, M. and Atkinson, P. (1983) *Ethnography: Principles in Practice*. London: Tavistock.

Hartmann, F.G.H. and Moers, F. (1999) 'Testing Contingency Hypotheses in Budgetary Research: An Evaluation of the Use of Moderated Regression Analysis', *Accounting, Organizations and Society*, 24 (4): 291–315.

Hartmann, L. (2000) 'Ethics in Business Research: Some Issues', University of South Australia Working Paper Series, Adelaide.

Lapsley, I. (2004) 'Making Sense of Interactions in an Investigation of Organisational Practices and Processes', in C. Humphrey and B. Lee (eds), *The Real Life Guide to Accounting Research*. London: Elsevier. pp. 175–90.

Smith, M. and Taffler, R.J. (1996) 'Improving the Communication of Accounting Information through Cartoon Graphics', *Accounting, Auditing and Accountability Journal*, 9 (2): 70–87.

Trotman, K.T. (1996) *Research Methods for Judgment and Decision-Making Studies in Auditing*. Melbourne: Coopers & Lybrand.

FIVE

Data Collection

Chapter Contents

- Choosing a research method
- Sample selection
- Measurement issues
- Data management
- Qualitative research

This chapter is concerned with the collection and analysis of qualitative and quantitative data for use in the subsequent methods described in Chapters 8 (experimental), 9 (surveys), 10 (qualitative) and 10 (archival). The emphasis in this chapter is unapologetically on quantitative methods, since I see so many research candidates adopting (arguably, more difficult) qualitative methods, mainly because either they are not confident with numerical methods, or they are just plain scared of numbers! One of the primary aims here is to reduce levels of confusion surrounding alternative quantitative methods by demonstrating the circumstances in which particular statistical methods are the most appropriate.

A logical sequence is observed in that we first consider sample selection and measurement issues here in Chapter 5, before proceeding to questions of data analysis, descriptive statistics and, where appropriate, significance testing in Chapters 6 and 7. As we shall see, many of the problems which can arise at the analysis and testing stages do so because too little attention has been paid earlier to questions of sample selection and measurement.

Choosing a research method

There is no single research method which can be considered the 'best' in all circumstances. The choice will depend on the research question, data access and precisely what we want to do. If we have access to large sets of quantitative data (cross-section or time series), then we have the opportunity to answer 'how much' questions; we can model relationships and use regression-type methods of analysis to assess how much of a change in one variable will produce a specified change in another. Such studies are ideally suited to archival research using reliable secondary data sources.

If we want to know 'what' individuals will do in particular circumstances, what decisions they will make, what information they will use etc., this is an ideal situation for an experimental study. We must recognise the limitations of the situation, and the unavoidable simplifications, but we control the variables in order to be able to specify causation.

If we want answers to a 'what do you think' question, seeking opinions, preferences and beliefs – even factual information not easily gleaned by other means – then survey methods are appropriate. Whether surveys or interviews are most likely to yield the more reliable responses will depend on the nature of the questions being posed.

In each of these approaches we are trying to generalise from the sample to the population, using the observed averages and variances to infer the existence of universal truths. What we are not able to do is to make empirical generalisations – to infer when the relationships will and will not hold. This is what we can do in fieldwork and case study research. By taking advantage of a sample that will rarely be representative, we can exploit the anomalies and outliers, so despised by the other methods, to provide a rich analysis of the situation. Such an analysis is likely to have practical implications, and to be sufficiently interesting to facilitate communication through multiple media.

Case study research is particularly useful where:

- the scenario under consideration is complex: there are many variables, many of them not quantifiable, and the interrelationships between the variables are unclear, so that formal modelling is not feasible;
- the opportunity arises to examine actual practice, and changes in practice in response to events; and
- the interaction between events and context is critical for both process and outcome, providing a potentially unique situation.

Subsequent chapters will provide a detailed discussion of each of the above research methods (archival, experimental, surveys and field studies) to enable a more informed initial choice to be made, while providing some assurance of the validity of the resulting data sets.

An important element of the advantages of case research is the element of control – control over who is interviewed and how. We will see in Chapter 9 how there might be doubts about our survey respondents:

- We may not know who has actually completed the questionnaire.
- The actual respondent may not be competent to participate.
- Where we delegate responsibility for data collection to a sponsoring body (in order to increase the response rate) then they will normally be responsible for both distributing and collecting the research instruments. But we have no knowledge of how the sample has been selected, and certainly no assurance of either randomness or representativeness.

With a case study situation, the researcher will choose whom to interview, in order to optimise their suitability to the research process as a whole. Thus, Barrett et al. (2005) report on how they selected their interview targets, and how they decided on what questions to ask – given that a 'blanket' interview schedule, common to all participants, would have been totally inappropriate.

Sample selection

Although random selection of samples is usually deemed desirable, it may not produce a sample that is either representative or 'useful'. Thus, random sampling of companies may not give us any representatives of a particular industry (in failure prediction studies it would quite likely give us few, if any, actually failed cases). A systematic sampling approach is often preferred in practice (e.g., choosing every 20th item, say, from the sampling frame) but this may still not solve the problems alluded to above. Directed sampling obtained from specified groupings, perhaps random or systematic at this lower level, may therefore be preferred in practice. We are usually violating the stated assumptions of statistical techniques to some extent straight away, though often without causing great harm. As we recognised earlier, we may even be forced to advertise to raise a sample, but in any event most samples that we achieve are voluntary (for experimental conditions) and convenient (for field studies), so they are scarcely random.

The determination of the most appropriate sample size is largely a cost–benefit exercise. We want the biggest sample size that we can afford to collect, in terms of both time and money. Larger sample sizes are usually more expensive in every aspect of performing the research. The representativeness of the research findings and their statistical significance will generally increase as the sample size increases, in all but the most exceptional circumstances. At the very least we should have a sample size large enough to allow us to conduct the required tests of the research question, and we should be aware of this minimum requirement at the outset. In qualitative research such restrictions may not apply, since we may be content with a sample drawn, such that further cases would yield no new information. Thus, Tucker and Parker (2014) report that they reached 'theoretical saturation', that is, were collecting no significantly new observations after sampling only 42 of their planned 64 participants.

Large samples may permit the use of sophisticated parametric testing (see Chapter 6), but many of these tests will demand that the data set conforms to some prescribed form of distribution. If it does not, because of the existence of a number of extreme observations, manipulation, in the form of data transformations or 'winsorising' of the data (e.g., Taffler, 1983; McLeay and Omar, 2000) may be required. These outliers can be removed from the data set, either by deletion, or by winsorising, which involves changing the value of the outlier to that of the value of the closest non-outlier. It is a particularly useful procedure when complete elimination would impact on either a small data set, or upset a case-matching process.

Issues of sample selection are fundamental to our subsequent choice of research method and the most appropriate form of hypothesis testing. Parametric tests of significance necessitate the assumption of independent random samples drawn from normally distributed populations. These conditions are rarely satisfied in practice, so, strictly, we should be choosing the non-parametric alternatives. Similarly, the experimental methods of Chapter 8 require the random selection and assignment of subjects to experimental treatments. Where we are unable to achieve such random selection standards, then we may not have a 'true' experiment.

Measurement issues

Kidder and Judd (1986) differentiate four types of measurement scale – nominal, ordinal, interval and ratio – each with implications for the most appropriate methods for data analysis. For example, techniques like regression analysis depend on numerically ordered data and are unsuitable for ordinal variables, which convey categories rather than levels (e.g., manufacturing, retailing, financial services). Analysis of variance (ANOVA) is preferred in such circumstances. Confusingly, Likert scales are strictly ordinal variables, but they are usually considered as interval variables for analytical purposes because of their relatively large number of categories (i.e., usually five or seven in practice) and the incidence of averaging.

- **Nominal:** mutually exclusive and collectively exhaustive categories conveying no ordering message (e.g., male/female; manufacturing/retailing/other). Where these are treated as other than (0, 1) variables, care must be exercised in their use as independent variables in a regression analysis, since ordinary least squares (OLS) analysis will treat them as ordered variables. The most common test of statistical significance for use with this data is the chi-squared (χ^2) test. Phi and Cramer's V are the most appropriate measures of association.
- **Ordinal:** mutually exclusive categories which can be ordered (e.g., large/medium/small). Rank-order methods (e.g., Spearman's 'rho') are the most appropriate measures of association for this data, and measures of statistical significance are confined to non-parametric methods (e.g., the Mann–Whitney U-test). Although the use of parametric methods (e.g., t-test, F-test) is theoretically incorrect for ordinal data, some researchers will still adopt these techniques on the grounds that the difference in outcomes is miniscule. Together, nominal and ordinal variables are often called *non-metric* variables.
- **Interval:** mutually exclusive ordered categories where specific intervals have the same meaning but no ratio relationship exists (i.e., a score of 2.0 is not double the size of a score of 1.0). Thus, a temperature of 30 degrees is not twice as hot as 15 degrees; a Z-score of 4.0 is not four times better than a Z-score of 1.0. The product–moment coefficient of correlation (Pearson's 'r') can be used here to measure association, and parametric tests of significance are employed.

- **Ratio:** continuous data, where specific intervals have the same meaning, and multiples have the same meaning (e.g., age, height, weight, dollars). Again Pearson's 'r' is an appropriate measure of association and parametric significance tests can be used. Interval and ratio measures, together, are often called *metric* variables.

Many data items in the accounting environment (notably dollar-based variables) are ratio-scaled. However, there are few situations in the behavioural and organisational arena where the data are so powerful. This causes problems in accounting research where the mix of variables from different measurement levels precludes the use of optimal analytical techniques. The solution is often the scaling-down of the ratio variables so that they are compatible with the other variables of interest, and the adoption of non-parametric methods of analysis (e.g., asset data are often re-scaled to high/low or high/low/medium to make them more compatible with behavioural data, like task complexity levels, in contingency studies). We must recognise the loss of measurement power and information content, which accompanies such re-scaling decisions, along with the associated testing restrictions. Even though they are ratio-scaled, many financial variables (notably accounting ratios and stock returns) will rarely be normally distributed, which means that they may violate the assumptions for the use of parametric methods anyway! In such circumstances we may need to turn to non-parametric alternatives like the Mann–Whitney U-test (for two sample situations) and the Kruskal–Wallis test (for multiple sample situations). Both of these tests are discussed later in the chapter.

Within our ordinal level measures, alternative rating scales are frequently employed in the accounting literature:

- **Linear (sometimes called graphic scales):** e.g., strongly agree/disagree and points in between these extremes, as long as they are not labelled verbally. But respondents may be unwilling to select the extremes on a continuous scale (i.e., a 1 to 7 scale may induce subjects to generate responses confined to the 2 to 6 range).
- **Itemised (sometimes called categorical scales):** as above, but with labels to denote specific ordered categories, i.e., Strongly Agree, Agree, Neutral, Disagree, Strongly Disagree. The word 'Neutral' is often replaced in practice by the phrase 'Neither Agree nor Disagree'.
- **Comparative:** measures ask for judgements to be made with reference to specific levels of performance with the objective of providing a comparative base.
- **Multiple-item (of which the Likert scale is much the most commonly adopted):** the numerical scores on the Likert scale permit items measuring the same construct to be added. In so doing it facilitates the investigation of the impact of individual items and sub-groups as well as any incidence of multicollinearity.
- **Semantic differential:** following Osgood et al. (1957), who developed a semantic differential to measure individuals' perceptions of the meaning of different terms. A set of seven-point bipolar scales allows respondents to rate concepts between the extremes of good/bad, passive/active, positive/negative etc. The method has been employed in the accounting environment (most notably by Houghton, 1987, 1988) to measure understanding of accounting terminology.

Measurement issues are fundamental to the availability of optimal analytical techniques. As we will observe in subsequent sections, the absence of ratio-scaled variables may necessitate the use of non-parametric statistical methods. The non-normality of the variables will violate ordinary least squares regression assumptions, and the incidence of measurement error may preclude the adoption of our preferred methods for model-building.

Measurement issues are central to many areas of accounting research, none more so than that of **earnings management**. Many firms make accounting policy choices which have income increasing or decreasing effects; Hepworth (1953) and Gordon (1964) were the first to observe this as income smoothing behaviour which might have been attempted because investors viewed earnings variability as an indicator of firm-risk, potentially impacting on future earnings and dividends (Burgstahler and Eames, 2003). Griffiths (1986) ranked companies based on the number of income-increasing accounting policy changes being introduced, while Smith et al. (2001) – in Appendix 2 – examined auditor tolerance of such practices. But these studies rely on the firm disclosing the changes so the data will not be comprehensive, nor will it provide an accurate indication of the quantitative impact of the changes. But management of earnings is not confined to accounting policy changes: revenues can be recognised early, expense recognition delayed, delivery schedules altered, in the manner observed by Smith's (2005) case study. Graham et al. (2005) suggest that such changes are the most popular forms of manipulation in practice since they are not easily discernible by the readers of financial reports; they may be legally permissible within generally accepted accounting principles, but they may also be evidence of financial fraud. Thus, the detection and measurement of earnings management has continued to interest accounting researchers.

Beneish (1997, 1999) suggests discriminant-type models to distinguish earnings manipulators from non-managers based on their individual characteristics in a similar manner to the failure prediction models of Altman (1968) and Taffler (1983). But this time the Type I and Type II errors were unacceptably high – unsurprising, given the difficulty of specifying definite non-managers. The Jones (1991) model used time-series data to distinguish between discretionary and non-discretionary accruals and proved to be extremely robust, especially when re-specified (to the Modified Jones Model) by Dechow et al. (1995). Alternative models using cross-section data (e.g., Defond and Jiambalvo, 1994) have attempted to overcome the requirement for extensive data sets in time-series models, but the latter have remained the preferred form of measurement. Gerakos (2012) criticises existing methods used to identify earnings management (notably Jones, 1991; Dechow and Dichev, 2002) since they assume that unexplained accruals represent either poor quality earnings or explicit earnings management and incorporate unreliable cross-section estimates; he suggests that the resulting increase in both Type I and Type II prediction errors might be avoided by adopting the improved Dechow et al. (2012) model.

Even so Roychowdhury (2006) suggests that the power of the **earnings management** measurement models is now such that the manipulation of discretionary accruals has become relatively easy to detect, so much so that firms now seek to avoid detection through more complex methods. Höglund (2012) suggests the use of non-linear models using neural networks to provide further improvement, while Kighir et al. (2014) see this as a potential means of advancing fraud detection through more reliable measurement.

It is not possible to consider the role of 'measurement' without also considering the manner in which it impacts on the scope of accounting research. In citing another sporting analogy, we can clearly measure fastest, highest, longest and heaviest with great accuracy – so measurement of achievement in athletics, swimming, cycling and weight-lifting, for example, are not normally problematic – though we still need arbitrary points allocations to combine the elements of heptathlon and decathlon events. But what of diving, gymnastics, dressage and even synchronised swimming? Here the evaluation is more qualitative, and arguably more subjective – and we may need to convert qualitative assessment into numerical scoring to make relative performance achievement even remotely acceptable. Does this make this latter group 'lesser' sports in some way? Were those editors of quantitative journals, who view qualitative research as 'inferior', in charge of international competition, then surely the latter group would not be acceptable as Olympic sporting events!

Data management

Ideally, before we commence the data collection, and certainly before the data analysis stage, we need to address issues concerning data management. We will likely have large volumes of data, perhaps quantitative and qualitative, and possibly emanating from alternative sources (e.g., experiments, surveys and documentary materials). We need to have systems in place early to establish the accuracy of the data, and to establish an audit trail should we need to check the sources and/or content of particular data items. My hoarder's mentality leads me to establish an early rule: 'never throw anything away'. This guideline naturally applies to final versions of experimental instruments and completed survey documents, but can usefully be extended to personal notes, 'post-it' reminders and drafts of both pilot instruments and papers for publication. All of these can act as memory aids should we need to return to source materials in order to establish the precise progress of the research process. Most university ethics protocols for research processes will dictate the safe storage of original research materials, including audio-tapes and associated transcripts, for periods of up to seven years.

Prior to data collection we need to establish precise variable definitions and easy-to-remember variable labels. Where we have a complex questionnaire, then we need to establish a coding system for the recording of answers. All of these issues need to be addressed early, and solutions carefully documented. Thankfully, computer-based help is at hand to provide assistance, but we must also guard against the perils associated with advanced technology.

Spreadsheet and database software (e.g., Excel and Access, respectively) are now well developed to handle large volumes of numerical data. They can also be used to conduct statistical descriptions without recourse to more sophisticated statistical packages (e.g., SPSS), and also to construct new variables as transformations of existing variables. But opportunities for error will exist, for example:

- How will the software treat missing data values? If we leave a blank, will it be treated as a zero entry? This needs to be checked.
- How do we check for data entry errors? Ideally, we input the data twice, independently and check for variation, though in practice this can be both expensive and time-consuming. Random spot-checks and eye-balling of columns vertically will usually reveal errors because they are most often associated with too many or too few key depressions. Alternatively, we can introduce check columns to highlight data irregularities (e.g., in ratio analysis, computing both the current assets ratio and the quick assets ratio to verify the existence of an intuitive relationship between the two). A quick alternative is to make use of simple descriptive statistics: compute the mean and standard deviation of each column with the formula function, and establish a range of values three standard deviations either side of this mean which we would expect to embrace all of the data values. Monitoring the columns will then establish which data items lie outside of this range so that we can quickly establish whether they are genuine outliers or data errors. If the latter, we should be able to correct the entry; if the former, we may need to make a decision about the inclusion of wild outliers which could potentially distort the research outcomes.
- How do we avoid data corruption? Keep multiple files in different places and never tamper with the master copy! Anyone who has had to reconstruct a spreadsheet file from scratch will echo these principles. This applies particularly to the use of data-sort routines where it is easy to exclude columns on the far-right of the sheet from the sort procedure, with the potentially disastrous consequences of mismatched results.

The management of narrative data poses particular problems. If we are dealing with relatively small numbers of cases, then manual solutions (e.g., the use of different coloured paper for different narrative sources) may be an efficient means of keeping track of individual contributions and, where appropriate, generalising overall. Large numbers of long narrative transcripts almost necessitate the use of dedicated software (e.g., NUD*IST – Non-numerical Unstructured Data: Indexing, Searching and Theorising) for classifying and categorising the data and facilitating keyword searches.

The basic principles of care in recording and documenting change are well known to accountants, and should make accounting researchers particularly proficient in this aspect of the research process.

Qualitative research

Because data collection for qualitative research can differ so markedly from that in corresponding quantitative studies, it is considered separately here. Having said that, Chapters 7, 9 and 10, relating to surveys, interviews and fieldwork, will complement the content of this section.

Quantitative analysis of large data sets permits modelling, which can yield complex predictive models. But rarely do such models consider how the data have been generated, or the motives, values and contexts that will guide the numerical outcome. Qualitative research looks to fill this gap, by examining the behaviour of 'actors' in actual settings, and asking how, and why, they react as they do to the circumstances and phenomena of the workplace. But this examination is not devoid of theory; a review of theoretical concepts provides the natural starting point for the development of research questions, and for the preferred approach to data collection. Nor is the process value-free, since the researchers are inextricably entwined with both the research instrument(s) and the case study actors. Any stance that places *science* in a neutral position, somehow above all this value-ridden participation, must be firmly rejected. The example in Chapter 2 (discovering DNA) and that referred to in Chapter 3 (developing penicillin) as well as the controversy concerning the science of climate change (e.g., Leake, 2009) all show how ethics, politics and funding considerations impact on the way in which research and researcher interact.

Qualitative researchers may be tempted to view their area as sacrosanct, and not to be poisoned by the imposition of numbers. This is a mistake; case study researchers will frequently make use of diverse data sources – making already rich qualitative outcomes even richer. Thus, for example, Lys and Vincent (1995) make use of annual reports, share price data and newspaper reports, as well as interview data from key organisational participants. This prior review of important documents makes their study an 'informed' case study approach, which uses both qualitative and quantitative data, and applies theories from both streams. The result is a more polished paper – and one which opens up more potential publication avenues than would otherwise be the case. However, this may not always be the case, especially (as recognised by Parker, 2012) where qualitative sources are viewed as somehow 'inferior' in mixed-method research studies.

Qualitative research tends to be both costly and time-consuming. External funding may be problematic, especially if potential benefits are unclear. Similarly, ethics approval can be tedious if the research question is vague, if there is the potential for participants to be treated inequitably or if their participation could damage their future organisational prospects. Saunders et al. (2009: 481) liken qualitative analysis to completing a jigsaw puzzle without knowing what the picture on the box is! Thus, we adopt strategies that link similar aspects (i.e., for jigsaws colour and shape) so that connections can be established and the final picture can begin to emerge.

Chapter 10 provides us with a more detailed discussion of qualitative methods, and the use of mixed methods in accounting research. The choice of method will often determine the choice of target journal, since a number of high-ranking journals remain resistant to the charms of qualitative research.

Further reading

Altman, E.I. (1968) 'Financial Ratios, Discriminant Analysis and the Prediction of Corporate Bankruptcy', *Journal of Finance*, 23 (4): 580–609.

Beneish, M.D. (1997) Detecting GAAP Violation: Implications for Assessing Earnings Management Among Firms with Extreme Financial Performance', *Journal of Accounting and Public Policy*, 16 (3): 271–309.

Beneish, M.D. (1999) 'The Detection of Earnings Management', *Financial Analysts Journal*, 5 (5): 24–36.

Burgstahler, D. and Eames, J. (2003) 'Earnings Management to Avoid Earnings Decreases and Losses: Are Analysts Fooled?', *Contemporary Accounting Research*, 20 (2): 253–94.

Dechow, P.M. and Dichev, I. (2002) 'The Quality of Accruals and Earnings: The Role of Accrual Estimation Error', *The Accounting Review*, 77: 35–59.

Dechow, P.M., Hutton, A., Kim, J. and Sloan, R. (2012) 'Detecting Earnings Management: A New Approach', *Journal of Accounting Research*, 50: 275–334.

Dechow, P.M., Sloan, R.G. and Sweeney, A.P. (1995) 'Detecting Earnings Management', *The Accounting Review*, 70 (2): 193–225.

Defond, M. and Jiambalvo, J. (1994) 'Debt Covenant Violation and Manipulation of Accruals', *Journal of Accounting and Economics*, 17 (1–2): 145–76.

Gerakos, J. (2012) 'Discussion of Detecting Earnings Management: A New Approach', *Journal of Accounting Research*, 50: 335–47.

Gordon, M.J. (1964) 'Postulates, Principles and Research in Accounting', *The Accounting Review*, 39: 251–63.

Graham, J.R., Harvey, C.R. and Rajgopal, S. (2005) 'The Economic Implications of Corporate Financial Reporting', *Journal of Accounting and Economics*, 40 (1–3): 3–73.

Hepworth, S.R. (1953) 'Smoothing Periodic Income', *The Accounting Review*, 28 (1): 32–9.

Höglund, H. (2012) 'Detecting Earnings Management with Neural Networks', *Expert Systems with Applications*, 39 (10): 9564–70.

Jones, J. (1991) 'Earnings Management During Import Relief Investigations', *Journal of Accounting Research*, 29 (2): 193–228.

Kighir, A., Omar, N. and Norhayati M. (2014) 'Earnings Management Detection Modelling: A Methodological Review', *World Journal of Social Sciences*, 4 (1): 18–32.

Modell, S. (2005) 'Triangulation Between Case Study and Survey Methods in Management Accounting Research: An Assessment of Validity Implications', *Management Accounting Research*, 16 (2): 231–54.

Roychowdhury, S. (2006) 'Earnings Management Through Real Activities Manipulation', *Journal of Accounting and Economics*, 42 (3): 335–70.

Saunders, M., Lewis, P. and Thornhill, A. (2009) *Research Methods for Business Students*, 5th edn. London: Prentice Hall.

Smith, M. (2005) 'Borthwick Construction: A Case Study of Dysfunctional Bonus Schemes', in M. Smith (ed.), *Performance Measurement and Management*. London: SAGE. pp. 215–23.

Taffler, R.J. (1983) 'The Assessment of Company Solvency and Performance Using a Statistical Model: A Comparative UK-based Study', *Accounting and Business Research*, 15 (5): 295–308.

Tucker, B.P. and Parker, L.D. (2014) 'In Our Ivory Towers? The Research–Practice Gap in Management Accounting', *Accounting and Business Research*, 44 (2): 104–43.

SIX

Quantitative Data Analysis

Chapter Contents ---

- Descriptive statistics
- Differences in sample means
- Measures of association
- Analysis of variance
- Multivariate model-building

Having considered sample selection and measurement issues in Chapter 4, we now proceed to questions of data analysis, descriptive statistics and, where appropriate, significance testing. As we shall see, many of the problems which can arise at the analysis and testing stages do so because too little attention has been paid earlier to questions of sample selection and measurement.

Descriptive statistics

What we are trying to do with statistical testing is essentially very simple; we want to compare an **observed** value with what we **expected** to find, and judge whether this difference is big enough to be attributed to chance or not. If the variation between two samples is bigger than the variation within the samples then we shall observe a difference which is statistically **significant** – it cannot be attributed to a chance occurrence. But if that inter-sample variation is small, then it is feasible that these samples may be drawn from a common population, with observed 'differences' being just random.

We require a standard by which to judge whether an observed difference is significant or not, and this is where statistics come in. There are a number of distinct stages that we adopt in the test procedure:

- state the Null Hypothesis;
- identify the most appropriate statistical test for the size and nature of sample, and the measurement scale;

- choose the level of significance (almost always 5% or 1%);
- choose an appropriate test statistic;
- compare the 'observed' and 'expected' values of the variable, and compute the test statistic for the difference between the two;
- look up the critical value of the test statistic for the appropriate statistical distribution and number of degrees of freedom (df) – where df = the difference between the size of sample and the number of coefficient values (parameters) that the sample has been used to estimate; and
- compare the 'test statistic' with the 'critical value' and come to a decision. Normally, if the 'test statistic' is greater than the 'critical value' then we should reject a Null Hypothesis of no significant difference.

Statistical tests can be classified into two major categories: **parametric statistics** and **non-parametric statistics**. They differ in the assumptions that they make about the underlying distribution of the data under analysis. Parametric statistics require that data be drawn from normal distributions, which are smooth, bell-shaped symmetrical curves, defined by mean and standard deviation measures. Non-parametric statistics make no such assumptions regarding the underlying distribution; they describe relationships in terms of frequencies, rankings and directional signs, rather than means and standard deviations. Parametric tests are the more powerful, so we would normally prefer to use them; but if there is any doubt about the quality of the data, or the underlying assumptions, then we would move to the non-parametric alternative. Although this is technically required, the outcomes are usually no different, because standard statistical techniques are incredibly robust in practice despite the violation of the underlying assumptions.

We may be conducting an essentially descriptive study, with very few numbers involved, but we still have at our disposal a powerful statistical armoury to add to the integrity of our findings. Descriptive studies often record simple proportions, cross-tabulations and measures of association, even where there is no formal hypothesis testing or model-building. We want to know if the **observed** values differ significantly from what we would **expect** if, in fact, no relationship existed at all, and simple statistics allow us to draw such inferences. Table 6.1 provides a summary of the statistical tests at our disposal for typical descriptive situations. Examples of each are provided below.

Table 6.1 Summary of significance tests by measurement level

| MEASUREMENT LEVEL | SINGLE SAMPLE | TWO SAMPLES | | MULTIPLE SAMPLES |
		Independent	Related	Independent
NOMINAL	χ^2 test	χ^2 test	–	χ^2 test
ORDINAL	–	Mann–Whitney U-test	Sign test	Kruskal–Wallis test
INTERVAL and RATIO	t-test Z-test	t-test Z-test	Paired-case t-test	Analysis of variance (ANOVA)

Table 6.1 is inspired by Cooper and Emory (1995: 445) but includes only those non-parametric tests in common use in the accounting literature. Cooper and Emory also discuss, among others, the use of the Kologorov–Smirnov test and Runs Test (for single-sample ordinal combinations), the Wilcoxon matched-pairs test (for related samples/ordinal) and the McNemar test (for related samples/nominal), none of which is considered further here.

Observed proportions

Consider first the use of a single sample to generate the proportion of observations which meet our requirements. We can use the Z-test of the normal distribution to test the significance of the observed proportion detailed in Figure 6.1. Effectively we are asking the question: is a proportion of 64% from a sample of 100 observations big enough to convince us that it is not a chance sample from a population with an actual proportion of 50%?

OBSERVED PROPORTION [O]   64% based on sample size of n = 100 observations

EXPECTED PROPORTION [E]   50%

      for a Null Hypothesis of no actual difference

      i.e., $p = 0.50$

      $q = (1 - p) = 0.50$

Mean $= np = 100(0.50) = \underline{50}$

Standard deviation $= \sqrt{npq} = \sqrt{100(0.50)(0.50)}$

      $= \underline{5.0}$

95% confidence interval for the sample mean:

      $50 \pm (1.96)5.0 = 50 \pm 9.80$

      i.e. a range from <u>40.20 to 59.80</u> is consistent with the Null Hypothesis

<u>But</u> the observed proportion of 64% is outside this range and so is unacceptably large to be consistent with the Null Hypothesis. i.e. reject the Null Hypothesis – 64% is a significant finding.

The equivalent Z test for these data is:

Test statistic: $\dfrac{[O] - np}{\sqrt{npq}} = \dfrac{64 - 50}{5.0} = \underline{2.80}$

Critical value: $Z_{0.05} = \underline{1.96}$

Since test statistic (2.80) exceeds the critical value (1.96) reject the Null Hypothesis at a 5% level of significance.

Figure 6.1 Significance of test of proportion

Cross-tabulations

The use of cross-tabulations to generate contingency matrices represents the most popular of analytical tools. A focus on the individual cells of the matrix allows us to compare the **observed** frequencies with those we would **expect** to see, should there be no relationship between the categories (the Null Hypothesis). We use a chi-squared test (χ^2) usually with a 5% level of significance. In using the χ^2-test no cell should have an expected value which is less than one, and expected frequencies should be rare (i.e., less than one in five cells). If this is not the case we will either require a small sample correction, or more likely need to aggregate some cells by reducing the size of the matrix, in order to be able to conduct the test. Figure 6.2 details the conduct of this test, comparing 'observed' and 'expected' numbers of accounting policy changes.

[O] <u>OBSERVED FREQUENCIES</u> (from figure 2a: Smith et al., 2001)

		ACCOUNTING POLICY CHANGE			
		NO CHANGES	SOME CHANGES	TOTAL	
COMPANIES	BIG 8	97	118	215	a = 2 rows
AUDITED BY	NON-BIG 8	94	58	152	b = 2 columns
	TOTAL	191	176	367	

[E] <u>EXPECTED FREQUENCIES</u> (assuming no relationship between auditor/changes)

$\dfrac{(191)(215)}{367}$	$\dfrac{(176)(215)}{367}$
$\dfrac{(191)(152)}{367}$	$\dfrac{(176)(152)}{367}$

=

111.9	103.1
79.1	72.9

Test statistic:

$$\chi^2 = \Sigma \frac{(O-E)^2}{E} = \frac{(149)^2}{111.9} + \frac{(14.9)^2}{79.1} + \frac{(14.9)^2}{103.1} + \frac{(14.9)^2}{79.2}$$

$$= \underline{\underline{9.98}}.$$

Critical χ^2 value at 5% level of significance $= \chi^2_{(a-1)(b-1)^{0.05}}$

$$= \chi^2_{1,0.05} = \underline{3.84}$$

Figure 6.2 χ^2-test for difference in frequencies

Since the test statistic (9.98) is greater than the critical value (3.84) we can reject a Null Hypothesis of no link between auditor grouping and the incidence of accounting policy changes.

Correlation coefficients

Measures of association are dealt with in more detail later, but it is opportune to ask and answer another simple question: is the observed correlation coefficient big enough for us to be confident that we have a real, not illusory, relationship here? That is, is a coefficient of 0.554 based on a sample of just 17 paired observations big enough for us to recognise a significant relationship? Although it may not appear to be a high measure of association, and the sample size is relatively small, as we see in Figure 6.3 it is too big for us to expect by chance.

The data of Figure 6.7 shows a correlation coefficient of r = 0.554

calculated from a sample size of n = 17

Mean (r) = 0.554

$$\text{Standard deviation} = \sqrt{\frac{1-r^2}{n-2}} = \sqrt{\frac{1-(0.554)^2}{15}} = 0.2150$$

$$\text{Test statistic} = \frac{\text{Mean}}{\text{Standard deviation}} = \frac{0.554}{0.2150} = 2.577$$

Critical t-statistic = $t_{n-2,0.05} = t_{15,0.05} = 2.131$

Test statistic is greater than the critical value so we should reject a Null Hypothesis of zero population correlation coefficient.

[Equivalent 95% confidence interval: 0.554 ± (2.131)(0.2150) giving a range of: 0.096 to 1.012 which does *not* include r = 0 as a possible value.]

Figure 6.3 Test of significance of correlation coefficient

Differences in sample means

Tests of differences of means between pairs of variables provide a major focus for accounting research. A variety of tests are available depending on the measurement level involved and the way in which the sample has been drawn.

Independent samples

Figure 6.4 illustrates the calculations for two samples (X) and (Y) each of size 17, of ratio scale data drawn as independent samples from normal populations. The question we want to answer is: are these samples similar enough to each other for us to judge that they could conceivably have been drawn from the same population? We answer this by testing the difference between the two sample means, relative to the variation that exists within the samples. If the difference between the samples is greater than that within the samples then we would infer that the samples are drawn from different populations, and reject the Null Hypothesis.

(1)	(2)	(3)	(4)	
X	Y	X²	Y²	$n_1 = n_2 = 17$
13	16	169	256	$N = (n_1 + n_2) = 34$
14	18	196	324	MEANS
15	19	225	361	
17	21	289	441	
18	20	324	400	
26	27	676	729	
28	17	784	289	
29	24	841	576	
30	12	900	144	SAMPLE VARIANCES
27	23	729	529	
31	11	961	121	
32	22	1024	484	
33	23	1089	529	
34	35	1156	1225	
36	25	1296	625	
37	38	1369	1444	
39	40	1521	1600	

$$\bar{X} = \frac{\Sigma X}{n_1} = \frac{459}{17} = \underline{\underline{27}}$$

$$\bar{Y} = \frac{\Sigma Y}{n_2} = \frac{391}{17} = \underline{\underline{23}}$$

$$\overline{(X+Y)} = \frac{\Sigma X + \Sigma Y}{n_1 + n_2} = \frac{850}{34} = 25$$

$$S_X^2 = \frac{\Sigma X^2 - n_1 \bar{X}^2}{n_1 - 1} = \frac{13,549 - 17(27)^2}{16}$$
$$= 72.25$$

$$S_Y^2 = \frac{\Sigma X_2 - n_1 \bar{Y}^2}{n_2 - 1} = \frac{10,077 - 17(23)^2}{16}$$
$$= 67.75$$

$\Sigma X = 459$ $\Sigma Y = 391$ $\Sigma X^2 = 13,549$ $\Sigma Y^2 = 10,077$

$$\text{test statistic} = \frac{\bar{X} - \bar{Y}}{\sqrt{\dfrac{S_X^2}{n_1 - 1} + \dfrac{S_Y^2}{n_2 - 1}}} = \frac{27 - 23}{\sqrt{\dfrac{72.25}{16} + \dfrac{67.75}{16}}} = \underline{\underline{1.352}}$$

$$\text{Critical value } t_{n_1 + n_2 - 2, 0.05} = t_{32, 0.05} = \underline{\underline{2.04}}$$

Since test statistic (1.352) < critical value (2.04) we cannot reject a Null Hypothesis of insignificant difference between the groups at a 5% significance level.

Figure 6.4 t-test for difference in means

Paired cases

Where the samples drawn are not independent, but represent a before-and-after situation involving the same subjects (usually people), then we have a repeated measures situation for which more powerful statistical tests are available. The paired-case t-test effectively controls for individual differences between subjects, so that the observed differences are wholly attributable to the treatments (changed conditions), assuming that there are no carry-over effects between the two conditions. In this case we can observe non-zero differences between the two samples, but are these differences in the same direction and big enough not to be attributed to chance?

(1)	(2)	(3)	(4)	
X	Y	$d = (X - Y)$	d^2	$n = 17$
13	16	-3	9	
14	18	-4	16	
15	19	-4	16	
17	21	-4	16	MEAN
18	20	-2	4	
26	27	-1	1	
28	17	11	121	$\bar{d} = \dfrac{\Sigma d}{n} = \dfrac{68}{17} = 4$
29	24	5	25	
30	12	18	324	SAMPLE
27	23	4	16	VARIANCE
31	11	20	400	
32	22	10	100	$S_d^2 = \dfrac{\Sigma d^2 - n\bar{d}^2}{n_1 - 1}$
33	23	10	100	
34	35	-1	1	$= \dfrac{1272 - 17(4)^2}{16}$
36	25	11	121	
37	38	-1	1	$= 62.5$
39	40	-1	1	
		$\Sigma d = 68$	$\Sigma d^2 = 1272$	

Figure 6.5 t-test for paired-case difference in means

Figure 6.5 details the measurement (in Column 3) of the differences in scores between the two samples, allowing the calculation of the mean and standard deviation for the d-score. A Null Hypothesis suggests a population mean of zero and a test statistic of:

$$\text{Test statistic: } \frac{d - 0}{\sqrt{\dfrac{s_d^2}{n-1}}} = \frac{(4)(4)}{\sqrt{62.5}} = \underline{\underline{2.02}}$$

$$\text{Critical value: } t_{n-1,0.05} = t_{16,0.05} = \underline{\underline{2.12}}$$

Despite the increased power of the test in the paired-case situation, the test statistic still does not exceed the critical value, so the Null Hypothesis cannot be rejected at the 5% level of significance.

Non-parametric alternatives

Where the sampling is not random, the resulting samples will be potentially unrepresentative. If assumptions about the population distribution are unwarranted, then parametric tests may be unreliable and we should adopt non-parametric tests. If we return to the data of Figure 6.5, but regard the data as ordinal, perhaps because of potential measurement error, which might distort the outcome of conventional t-tests, then we can use the **sign test** as a non-parametric alternative (for the before-and-after paired situation) and the **Mann–Whitney U-test** (where we have independent samples).

The sign test

When using the sign test, we simply monitor Column 3 of Figure 6.5 to determine the number of positive and negative differences we have in the paired cases. For the 17 pairs, we observe nine negative and eight positive differences; there are no ties (i.e., no instances of no-change) cases, which would otherwise be eliminated from the analysis.

A Null Hypothesis would lead us to expect $17/2 = \underline{\underline{8.5}}$ signs of each direction. Our test statistic would be:

$$\text{Test statistic: } \frac{\text{Observed} - \text{Expected}}{\text{Standard deviation}} = \frac{9 - 8.5}{\sqrt{17\left(\dfrac{8.5}{17}\right)\left(\dfrac{8.5}{17}\right)}} = \underline{\underline{0.243}}$$

$$\text{Critical value} = Z_{0.05} = \underline{\underline{1.96}}$$

Clearly the test statistic (0.243) is well below the critical value (1.96) so again we cannot reject the Null Hypothesis.

The Mann–Whitney U-test

Figure 6.6 details the conduct of this test, which is based on the rank order of the sample values.

(1)	(2)	(3)	(4)	
X	Y	R_X	R_Y	n = 17
13	16	32	29	
14	18	31	25.5	m = 17
15	19	30	24	
17	21	27.5	22	
18	20	25.5	23	MEAN
26	27	16	14.5	
28	17	13	27.5	$\bar{U} = \dfrac{n}{2}(n+m+1)$
29	24	12	18	
30	12	11	33	$= \dfrac{17}{2}(35) = \underline{297.5}$
27	23	14.5	19.5	VARIANCE
31	11	10	34	
32	22	9	21	$S_u^2 = \dfrac{nm(n+m+1)}{12}$
33	23	8	19.5	
34	35	7	6	$= \dfrac{(17)(17)(35)}{12}$
36	25	5	17	
37	38	4	3	
39	40	2	1	$= \underline{842.92}$
		$\Sigma R_X = 257.5$	$\Sigma R_Y = 337.5$	

Figure 6.6 Mann–Whitney U-test for difference in means

The test statistic is:

$$\text{Test statistic: } \frac{R_x - \bar{U}}{\sqrt{S_U^2}} = \frac{257.5 - 297.5}{\sqrt{842.92}} = \underline{1.38}$$

$$\text{Critical value} = Z_{0.05} = \underline{1.96}$$

So, once again, the Null Hypothesis cannot be rejected; the critical value (1.96) comfortably exceeds the test statistic (1.38).

Strictly speaking, to employ this version of the Mann–Whitney test, one of the two samples (n or m) should be greater than 20 to invoke the 'Normal' approximation. The proximity of our sample sizes (n = m = 17) suggests that it will make little difference, but for technical accuracy we will compute the small sample test:

$$U_X = nm + \frac{n(n+1)}{2} - R_X = (17)(17) + \frac{(17)(18)}{2} - 257.5 = \underline{\underline{184.5}}$$

$$U_Y = nm + \frac{n(n+1)}{2} - R_Y = (17)(17) + \frac{(17)(18)}{2} - 337.5 = \underline{\underline{104.5}}$$

We compare the smallest of these two U values ($U_Y = 104.5$) with a critical value taken from Mann–Whitney tables (87 for $n = m = 17$). In this case the test statistic must be **smaller** than the critical value in order to reject the null hypothesis, so since 104.5 exceeds 87 we still cannot reject the Null Hypothesis.

Measures of association

The most appropriate measure of association is again determined by the measurement level, as detailed in Table 6.2. Each of the measures in the table are considered below.

Table 6.2 Measures of association by measurement level

Measurement level	Measure of association
NOMINAL	Phi
	Cramer's V
ORDINAL	Spearman's 'rho'
	(coefficient of rank correlation)
INTERVAL	Pearson's 'r'
and	(product–moment coefficient of correlation)
RATIO	

Pearson correlation coefficient (r)

The correlation coefficient matrix is, arguably, the single most useful piece of preliminary diagnostic information. It serves three vital functions:

- it establishes the direction of any relationship, which should be intuitively correct and which must correspond with the sign of this variable in any regression equation;
- it suggests those variables which are likely to be useful explanatory variables, because they are highly correlated with the dependent variable; and
- it highlights potential multicollinearity problems by quantifying the strength of association between competing explanatory variables.

Figure 6.7 illustrates the calculation of the coefficient for interval/ratio data, so that it yields a value in the range +1 (for a perfect positive correlation) and –1 (for a perfect inverse relationship).

(1)	(2)	(3)	(4)	(5)	
X	Y	XY	X²	Y²	n = 17
13	16	208	169	256	MEANS
14	18	252	196	324	$\bar{X} = \dfrac{\Sigma X}{n} = \dfrac{459}{17} = \underline{\underline{27}}$
15	19	285	225	361	
17	21	357	289	441	$\bar{Y} = \dfrac{\Sigma Y}{n} = \dfrac{391}{17} = \underline{\underline{23}}$
18	20	360	324	400	
26	27	702	676	729	
28	17	476	784	289	SAMPLE VARIANCES
29	24	696	841	576	$S_X^2 = \dfrac{\Sigma X^2 - n\bar{X}^2}{n_1 - 1} = \dfrac{13{,}549 - 17(27)^2}{16}$
30	12	360	900	144	
27	23	621	729	529	$= \underline{72.25}$
31	11	341	961	121	$S_Y^2 = \dfrac{\Sigma Y^2 - n\bar{Y}^2}{n - 1} = \dfrac{10{,}077 - 17(23)^2}{16}$
32	22	704	1024	484	
33	23	759	1089	529	$= \underline{67.75}$
34	35	1190	1156	1225	Pearson's r =
36	25	900	1296	625	$\dfrac{\Sigma XY - n\bar{X}\bar{Y}}{\sqrt{(n-1)^2 . S_X^2 . S_Y^2}} = \dfrac{(11{,}177) - 17(27)(23)}{\sqrt{(256)(72.25)(67.75)}}$
37	38	1406	1369	1444	
39	40	1560	1521	1600	$= \underline{0.554}$

ΣX = 459　ΣY = 391　ΣXY = 11,177　ΣX² = 13,549　ΣY² = 10,077

Figure 6.7 Product–moment correlation coefficient (Pearson's r)

The statistical significance of this coefficient was tested earlier (in Figure 6.3). The square of this correlation coefficient is called the coefficient of determination (R^2), and indicates the percentage of the variation in one variable explained by changes in the other. Thus, for $r = 0.554$, $R^2 = 0.307$, i.e., 30.7% of the variation in Y is explained by changes in X (and vice versa). The other 69.3% of variation is currently unexplained, and will remain so until we have the opportunity to build multivariate causal models surrounding these variables.

Spearman coefficient ('rho')

As before, where we are unsure of the quality of the data, or of the populations from which they are drawn, we prefer to use rank-order methods.

(1)	(2)	(3)	(4)	(5)	(6)
X	Y	R_X	R_Y	d $(R_X - R_Y)$	d^2
13	16	17	15	2	4
14	18	16	13	3	9
15	19	15	12	3	9
17	21	14	10	4	16
18	20	13	11	2	4
26	27	12	4	8	64
28	17	10	14	−4	16
29	24	9	6	3	9
30	12	8	16	−8	64
27	23	11	7.5	3.5	12.25
31	11	7	17	−10	100
32	22	6	9	−3	9
33	23	5	7.5	−2.5	6.25
34	35	4	3	1	1
36	25	3	5	−2	4
37	38	2	2	0	0
39	40	1	1	0	0
					$\Sigma d^2 = 327.5$

For n = 17

$$\rho\text{(rho)} = 1 - \frac{6\sum d^2}{n(n^2 - 1)} = 1 - \frac{6(327.5)}{17(288)} = 0.5987$$

Figure 6.8 Coefficient of rank correlation (Spearman's rho)

The conversion of continuous data to ranks (and the corresponding move from Pearson's r to Spearman's rho) is convenient if we are suspicious of the presence of measurement error. Rho is unaffected by data transformations and deals equitably with problems associated with outliers, without the necessity for winsorising the data. Its only major deficiency is with regard to tied ranks: too many of these in small samples may distort the size of the coefficient.

As is evident from Figure 6.8 the Spearman coefficient is simple to calculate and yields similar answers to the Pearson coefficient.

Phi and Cramer's V

For the 2 * 2 contingency table of Figure 6.2

where

a	b
c	d

=

97	118
94	58

and $\chi^2 = \underline{9.988}$ and $N = (a + b + c + d) = \underline{367}$

Cramer's V = $\sqrt{\dfrac{\chi^2}{N * \min[r - 1, c - 1]}}$ for r, rows – c, columns

$= \sqrt{\dfrac{9.988}{367 * 1}} = \underline{\underline{0.165}}$

a very low measure of association reflecting large cell differences

Phi coefficient = $\dfrac{ad - bc}{\sqrt{(a + b)(c + d)(a + c)(b + d)}} = \dfrac{(97)(58) - (118)(94)}{\sqrt{(215)(152)(191)(176)}}$

$= \underline{\underline{-0.165}}$

A very low inverse measure of association reflecting large cell differences

[Cramer's V and Phi equivalent for 2 * 2 contingency table].

Figure 6.9 Measure of association within contingency tables

In Figure 6.2 we were able to reject a Null Hypothesis for the data set relating auditor grouping to accounting policy changes. The very low measures of association in Figure 6.9 reflect the earlier findings. Where the contingency table reflects an ordered set of categories on each axis then the chi-squared test is marginally less powerful than alternatives (e.g., Goodman and Kruskal's **gamma** statistic or Kendall's **tau** statistic). Neither of these is considered further here, except to note that Figure 2c of the Smith et al. (2001) paper of Appendix 2 makes use of the latter.

Analysis of variance

If we return to Table 6.1 briefly we note that there are two tests that we still need to address – the analysis of variance (ANOVA) and the Kruskal–Wallis test – for multiple independent samples of, respectively, ratio and ordinal data. We consider a three-sample illustration in Figure 6.10.

TREATMENT OUTCOMES

SAMPLE (Y_1) $(n_1 = 10)$	SAMPLE (Y_2) $(n_1 = 10)$	SAMPLE (Y_3) $(n_1 = 10)$	TOTAL OBSERVATIONS $n_1 + n_2 + n_3 = N = 30$
32	35	44	
30	38	46	
35	37	47	
33	40	47	
35	41	46	
34	35	43	
29	37	47	
32	41	45	
36	36	48	
34	40	47	
$\Sigma Y_1 = 330$	$\Sigma Y_2 = 380$	$\Sigma Y_3 = 460$	$\Sigma(Y_1 + Y_2 + Y_3) = 1170$

Means: $\overline{Y}_1 = 33$ $\overline{Y}_2 = 38$ $\overline{Y}_3 = 46$ $\overline{Y} = 39$

Variance: $S_1^2 = 4.6$ $S_2^2 = 5.0$ $S_3^2 = 2.2$

where $S^2 = \dfrac{\Sigma(Y_i - Y_i)^2}{n_i}$ for each of $i = 1, 2, 3$

Between sample variance $= \dfrac{\Sigma n_i(\overline{Y}_i - \overline{Y})^2}{K - 1}$ for K = no. of samples

$$= \frac{10(33 - 39)^2 + 10(38 - 39)^2 + 10(46 - 39)^2}{3 - 1} = \underline{\underline{430}}$$

Within sample variance $= \dfrac{\Sigma n_i S_i^2}{N - K} = \dfrac{10(4.6) + 10(5.0) + 10(2.2)}{30 - 3} = \underline{\underline{4.37}}$

Test statistic $= \dfrac{\text{Between sample variance}}{\text{Within sample variance}} = \dfrac{430}{4.37} = \underline{\underline{98.4}}$

Critical F-value $= F_{K-1, N-K, 0.05} = F_{2, 27, 0.05} = \underline{\underline{3.37}}$

(i.e. 5% level of significance, with 2 (nominator), 27 (denominator) degrees of freedom)

Since the test statistic (98.4) is greater than the critical value (3.37) we must **reject** the Null Hypothesis. There is a significant difference in the outcomes from the three treatments.

Figure 6.10 One-way analysis of variance (ANOVA)

Three samples, each of size $n_1 = n_2 = n_3 = 10$ are drawn (initially) from normal populations. The question we want to answer is: could these three samples conceivably have been drawn from the same population, or are the differences between them too large for that to be realistic? We could address the question by conducting separate t-tests between each pair of samples, but that would not be an efficient method, nor an appropriate one were the samples not to prove independent. We therefore conduct a single test – a one-way ANOVA – to determine whether the variation between the three samples is greater than the variation evident within the samples.

The analysis of Figure 6.10 demonstrates that the between-sample variance is sufficiently greater than the within-sample variance for us to reject the Null Hypothesis and infer that the samples are indeed drawn from different populations.

ANOVA was introduced to the accounting literature by Ashton (1974) as a model for measuring the significance, and percentage variance, explained by the main effects of treatments and interactions between treatments. It was immediately widely adopted as a means of eliminating multicollinearity problems, heteroscedasticity problems when group sizes are equal, and facilitating an unbiased estimation of both main and interactive effects. In theory the size of the factorial design can be expanded greatly, but in practice it quickly becomes unmanageable; frequently third and fourth order interactive effects cannot be explained satisfactorily, limiting their contribution to the development of theory. The dichotomisation of data necessary to conduct ANOVA reduces the effects of measurement errors, but it may incur information loss.

Table 6.3 details the manner in which ANOVA results would typically be presented. It includes the sources of variation, the degrees of freedom, sums of squares, mean squares and the calculated value of the F-test statistic for the data of Figure 6.10.

Table 6.3 ANOVA summary table

Source of variation	Degrees of freedom	Sums of squares	Mean square	Test statistic
Model	2	860	4.30	98.4
Residual error	27	118	4.37	
TOTAL	29			

If we now relax our assumptions we move to the case detailed in Figure 6.11. We are still operating with the three-case sample of Figure 6.10, but this time our doubts about the quality of the data dictate that we treat the data as ordinal, rather than ratio, and employ non-parametric methods. This means we need to use the rank order of the data, rather than actual values, and the Kruskal–Wallis test. First, all of the sample observations are ordered (from 1 to 30) taking care to average appropriately where ties occur. We then sum the ranks appropriate to each sample and compute the test statistic (see Figure 6.11).

Once again our test statistic exceeds the critical value, leading us to reject the Null Hypothesis and infer that the samples are indeed drawn from separate populations.

Y$_1$	RANK	Y$_2$	RANK	Y$_3$	RANK
32	3.5	35	9.5	44	22
30	2	38	16	46	24.5
35	9.5	37	14.5	47	27.5
33	5	40	17.5	47	27.5
35	9.5	41	19.5	46	24.5
34	6.5	35	9.5	43	21
29	1	37	14.5	47	27.5
32	3.5	41	19.5	45	23
36	12.5	36	12.5	48	30
34	6.5	40	17.5	47	27.5
$\Sigma R_1 = 59.5$		$\Sigma R_2 = 150.5$		$\Sigma R_3 = 255.0$	

Test statistic $= H = \dfrac{12}{N(N-1)} \Sigma \dfrac{T^2}{n} - 3(N+1)$

where T = sum of ranks in any column

n = no. of cases in that sample; N = total number of cases (30)

K = no. of samples (3)

$H = \dfrac{12}{30(29)} \Sigma \dfrac{(59.5)^2 + (150.5)^2 + (255)^2}{10} - 3(31)$

$= \dfrac{12}{870} * \dfrac{91,215.5}{10} - 93 = 125.81 - 93 = \underline{\underline{32.81}}.$

However, where there are a large number of tied ranks (as in this case),

i.e., 7 in sample 1; 9 in sample 2; 6 in sample 3

an adjusting factor 'C' is applied where $C = 1 - \Sigma \dfrac{t^3 - t}{N^3 - N}$,

i.e., $C = 1 - \Sigma \dfrac{(7^3 - 7) + (9^3 - 9) + (6^3 - 6)}{30^3 - 30} = 1 - \dfrac{1266}{26,970} = \underline{\underline{0.96}}.$

Revised test statistic $= \dfrac{H}{C} = \dfrac{32.81}{0.96} = \underline{\underline{34.17}}.$

Critical value $\chi^2_{K-1, 0.05} = \chi^2_2 = \underline{\underline{5.99}}.$

Since the test statistic (34.17) easily exceeds the critical value (5.99) we must again reject the Null Hypothesis.

Figure 6.11 The Kruskal–Wallis multiple sample test

Multivariate model-building

Depending upon the measurement level of the data and the role played by the associated variables (whether dependent or explanatory), a variety of model-building methods will be available, as detailed in Table 6.4.

Table 6.4 Summary of multivariate model-building methods by measurement level

		Independent variables	
		NOMINAL AND ORDINAL	**INTERVAL AND RATIO**
Dependent variables	NOMINAL AND ORDINAL	Conjoint analysis Canonical analysis	Discriminant analysis logit and probit
	INTERVAL AND RATIO	Multivariate analysis of variance (MANOVA) Multiple regression	Canonical analysis Multiple regression

Adapted from Cooper and Emory (1995) flow chart, p. 521 (http://www.irwin-pub.com).

Table 6.4 is adapted from the flow chart provided by Cooper and Emory (1995: 521). Conjoint analysis and canonical analysis are rarely used in the accounting literature (they are mainly to be found in the marketing literature) and so are not discussed further. LISREL (linear structural equations model for latent variables) is omitted from Table 6.4 because its allocation to any cell would be arbitrary. LISREL embraces path analysis and structural equation modelling, among others, and can handle dependent and independent variables, which may be nominal, ordinal, interval or ratio scale measures.

Regression analysis

Whereas time-series analysis can provide us with trend projections for a key variable, in practice this may not be enough. If we wish to influence future values, through appropriate management action, we need to know which variables impact on the values assumed by the key variable. In essence we wish to establish the degree of association between variables and any causal relationships between those variables, in order to develop an explanatory relationship which allows us to show how and why key variables are changing.

Alternative forms of regression analysis may be adopted depending on the nature of the causal model:

- ordinary least squares regression (for standard causal relationships);
- ordinary least squares regression with dummy variables (for simple conditional relationships);

- moderated regression (for moderating variables); and
- path analysis (partial regression for intervening variables).

For the simple two variable (X,Y) situation a scatter diagram with Y on the vertical axis and X on the horizontal would reveal the strength of any linear relationship between the two variables. We might speculate on the existence of a linear relationship of the form:

Y = a + bX. To specify the values of the parameters 'a' and 'b' we need to fit a straight line to the points – effectively averaging out their position and establishing the average to which they regress.

The OLS solution to this problem measures the vertical deviation of points away from a fitted line, and ensures that the optimum fit is such that the sum of the squares of these distances, over all the points, is as small as possible.

The fitted line is designated $\hat{Y} = \hat{a} + \hat{b}X$ with 'hats' (^) added to signify that we are dealing with estimates based on a sample of observations. The line is fitted with reference to the vertical distances $(Y - \hat{Y}_i)$ of the points from the line, where $e_i = Y - \hat{Y}_i$ signifies the 'error' involved in fitting.

The OLS regression line is fitted to satisfy simultaneously two conditions:

i. $\Sigma e_i = \phi$

Positive and negative deviations must exactly balance, and

ii. Σe_i^2 is a minimum

The sum of the squares of the vertical deviations from the line is as small as possible.

The specification of the 'a' and 'b' parameters to minimise Σe^2 can be derived using differential calculus such that:

$$\hat{b} = \frac{\Sigma XY - n\overline{X}\overline{Y}}{\Sigma X^2 - n\overline{X}^2}$$

for n pairs of observations, and

$$\hat{a} = \overline{Y} - \hat{b}\overline{X}$$

For example the data of Figure 6.4 would generate a regression equation of the form:

$$\hat{Y} = 37.48 + (0.5363)\hat{X}$$

on the assumption that we had a theory to justify changes in Y being caused by changes in X. Fortunately, most spreadsheet software will calculate regression and correlation coefficients, as well as providing a graphic plot of the extent of the linearity, without the user needing recourse to the above formulae!

We know from Figure 6.7 that the Pearson correlation coefficient is: $r = 0.554$, and from Figure 6.3 that this coefficient is significant at the 5% level of significance. However, if we had $r = 0$ it would not necessarily mean that no relationship exists, only that no meaningful **linear** relationship exists. For example, a circular relationship between X and Y would generate a linear correlation coefficient, $r = 0$ even though a perfect non-linear relationship would be in existence.

Similarly, a non-zero correlation coefficient does not necessarily mean that a real linear relationship exists. Two totally unrelated variables will inevitably yield small, but non-zero, spurious correlation coefficients by chance. Statistical tests of significance like those in Figure 6.3 will demonstrate whether or not such values are small enough to constitute non-zero sample estimates from a zero population.

When we come to perform statistical tests of the significance of the parameter estimates, a rule of thumb for sample sizes in excess of thirty, is the ratio:

$$\frac{\text{Sample estimate}}{\text{Standard error of the estimate (se)}} > 2$$

then the sample estimate is statistically significant (i.e., it is too big to be a chance estimate of a non-existent relationship). Our standard 'normal' ordinate has been 1.96 (just as the standard chi-squared ordinate χ_1^2, is 3.84, where this is the square of 1.96). For smaller samples the t approximation is about 2.0, and the standard F-value about 4.0 (since $F = t^2$ for one degree of freedom).

These critical values (2 for the t-test and 4 for the F-test) will each vary depending on the size of sample (n) used, and the number of parameters (k) which the data have been used to estimate. As (n–k) gets smaller the critical values of the t-test and F-test will increase.

OLS regression methods attempt to estimate the actual relationship $Y_i = a + bX_i + \mu_i$ with an estimated relationship based on a finite sample size of n observations. The error term μ_i in the relationship is estimated by the residual of the equation e_i.

OLS fits make a number of assumptions, the violation of which can result in unreliable equations:

1. μ is a random variable;
2. the mean value of μ is zero;
3. the variance of μ is constant;

4. the variable μ is normally distributed;
5. the random terms from different observations (μ_t, μ_{t-1}) are independent;
6. μ_i is independent of the explanatory variables;
7. the explanatory variables are measured without error;
8. the explanatory variables are not perfectly linearly correlated;
9. any variable aggregation has been carried out appropriately;
10. the identified relationship has a unique mathematical relationship; and
11. the relationship has been correctly specified.

For analysis, the assumptions fall conveniently into two groups. The first six assumptions (numbers 1 to 6) concern the error term μ_i, as estimated by the residual term e_i. The last six assumptions (numbers 6 to 11) concern the behaviour of the explanatory variables. Several of the assumptions may be difficult to test, especially when only limited data are available. In practice, the verification of assumptions 2, 3, 5, 6 and 8 is the most critical.

Assumption 2 suggests that $\bar{\mu} = 0$ and assumption 6 that $r_\mu.x_i = 0$. If either is violated then parameter estimates will be both biased and inconsistent, i.e., OLS will generate wrong answers, which will not be improved upon by seeking a larger sample size. In practice, we will fit the regression to ensure that $\bar{e}_i = 0$ so that we need only observe $r_{e^2.x_i}$ to verify assumption 6.

Assumption 3 suggests that S_μ^2 is constant, verified in practice by observing any variance in the estimate $\Sigma e^2/(n-k)$ around a fitted regression equation embracing the estimation of k parameters. If this assumption is not satisfied then heteroscedasticity exists and formulae for parameter estimates, and hence associated significance tests, may be inefficient. Assumption 5 suggests that $re_t.e_{t-1} = 0$ and applies only to time-series data. If not satisfied, autocorrelation exists, resulting in incorrect estimates of both parameter values and their variances. Most critically of all, assumption 8 suggests that $r_{x1.x2} = 0$. If this condition is violated then multicollinearity exists, which, where the incidence is serious, may again result in parameter estimates that are both biased and inconsistent.

The potential violation of Assumption 7 is a problem in accounting research, and one which is frequently overlooked. This is particularly so when dealing with **latent** explanatory variables (i.e., those which cannot be measured directly but which are founded on multi-item measurement constructs); this would include such familiar variables in behavioural and organisational research as organisational effectiveness, job satisfaction, budgetary participation etc. If the instrument used to measure the variables displays a Cronbach alpha of less than one (which it always will!) then we have a measurement error; if, more realistically, we have an alpha of only 0.8, then this might be acceptable on other grounds, but the significance of the measurement error could lead to biased regression coefficients and inefficient tests of statistical significance. Shields and Shields (1998) suggest that multiple regression methods may be inappropriate in such circumstances and that structural equation modelling might provide a more suitable alternative.

After fitting a regression equation we must conduct at least three tests of the violation of OLS assumptions, all of which may provide evidence of the misspecification of the OLS equation:

- Monitor the size of correlation coefficient between X variables
- Confirm that the explanatory variables (X_i) are independent of the residuals (e_i), and the absence of heteroscedasticity by ensuring that the correlation coefficient $r_{e^2 \cdot x_i}$ is not statistically significant for any explanatory variable. Graphically this may be apparent from a wedge-shaped X–Y scatter indicative of a size relationship so that e_i increases as X_i increases.
- Ensure that for time-series data $r_{e_t \cdot e_{t-1}}$ is not statistically significant, or alternatively that tabular values of the Durbin–Watson d-statistic are within acceptable bounds. Graphically, plots of e_t against e_{t-1} in successive time periods should be random but they may reveal a positive relationship (through clearly increasing or decreasing trends) or a negative relationship (through a saw-tooth pattern). Both are indicative of key variables omitted from the regression equation.

In a multivariate situation, where we have more than one explanatory variable, we seek to improve on the explanatory power of the equation (R^2) while at the same time ensuring that:

- coefficients remain statistically significant;
- coefficients and standard errors remain relatively stable; and
- signs of coefficients remain intuitively correct.

Unless there is convincing evidence to the contrary we begin by fitting a linear relationship of the form:

$$Y = a + bX_1 + cX_2 + dX_3 + \ldots\ldots$$

A forwards or backwards stepwise regression procedure can be employed for the purpose (e.g., Burns and Burns (2008) with SPSS), with additional variables appearing in the equation, as long as they add to the explanatory power of the equation, and they are individually statistically significant.

The resultant equation should:

- have the highest possible explanatory power (using the adjusted R^2 feature to filter out useless variables making a negligible contribution);
- have a combination of variables for which appropriate tests ensure that all variables in the set are statistically significant; and
- demonstrate the non-violation of the assumptions implicit in the use of ordinary least squares regression.

MODEL SUMMARY

R	R Square	Adjusted R Square	Standard Error of the Estimate	Change Statistics				
				R Square Change	F Change	df1	df2	Sig. F Change
0.684	0.468	0.438	17.984	0.468	15.272	3	52	0.000

Predictors: (constant), HELPERS, POPULATION, DÉCOR

ANOVA

	Sum of Squares	df	Mean Square	F	Sig.
Regression	14,819.081	3	4939.690	15.272	0.000
Residual	16,818.929	52	323.441		
TOTAL	31,638.010	55			

Predictors: (constant), HELPERS, POPULATION, DÉCOR

Dependent variable: TURNOVER

COEFFICIENTS

	Unstandardised Coefficients		Standardised Coefficients		
	B	Standard Error	Beta	t	Sig.
(Constant)	8.946	6.6447		1.383	0.172
DÉCOR	6.039	1.646	0.407	3.668	0.001
POPULATION	0.112	0.042	0.269	2.651	0.011
HELPERS	0.920	0.280	0.363	3.282	0.002

Dependent variable: TURNOVER

Figure 6.12 Summary of regression results for charity shops case study

Figure 6.12 details the typical output from statistical software for regression results. The data for the illustration are drawn from Smith (1997) and his charity shops case study, which relates retail turnover performance to store characteristics. The key features of the output are:

- The inclusion of the three explanatory variables (DÉCOR, helpers and population) which correlate well with turnover (R = 0.684).

- The R^2 of 0.468 indicates that 46.8% of the variation in turnover for this sample of 56 cases is explained by the three independent variables.
- The adjusted R-square = 0.438. R^2 is adjusted to reflect the goodness of fit of the model by scaling-down the R-square value in accordance with the number of explanatory variables in the equation.
- Standard error = 17.984, which is the standard deviation of the actual values of Y (turnover) about the regression line of estimated Y values.
- ANOVA shows that the complete set of regression coefficients (i.e., the equation as a whole) is statistically significant (F = 15.272 significant at the 0.000 level).
- The column headed B gives the regression coefficient for the equation and establishes the equation as:

    TURNOVER = 8.946 + (6.039) * DÉCOR + (0.112) * POPULATION + (0.920) * HELPERS

- The column headed Beta gives the regression coefficients in a standardised form, with a zero intercept term. Standard error of B is a measure of the sampling variability of each regression coefficient.
- Column 't' measures the statistical significance of each of the regression coefficients by computing the ratio of (B/standard error of B) for each variable. Its level of significance is also displayed.

Moderated regression analysis (MRA)

While the normal multiple regression equation looks like:

$$Y = a_0 + b_1 X_1 + c_2 X_2 + e$$

that for moderated regression analysis looks like:

$$Y = a_0 + b_1 X_1 + c_2 X_2 + d_3 (X_1 * X_2) + e$$

and contains an additional 'interaction' term. The product term $(X_1 * X_2)$ represents the 'moderating' effect of X_2 on the relationship between Y and X_1. That is, the relationship between Y and X_1 is conditional on the value of X_2. The variables X_1 and X_2 represent the main effects, and $(X_1 * X_2)$ the two-way interaction effect.

Where the coefficient 'd_3' is statistically significant, then the variable X_2 has a significant moderating effect on the relationship between X_1 and Y (as correspondingly does X_1 on the relationship between X_2 and Y). Adding further explanatory variables to the equation facilitates the evaluation of three-way, and even four-way, interaction effects. Where d_3 is significant it shows that the moderated regression indicates that X_1 and X_2 are interacting to influence the dependent variable Y, even though b_1 and c_2 may themselves be insignificant. The main effects may not be interpretable without the adoption of ratio scales, following Southwood (1978) and Dunk (1995). Thus, Cheng (2012) follows Dunk in dichotomising her X_2 scores at the mean, with scores lower than that termed 'low' and those above the mean termed 'high'. Running two further regressions of Y on X_1 – the first with low X_2 and the second with high X_2 – will highlight the divergence in slope coefficients and demonstrate the circumstances in which X_1 will have the greatest impact on Y, and indeed may demonstrate relationships of opposite signs. Together they show the mediating role of X_2 on the relationship between Y and X_1.

In the accounting literature moderated regression analysis has been widely used in contingency research, most notably in association with budgetary behaviour (e.g., Otley, 1980; Brownell, 1982). Hartmann and Moers (1999) provide examples of this type of research together with a critique of the application of MRA methods.

Further problems might arise when the moderated regression equation involves latent (i.e., unobserved) explanatory variables. Interaction terms are then likely to include significant measurement errors, suggesting that this form of regression analysis might not be the most appropriate method of estimation in such circumstances.

Structural equation modelling and partial least squares

The development of SEM follows Anderson and Rubin's (1949) initial discussion of the use of maximum likelihood methods in the estimation of parameters for single equations, which form a complete set of stochastic equations. There is general acceptance (e.g., Hair et al., 1995; Schumacker and Lomax, 1996; Kline, 1998) of the two-stage technique suggested by Jöreskog (1969) for explaining the relationships between latent variables:

1. a measurement model which uses confirmatory factor analysis of covariance structures to demonstrate the relationships between the observed variables and the constructs (latent variables); and
2. the development and estimation of a structural equation model, which is the representation of a causal path diagram through a set of linear equations.

SEM permits interpretation even in the presence of multicollinearity. We would normally test two or more causal models, all consistent with existing theory, to determine which has the best fit. The SEM software is itself helpful in suggesting modifications that will improve model fit – but it is down to the researcher to decide whether or not such modifications are theoretically justifiable.

Hult et al. (2006) suggests that about 300 observations are ideal for SEM use, but that in practice fewer will do as long as we have about 20 observations for each parameter that is to be estimated.

There is no single measure of the goodness of fit of structural equation models that is acceptable under all circumstances (i.e., method of estimation, sample size, software employed). Accordingly, most published papers will report multiple fit measures; this extends to the reporting of eight different fit indicators in Fogarty et al. (2000)! Smith and Langfield-Smith (2004) note the importance of reporting the specific modelling software employed, since this will likely impact on the relationships explored; thus the AMOS software (see Byrne, 2001) would not permit some of the relationships adopted by Collins et al. (1995) when using LISREL, on the grounds of logic. SEM software permits the adoption of a 'model generating approach', which suggests additional paths to be evaluated – even though these might not have been specified initially on theoretical grounds. Such a facility has led to widespread accusations of 'data mining' in the use of this approach; insignificant paths will usually be eliminated unless their removal results in a drastic reduction in the goodness of fit of the model. Thus, Jaworski and Young (1992), Smith et al. (1993) and Baines and Langfield-Smith (2003) all add and drop paths to or from their initial models to improve the model fit, where such procedures still preserve theory and logic.

Bollen and Long (1993) regard structural equation modelling as an umbrella classification which covers path analysis, partial least squares and latent variable SEM, each as a preferred alternative to OLS regression in prescribed circumstances.

Traditional multiple regression is confined to a single dependent variable and a number of explanatory variables. Path analysis (see Pedhazur, 1982) provides a natural extension by facilitating an analysis of the interrelationships in the variables, so that the dependent variable from one equation can become the explanatory variable in a second equation. However, Maruyama (1998) observes a problem common to both path analysis and conventional regression methods in that only one direction of causation is permissible. While estimating the strengths of specified relationships, it says nothing about direction; theory remains paramount in dictating causation. The path diagram shows the likely causal directions between variables, consistent with theory, so that the path coefficients can be separated to indicate both 'direct' and 'indirect' effects in a linear relationship. Path analysis is subject to all the usual assumptions associated with regression analysis – notably the normality of variables, correct specification of the relationships and absence of multicollinearity. Chong and Chong (1997) provide an early example of the application of the use of path analysis in the accounting literature.

There are two distinct branches of SEM – covariance-based and variance-based SEM. Covariance-based SEM (e.g., as offered by AMOS) emphasises the confirmatory nature of a research model. This is done in a way that minimises the covariance matrix difference, thus confirming that the underlying data structure 'conforms' to the hypothesised relationships of the latent variables.

The variance-based SEM on the other hand, seeks to maximise variance in the criterion (dependent) variable, allowing researchers to measure the predictive capacity of a given model, making it useful in theory-building.

The most popular variance-based SEM is the PLS method, which is built on the work of Wold (1985). Despite early doubts about the applicability of PLS to accounting research, it is now viewed as a valid alternative to the widely acclaimed covariance-based approach. Indeed, current trends suggest that PLS might be a 'silver bullet' (Hair et al., 2011) when used appropriately. The extant accounting literature emphasises confirmatory estimates by the covariance-based SEM and has neglected one of the most pressing issues in research – theory-building and the associated prediction. This is an area where PLS has proved to be most useful (Hair et al., 2014).

PLS was once viewed as the 'poor man's' SEM (e.g., Smith, 2011), in that it is the alternative sought when we cannot satisfy the stringent assumptions of SEM. PLS might be preferred when we have a weak theory, small sample sizes (less than 100) and data which are likely to violate assumptions of normality. The weakness of theory often leads to PLS being referred to as 'soft modelling', being used for predictive rather than explanatory purposes. 'Latent' variables are theoretical constructs, which might be considered to resemble (but not be equivalent to) a factor label – representing the theme, in a factor analysis, to which a number of the observed variables belong. The use of the word 'latent' necessarily implies that there is no opportunity for measurement error; thus, PLS attracts further criticism on technical grounds in that its construction of **latent** variables means that they are not latent in the conventional sense, but merely weighted linear additive combinations of observed variables. There are now a number of instances of the use of PLS in the accounting literature (e.g., Ittner et al., 1997; Smith and Chang, 2009; Djajadikerta et al., 2015).

Djajadikerta et al. (2015) describe the criteria to be observed when reporting the results of PLS modelling. These can be divided into two parts – measurement model estimates and structural model parameters. The measurement model is the outer model that specifies the relationship between a latent variable and its indicators (observed variables), while the structural model is the inner model where the paths indicate the relationship among the latent variables in a given model. Table 6.5 and Table 6.6 summarise their suggested reporting requirements for both measurement and structural models.

Table 6.5 PLS measurement model assessment criteria

Assessments	Criteria	Notes
Item reliability	Individual item standardised loading on parent factor	Min. of 0.50
Convergent validity	Individual item standardised loading on parent factor, and	Min. of 0.50
	Loadings with sig. p-value	$p < 0.05$
	Composite reliability	> 0.70
	Average variance extracted (AVE)	> 0.50
Discriminant validity	Square-root of AVE	More than the correlations of the latent variables
Reliability	Cronbach's alpha	> 0.70
	Variance inflation factor (VIF)	< 5

Table 6.6 PLS structural model criteria

Criteria	Notes
Coefficient of determination, R^2	0.67 substantial
	0.33 average
	0.19 weak
Predictive relevance, Q^2	> 0
	Stone–Geisser test
Effect size, f^2	0.02 small
	0.15 medium
	0.35 large
Path coefficient	Assessed on:
	Magnitude
	Sign
	p-value

Smith and Langfield-Smith (2004) report the results of a survey of the use of SEM in the accounting literature, noting the increasing penetration of the technique, though it still remains at low levels relative to that of other behavioural disciplines.

A focus on the behavioural aspects of accounting research, stressing the importance of latent variables, has advanced the prominence of structural equation modelling research in the accounting field. Existing knowledge of the complex inner workings of latent variables has been advanced, both to confirm existing theories and propose new ones.

Panel data methodology

Panel data, often referred to as longitudinal data, typically provide time observations for a number of different individual variables. Thus, at least two dimensions, a cross-sectional dimension and a time-series dimension, are involved in the observations (Hsiao, 2007). A number of accounting studies (e.g., Bai et al. 2004; Black et al. 2006; Xia and Zhu, 2009; Shan and McIver, 2011) have relied on the use of panel data, frequently employing STATA statistical software for data analysis because of its suitability for panel data regression.

Panel data analysis provides the researcher with a large number of data points, increasing the degrees of freedom and normally reducing the degree of collinearity between explanatory variables (Hsiao, 2003). Baltagi (2005: 4) identifies six advantages of panel data over the more traditional cross-section and time-series data analyses:

1. Reducing the impact of potential bias resulting from heterogeneity. This heterogeneity cannot be controlled easily by time-series or cross-sectional approaches alone.

2. Reducing the degree of multicollinearity so typical of time-series data-based studies. Panel data are less likely to suffer this problem since the cross-sectional element provides greater variability, making the data more informative.

3. Better representing the dynamics of the data. Cross-sectional distributions may appear stable, but can hide multiple changes; panel data are better able to study the nature and extent of adjustments.

4. The additional dimension means that panel data can identify and measure effects that cannot be detected in either pure cross-section or time-series data.

5. The relaxation of regression restrictions means that panel data can be used to construct and test more complicated models than is possible with cross-section or time-series studies.

6. Panel data can reduce the potential bias arising from aggregation of data over many individuals or firms. Data collection from individual cases, at the micro level, often results in more accurate data measurement.

However, Wooldridge (2009) observes that the econometric analysis of panel data cannot assume that observations are independently distributed across time, suggesting that new methods need to be developed for panel data analysis. Baddeley and Barrowclough (2009) suggest that simple OLS is not likely to be valid for samples that have some fixed effects (i.e., firm-specific effects) which are time invariant, since if these fixed effects were to be ignored, then heterogeneity bias would be increased. Such bias can occur because the time-invariant fixed effects, affecting individual cross-sectional units, are not included in the model. Heterogeneity bias might thus be considered to be a form of 'omitted variable' bias increasing autocorrelation errors. The panel estimation technique can eliminate heterogeneity bias, through the adoption of alternative models: a 'fixed effects' model or a 'random effects' model.

Fixed effects model

The fixed effects model is a form of regression that can control for variables that have not been measured or which cannot be measured. The model treats unobserved time-invariant differences of individuals as a set of fixed parameters, which can be directly estimated. Allison (2009) suggests two basic data requirements for the use of a fixed effects model: first, there should be at least two separate measures of the dependent variables for each individual case; second, there must be significant variation in the value of the dependent variables across the sample.

However, Baltagi (2005) identifies potential disadvantages of the fixed effects method: First, the regression model will not permit the examination of time-constant independent variables, and second, standard errors of fixed effects estimates may be larger than those for random effects estimates. Despite this Jager (2008) suggests that for accounting researchers, the most serious problems are those associated with omitted variables, and the resulting inconsistent estimates for regression parameters, both of which can be controlled with a fixed effects model.

Allison (2009) suggests two alternative methods to achieve a fixed effects approach: by creating dummy variables, or through constructing mean deviations. The creation of a set of dummy variables to distinguish each individual in a data set allows the estimation of the unobserved time-invariant variables; however, Allison (2009) suggests that this method may be beyond the computational capacity of the software common to accounting research. Additionally, Wooldridge (2009) argued that the complexity of this method makes it impractical for panel data sets with multiple cross-sectional observations.

The mean deviation method is a simpler method: for each time-varying variable, the means over time are computed for each individual case; the individual-specific means are then subtracted from the observed values of each variable. Where zero values result, these time-constant explanatory variables must be dropped from the equation, though their effects are still being controlled.

Random effects model

One advantage of a random effects approach is that time-constant explanatory variables need not be eliminated, because the random effects model assumes that the unobserved variable is uncorrelated with each explanatory variable, regardless of whether they are fixed over time (Wooldridge, 2009). This approach is therefore appropriate when drawing individuals randomly from a large population in order to make inferences about the characteristics of the population (Jager, 2008). This model is a simpler model than the fixed effects model and will lead to more efficient estimates. However, Allison (2009) has suggested that the random effects model does not really control for unobserved heterogeneity because it assumes no correlation between the unobserved variables and the observed variables – assumptions that may introduce bias if they are shown to be false. He, therefore, suggests the use of the **Hausman specification test** to determine whether the biases inherent in the random effects approach are small enough to ignore, or whether the less restrictive fixed effects model is more appropriate. The Hausman test posits a Null Hypothesis that the random effects estimates are identical to the fixed effects estimates. If the Hausman tests are significant, so that we reject the Null Hypothesis, then the fixed effects model should be used.

An increasing panel data literature indicates that panel data models are likely to have substantial **cross-sectional dependence** in the errors, which may arise because of the presence of common shocks and unobserved components (Hoyos and Sarafidis, 2006). If left untreated, cross-sectional dependence could cause bias and inconsistency estimation (Bai and Kao, 2006). Pesaran's (2003) cross-sectional dependence test is frequently employed within STATA.

Homoskedasticity refers to the assumption that dependent variables have equal levels of variance across the range of explanatory variables (Hair et al., 2006). The assumption of homoskedasticity is restrictive for panel data where the cross-section units may be of varying size and thus may have different variation (Baltagi, 2005). If the variance is unequal across values of explanatory variables, then the situation is known as **heteroskedasticity**. With the presence of heteroskedasticity, consistent estimates of the regression coefficients can still be produced; nevertheless, these estimates are inefficient and the standard errors of the estimates will be biased (Baltagi, 2005).

In a panel data set, the serial correlation is likely to have a more substantial influence on the estimated covariance matrix of the least squares estimator than heteroskedasticity. A new test for serial correlation in the panel data model produced by Wooldridge (2002) is very attractive since it requires relatively few assumptions and implements easily.

Discriminant analysis

The use of OLS regression methods in the previous section requires a dependent variable which can be measured continuously. However, there will be occasions where the variable that we want to explain and predict is not of a continuous nature. It may be categorical of the form high/medium/low, good/bad or success/failure. These can be quantified by assigning dummy variables of the (1,2,3) or (0,1) variety to reflect the alternative states, but in each case these are the only values that the dependent variable can take. Changes in the value of the explanatory variable cannot change the continuous value, only its classification into one or other of the categories. In such circumstances we cannot use simple regression methods, but must seek an alternative. Linear discriminant analysis (LDA) can be used when:

- the groups being identified are clearly separate;
- the explanatory variables are close to being normally distributed, or can be transformed to be so. This ensures 'univariate normality', where the stricter requirement of 'multivariate normality' is more difficult to test in practice; and
- there is no multicollinearity between the explanatory variables.

We seek to construct an equation of the form:

$$Z = a + bX_1 + cX_2 + dX_3 + \dots$$

such that the resulting value of Z allows the categorisation of cases. Effectively we are generating the equation of a line (or lines), which can be positioned to divide the cases into the required groups. For example, in a failure prediction scenario, the construction of a three-variable discriminant model using financial ratios representing profit, debt and liquidity might be visualised relative to the space in a rectangular room where axes are constructed in the corner of the room: the profit ratio stretches vertically towards the ceiling, and liquidity and debt axes are at right angles along the skirting boards. The company cases under consideration appear as points in space, representing three-ratio combinations, and discriminant analysis would try to position a plane in this space such that all the failed companies were on one side of this plane and all the healthy ones on the other. The equation of the optimum plane, even if it were impossible to classify all company cases correctly on either side, would be given by:

$$Z = a + (b * \text{Profit}) + (c * \text{Liquidity}) - (d * \text{Debt})$$

where b, c and d are the weighting attached to each of the ratios;

a is a constant term whose value determines the cut-off between failed and non-failed groups; and

Z is the value of the composite function, such that

Z > 0 corresponds with a state of financial health and

Z < 0 corresponds with a state of financial distress, in that the company has a financial profile similar to that of a previously failed company.

The exhibition of a negative score does not necessarily foreshadow bankruptcy, but gives an indication of financial distress, in that the company has the profile of a previously failed company. The negative score therefore provides early warning, in that future failures will almost certainly come from this distressed group, members of which require close attention (Smith, 2005: 263).

Multivariate techniques such as linear discriminant analysis (e.g., Altman, 1968; Altman et al., 1977; Taffler, 1983) or LOGIT (e.g., Ohlson, 1980; Zavgren, 1985) have been used to generate appropriate models that best discriminate between samples of failed and non-failed firms based on a set of computed financial ratios. The derived model can then be used to classify (predict) other firms as potential failures or as financially healthy. Typically such models are able to distinguish between failed and non-failed firms with very high degrees of accuracy (e.g., Altman, 1993: 219–20; Taffler, 1995), and are widely used in practice (e.g., Altman, 1993: 218–19; Taffler, 1995).

Thus, the original Taffler (1983) model can be specified (according to Agarwal and Taffler, 2007) as follows:

$$Z = 3.2 + 12.18X_1 = 2.5X_2 - 10.68X_3 + 0.0289X_4$$

where X_1 = profit before tax/current liabilities

X_2 = current assets/total liabilities

X_3 = current liabilities/total assets

X_4 = the no-credit interval = $\dfrac{\text{defensive assets} - \text{actual liabilities}}{\text{projected daily expenditure}}$

$= \dfrac{(\text{current assets} - \text{inventory} - \text{current liabilities}) * 365}{\text{sales} - \text{profit before tax} + \text{depreciation}}$

Smith and Taffler (2000) detail the classification of failed and non-failed companies on the basis of their narrative content within the context of two-group LDA. Their discriminant function is of the form:

$$Z = d_0 + d_1 v_1 + d_2 v_2 + d_3 v_3 + \ldots$$

where Z is the discriminant score, $\{v_j\}$ are the variables selected for inclusion in the analysis and $\{d_j\}$ are the optimal coefficients, with d_0, the constant term, representing the cut-off criterion between the two groups.

To take account of the differential costs of Type 1 and Type 2 errors, C_1 and C_2, i.e., classifying a failed firm as non-failed and vice versa, and the differential proportions of potential failures and solvent firms in the corporate population, p_1 and p_2, d_0 is adjusted according to $\ln\left(\dfrac{p_1}{p_2} \cdot \dfrac{C_1}{C_2}\right)$.

Altman (1993: 254–63) provides empirical evidence that for the commercial bank loan decision in the US the ratio of p_1/p_2 is 2/98 and the C_1/C_2 ratio is around 31 times.

While alternative multivariate methodologies such as quadratic discriminant analysis (Altman et al., 1977), LOGIT and PROBIT (e.g., Ohlson, 1980; Zavgren, 1985), non-parametric methods such as recursive partitioning (Frydman et al., 1985) and neural nets (e.g., Altman et al., 1994) are detailed in the literature, there is no evidence of significantly superior performance associated with such approaches compared with traditional LDA (e.g., see Hamer, 1983; Lo, 1986). This is probably because the classical linear discriminant model is quite robust in practice (e.g., Bayne et al., 1983).

Ideally, the validity of a classification model needs to be tested by seeing how well it predicts (classifies) other cases in a 'hold-out' sample. If a model fails to perform well for the hold-out sample, two possibilities exist: (1) the model is sample-specific, or (2) the hold-out sample is not representative of the population from which it was drawn. Since data are difficult to collect, especially matched samples, hold-out samples are often seen as a luxury. A common solution to the problem is to test the validity of the model by varying the cases on which the model is based.

Validation of the derived models is undertaken using the Lachenbruch (1967) jack-knife hold-out test approach, which provides almost unbiased estimates of the true misclassification probabilities. In this approach, $(n_1 + n_2)$ discriminant functions are computed from the original data samples of size n_1 and n_2 observations, with a different observation held out each time, which is then reclassified by the function computed from the remaining $(n_1 + n_2 - 1)$ cases. If m_1 and m_2 observations, respectively, are misclassified in the two groups, then the ratios m_1/n_1 and m_2/n_2 will provide the almost unbiased estimates of the true misclassification probabilities.

Simnett and Trotman (1992) identify three key reasons for non-use of financial distress models in practice:

1. lack of formal training of most practitioners;
2. criticism of the statistical assumptions underlying the models; and
3. failure to include non-financial variables widely accepted as useful discriminators.

More research is necessary to address the third of these issues; while limited evidence has been provided (e.g., Smith and Graves, 2005) to demonstrate the potential usefulness of such models in the appraisal of financial performance, further studies are necessary to overcome the acknowledged implementation difficulties.

LOGIT and PROBIT

Discriminant analysis may not be the most appropriate method of estimation in some circumstances, because the data violate key assumptions of its application:

*   The explanatory variables are assumed to have a multivariate normal distribution. However, many financial variables – notably financial ratios used in failure prediction – are not normally distributed (Eisenbeis, 1977; McLeay, 1986). Variables which have a lower bound of zero are inevitably non-normal.
*   Samples are assumed to have been drawn randomly from their respective populations. These conditions are rarely satisfied in failure prediction studies because of the rarity of the failure event and the likelihood that a random sample would generate few if any failed cases. The widely used matched-pairs technique for case selection specifically violates this assumption.
*   Group covariance matrices should be equal if a linear classification method is to be used – an assumption which is rarely satisfied.

Logistic (LOGIT) and probabilistic (PROBIT) regressions do not necessitate such restrictive assumptions, and are thus often more appropriate estimation methods, even though, as we saw earlier, the predictive outcomes may be little affected. Importantly, sampling techniques which do not involve case-matching permit the inclusion of variables like size, industry and economic cycle to be included in the analysis of business failure. A number of researchers (e.g., Ohlson, 1980; Zmijewski, 1984; Koh, 1991; Lennox, 1999) have adopted LOGIT and PROBIT methods in the accounting literature.

The logistic regression model estimates the model:

$$Log[P_i/(1 - P_i)] = a + B_1X_1 + B_2X_2 + \dots B_kX_k$$

where P_i is the probability of the event under study.

LeClere (2000) observes that the elasticities of probability provide the best indication of the effect of independent variables on the probability of bankruptcy. Following Ohlson

(1980), Shumway (2001) uses logistic regression to model financial distress, on the basis of the probability of subsequent bankruptcy as:

$$\text{LN (odds ratio)} = -7.811 + (4.068)X1 - (6.307)X2 - (0.158)X3 + (0.307)X4$$

where X1 = TL/TA

  X2 = NI/TA

  X3 = CA/CL

  X4 = LN (AGE)

The coefficient of –6.307 for the NI/TA (net income variable) allows the exponent to be interpreted: $e^{-6.307} = 0.0018$; so that a one unit increase in NI/TA decreases the odds of bankruptcy by 0.18%, when the other covariates of the model are controlled.

In other than failure prediction environments, Trubik and Smith (2000) use logistic regression to develop a model which explains customer defection in retail banking. They report a four variable model to examine the odds of staying versus leaving:

$$\text{LN (odds ratio)} = -7.9439 + (0.7031)X1 + (3.8607)X2 + (2.4333)X3 + (0.9933)X4$$

where X1 = time in years an account has been held with the bank

  X2 = fee exemption levels

  X3 = number of bank products held

  X4 = delivery channels used

As with linear discriminant analysis, the cut-off for classification purposes is determined by the relative costs of misclassification. Thus, for failure prediction modelling we might be guided by the relative cost of Type 1: Type 2 misclassification errors. In our customer defection example the literature suggests a 10:1 cost comparison between attracting a new customer and retaining an existing customer, and a cut-off value of 0.05, which correctly classifies 83.2% of bank customers.

Multivariate analysis of variance (MANOVA)

If ANOVA were employed consecutively for dependent variables that were eventually shown to be interrelated then unreliable inferences would result. In such circumstances it is better to use a method (MANOVA) which simultaneously tests all of the variables and their interrelationships. MANOVA is thus very similar to ANOVA and operates on the same basic principles, except that it can handle more than one dependent variable. As with ANOVA,

MANOVA uses the F-test to measure the differences between groups by comparing within-group variance to between-group variance.

MANOVA evaluates the differences between the multivariate means (centroids) of several populations, on the null hypothesis of equality. When the null hypothesis can be rejected, follow-up tests can be performed to pinpoint the source of the difference, namely:

- univariate F-tests run on each of the dependent variables, or
- multiple discriminant analysis.

The dependent variables for use in such an analysis must be correlated with each other, otherwise there is no justification for using MANOVA; ANOVA with separate F-tests would then be more appropriate.

The content of this chapter is inevitably a compromise, both in terms of the techniques addressed and the depth of coverage attempted. A search of the recent accounting literature, especially those journals favouring a quantitative approach, will reveal more complex methods and tests than are described here. However, those considered above still represent the analytical tools most likely to be employed and reported. The mathematics of quantitative methods can be intimidating, and can cause some researchers to neglect the potential benefits of carrying out even the most cursory of tests of hypothesis. However, the most important elements of this chapter are, arguably, the least quantitative:

- the recognition of a theory which allows us to establish 'expected' frequencies and outcomes, with which to compare our observations;
- the basic principles of sample selection; and
- measurement issues.

The number-crunching, of ever-increasing sophistication, to handle increasingly complex experimental designs, is secondary, building on these foundations to demonstrate the potential which exists for significance testing and model-building.

Further reading

Agarwal, V. and Taffler, R.J. (2007) 'Twenty-five Years of the Taffler Z-Score Model: Does It Really Have Predictive Value?', *Accounting and Business Research*, 37 (4): 285–97.

Altman, E.I. (1968) 'Financial Ratios, Discriminant Analysis and the Prediction of Corporate Bankruptcy', *Journal of Finance*, 23 (4): 580–609.

Ashton, R.H. (1974) 'An Experimental Study of Internal Control Judgments', *Journal of Accounting Research*, Spring: 143–57.

Baines, A. and Langfield-Smith, K. (2003) 'Antecedents to Management Accounting Change: A Structural Equation Approach', *Accounting, Organizations and Society*, 28 (6): 675–98.

Baltagi, B.H. (ed.) (2005) *Econometric Analysis of Panel Data*. Chichester: John Wiley.

Burns, R.P. and Burns, R. (2008) *Business Research Methods and Statistics Using SPSS*. London: SAGE.

Byrne, B.M. (2001) *Structural Equation Modelling with AMOS: Basic Concepts, Applications and Programming*. Mahwah, NJ: Lawrence Erlbaum.

Cheng, M.-T. (2012) 'The Joint Effect of Budgetary Participation and Broad-scope Management Accounting Systems on Management Performance', *Asian Review of Accounting*, 20 (3): 184–97.

Cooper, D.C. and Emory, C.W. (1995) *Business Research Methods*. New York: Irwin.

Djajadikerta, H.G., Mat Roni, S. and Trireksani, T. (2015) 'Dysfunctional Information System Behaviors Are Not All Created the Same: Challenges to the Generalizability of Security-based Research', *Information and Management*, 52 (8): 1012–24.

Dunk, A.S. (1995) 'The Joint Effect of Participative Budgeting and Managerial Interest in Innovation on Departmental Performance', *Scandinavian Journal of Management*, 11 (1): 75–85.

Eisenbeis, R.A. (1977) 'Pitfalls in the Application of Discriminant Analysis in Business, Finance and Economics', *Journal of Finance*, 22 (3): 875–90.

Geisser, S. (1974) 'A Predictive Approach to the Random Effects Model', *Biometrica*, 61: 101–7.

Hair, J.F., Anderson, R.E., Tatham, R.L. and Black, W.C. (1995) *Multivariate Data Analysis with Readings*, 4th edn. Upper Saddle River, NJ: Prentice Hall.

Hair, J.F., Black, W.C., Babin, B.J., Anderson, R.E. and Tatham, R.L. (2006) *Multivariate Data Analysis*, 6th edn. Upper Saddle River, NJ: Pearson Prentice Hall.

Hair, J.F., Ringle, C.M. and Sarstedt, M. (2011) 'PLS-SEM: Indeed a Silver Bullet', *Journal of Marketing Theory and Practice*, 19 (2): 139–51.

Hair, Jr, J.F., Sarstedt, M., Hopkins, L. and Kuppelwieser, V.G. (2014). 'Partial Least Squares Structural Equation Modeling (PLS-SEM)', *European Business Review*, 26 (2): 106–21.

Hartmann, F.G.H. and Moers, F. (1999) 'Testing Contingency Hypotheses in Budgetary Research: An Evaluation of the use of Moderated Regression Analysis', *Accounting, Organizations and Society*, 24 (4): 291–315.

Hsiao, C. (2007) 'Panel Data Analysis – Advantages and Challenges', *Test*, 16 (1), 1–22.

Hult, G.T.M., Ketchen, D., Cui, A.S., Prudhomme, A.M., Seggie, S.H., Stanko, M.A., Xu, A.S. and Cavuseil, S.T. (2006) 'An Assessment of the Use of Structural Equation Modelling in International Business Research', *Research Methodology in Strategy and Management*, 3: 385–415.

Jager, P. D. (2008). 'Panel Data Techniques and Accounting Research', *Meditari Accountancy Research*, 16 (2): 53–68.

Kline, R.B. (1998) *Principles and Practice of Structural Equation Modeling*. New York: Guilford Press.

Schumacker, R.E. and Lomax, R.G. (1996) *A Beginner's Guide to Structural Equation Modeling*. Mahwah, NJ: Lawrence Erlbaum.

Smith, D. and Langfield-Smith, K. (2004) 'Structural Equation Modeling in Management Accounting Research', *Journal of Accounting Literature*, 23: 49–86.

Southwood, K.E. (1978) 'Substantive Theory and Statistical Interactions: Five Models', *American Journal of Sociology*, 83 (5): 1154–230.

Stone, M. (1974) 'Cross-Validatory Choice and Assessment of Statistical Predictions', *Journal of the Royal Statistical Society*, 36: 111–47.

Taffler, R.J. (1983) 'The Assessment of Company Solvency and Performance Using a Statistical Model: A Comparative UK-based Study', *Accounting and Business Research*, 15 (5): 295–308.

Wold, H. (1985) 'Partial Least Squares', in S. Kotz and N.L. Johnson (eds), *Encyclopedia of Statistical Sciences*, Volume 6. New York: Wiley. pp. 581–91.

Wooldridge, J.M. (2002) *Economic Analysis of Cross Section and Panel Data*. London: The MIT Press.

SEVEN

Qualitative Data Analysis

─── Chapter Contents ───

- Data management
- Validity concerns
- Content analysis
- Protocol analysis

Qualitative data analysis implies that the focus is on **meaning** rather than on **numbers**. Sample sizes are thus relatively small, but the data collection is intensive.

Patton (2002: 432) notes that there is no single, all-embracing, method for the analysis of textual data: 'Qualitative analysis transforms data into findings. No formula exists for that transformation. Guidance, yes. But no recipe. Direction can and will be offered, but the final destination remains unique for each inquirer, known only when –and if – arrived at.'

Malsch and Salterio (2016: 5) specify five areas of concern that authors of field research studies must address:

- the role played by theory;
- sample size requirements sufficient to demonstrate the conduct of a credible study;
- evaluation of the quality of the data, so that the findings can be trusted;
- how the research demonstrates an appropriate presentation of the findings; and
- how the research constitutes a contribution to the field of study.

Data management

Silverman (2005: 138) suggests the adoption of three processes: data reduction, data display and data interpretation. This can be done using **inductive** methods (e.g., grounded theory) or through a **deductive** approach, which relies on an established theory to provide guidelines or a conceptual framework needs to be made, both of which are beyond the scope of the software.

Basic analysis of qualitative data takes place at the **observation** stage during data collection. Initial impressions are formed and the subsequent write-up of notes (from interviews, documents etc.) will reveal initial ideas about emphases and relationships. These early impressions are helpful in the establishment of an initial **coding** system, whereby we can start to organise the data by interpreting the content and making connections between different pieces of information. It is easy for the researcher, especially the inexperienced researcher, to be overwhelmed by the sheer volume of narrative information to be analysed. Transcripts of even short interviews may produce pages of data! A disciplined and systematic approach is therefore essential in overcoming such information overload, and a good coding system can do this. However, care must be exercised at the coding stage to ensure that we are still conducting qualitative research! We do not wish to attach codes that become mere quantitative labels; it is essential that the coding system retains the variety and character of the data set so that the richness of the environment is retained.

Formulation and modification of the initial coding system is a critical function, and one that needs to be carried out by the researcher. Computer software is of little help here, but it is of immense help when we come to the efficient codification of masses of narrative data. The software can help to facilitate a consistent approach to codification, and to reduce the opportunities to introduce bias. Initial attempts at coding may be flawed – usually by constructing categories which are too wide, and which do not adequately reflect the particular nuances of the data. Other codes may be too narrow, or partially overlapping, necessitating aggregation. Here the computer software can be helpful with a sensitivity analysis of alternative coding systems, or with testing hypotheses about possible relationships between codes.

Recent studies have recognised the potential help provided by a number of software packages: NUD*IST (e.g., Richards et al., 1992), NVivo (e.g., Welsh, 2002) and ATLAS/ti (e.g., Muhr, 1992), which have been used to assist in sorting and managing qualitative data. Fielding and Lee (1998) and Kelle (1995) also provide useful sources for computer-based approaches. But manual methods often prevail because decisions which are beyond the scope of the software frequently need to be made. For example, the researcher might need to establish 'themes' or 'keywords' for categorisation purposes; the software is great at sorting, but the establishment of the key elements for searching must be researcher-driven. Fogarty (2006) questions the continued focus on quantitative data in accounting research, and suggests that the future focus should be on qualitative research concerned with the 'words' and 'language' of accounting. He recommends more emphasis on projects using NUD*IST and DICTION for the content analysis of accounting narratives.

Miles and Huberman (1994) recommend the use of a matrix approach to data analysis, which facilitates a comparison of themes across cases in order to readily highlight patterns and variations. Abernethy et al. (2005) suggest an alternative approach to this task, recommending a triangulation method, which incorporates causal maps, researcher intuition, participant feedback and documented word-based codes. These approaches seek to adopt structured methods for identifying patterns that overcome the danger of the researcher overtly seeking patterns that happen to fit an existing theory! Indeed the findings may be more interesting (e.g., Merchant and Manzoni, 1989) if the findings come as a surprise and appear to question existing theory.

After the coding stage, a number of alternative approaches might be adopted to aid interpretation, explanation and theorising, most notably:

- grounded theory, using a constant comparison of categories, and an inductive approach to generate hypotheses (see Chapters 3 and 10);
- discourse analysis, examining patterns of communication between individuals over time, like a time-series analysis of content; and
- content analysis, to identify key themes, considered in detail below, and in Chapter 11.

Validity concerns

Each piece of qualitative evidence (e.g., documents, observational notes, interview transcripts) should first be evaluated for reliability and validity. Lillis (2006) observes that, in the absence of control groups, validity can be problematic. However, she recommends that qualitative researchers seek to address issues of construct validity, internal validity, external validity and reliability. Ahrens and Dent (1998) emphasise that field study researchers are obligated to be as rigorous and unbiased in conducting and reporting their research as are quantitative researchers.

Atkinson and Shaffir (1998) suggest that field research can yield construct validity to a far greater extent than quantitative alternatives by capturing richer and more subtle complexities – but field research still needs multiple sources of evidence if it is to be successful in mapping theoretical constructs onto empirical observations. Lillis (2006) notes that while field research facilitates the formation of rival explanations for observations, the demonstration of internal validity remains a problem because of the inability to reach unbiased conclusions about the nature of relationships between variables.

Lillis (2006) distinguishes threats to reliability at two major stages of the data analysis process: (i) when attaching data to particular constructs, and (ii) when making linkages between the constructs. Clear decision rules must guide both processes, and multiple coders are helpful in ensuring that these decision rules are appropriately implemented. Measures of inter-coder reliability (e.g., Malina and Selto, 2001; Abernethy et al., 2005) become a helpful necessity in such circumstances. However, Lillis (1999, 2006) considers the use of multiple coders a necessary, but not sufficient, means of generating internal validity, because of the absence of independent supporting evidence. The quest for **external validity** poses different problems, because field study research seeks to examine the links between findings and theory. It does not seek to offer findings that are generalisable to other situations, since the context and timing of the data collection would render this near impossible. Where generalisability between sites is sought this is best accomplished through multiple case studies which permit the observation of similar events at different locations (e.g., Eisenhardt, 1989, 1991; Scapens, 1990).

The question of reliability is also problematic in field research, since it is most unlikely that independent researchers using common procedures will produce exactly the same outcomes; the recorded observations will be 'coloured' by the perceptions, attitudes and personal characteristics of participants and researchers at that particular time and place (Otley, 2001: 248). This major threat to reliability must be addressed through greater vigilance and strict attention to detail during the data collection phase. As Lillis (2006: 470) notes, there is a requirement for

> not only a record of procedures undertaken, but also an audit trail of decisions made as multiple sources of evidence are evaluated and compared, definitions are revised, decision rules created and modified, coding schemes tested and altered, and productive and unproductive thematic analysis undertaken.

Content analysis

Content analysis is defined as a method that uses a set of procedures to make valid inferences from texts. The inferences are about the sender(s) of messages, the message itself or the audience of the message, and the rules for the inferential process vary with the interests of the investigator (Weber, 1985). Statistical studies of literary style, particularly those that solve disputes about the authenticity of writings, date back to the 1850s, and are well illustrated by Mosteller and Wallace's (1963) model, which allows a distinction between disputed authors of the Federalist Papers based on the incidence of the words 'whilst', 'upon' and 'enough'. Similar approaches were adopted by Osgood and Walker (1959) and Stone and Hunt (1963) to distinguish between fake and genuine suicide notes, based on their reference to things and persons. The analysis of word patterns and sequences to detect hidden messages came to the fore during wartime, with their use in exposing propaganda in political speeches (Laswell, 1948; Berelson, 1952).

Content analysis has traditionally been applied to the analysis of archival data, but is becoming increasingly popular in the analysis of interview transcripts. Typically, quantitative methods have been applied to archival data and qualitative methods to interview transcripts. Where quantitative methods have been employed, they have usually been limited to the manifest characteristics of text (e.g., the number of occurrences of words, or the number of words relating to particular themes). The quantitative results in the form of variables referring to particular words and themes are then available for statistical analysis.

More recently, the techniques have been applied to the qualitative analysis of open-ended survey responses with the aim of corroborating survey data. In these applications, content analyses may examine latent characteristics of the data such as the underlying meaning of the phrases used (Holsti, 1969). A further issue relates to the connection between the manifest and latent content of a narrative. Content analysis rests on the belief that it is possible to go behind the text as presented and infer valid hidden or underlying meanings of interest to the investigator (Weber, 1990: 72–6). Content analytic procedures that restrict themselves to manifest content alone would thus be of very limited value. Salancik and Meindl (1984: 243, footnote 2), however, argue that whether or not the attributions expressed are the 'true' beliefs of the authors is irrelevant.

Two alternative generic approaches to content analysis are usually taken where quantitative analysis is contemplated: **form oriented** (objective) analysis, which involves routine counting of words or concrete references; and **meaning oriented** (subjective) analysis, which focuses on analysis of the underlying themes in the texts under investigation.

In the managerial literature, Bettman and Weitz (1983), Staw et al. (1983), Salancik and Meindl (1984), Clapham and Schwenk (1991) and Abrahamson and Park (1994) all adopt a content analysis approach to explore the causal attributions made by firm managements in their letters to shareholders that explain or account for company performance. Jones and Shoemaker (1994) provide a general overview of empirical accounting narrative analytic studies. Kelly-Newton (1980) adopts a content analysis procedure to the measurement of themes in her analysis of the general comments section of a sample of replacement cost footnotes examining management reaction to disclosure requirements. Ingram and Frazier (1980) conduct a content analysis of firm environmental disclosures, and also report an explanatory study linking narrative disclosures with firm performance across three industries (Ingram and Frazier, 1983).

Abrahamson and Amir (1996) study the information content of the president's letter to shareholders, and highlight the importance of textual portions of annual reports to investors. Bowman (1984) uses the number of occurrences of the word 'new' in the president's letter as a measure of managerial risk in addressing questions of firm strategic risk and uncertainty. He also emphasises the advantages of content analysis as an unobtrusive measurement, since the statements are written for purposes and audiences different from those constituted by content analysts. There is little danger that the measurement process will confound the data (Weber, 1990: 10).

D'Aveni and MacMillan (1990) use content analysis of shareholder letters to analyse the differential strategic responses to demand crises by the top managements of surviving and bankrupt firms. Successful firm managements are distinguished by their focus on critical success factors in their output environment (e.g., customer needs and demand growth), whereas failing firm managements deny crises, look inwards and focus on the short term.

Building on Frazier et al. (1984), McConnell et al. (1986), Swales (1988) and Yoon and Swales (1991) all use a content analysis approach to explore whether qualitative data found in the firm's annual report can forecast stock price performance. In contrast to Bowman (1984), who focuses on positive references, Abrahamson and Amir (1996) restrict consideration to negative references only. Tennyson et al. (1990) explore the relationship between the firm's narrative disclosures and bankruptcy, using a content analysis approach, but they do not differentiate between positive/negative or good/bad references in their statistical models.

Weber (1990: 37) argues that word categories inferred from co-variation among high-frequency words are more reliable than themes. However, Krippendorff (1980: 63) suggests that for many content analyses, thematic units requiring user judgement in the determination of the hidden messages conveyed in the narratives may be preferable despite application difficulties. The term 'word' is taken to indicate semantically equivalent textual units, including word synonyms, idioms and phrases (Weber, 1990: 22), and 'theme' is taken to mean clusters of words with different meanings or connotations that, taken together, refer to some theme or issue (Weber, 1990: 37). Smith and Taffler (2000) adopt these basic definitions in their conduct of both form-oriented (word-based) and meaning-oriented (theme-based) analyses. The qualitative content of the narrative is transformed into quantitative variables for subsequent analysis with simple formulae. Thus, for words:

$$\text{Word variable} = \frac{\text{Number of common occurrences}}{\text{Total number of words in the narrative}}$$

Ratio variables can then be computed from the narrative for each theme on the basis of the importance of those themes in the narrative. Thus, if a sentence comprises four themes, each is accorded a theme score of 0.25. The overall score summed across all sentences accorded any particular theme is taken to be indicative of its importance within the narrative.

$$\text{Theme variable} = \frac{\text{Sum of theme scores}}{\text{Total number of sentences in the statement}}$$

Reliability and limitations

Krippendorff (1980: 130–54) warns against the potential unreliability of self-applied investigator-developed recording instructions, emphasising three aspects of the process:

- stability – inter-temporal coding differences in the same coder should be insignificant;
- reproducibility – coding rules should be such as to allow different coders in different locations to agree substantially on their assignments; and
- accuracy – the performance of coders should largely comply with a known 'right' answer, although this is frequently impossible to assess in practice.

There is no generally agreed level of performance inter-correlations that is deemed to be satisfactory, but Krippendorff (1980: 146–7) suggests that inter-coder reliability correlations in excess of 80% should be sought. Nonetheless, however careful the researchers are, as Weber (1990: 62) emphasises, content analysis is partly an art and depends on the judgement and interpretation of the investigator. 'Texts do not speak for themselves... The investigator must do the speaking and the language of that speech is the language of theory' (Weber, 1990: 80). Researcher bias cannot be avoided.

Another major limitation of content analysis is that it assumes that frequency of occurrence directly reflects the degree of emphasis accorded to words or themes, but this may not always be so (e.g., see Weber, 1990: 71–3). In addition, words or sentences classified in the same category for data reduction purposes may not reflect that category to the same extent (Weber, 1990: 72).

More recent publications concerned with the analysis of narratives have moved beyond 'words' and 'themes' to address alternative stylistic features. Thus, Amernic and Craig (2006, 2008) examine the use of rhetoric in corporate statements; Beattie et al. (2004) examine alternative narrative disclosure indices; Aerts (2005) examines the selectivity of performance measures for disclosure emphasis; Brennan et al. (2009) develop a model to permit the analysis of six narrative characteristics: keywords, amounts, selectivity of P&L amounts, keyword reinforcement, performance comparisons and ambiguity; and Merkl-Davies and Brennan (2007) focus on the use of narrative manipulation for the purposes of impression management.

Content analysis, and related methods like discourse analysis and document analysis, have become popular methods across a whole range of research topics. Beattie and Thomson (2007) provide an excellent example of the wider applicability of the method.

Protocol analysis

The fundamentals of protocol analysis lie in psychology (e.g., Ericsson and Simon, 1980, 1993) and can be linked to management (work study) and ethnomethodology. Newell and Simon's (1972) early protocol method is essentially an information processing tool examining process tracing. It provides the basis for audit research examining the audit process (e.g., Ashton and Kramer, 1980; Lauer and Peacock, 1989). The method has subsequently been extended to address applications concerning financial analyst decision-making (e.g., Bouwman, 1984; Anderson and Potter, 1998) and loan decisions (Campbell, 1984).

Campbell (2006) highlights thematic coding as the major problem of protocol analysis – just as it is with theme-based content analysis. But protocols have one further problem in that participant behaviour might be influenced by the presence of the researcher – even so, concurrent (rather than retrospective) protocols appear to be preferred in the literature. Campbell (2006) also questions the specifics of the protocol and notes that Bouwman (1984) begins by defining a verbal protocol in terms of activities, goals etc., before deciding how they might be narrowed down.

Further reading

Abernethy, M., Horne, M., Lillis, A.M., Malina, M.A. and Selto, F.H. (2005) 'A Multi-Method Approach to Building Causal Performance Maps from Expert Knowledge', *Management Accounting Research*, 16 (2): 135–55.

Amernic, J.H. and Craig, R. (2008) 'A Privatization Success Story: Accounting and Narrative Expression over Time', *Accounting, Auditing and Accountability Journal*, 21 (8): 1085–115.

Atkinson, A.A. and Shaffir, W. (1998) 'Standards for Field Research in Management Accounting', *Journal of Management Accounting Research*, 10: 41–67.

Beattie, V. and Thomson, S. (2007) 'Lifting the Lid on the Use of Content Analysis to Investigate Intellectual Capital Disclosures in Corporate Annual Reports', *Accounting Forum*, 31 (2): 129–63.

Brennan, N.M., Guillamon-Saorin, E. and Pierce, A. (2009) 'Impression Management: Developing and Illustrating a Scheme of Analysis for Narrative Disclosures – A Methodological Note', *Accounting, Auditing and Accountability Journal*, 22 (5): 789–832.

Holsti, O.R. (1969) *Content Analysis for the Social Sciences and Humanities*. Reading, MA: Addison-Wesley.

Ingram, R.W. and Frazier, K.B. (1983) 'Narrative Disclosures in Annual Reports', *Journal of Business Research*, 11: 49–60.

Jones, M.J. and Shoemaker, P. A. (1994) 'Accounting Narratives: A Review of Empirical Studies of Content and Readability', *Journal of Accounting Literature*, 13: 142–84.

Krippendorff, K.H. (1980) *Content Analysis: An Introduction to its Methodology*. Beverley Hills, CA: SAGE.

Krippendorff, K.H. (2004) Content Analysis: An Introduction to its Methodology, 2nd edn. Thousand Oaks, CA: SAGE.

Lillis, A.M. (1999) 'A Framework for the Analysis of Interview Data from Multiple Field research', *Accounting and Finance*, 39 (1): 79–105.

Malsch, B. and Salterio, S.E. (2016) 'Doing Good Field Research: Assessing the Quality of Audit Field Research', *Auditing: A Journal of Practice and Theory*, 35 (1): 1–22.

Merkl-Davies, D.M. and Brennan, N.M. (2007) 'Discretionary Disclosure Strategies in Corporate Narratives: Incremental Information or Impression Management', *Journal of Accounting Literature*, 26: 116–94.

Patton, M.Q. (2002) *Qualitative Research and Evaluation Methods*. Thousand Oaks, CA: SAGE.

Silverman, D. (2005) *Doing Qualitative Research: A Practical Handbook*. London: SAGE.

Smith, M. and Taffler, R.J. (2000) 'The Chairman's Statement: A Content Analysis of Discretionary Narrative Disclosures', *Accounting, Auditing and Accountability Journal*, 13 (5): 624–46.

EIGHT

Experimental Research

Chapter Contents

- The problem statement
- Theory and context
- Experimental design
- The validity trade-off
- Quasi-experimental research

Abdel-Khalik and Ajinkya (1979) provide a precise definition of the nature of an experiment in that the researcher manipulates one or more variables with subjects who are assigned randomly to various groups. These groups receive different combinations of the variables (termed 'treatments'); in some cases a control group may exist which receives no such treatments. The major advantage of experiments lies in the researchers' ability to ensure high internal validity, defined in terms of how well they can eliminate rival explanations for their results. Experiments are, thus, particularly suited to research questions that investigate causal relations between variables.

Gibbins and Salterio (1996: 24) suggest four guidelines for good experimental research in accounting:

1. A clear statement of the problem, its importance and the contribution to knowledge that its solution will make.
2. A clear statement of the theory that underlies the process, in particular the theory that drives the behaviour and the impact of context on theory.
3. A sound experimental design – since fatal flaws can be introduced by inappropriate or inadequate designs.
4. Recognition of the importance of external validity. If this means that we need more realistic experimental settings, then we need correspondingly richer theoretical explanations of resultant behaviour.

These guidelines provide an excellent framework for the consideration of research issues in accounting experimentation, and are adopted here.

The problem statement

The variables of interest are:

Y = the dependent variable or observation

X_i = the independent variable (or treatment), which can be either manipulated in value, as in an experiment, or measured from archival data, as in econometric studies. A laboratory experiment will normally have more internal validity than other research methods (particularly field studies or archival research). As we move away from the high-control environment of an experimental setting, the various threats to internal validity grow, with the consequence that tests of causality cease to be so reliable. We may then only be able to attribute association (through correlation measures), rather than the direction of the association.

Theory and context

With the explosion of experimental research in auditing in the mid-1970s, the use of experienced subjects or expert practitioners as participants was thought to be essential to provide the necessary external validity to the research. As a result, most journals have expressed a preference for the use of practitioners in any experimental research. This has imposed a serious constraint on the implementation of experimental work, particularly over recent years, because it has become increasingly difficult to secure the participation of accounting practitioners for experimental research. This participation remains essential for the publication of auditing research in the top journals; but, fortunately, for experimental work outside the auditing sphere there is increasing recognition that surrogate participants may have the necessary skill base to participate. The use of a large proportion of students in a study has been justified by a number of authors: Ashton and Kramer (1980), in a review of research in both business and psychology, report that the information processing behaviour of students and 'real-world' decision makers does not differ; Abdolmohammadi and Wright (1987) argue that for highly structured decision tasks the performance of a student should not differ significantly from that of real-world decision makers; and past research has reported that there are no differences between subjects with and without work experience in experiments using financial information data sets (MacKay and Villarreal, 1987; Stock and Watson, 1984). Brownell (1995: 83) suggests that the alleged shortcomings of using students in laboratory-based experiments are overstated. He likens the situation to that of non-response in survey work, suggesting that we need to demonstrate both that systematic differences do exist and that such differences matter before we rule out the use of student surrogates.

The role of theory in real judgement settings

In order to take advantage of the potential strength of experimental settings in testing causal relations, a well-developed theoretical framework is essential. Once the theoretical framework has been established, the researcher can decide which variables should be manipulated and measured, and which controlled. Libby et al. (2002) stress the importance of careful hypothesis development and research design in producing efficient and effective experiments, highlighting internal and external validity as the key aspects of effectiveness. Bisbe et al. (2007) follow Libby in emphasising the need to establish the nature and direction of constructs before attempting to build predictive models. They focus on the constructs widely adopted in quantitative research, concerning management accounting control systems, and in doing so question the conceptual foundations and imprecise definitions of much survey-based research.

Early experimental research in accounting was highly criticised for its atheoretical approach, but more recently we have seen the application of psychological theories to decision-making research, following the work of Kahneman and Tversky (1972) in the exploration of heuristics and biases (e.g., Ashton, 1983; Smith, 1993) and more recently in the use of theories of knowledge, memory and learning (e.g., Libby and Frederick, 1990). Economics-based theories (notably agency theory) have also evolved to explain experimental settings in management accounting (e.g., Demski and Feltham, 1976).

The embedding of judgement within the context of a particular task

The question of context is a potentially great threat to the external validity of judgement in experimental tasks. We may be unsure whether the observed findings are attributable to the variables subject to manipulation, or to the impact of such variables as task complexity, location, time constraints, incentives etc. A well-designed experiment should attempt to address each of these issues, but even so, it remains difficult to control for all potential extraneous variables successfully with 100% certainty in any experiment. Great care must be taken in assembling a literature of comparative findings to support a particular research direction, especially without returning to the original papers; inconsistent or contradictory findings may be attributable to different research contexts rather than to the key variables at issue.

The role of incentives to participants

One contextual issue is of particular concern and has raised a number of associated issues: the availability of incentives to motivate participants to expend effort in the performance of the task may create more problems than it solves. Libby and Lipe (1992) provide an interesting example of this where they suggest that the conceptual noise introduced by the incentive scheme is influenced by unmeasured factors. For student participants, modest monetary incentives might be necessary to induce attendance, participation and attention, but the impact of these on the eventual outcomes is unclear. We may need to examine a theory of incentives, and the way they influence individuals with differing personal characteristics, before we can measure their effect. Libby and Luft (1993) suggest that any extra effort induced by incentives may be related to ability and knowledge characteristics of the participants. Ethical requirements may impose a further constraint in that while incentives to participate may be acceptable, performance-related incentives (where differential rewards are provided) may be disallowed on equity grounds. Hence, we may reasonably try to avoid the availability of incentives wherever possible. The use of incentives appears to be unnecessary where the participants are skilled professionals. Bonner and Sprinkle (2002) establish a theoretical framework for incentive payments, which has guided subsequent work in this area.

The use of professionals as research participants

As discussed above, some journals and some experimental settings demand the use of skilled professional participants. It is becoming increasingly difficult, even outside the top-tier journals, to publish experimental research using wholly student audiences. This is particularly so for undergraduate audiences. Student audiences may still be acceptable for the conduct of pilot studies, but practitioner/professional subjects will be required for the main study.

The use of deception to create appropriate research settings

The mere fact that subjects are placed in a laboratory setting may create an effect resulting in an outcome that would not have arisen outside the experimental setting. This can occur for a variety of reasons, including where the subjects may adopt an attitude whereby they try to please the experimenter: Weber and Cook (1972) and Schepanski et al. (1992) report on situations where the participants in experiments want to help the experimenter by apparently trying to deliver what is expected of them.

Under such circumstances it may be necessary to deceive the subjects as to the objectives of the experiment, so that they are unaware of the predicted outcomes of the study, in order to deliver valid results. Thus, Smith and Taffler (1996) inform their subjects that they are making judgements on 60 separate companies, to secure separate decisions for each of the 20 company cases being employed with three different treatments. Only on completion of the experiment is the deception revealed. Such behaviour, however, may generate cynicism among participants so that they are in such a state of disbelief regarding experimental settings that it may preclude future participation. There are also ethical considerations in that participation in the experiment has been achieved in a potentially undesirable manner, with the result that researcher trust and honesty have been sacrificed in order to deliver experimental outcomes.

Experimental design

Trotman (1996), following Campbell and Stanley (1963) and Libby (1981), suggests a number of simple alternatives.

Post-test only control group design

Subjects are randomly assigned to treatments; that is, to different levels of the independent (explanatory) variables. For two levels of the independent variable, X1 and X2 (one of which may be a control group with no treatment), two corresponding outcomes are observed, OO_1 and OO_2, say. These outcomes are measured after each of the subjects has received the treatment. A comparison of OO_1 and OO_2 will reveal the impact of the different treatments. The basic form of this design could easily be expanded to cover many other levels of the treatment. Joyce and Biddle (1981) provide an example of this type of design.

Pre-test/post-test control group design

Subjects are measured to see how they react to successive treatments, but this time a before-and-after experimental design is used, which allows the research design to control for individual differences. A treatment X_1 is applied to a subject, producing an observed outcome OO_1; a further treatment X_2 (which may be something as simple as the provision of additional information) is then applied to the subject and a new outcome OO_2 observed, facilitating the comparison of the two observed outcomes.

Despite the advantages of the control of individual differences, the repeated use of the same individuals for successive treatments also causes potential problems: there may be a 'learning' effect as well as an 'order' effect. Heiman (1990) provides an example of this type of design.

Factorial design: between subjects

This involves the simultaneous variation of two or more treatments (explanatory variables) so that we can monitor their separate impacts on the dependent variable, and any potential interactive effect between the explanatory variables (i.e., the extent of any conditional relationship such that treatment X_1, say, only has an effect for certain levels of the X_2 treatment).

The simplest 2×2 design manipulates two treatments across two levels to give four different possible combinations. Subjects are randomly assigned to each of these four cells, and each receives only one treatment. Trotman (1996: 19) identifies a number of distinct advantages for using a factorial design of this type:

1. The interaction effects can be evaluated. This is particularly important where there are competing alternative explanations for the observations. Brown and Solomon (1993) provide an example of this type of design in testing three competing theoretical explanations from the psychological literature.
2. Potentially confounding variables (e.g., gender, work experience) can be held constant within a cell so that their influence can be evaluated.
3. External validity can potentially be enhanced by findings which demonstrate similar effects across a number of subject characteristics.
4. Designs of this kind are more economical than the simpler post-test only designs in their use of subjects. Fewer subjects are required to conduct the same tests, which is an important consideration where practitioners willing to participate are difficult to locate.

Factorial design: within subjects

As with the simpler designs, we can also introduce a 'before-and-after' factorial design. Whereas in a 'between-subjects' design subjects receive only one treatment, in a 'within-subjects' design each subject receives all the successive treatments. This constitutes what is often called a 'repeated measures' design. Such designs can have further advantages:

1. They require many fewer subjects.
2. The statistical power of the outcomes is potentially greater because of the controls implicitly introduced for individual characteristics, assuming that the characteristics of the individual have not changed significantly between successive treatments (see also the maturation effect, regarding internal validity concerns).
3. They are particularly useful for examining differences in information use and the impact of different treatments in learning and training environments.

But there are also a number of potentially serious disadvantages associated with this research design, which have been identified by Brownell (1995: 11) and Trotman (1996: 30):

1. Demand effects, such that the subject is able to glean the details of the experiment (e.g., the hypotheses under test, or the number of failed companies in a sample) to such an extent that his/her behaviour becomes different from that which would be expected (under real-world conditions).
2. One of the major downsides is that subject variables cannot be used as explanatory variables in a within-subjects design because individual characteristics cannot be altered across treatments.
3. Practice effects, such that subjects' behaviour changes as the experiment proceeds – they may perform better because of skills learning and knowledge accumulation, or worse because of fatigue or waning enthusiasm.

4. Carry-over effects, such that the way a second treatment is considered is highly depend-ent on experience from the first one (e.g., in successive failure prediction tasks, the expectation, justified or otherwise, that the number of failed cases will be identical). This may mean that independent decision-making may be impossible without using counterbalancing measures associated with the re-ordering of the tasks. Even with re-ordering, Schepanski et al. (1992) suggest that there may still be a problem, which may be overcome by introducing 'filler' tasks and lengthening the experimental period. However, this is a solution that will itself pose further problems. Maturation effects may also be apparent here in that within-subjects designs must inevitably involve some time lag, namely that between successive treatments, which will make them more vulnerable to this kind of internal validity threat.
5. Statistical effects, such that the equality of variances assumption is violated in within-subjects analysis of variance (ANOVA), making the F-tests biased. The outcome may not be serious but should be acknowledged by performing alternative checks.
6. A cue salience effect, such that the number of variables under focus in a within-subject experiment will be fewer than in the corresponding between-subjects exper-iment. Schepanski et al. (1992) suggest that this may pose an external validity threat. A major constraint in most experiments is the amount of time available to subjects for participation in the experiment, and the variability in the time taken by individual subjects. All researchers are constrained to some extent by the number of variables they can consider given the number and amount of time the subjects are available.

There will almost always be other potentially influential variables that threaten internal validity, and these must be dealt with by exercising some form of control. A number of alternative procedures exist.

1. **Control groups:** to hold extraneous variables constant. A controlled environment is established by the researcher being present during the conduct of the experiment, in contrast to the non-controlled settings like those used by survey researchers. Where control groups are not feasible, we may seek to control those variables not directly involved in the relationships under investigation.
2. **Randomisation:** so that the distribution of the variable is equally likely across all of the independent variables. Subjects will be assigned randomly to each of the treatment cells. Random assignment assumes that the same factors will influence each treatment group, and that each should contain an approximately equal mix of these factors. The larger the sample size, the more likely this is to be the case. Where we have a small sample, and very small cell sizes, we must doubt whether randomisation will effectively dull the impact of individual differences among subjects.
3. **Holding constant:** so that the variable has the same value across all values of the independent variable.

4. **Matching:** so that the distribution of the variable is common across each of the independent variables. Thus, for auditing experiments, we may match the participants based on their experience; in financial accounting, companies may be matched on size. Matching effectively precludes the study of the 'matched' characteristic. Where this is a problem we may seek to include matched variables (e.g., size) as explanatory variables. However, such inclusion is not a completely satisfactory solution because the matched variables cannot then be randomly assigned to experimental groups. Thus, if they are found to be influential, we cannot rule out an alternative hypothesis that some unknown variable (proxied by the included variable) is responsible for the relationship.

5. **Counterbalancing:** using all combinations of ordering of treatments will overcome the impact of any order effect, but will necessitate the preparation of many different versions of the experiment. Thus, Trotman and Wright (1996), in an audit environment, had half the subjects processing internal control aspects, followed by going concern aspects, while the other half conducted the going concern part first, followed by the internal control. Similarly, Smith and Taffler (1995), in a financial accounting environment, address three different information processing formats (narratives [N], ratios [R], graphs [G]) which require six different instruments, one for each of the possible order combinations (NRG, NGR, RNG, RGN, GNR, GRN). However, counterbalancing may not solve all the problems of order effects. Smith and Taffler (1996) observe that for tasks of similar difficulty, the 'last' test performed, whichever it was, was often performed the quickest.

6. **Ignoring variables:** either intentionally (if the variable is considered to have an inconsequential impact) or unintentionally (if its impact has not been considered at all!).

Each of the alternatives has potential pitfalls. In archival studies, for example, it is usually impossible to hold constant a large number of variables, or to match on many others. Matching can create almost as many problems as it is attempting to solve. For example, in accounting studies (e.g., Smith and Taffler, 1992) it is common to match companies on the basis of industry; some measure of size; and even financial year-end. Such a process may severely constrain the sample size achievable, and may effectively eliminate the consideration of the influence any of the matched variables (notably size) may have. Some variables can safely be ignored on the basis of prior literature, but many others may still have to be ignored even though we are uncertain of their potential impact. Thus, it is common (e.g., Schulz, 1999) for variables associated with individual differences between participants to be ignored, other than those for age, gender and experience. This is despite the growing evidence for the influence of numerous other factors (e.g., cognitive style, tolerance of ambiguity) on behaviour in accounting environments. Some variables may be so difficult to measure that we seek to employ proxy variables instead – for example, the use of size measures to proxy for political influence. Failure to include potential variables may result in a selection bias at the data sampling stage.

Manipulation checks can be used to help ensure that subjects really understand both the instrumentation and what is required of them, and to monitor the course of the experiment (especially at the pilot stage, where one is feasible) to ensure that the different treatments are producing changes in the same direction as anticipated. Maines and Wahlen (2006), Magilke et al. (2009) and Elliott et al. (2014) provide examples of experimental research focusing on the reliability and objectivity aspects of accounting information.

The validity trade-off

We can identify three distinct validity concerns in the conduct of experiments: construct validity, internal validity and external validity.

Threats to construct validity

Construct validity describes the extent to which abstract constructs are successfully operationalised. This definition embraces both the extent to which the constructs are measured reliably and the extent to which they provide measures that effectively capture the essence of the abstraction. We attempt to interpret theory through the development of abstract constructs, and then seek to operationalise these constructs with measurable variables. Where this is not possible we must substitute proxy variables, which are measurable but which may be less than perfect proxies. Imperfect proxies will mean flawed tests of hypotheses.

Nunnally (1978) describes three aspects of establishing construct validity:

1. Specify those variables that are both observable and related to the construct – this tells the researcher which items to measure and evaluate in the next step.
2. Determine the extent to which these observable variables are reliable measures of one or more constructs and the extent of interrelationships among measured items.
3. Determine the extent to which those measures of the constructs employed will produce predictable results.

Most of the attention in designing laboratory research is on the experimental treatment with typically little attention paid to the construct validity issues associated with the measured variables. Where there is any attention being paid, it is usually to the second of Nunnally's stages alone.

The consequences of errors here are potentially serious. For example, Brownell (1995: 112) reveals that in his earlier paper (Brownell, 1982) he used the widely accepted Milani (1975) instrument to measure budgetary participation. However, he perceives 'participation' to be a combination of both 'influence' and 'involvement', and is not convinced that the Milani instrument adequately addresses both dimensions. The instrument used may not be measuring the construct in a reliable way, but the alternative is to develop a new and completely untested instrument. Brownell is apparently prepared to trade construct validity for reliability in this instance.

Threats to internal validity

Cook and Campbell (1979) identify nine separate internal validity concerns.

1. **Maturation:** This concerns any impact associated with the passage of time. This would relate to changes to subjects between successive experiments, or even during a single experiment or interview. It would also relate to the characteristics of company cases, say, where growth or restructuring over time means that we are no longer comparing like with like. Thus, the researcher must be aware of the potential impact on subjects of the likes of learning, fatigue and boredom.

2. **History:** This is similar to that above but is more concerned with environmental changes that may impact the research, rather than with those changes in the subject. These environmental changes will impact significantly on longitudinal studies and those where the data collection (e.g., interviews or experiments) is conducted over an extended period.

3. **Testing:** The outcomes of a set of tests may be partly attributable to the outcomes of prior tests. The effect of repeated measures may therefore extend over a lengthy period.

4. **Subject mortality:** Subjects may die or, more likely, absent themselves part way through a series of experiments or interviews. This will cause data loss but, more seriously, the absence may be dependent on systematic factors: the least-motivated subjects may drop out of an experiment so that we are left with an unrepresentative group. Brownell (1995: 11) observes that in experimental settings, failure to recruit participants, and their failure to re-appear, may be related to the treatment, especially if some treatments are perceived to be less desirable than others.

   Similar effects are reported by users of other methods; thus, Casey (1980) reports different response rates to his survey; those with the greatest information load were least likely to respond. Similarly, in archival studies on company cases, the failure, merger or acquisition of some companies means that they will be removed from the sample and will be under-represented in time-series studies.

5. **Experimental mortality:** The passage of time can have numerous effects on the subject companies. For example, the companies may have grown, merged or shifted from public to private status. A survivorship bias can arise because failed companies have been omitted from an all-company analysis due to unavailable information.

6. **Instrumentation:** Identical materials, instructions and procedures must be used throughout the study, other than where treatments are being deliberately varied. If an instrument generates different measures of the same thing under different conditions, then this suggests that contextual problems associated with the instrument, and its administration, have threatened internal validity.

   Accidents or poor planning that cause inconsistencies threaten internal validity and may necessitate the 'scripting' of researchers to ensure there are no unintended distractors, as well as the use of the same researcher for the administration of all experiments or interviews in a cluster to minimise researcher bias. When the impact of several different variables is being tested simultaneously, many different versions of the test instrument must be prepared. These must be checked meticulously (in the same way as examination papers) because a missing page, or a case error, can invalidate the whole experiment. If errors of this type are to be made, then they must occur at the pilot stage with student audiences – the researcher cannot afford the risk of wasting a data set with a practitioner audience because of an untested instrument. For example, in the pilot stages of Smith and Taffler (1996) it became apparent that while one treatment included 'mean' data, another had implicitly included both 'mean' and 'standard deviation' data. Differences in group performance might have been attributable to data differences, rather than to the substantive treatment, which would have invalidated the results of the experiment (even though in practice subjects would tend to ignore standard deviation data). The instrument had to be corrected and the whole experiment re-run to ensure the integrity of the outcomes.

7. **Selection:** Subjects should be allocated randomly to cells (groups for comparison purposes), but this may be either impossible to achieve in practice or insufficient to control for all the variation in the sample. For example, an assumption that control for experience and gender, prior to allocation to random cells, will be sufficient may be unrealistic if there are wide disparities in individual characteristics among the subjects. In some studies, notably in field research, randomisation may be impossible to achieve. In exceptional others it may be undesirable. Thus, Cheng et al. (2003) chose experimental participants based on their cognitive style in order to explore the impact of this particular characteristic. A selection bias can also interact with the variables of interest to the researcher in a manner that precludes the ability to generalise to other subjects. For example, if the selection of subjects was based on volunteers interested in accounting topics, then these individuals may be expecting change and reacting to it, in a way at variance to that of a 'real-world' decision maker who is less interested in accounting. Where the subject selection is essentially a self-selection process (very commonly the case in accounting experiments), then the personal experiences and expectations of those so attracted may not correspond with those of a more representative set of individuals.

8. **Statistical regression:** There will be a statistical tendency for successive results from individuals to regress towards the mean. This should be reflected in the interpretation of the pattern of successive results over time. Thus, where subjects generate extremely high/low scores in one test, they are less likely to do the same on a subsequent one; they are more likely to regress towards the mean.

9. **Imitation of treatments:** Where subjects can communicate with each other it is possible that we will not achieve independent responses. This can be overcome in experimental settings by asking subjects not to collaborate, or by manipulating instrumentation orders to preclude useful comparisons, or by providing 'filler' processes to occupy potentially disruptive subjects.

10. **Resentful demoralisation:** Different treatments may cause different levels of motivation among subjects, with a consequent impact on outcomes. For example, those subjects receiving feedback on one experiment may be better motivated for subsequent experiments, than those who do not.

Threats to external validity

Christensen (1994) specifies three forms of external validity concern:

1. **Population validity:** Research findings should be generalisable to other people, companies, countries and/or cultures, as appropriate. But many research samples are not representative – often because of access problems in field study settings – making extension of the findings problematic. Trotman (1996) suggests that case variability constitutes a significant external validity threat, especially if the number of extreme cases employed in an experiment is at variance with those confronted in practice. Failure prediction studies (e.g., So and Smith, 2002, 2004) are particularly vulnerable to such criticism, since the proportions of failed cases employed in experimental situations will necessarily be far in excess of those experienced in the real world.
2. **Ecological validity:** Research findings can be generalised to other situations and environmental settings. This requirement spurs the search for greater reality in experiments and increased attention to the context of the experiment. Data limitations often provide a constraint in experimental research since the design is accompanied by a removal of the richness of the data. Analytical requirements also necessitate the use of data categorisation methods in order to use the simplified treatment levels of ordinal variables (e.g., yes/no, high/low, structured/unstructured) in order to accentuate the observed variation in ANOVA-type analyses.
3. **Temporal validity:** Research findings can be generalised across time.

Brownell (1995: 13) identifies three further external validity threats:

1. **Treatment/selection interaction:** Managers of organisations usually choose those members of staff who will participate in research; they will usually be the 'better' performers and they will always be those who have some spare time!
2. **Treatment/setting interaction:** Without replication (which would normally be impossible to achieve) we cannot generalise the findings from a particular group of people in an organisation to other people at different levels or in other locations or different organisations.
3. **Treatment/treatment interaction:** Where prior treatments appear to impact on subsequent ones (in within-subject experimental designs), there may be a conditional relationship which requires a redesign of the research model.

Experiments are designed to achieve internal validity in order to confirm or disconfirm existing theories. Such theories may then be generalised to provide some external validity. However, the experimental conditions may be so extreme that they bear little resemblance to actuality, making generalisations difficult. Replications would help in the verification of outcomes, but the accounting literature is extremely unwilling to publish replications of this nature, so they tend not to be conducted.

The possibility therefore exists that research will produce sample-specific findings. This can be the result of a non-representative sample selection process or the fact that the unusual combination of various internal validity problems has led to peculiar results for the specific research project.

Quasi-experimental research

Experiments conducted in the field still appear very rarely in the literature, largely because of the constraints imposed by access, ethical considerations and even trade unions. Such constraints were by no means as restrictive in 1924, when a series of experiments commenced which have become one of the most celebrated examples of experiments in the field, though largely for the wrong reasons. The Hawthorne Experiments (Mayo, 1933; Roethlisberger and Dickson, 1939) remain a classic indicator of what can go wrong under experimental conditions when planning does not adequately anticipate the range of possible responses. The experiments were conducted in the period 1927–32 in Western Electrics' Hawthorne works in Chicago, and examined a supposed causal relationship between productivity, as the dependent variable, and physical working conditions. The latter was defined in terms of a combination of illumination, temperature, humidity and frequency of rest periods. Productivity levels prior to the experimental period were used to match two groups – an experimental group and a control group – and alternative treatments were applied to observe the impact of varying the four dependent variables. But output in the experimental group increased for all treatments (even those meant to induce lower productivity), and the output of the control group increased without the application of any treatments. Further manipulations, including lengthening the working day and eliminating rest periods, also failed to constrain the observed increase in productivity! Uncontrolled mediating variables associated with employee behaviour (notably attitudes, values and norms), together with the conduct of the experiment, apparently colluded to produce outcomes the opposite of those anticipated. A number of important issues emerge from this, which have wider implications for experimental research:

- The 'matching' process employed leads us to believe that we may not be comparing like with like. Randomisation in the assignment of subjects to groups is much preferred, especially if we wish to conduct any statistical analysis.
- The failure to isolate experimental and control groups under identical experimental conditions provides a threat to internal validity.
- Initial experiments included only six female personnel (even though in excess of 40,000 people in total were employed at Hawthorne), suggesting that the samples were scarcely representative.
- Potentially uncooperative subjects were excluded from the experiment, so we may be dealing with a biased and unrepresentative group.

- Experimental mortality is a serious problem with longitudinal studies of this kind; absenteeism and terminations produce discontinuities of data collection.
- A large number of intervening variables associated with employees' attitudes to work and each other have been overlooked (e.g., the influence of job security).

The peculiar experimental outcomes may in part be explained by the sort of behaviour referred to by Weber and Cook (1972); the employees are so glad that someone is taking an active interest in their work that they seek to deliver what the researchers are looking for – namely, increased productivity. The 'surprising' outcomes experienced by the researchers, subsequently termed the 'Hawthorne Effect', have become associated with occurrences where the behaviour of groups derives from them seeing themselves as 'special' in novel situations. The outcomes were therefore attributable to the experimental conditions, with mediating variables obscuring the causal relationship under investigation and threatening the internal validity of the experiment. We may argue that the researchers should not have been 'surprised' by these outcomes because Myers (1924: 28) had earlier reported almost identical outcomes in a substantially similar context. In an accounting parallel, Smith and Taffler (1995) report unexpected subject behaviour during the conduct of their experiment in that respondents all chose to adopt decision-making heuristics to reduce the decision-making burden under conditions of information overload. They had been expected to re-evaluate decision outcomes separately, and hypothesis testing required them to do so, but none did. The analysis of the experimental findings and conclusions are therefore restricted in a manner which may not have happened had the authors anticipated this occurrence and redesigned the experiment accordingly. Further, they require the additional, and unplanned, analysis of the different time-saving heuristics being employed. Svenson (1979), in the psychological literature, had foreshadowed just this kind of behaviour in information overload situations.

The observed threats to validity associated with a 'Hawthorne Effect' can conveniently be split in three ways:

- Indexicality: the variation of day-to-day behaviour by individuals in a longitudinal experiment.
- Experimenter effects: bias introduced from the researcher behaving differently from day to day and between groups, providing unintended information which results in different outcomes.
- Subject mediation: differences associated with individuals interpreting the task requirements differently.

The implications for these three effects on accounting research may be described respectively as:

- external validity threats because subjects will not behave similarly in different contexts, or even in the same context at subsequent time periods;

- internal validity threats associated with using different researchers for the administration of the experiment, when they are neither scripted nor approach the experiment in identical fashions (see Rosenthal, 1966); and
- internal validity threats, derived from assumptions about the personal characteristics, abilities and motivation of research subjects, and their understanding of the experimental task and instrumentation.

The kinds of outcomes that were observed in the Hawthorne studies provide a warning of the care that is needed if we are contemplating the search for greater external validity in experimental settings. Quasi-experimental designs, associated with moving out of the laboratory, aim to reduce the artificiality of the situation. A trade-off of internal validity is inevitable, for lack of control over both extraneous variables and participating groups may make manipulation of treatments impossible, which may, as a consequence, threaten internal validity. Quasi-experimental designs usually preclude the random assignment of subjects to treatment groups. This absence necessitates sound theory at the outset, and the use of pre-tests prior to the manipulation of treatments, so as to establish a base for the evaluation of judgements. The use of a control group – with no treatment – is also helpful, but may be impossible to achieve.

Additional problems, over and above those already noted for true experiments, arise in the field because of the need to collaborate closely with the organisation that is providing access. Managers are often not very concerned about research, but are interested more in findings that may be useful to their organisation. They may treat the study as a problem-solving exercise or consultancy assignment, and be indifferent to research niceties. They may insist on their allocation of employees to treatment groups (without random assignment) and view groups that are not testing out some improvement opportunity as a waste of resources (which will mean no control groups either).

Such difficulties may persuade some researchers to adopt a covert approach, leading them to introduce manipulations without management or employees being fully aware of them. Apart from the ethical problems associated with such actions, the outcomes are often not worthwhile because the manipulations to the treatment may have to be so small, in order for them to be introduced covertly, that they go unnoticed and will produce no effects. Worse, if trust is lost with the sponsoring agency, then access may be denied and employees may refuse to cooperate appropriately.

Given the difficulties, it is hard not to read some reports of quasi-experimental studies and form the impression that the research has run away from the researcher! The findings are interesting, but the researcher is struggling to justify both their methods and their degree of control over the whole research study.

Detailed planning at the design stage is imperative in experimental settings. Even so, it is very difficult to be 100% certain of covering everything that may cause a difficulty, meaning that additional experiments may be necessary to correct flaws. Where access to subjects is highly restricted, based on either time or availability, this can be problematic, and at the very least will delay the analysis.

Further reading

Bisbe, J., Batista-Foguet, J.-M. and Chenhall, R.H. (2007) 'Defining Management Accounting Constructs: A Methodological Note on the Risks of Conceptual Misspecification', *Accounting, Organizations and Society*, 32: 789–820.

Elliott, W.B., Jackson, K.E. and Peecher, M.E. (2014) 'The Unintended Effect of Corporate Social Responsibility Performance on Investors' Estimates of Fundamental Value', *The Accounting Review*, 89 (1): 275–302.

Kahneman, D. and Tversky, A. (1972) 'Subjective Probability: A Judgment of Representativeness', *Cognitive Psychology*, July: 430–54.

Libby, R., Bloomfield, R. and Nelson, M.W. (2002), 'Experimental Research in Financial Accounting', *Accounting, Organizations and Society*, 27: 775–810.

Liyanarachichi, G.A. (2007) 'Feasibility of Using Student Subjects in Accounting Experiments: A Review', *Pacific Accounting Review*, 19 (1): 47–67.

Magilke, M.J., Mayhew, B.W. and Pike, J. (2009) 'Are Independent Audit-Committee Members Objective? Experimental Evidence', *The Accounting Review*, 84 (6): 1959–82.

Maines, L.A. and Wahlen, J.M. (2006) 'The Nature of Accounting Information Reliability: Inferences from Archival and Experimental Research', *Accounting Horizons*, 20 (4): 399–425.

Schepanski, A., Tubbs, R.M. and Grimlund, R.A. (1992) 'Within-subjects and Between-subjects Designs in Behavioral Accounting Research: An Examination of Some Issues of Concern', *Journal of Accounting Literature*, 11: 121–50.

Schulz, A.K.-D. (1999) 'Experimental Research Method in a Management Accounting Context', *Accounting and Finance*, 39 (1): 29–52.

Smith, M. and Taffler, R.J. (1995) 'The Incremental Effect of Narrative Accounting Information in Corporate Annual Reports', *Journal of Business Finance and Accounting*, 22 (8): 1195–210.

So, S. and Smith, M. (2002) 'Colour Graphics and Task Complexity in Multivariate Decision Making', *Accounting, Auditing and Accountability Journal*, 15 (4): 565–93.

Trotman, K.T. (1996) *Research Methods for Judgment and Decision-Making Studies in Auditing*. Melbourne: Coopers & Lybrand.

NINE

Survey Research

Chapter Contents

- Mail surveys
- Design and planning issues
- Pilot testing
- Data collection
- Measurement error
- Interview methods

Survey methods are often criticised as being the 'poor man's experiment' because of their inability to assign subjects randomly to treatments, and their consequent inability to rule out rival hypotheses. Brownell (1995: 31), among others, recognises the internal validity threats, but he suggests that survey studies can be designed to minimise such threats, while optimising their external validity benefits. He emphasises the need for good theory in order to underpin the specification of causal relationships.

Surveys can be conducted via mail, telephone, e-mail, internet or face-to-face interview. There is still very little literature in the accounting domain with respect to e-mail-based research, though internet-based studies are becoming more prominent (e.g., Hutchison et al., 1998; Northcott and Linacre, 2010). The two predominant methods for survey data collection are traditionally the mail survey and face-to-face interview, each with its own advantages and disadvantages. These two methods provide the focus of this chapter, with the emphasis on the former, although electronic versions (e-mail, internet, Skype) are increasingly gaining prominence. Identical characteristics for rigour in data collection are common to all.

Mail surveys

Young (1996: 55) highlights the decline of mail survey methods in management accounting, after a period in excess of 25 years during which it has been the pre-eminent research method in use in the discipline. He attributes the decline to three major factors:

1. A growing interest in alternative forms of research, which can provide richer data sources.
2. The increasing difficulty of having mail survey studies published in major refereed journals.
3. Doubts about the usefulness of survey research in accounting since it has failed to yield a cohesive body of knowledge concerning accounting and control practices, despite 25 years of trying to do so.

Brownell (1995: 60) also questions the predominance of survey questionnaires in management accounting research, and the reliance on instruments taken from organisational behaviour. Together, these two provide potentially serious weaknesses, so that questions of context are 'typically handled either badly or not at all' in experimental survey studies in accounting. A fourth point may be added to the above list – the difficulty of achieving adequate levels of response to mail surveys, despite following stated guidelines. For example, Brown et al. (2004) report a response rate of only 13% despite using a personalised sample with support from a sponsoring organisation; similarly, Askarany and Smith (2008) report a response rate of only 11% despite having secured the collaboration of the relevant industry association. Indeed, both instances provide more recent support for Baruch (1999), who highlights a significant decline in the response rates to surveys in business since the 1970s. Colombo (2000), among others, attributes declining response rates to time and job pressure on respondents, and the increased volume of unsolicited mail. Anecdotal evidence in Australia also suggests that many large companies have in place codes of conduct which forbid participation in organisational surveys. Further declines in mean response rates appear inevitable and unavoidable, with the potential to threaten the validity of organisational analysis based on survey evidence. Indeed, Zimmerman (2001) has already controversially dismissed survey-based management accounting research.

The outcome of this debate has been restricted targets for survey research: few of the top-tier journals detailed in Appendix 1 now publish survey-based studies in management accounting; thus, Van der Stede et al. (2005) report that the following top journals (*Contemporary Accounting Research*, *Journal of Accounting Research*, *Accounting Review*, *Journal of Accounting Economics*) published their last such studies in 1988, 1990, 1993 and 1997, respectively.

Young's analysis of mail survey studies published in major journals (*Accounting Review*, *Accounting Organizations and Society*, *Journal of Management Accounting Research* and *Behavioral Research in Accounting*) over the period 1985–94 identifies a number of common difficulties:

*   low target populations (average only 207);
*   low numbers of respondents (average only 146);
*   few studies using follow-up procedures to increase the sample size;
*   absence of analysis of non-response bias;
*   absence of studies using both subjective and objective measures of performance;
*   absence of the use of sampling procedures; and
*   failure to collect both factual and psychological data within the same study, making it impossible to link practices with behavioural variables.

Such failings lead to the impression that survey research is rarely good research, and is therefore only exceptionally equipped for publication in the most prestigious outlets.

Young (1996: 67) identifies seven improvement opportunities:

1. **Research programmes to establish a framework for research.** There remains the pressing need to develop a coherent body of knowledge in management accounting, to match those in finance and financial accounting. Opportunistic research to date has limited developments in this regard, so 'budget impact' remains the major area in the discipline that has been extensively researched.

2. **Sampling methods leading to more powerful theory testing.** Random sampling is usually not practicable so convenience sampling predominates. Such criticisms apply to accounting research generally, and make the application of standard statistical testing fraught with danger.

3. **The use of Dillman-type methods to achieve larger sample sizes.** Follow-up procedures (Dillman (1978, 2007) suggests sending two reminders) and sponsorship by participating organisations may increase response, but will incur extra costs and a lack of research control. If we are to guarantee anonymity in the conduct of the survey, as ethical guidelines require, then the survey response should not include the name or position (or perhaps company) of the respondent, to prevent any link between a particular individual and a specific survey response. This will increase the costs associated with follow-up reminders since letters will be sent to both respondents and non-respondents (often much to the annoyance of the former). There is the temptation to adopt unethical numbering systems, colour coding, or even invisible ink(!) to identify participants, while appearing to deliver anonymity, but the use of a dual-response mechanism (anonymous questionnaire *plus* named postcard) usually satisfies both cost and ethical concerns. Tucker and Parker (2014) report the adoption of Dillman-type methods in examining the research–practice gap in management accounting; their research design incorporated pre-contact with potential participants, mail-outs with attractive cover letters, well-prepared surveys, follow-ups, reminders and phone-calls to encourage a high response rate.

4. **Addressing the issue of non-response bias.** The absence of any reference to non-response in many published papers, or the ubiquitous footnote to the effect that non-response was not considered a problem, are of concern. They suggest that no serious attempt has been made to examine the issue.

5. **Moving away from outmoded survey instruments.** It is still common to see papers published in 2016 using standard instruments like those developed by Mahoney et al. (1963) for self-reported performance; Milani (1975) for budgetary participation; and MacDonald (1970) for tolerance of ambiguity. Their age suggests that it must be possible to generate a more relevant current instrument, but the incentives to do so are slim. A new instrument is vulnerable and needs extensive testing, and there are no corroborative studies using the same instrument. We observe the classic trade-off between reliability and construct validity, the choice of a well-accepted and reliable

instrument that may only approximately capture the construct of interest. Thus, Merchant (in Brownell, 1995: 149) uses the LBDQ (leader behaviour description questionnaire) adapted by Aiken and Hage (1968) from Halpin's instrument developed in the 1950s. The LBDQ measures two dimensions of leadership (consideration and task orientation), while Merchant (1985) uses it to measure 'detail orientation', even though he subsequently suggests that this particular instrument may have been less than optimum.

6. **The development of surveys on the basis of improved organisational knowledge.** If the survey instrument does not correspond with the 'language' of the firms involved, then response will be limited because of the perceived irrelevance of the survey.

7. **Moving away from subjective self-reported measures to more objective evaluations.** Young observes an almost total absence of, arguably, more objective superior ratings. However, other authors (notably Brownell, 1995: 44) suggest that such criticism of self-rated performance is overstated, and that superior ratings are just as likely to be in error because of the range of subordinates under the control of a single supervisor.

A subsequent study involving Young (i.e., Van der Stede et al., 2005) over the 20-year period (1982–2001) assessed the quality of survey design in management accounting research according to the five key elements suggested by Diamond (2000):

- purpose and design of the survey;
- population definition and sampling;
- survey questions and other research method issues;
- accuracy of data entry; and
- disclosure and reporting.

They note that around 30% of empirical management accounting research over the period had used mail surveys, and that there had been a significant improvement in survey quality over that time period, as measured across these dimensions. However, they highlighted a number of interesting issues:

- Nearly all of the surveys (98%) were cross-sectional in nature, even though they were investigating causal relationships. They noted the almost total absence of longitudinal studies, which they attributed to time cost, and complexity factors. Askarany and Smith (2008) provide an example of such a survey.
- Most of the surveys addressed only one person in an organisation, who was taken to be representative of that organisation, and even where multiple respondents were addressed, corroboration of responses was rarely analysed.
- A detailed analysis of non-respondents in the sampling frame was rarely considered. Guilding et al. (2000) provided a notable example. Indeed, the manner in which non-response bias was considered (or rather dismissed) in most papers, was an area of concern to which we return below.

Nazari et al. (2006: 427) expand on the work of Van der Stede et al. (2005) to identify potential improvements in the way survey research is conducted. They focus on the most common form of survey research in accounting, that which combines closed-ended numerical responses regarding opinions, attitudes and beliefs, through a self-reported mail survey. They suggest:

- the use of a focus group or in-depth interviews with about ten people to help develop a survey instrument which embraces all perspectives;
- a survey design which ensures that the constructs are free from contamination – i.e., the constructs actually measure what they are supposed to measure;
- the use of a mid-point scale or a 'don't know' category on Likert scales to increase response rates, and relieve the frustration of respondents who cannot come to a decision, and fail to complete as a result;
- the use of clear and explicit meanings for response categories to ensure that all respondents are actually answering the same question;
- pilot testing of the draft instrument with a representative group of respondents to check for both content and length;
- effort be expended to ensure a response of at least 100 in order to demonstrate validity; and
- the need to demonstrate that the sample results can be generalised to the population, without unrealistic assumptions.

Despite the former pre-eminence of the mail survey, in recent years its dominance has been threatened by the online survey, conducted through platforms like that provided by SurveyMonkey. Such platforms considerably simplify the survey process by supplying an online survey site which offers a user-friendly, cost-effective and time-saving option. It facilitates the use of multiple-question formats (e.g., true–false, multiple choice and open-ended questions) and can track respondents and send reminders. It can thus avoid the issue encountered in mail surveys where reminders are sent out to those who have already responded anonymously. Importantly SurveyMonkey generates response frequencies, which can simply be exported to statistical packages like SPSS and SAS for further analysis. But there are some limitations on how questions can be asked, and some institutions may block e-mails from SurveyMonkey sources, so response rates will not necessarily be improved. Some loss of control is also evident (similar to that from using agencies to conduct a mail survey) in that only e-mails from SurveyMonkey sources can be used to track respondents. Symonds (2011) provides a discussion of the advantages and disadvantages of using SurveyMonkey in practice, while Northcott and Linacre (2010) provide an example of its adoption in the accounting literature. Hutchison et al. (1998) report that response rates for e-mail surveys are only marginally below those for conventional mail surveys, a difference more than made up for by the relative cost advantage of the former. They suggest that e-mail is an effective means of data collection in accounting research.

We might also anticipate an increased incidence of the use of Skype-type online platforms as a substitute for face-to-face interview methods. Tucker and Parker (2014) report on the use of Skype for data collection in their study and note the time-consuming problem of organising the conduct of Skype interviews – not dissimilar to the issues arising when setting the date and time for a face-to-face interview. The potential impact of whatever is going on behind the camera on the conduct and content of the interview also needs to be examined, as a further variable influencing outputs, in addition to interviewer behaviour.

Design and planning issues

A number of fundamental questions need to be answered at the design stage.

1. **What sort of survey are we contemplating?** The requirements of the research question and the impact of cost differentials, for example, will both be important in determining whether a conventional mail survey is appropriate, or if surveys conducted by telephone, e-mail or through the internet would yield superior and/or more cost-effective outcomes. Mail questionnaires allow a large enough sample to reduce sampling error to acceptable levels, at considerably lower costs than either telephone or face-to-face interviews. In addition, mail surveys provide no opportunity for interviewer bias, a potentially serious problem in both face-to-face and telephone interviews. Anonymity and confidentiality continue to be issues affecting e-mail and internet-based studies, especially the former.
2. **What sort of respondent are we targeting?** It will make a great deal of difference at the planning stage, depending on whether we are targeting the population in general or a very specific proportion – for instance, particular professional groupings, or even CEOs. The narrower the grouping, the more essential it is that we have up-to-date mailing details of the individuals who are to be contacted. If we wish to contact very specific members of the population (e.g., sets of twins for environmental studies where we wish to eliminate the impact of heredity), we may have to advertise for participants.
3. **What questions do we want answers to?** It may appear obvious, but it helps in this respect if we have carefully specified research question(s) and hypotheses to direct expected responses. Too often in research papers and dissertations it appears that the survey has been conducted first, perhaps because of the opportunistic availability of access, without the research question really having being thought through. This quickly becomes apparent when key questions that should have been asked are found not to have been asked in the subsequently developed research questions. Roberts (1999) suggests that best practice in the development of instruments and questionnaires dictates that an extensive review of related instruments is undertaken first, and that where instruments need to be purpose-built or adapted, pilot testing is required to address issues of relevance and wording. It cannot be overemphasised: the theory and literature drive the research question and hypotheses; the survey instrument is merely

the vehicle that we employ to test theory and hypotheses. There must be a direct and transparent link between the three.

4. **What response categories are we contemplating?** For example, are we asking for opinions, judgements or knowledge? Are we setting questions which are closed (requiring yes/no, Likert scale responses or tick-a-box type answers) or open (allowing a considered narrative response)? We need to address these issues early on or they can come back to haunt us. If we are expecting a narrative response, for instance, then we must provide the respondent with enough room to give it; if we have a mass mail-out, we need an efficient coding system to deal with all the closed questions; if we are asking for knowledge, then questions must refer to items that we can reasonably assume a respondent to know without having to search or look up the details. One of the most serious criticisms of survey research (e.g., Chua, 1996) is that the questions asked are often so complex that the survey questionnaire ceases to be the most appropriate method of data collection.

5. **What sequence of questions should we pursue?** There are varying opinions as to whether the easiest and shortest questions should be at the beginning of the questionnaire or at the end. Some authors (e.g., Parker, 1992) suggest that short and easy questions should be used at the beginning, leading to the meatiest questions in the middle of the survey, followed by relatively shorter and easier questions towards the end in order to encourage completion of the whole survey document; others (e.g., Bryman, 2001: 117) suggest that early questions should clearly be relevant to the research topic and should not address personal issues like age, experience and educational background. At this stage we must also consider whether there will be an order effect; that is, would we have generated different answers by ordering the questions differently? If we think that this is likely, we should re-run the survey with a smaller pilot audience to determine whether or not our fears are justified.

6. **What form should the layout of the survey instrument take?** Most authors concur that the survey should not be too long, but that, more importantly, it should be made interesting and relevant to the target audience. Long questionnaires are more cost-effective, but only if they are actually returned! The optimum length depends on the format of the survey instrument (e.g., the desire to leave white space, or the requirement to provide gaps for narrative inputs), but should not normally be greater than four pages for the general population. Specialist groups may tolerate something slightly longer, perhaps of the order of six pages. Maintaining interest and motivation mean that the typical respondent should be able to complete the instrument in less than 20 minutes.

7. **How do we select the sample?** This is important and a weakness in many papers, where the issues seem to have been brushed aside – probably because they have not been adequately addressed in the first place. There are several key considerations: Do we know the size of the population and its constituent items? In many accounting research projects the answer to this question is no. As a result scientific methods of sample selection are precluded, and we need to appeal to the opportunistic or convenience samples so common in the literature – even though they may be 'dressed

up' to look like something more systematic. If we have a known population, we will probably have a readily available sampling frame (a stock exchange yearbook, for example, for companies, or an electoral register for individuals). We can then sample randomly from this population (perhaps using a random number generator), or choose every nth item to deliver the required sample size, or stratify the population according to its characteristics in order to ensure that we deliver a representative sample. There are mathematical formulae for calculating the required sample size to deliver the necessary statistical accuracy of estimates, but it is usually easier to return to the research question and hypotheses. We should be able to specify the tests we intend to perform, and the number of ways that the data will be split; we can identify all the cells of the analysis and we would like at least ten (20 is better) items in each to give us confidence in conducting the intended statistical tests. If we cannot adequately resolve order issues at the pilot stage of the survey, then the requirement for multiple versions of the final instrument will expand the required sample size by the same multiple. For example, we do not want to be in the position where we want to test for gender effects, say, with data on individuals, and then find we have too few females in the sample (which happens more often than it should with accounting data). Similarly, when testing for industry effects with company data, we may have too few retail representatives, though with some countries (e.g., Australia and New Zealand) the populations themselves may not be big enough to yield the samples required to conduct tests of all desirable relationships.

Pilot testing

Extensive piloting of the survey instrument is essential to demonstrate that it is capable of generating the required responses from the target audience. Although surveys are often tested on academic colleagues or undergraduate students, it helps if members of the target population who have been excluded from the sample are used to gauge its viability. The pilot instrument should be an advanced draft of a document which adequately represents the progression of the research from abstract concepts, through the development of valid constructs, to the identification of reliable individual questions. A number of important issues will arise at this stage, which must be addressed satisfactorily:

- the questions must be clear, simple and easily understood;
- the questions and covering letter should be targeted towards the respondent's viewpoint so that they are clearly relevant to the target audience – any jargon or industrial terminology employed should be technology-specific so as to improve response rates;
- the choice of words must be careful, avoiding slang, abbreviations and any terms with potentially ambiguous meanings;
- there should be no 'double-barrelled' questions because if more than one answer appears to be sought, confusion will result;

- double negatives should be avoided, as they will frequently be misunderstood;
- however, wording reversals should be employed to prevent respondents from unthinkingly 'ticking the right-hand box', say, without paying due reference to the precise meaning of the question;
- respondents must have the knowledge and skills to equip them to answer the questions. This is currently an issue in auditing research which is targeted at subordinates in accounting firms – the levels of complexity in some surveys place unrealistic demands on those responding to the survey;
- those questions which are incapable of producing reliable answers must be eliminated. Thus, questioning individuals in social research about their sexual behaviour, gambling habits, drug or alcohol abuse are unlikely to produce accurate responses. In accounting research, questions relating to fraudulent practices, dysfunctional behaviour, income and even position may elicit misleading answers. Similarly, questions relating to religion may cause difficulties in cross-cultural research; and
- attention to the time taken by pilot respondents in completing the survey should give an early indication of whether individual questions, or whole sections, need to be pruned.

To improve the reliability and validity of individual questions the entire questionnaire should be evaluated at the pilot stage prior to conducting the survey proper. A large pilot study would also allow an evaluation of the reliability and validity of the measures to be used. In practice the pilot test will do more than validate the wording of the questions: it will give us a firm indication of the validity of the scope of the survey, and the priorities and preferences of the respondents. This can provide very important information, for example, where we are adapting an instrument from one country for use in another. The outcomes may even suggest that some lines of questioning are irrelevant, causing us to revise the instrument – and potentially modify the hypotheses. In view of the significance of the outcomes to pilot testing, it is therefore surprising that Van der Stede et al. (2005) report that only 23% of papers in their sample had made use of one at all!

Data collection

A number of further considerations arise when we focus in more detail on the collection of the data.

1. **A relevant and up-to-date mailing list is essential.** Use of an existing mailing list may require sponsorship by a host organisation (e.g., one of the professional accounting bodies). The 'cost' of sponsorship may be recognition of the host organisation in any publication and/or some loss of control in the conduct of the survey in that the host organisation handles completions and returns so that there are no guarantees as to exactly who has completed the survey. Alternatively, the purchase of a reputable database may be required. This can be expensive for a narrowly focused mailing list.

The development of a mailing list of one's own from 'scratch' is extremely time-consuming and labour intensive. It is also an ongoing involvement because vigilance must be exercised in the maintenance of the mailing list. There is nothing likely to cause more consternation among survey recipients than if one of the named targets is already deceased.

2. **The survey should target specific named respondents.** There is a wealth of evidence which suggests that surveys that are addressed to the 'occupant' or the 'manager' or some other unnamed individual are those most likely to be consigned to the waste bin. The research literature (e.g., Dillman, 1978, 2007) suggests that surveys should be targeted by both name and position, and that if there are any doubts in these respects they should be confirmed in advance by telephone (e.g., through the company exchange operator) before delivery of the survey. Dillman further suggests the use of a clear covering letter, ideally on headed notepaper and with a handwritten signature from a recognised dignitary; the letter should provide unambiguous instructions, a guarantee of confidentiality, and a demonstration of the importance of the survey and its relevance to the respondent. Merchant (1985) customises his research instruments by varying the technological terms to fit the target audience. In so doing he ensures the relevance of the survey to the recipient, increasing the response rate to 95%, but jeopardises reliability through variable instruments. Edwards et al. (2002) note the following factors to significantly increase the response rate to a mail survey:

   - use of a brown envelope (rather than white);
   - provision of monetary incentives for completion;
   - a short questionnaire; and
   - recorded delivery of mail-out and responses.

   All of these suggestions are consistent with creating an impression that the survey is important, and is deserving of urgent attention from the respondent; however, their adoption must be balanced against both cost and complexity – with respect to incentives, the inclusion of additional variables into the research!

3. **How do we record the answers?** This should be established early to make the most of the media employed. If we are dealing with a mail survey, then manual methods will predominate. However, if we have verbal (i.e., interview or telephone response) or written responses (i.e., narrative answers in a manual survey, or e-mail or internet responses), then opportunities exist to conduct a detailed qualitative analysis of the narrative through the content analysis of the text, even though this may have to be transcribed from tape recordings.

4. **Feedback to respondents?** The offer of aggregated results to respondents may provide an incentive, which encourages completion of the survey. This is often more successful than the offer of prizes or nominal rewards for return of the survey. In any event, a letter of thanks to respondents is good manners, and may elicit an increased willingness for further involvement. For example, it may encourage respondents to make themselves available for

follow-up interviews, to provide both clarification and detail. If response is still the major objective, then stamped addressed envelopes, preferably with real stamps rather than bar codes, are preferable. Dillman (1978) recommends the sending of two follow-up reminders to elicit further responses, as well as a careful monitoring of holiday or busy business periods so that these may be avoided for the survey distribution (e.g., avoidance of company surveys close to the financial year-end, the end of the tax year, Christmas or Easter).

5. **Organisation.** It is better to think ahead. At the planning stage we should be aware of the coding necessary for closed answers, and also of the methods of analysis to be employed. Ideally, the responses should readily be transferable to spreadsheets for manipulation, or to SPSS input, to facilitate more detailed analysis.

6. **Non-response problems.** The biggest concern in survey research is lack of response. If respondents are unrepresentative and response rates are extremely low, then doubts will arise about the validity of the findings and the potential for biases being introduced. Response rates of less than 25% are common in accounting research; the question that is difficult to answer is whether respondents differ significantly from non-respondents. Non-response is only a problem if we can demonstrate that there are systematic differences between respondents and non-respondents, and that such differences will impact on the findings. This latter condition may be difficult to demonstrate. Merchant (1985) uses a 'postcard' method both to guarantee the anonymity of respondents and to distinguish between respondents and non-respondents. Participants are asked to complete the questionnaire and a separate postcard, which are independently mailed back to the researcher. Assuming that respondents do indeed return both items, then the identities of non-respondents will be known and their characteristics can be compared with those of the known respondents. In the absence of such a device we are forced to estimate the characteristics of non-respondents by proxying their characteristics from those respondents who were the last to respond after the final reminder. The implication is that these last-minute, almost reluctant, respondents will resemble those who did not bother to respond at all.

Dillman's (1978, 2007) Total Design Method (TDM) pays particular attention to the reasons for non-response:

- a wrong address in the first place, or incorrect postage attached, resulting in non-delivery;
- the unopened letter is discarded because it looks too much like a circular or other junk mail;
- the delivery is to an inappropriate person, who fails to forward it appropriately;
- there is no motivation to complete the survey when opened, so it is discarded;
- the recipient cannot understand the completion instructions and/or the survey content;
- the survey instrument is temporarily 'shelved' because of time pressures; or
- the return address has been misplaced, so that even if completed, the survey instrument does not get returned.

He tackles each of these problems by ensuring that the instrument is 'right', that it reaches the correct person and that incentives for completion (prizes or monetary rewards) are provided. He also institutes a detailed series of follow-ups:

- one week after the initial survey – with a reminder postcard (some researchers suggest that this first reminder should be sent as soon as three days after the original mailing!);
- three weeks after the initial mailing – a new covering letter and questionnaire; and
- seven weeks after the initial mailing – a third covering letter and questionnaire.

The whole survey process is considerably lengthier and more expensive than those we may normally contemplate as a result, but Dillman can point to his response rates as a rejoinder.

Whatever the response there will always be missing data items, for which alternative strategies can be applied, within the range of draconian (cut all items with missing cases) to 'let the software sort it out'. Neither is likely to be appropriate and suggests that more attention be paid to the detailed occurrence. Tabachnick and Fidell (2001) suggest that the pattern of the omissions is important – so that if the missing items are focused within one or more particular sections for many respondents, this is of much greater concern than the odd omission throughout the instrument. They suggest a number of acceptable alternatives for dealing with the problem:

- delete all cases with a missing item – though this is rarely the optimum solution since much data will be lost, the sample severely curtailed and sample bias potentially introduced;
- replace all cases with a missing item with the 'mean' across all cases; or
- replace all cases with a missing item with the 'mean' for that particular respondent.

They suggest the use of sensitivity analysis to evaluate the impact on outcomes, running with three versions of the data – the two substitutions above, and with missing cases deleted. The objective is to increase the sample size by permitting substitutes, and this can be justified if the alternative approaches generate similar overall outcomes.

Initial analysis of survey data will reveal how well the instrument has operated in practice:

- If there is very little variation for some items (i.e., the question produces the same Likert score response nearly all the time) – then this is not a good discriminator, and the item should be eliminated. This might have been apparent at the pilot stage if the response there had been sufficient.
- Item responses should be approximately normally distributed. If not there may not be much we can do about it, but it may restrict subsequent statistical analysis.
- Items within a construct should be highly correlated – i.e., they are all measuring different aspects of the same thing.
- Items across constructs should not be highly correlated – if they are they might be alternative measures of the same construct.
- Cronbach's alphas should be calculated and reported to demonstrate validity of the instrument.

Van der Stede et al. (2005) note that sample size was the focus of most cases in their study rather than non-response bias; the latter was rarely addressed satisfactorily. They stress that sample size is not the key issue, as long as it is sufficient to test the hypothesised relationships. Indeed Sapsford (2000) observes that smaller sample sizes are actually biased against finding statistically significant differences, while Colombo (2000) suggests that non-response bias (determined by both sample size and response rate) is the key issue. Moore and Tarnai (2002) suggest that where response rates exceed 80% then non-response bias should no longer be considered a real threat to validity; but such response rates are rare in accounting survey research.

Van der Stede et al. (2005) are critical of the oft-used throwaway lines (or footnotes) to the effect that tests were performed for non-response bias, but no bias was evident! The most common type of test reported (in 72% of cases) was a comparison between early and late respondents, with the latter used as a proxy for non-respondents. (Krumweide (1998) was an exception in this regard in making detailed comparisons against the sampling frame). Van der Stede et al. (2005) follow Tomaksovic-Devey et al. (1994) in emphasising that timeliness is not the only issue in non-response (especially for organisational rather than individual studies) and that authority, capacity and motivation to respond should be considered: authority (depending on position in the organisation); capacity (depending on access to information); and motivation (depending on willingness to participate). In particular, 'authority' and 'capacity' impact on the decision to respond, but not necessarily the timeliness. Thus, survey requests for accounting information targeted to CEO or CFO, for example, could fail on either grounds – capacity or authority respectively. Thus, Tomaksovic-Devey et al. (1994) suggest that many organisational characteristics (e.g., size, structure, profitability, systems and competition) might impact on the decision to respond, and that these should be examined for non-respondents to determine the nature of any non-response bias.

Measurement error

Andrews (1984) specifies three kinds of measurement error: bias, random errors and correlated (or systematic) errors. He suggests that better questionnaire design will help to overcome the most serious effects of these errors, including:

- the use of as many answer scale categories as possible, consistent with parsimony and survey length;
- a 'don't know' option where appropriate;
- keeping the number of items grouped together (termed the 'battery length') small;
- the use of comparative scale questions where possible to provide an explicit judgement base;
- the use of a linear rating scale, with only the extreme categories labelled;

- care in the length of both 'battery' introductions and questions (recommended as between 16 and 24 words for the former, and more than 16 words for the latter); and
- positioning easy and less important questions at the beginning and end of the questionnaire.

Assal and Keon (1982: 114) suggest that non-sampling error is the major contributor to poor quality survey outcomes, and that the total error comprises: non-response error (because of an unrepresentative sample) and response error (that due to unreliable answers from respondents) perhaps because they are mistaken, dishonest or confused. In this regard Diamond (2000) suggests that guessing is a common reaction to questions which are poorly worded or too complex for the target audience. Hence the need for a dual focus: get the questions worded correctly for the target audience (with pilot testing on an *actual* pilot group), and use appropriate measures to optimise the response rate.

Measures of reliability

If we are to draw valid conclusions about the relationships under investigation it is important that the variable measures are both reliable and valid. Multi-item scales are preferable to single-item scales for two major reasons:

- many constructs represent complex concepts, and this complexity is better addressed by asking more than one question; and
- a number of related items can increase validity because of the possibility that individual questions may be misinterpreted or misunderstood, or they may contain missed wording reversals.

There are several commonly used methods of measuring reliability:

- Test–Retest Reliability Coefficient: the same instrument is completed twice by a single group of individuals within a short time period. A high correlation between the responses suggests reliability, but the outcome the second time around may have been influenced by the first completion.
- Split-Half Reliability Coefficient: the instrument is completed by one group and the correlation is measured between two halves of the instrument (usually between first and last to examine the effects of fatigue). But many errors are attributable to reversals in wording not picked up by respondents, suggesting a preference for the random selection of the two halves for testing. If the correlation between the two halves is high, then this suggests high reliability on an internal consistency basis; but the longer the test, the higher the reliability, and the way the split is performed is likely to impact on the measure of consistency/reliability. The logical extension to this method is then the generation of an Average Inter-Item correlation coefficient ($\bar{r}$) based on the average of all possible pairwise items.

- Cronbach's Alpha Coefficient is the most widely used measure, especially for newly developed instruments, and overcomes the splitting problem, though its value is still wholly dependent on the number of items (n) in the instrument. Thus, sensitivity to the number of items should be evaluated to demonstrate reliability.

$$\alpha = \frac{n * (\bar{r})}{(1 + (n-1) * \bar{r}}$$

where $\bar{r}$ would be calculated from averaging

$$\frac{(n!)}{(n-2)!2!}$$

correlation coefficients.

Thus, for a four-item construct, there would be six correlation coefficients to average to generate ($\bar{r}$). An alpha of 0.8 is normally deemed to be satisfactory, though figures slightly lower than this may be acceptable. Since the Cronbach alpha depends on the number of items included, the more items the higher the Cronbach coefficient. Very high coefficients, resulting from too many similar questions, may therefore reflect redundancy in the instrument. A sensitivity analysis of the alpha to deletion of successive items will reveal whether we have a parsimonious set which is consistent with reliability.

Interview methods

Many of the problems associated with self-completion mail questionnaires are also applicable to interview methods, but there are also additional and inevitable 'people' problems because of the interaction between interviewer and interviewee. However, if we can alleviate the difficulties, interviews offer greater opportunities for dealing with more complex and wide-ranging issues than do conventional mail surveys. A number of interview formats are common in the accounting literature, and are addressed here. Case studies and field research are considered separately in the following chapter.

1. **The structured interview.** This is the format which most closely resembles that of the self-completion mail questionnaire. Opportunities for interviewer bias are restricted by seeking a common context: the same questions, in the same order, with the same cues and prompts permitted, and all within a specific, closed-question framework. The use of closed questions makes the coding of answers easier and has advantages for the subsequent analysis. Closed questions also eliminate the opportunities for error associated with open questions, as well as the chance of 'missed' questions where order differences are permitted. But closed questions also sacrifice the comparative advantage of the interview method by failing to include the flexibility and richness of response offered by open-ended questions. In the accounting literature, Lowe and Shaw (1968),

Onsi (1973) and Marginson and Ogden (2005) provide examples of the adoption of a structured interview approach.

2. **The semi-structured interview.** This format allows a series of questions to be asked, but in no fixed order. Additional questions may also be asked, as the interviewer sees fit, to examine associated issues that arise in the course of the interview. Lillis (1999) provides an example of the use of the semi-structured approach.

3. **The unstructured interview.** This format commences with a series of topics for discussion, rather than specific questions to be asked. It may develop into a directed conversation, with the interviewer able to adopt a 'free-wheeling' approach, as long as the required topics are all covered. The actual words and phrases used may therefore vary significantly between interviews, but this approach may put interviewees at their ease sufficiently to induce them to make disclosures that would not have emerged under different conditions. The unstructured interview approach is illustrated by Merchant (1985) and Malina and Selto (2001).

A number of studies (e.g., Birnberg, Shields and Young, 1990; Chapman, 1998; Ittner and Larcker, 2001) have reported the use of multiple methods – usually a combination of questionnaire and interviews, both to elicit different information, and to provide confirmatory evidence, from the same audience.

Several areas of concern may arise, which may cause the outcomes of the interview process to be questioned:

- Poorly worded questions may cause confusion or misunderstandings among interviewees. It is possible that interviewer and interviewee have different interpretations of the terms used or the emphases accorded them – an extension of the sort of 'measurement of meaning' issues raised in the accounting literature by Houghton (1987, 1988) and Hronsky and Houghton (2001).
- Memory problems among interviewees can make instant responses unreliable. This may be associated with questions which are far too demanding for this mode of investigation.
- Questions may be asked in an inconsistent manner or a particular interviewer may behave differently over time and between respondents. Significant differences may exist between interviewers despite levels of training, guidelines and standardisation of questions. This within- and between-interviewer inconsistency may result in biased outcomes if, say, overly sympathetic or aggressive attitudes are linked to a particular group of interviewees.
- Problems may arise in the recording and processing of responses. This occurs particularly with open-ended questions, where interviewers may misinterpret or embellish responses in the course of hurriedly transcribing what has been said.
- Non-response bias can arise, as it does with mail surveys, but refusals are compounded by absenteeism. Face-to-face requirements may necessitate frequent call-backs (analogous to the reminder letter) and their success may depend on the gender, dress code and non-threatening attitude of the interviewer.

Parker (2008) highlights the importance of **silence** in the interview process; by employing lengthy pauses the interviewer gives respondents the chance to think, as well as the opportunity to divulge more than might otherwise have been the case, because they are uncomfortable with the silence. He also suggests the use of minimal comments and interjections to encourage explanation and elaboration.

A special category of problems for interviewers arises with regard to concern for ethical issues. While the covering letter demonstrates the purposes of the research in mail surveys, and the return of the instrument itself constitutes implicit 'permission to participate', the interview situation is different. Some ethical codes will even insist that the interviewee 'signs-off' at the completion of the interview to verify the content of the responses. Particular points that should be addressed include:

- interviewers must clearly identify themselves, their status, who they represent and the purposes of the interview;
- interviewees should be aware of how and why they have been chosen to participate;
- the confidentiality and anonymity of responses must be emphasised;
- voluntary participation is paramount so that interviewees are free to withdraw their cooperation at any time; and
- there should also be the opportunity for interviewees to ask questions of the interviewer. Interviewers need to be careful here because if they are off their guard they may be induced to reveal the research questions under examination. Such disclosures may threaten the validity of responses from subsequent interviewees.

Gill and Johnson (2010: 132) highlight some of the problems associated with e-mail research, which are likely to threaten the validity of the outcomes. There is no sampling frame, so the degree to which the sample is representative cannot be evaluated. The absence of anonymity for respondents, and confidentiality of responses, both run counter to what we would normally expect to achieve with surveys. It might be anticipated that the validity and honesty of the responses would be threatened as a result. Simsek and Veiga (2001) provide a detailed discussion of associated problems.

Morgan and Symon (2004) discuss the problems associated with telephone and e-mail interviews, highlighting the absence of visual cues to the interviewer, and lack of access to non-verbal behaviour. They refer to 'electronic interviews' as those conducted via the internet, and highlight a whole new set of issues to be addressed:

- software problems replace the technical problems so often confronted when taping one-to-one interviews;
- the richness of responses may be limited;
- anonymity of the respondents may increase candour, but also provides the opportunity for elaboration or dishonesty; and
- timeliness may be an issue because respondents no longer appreciate the urgency of the interaction; responses can be garnered over a long period of time and may necessitate e-mail reminders.

Saunders et al. (2009: 364) note that what would have been a 30% response rate for a traditional mail survey will likely be reduced to around 10% using the internet – presumably because 'click and flick' on the keyboard is accomplished far more easily than opening an envelope before disposal!

Well-designed surveys allow the relations between the variables of interest to be rigorously studied. However, internal validity is not as strong in surveys as it is in experimental research, though the extra realism provides higher external validity. Since surveys often embrace many cases, which necessarily limits the depth, they are often subject to criticism relative to case studies.

In this chapter we hope to have specified both the advantages of surveys and their limitations. Highly structured questionnaires, restricted to non-complex questions, cannot probe issues in depth, and there are no opportunities either to respond to queries or to ask appropriate follow-up questions. These limitations are not significant as long as the questions are well formulated and relatively narrow in scope; they can then provide valid responses to research questions. As with all of the research methods we examine in this volume, the question of theory cannot be understated. Good theory underpins everything that we do, and allows the development of clearly defined constructs. The demonstrable development of reliable research instruments to collect data is one of the great strengths of survey research in accounting. However competent the conduct of the research, when analysing publications in top journals using survey methods, Nazari et al. (2006: 438) note that they are largely confined to just three journals (*Accounting, Organizations and Society, Behavioral Research in Accounting, Journal of Management Accounting Research*) and that the survey methods were rarely used to develop theory, but were confirmatory in nature.

There is much confusion in the literature between surveys, field studies and case studies. For example, Merchant (1985) described his research as a 'field study' and Smith (1994a, 1994b) described his as 'semi-structured interviews' when they may more aptly have been described as an 'unstructured interview' and a 'field study', respectively. Brownell (1995: 156) suggests that a distinction between 'surveys' and 'field studies' may be determined by the degree of structure in the questioning, which is a necessary, but perhaps not sufficient, condition for the distinction. These issues are explored in the following chapter devoted to qualitative methods.

Further reading

Andrews, F.M. (1984) 'Construct Validity and Error Components of Survey Methods: A Structural Modelling Approach', *Public Opinion Quarterly*, 48: 409–42.

Dillman, D.A. (2007) *Mail Internet Surveys: The Tailored Design Method*, 2nd edn. Hoboken NJ: Wiley.

Hutchison, P.D., Fleischman, G.M. and Johnson, D.W. (1998) 'E-mail versus Mail Surveys: A Comparative Study', *The Review of Accounting Information Systems*, 2 (3): 43–56.

Lillis, A.M. (1999) 'A Framework for the Analysis of Interview Data from Multiple Field Research', *Accounting and Finance*, 39 (1): 79–105.

Northcott, D. and Linacre, S. (2010) 'Producing Spaces for Academic Discourse: The Impact of Research Assessment Exercises and Journal Quality Rankings', *Australian Accounting Review*, 20 (1): 63–79.

Sapsford, R. (2000) *Survey Research*, 2nd edn. London: SAGE.

Saunders, M., Lewis, P. and Thornhill, A. (2009) *Research Methods for Business Students*, 5th edn. London: Prentice Hall.

Symonds, E. (2011) 'A Practical Application of SurveyMonkey as a Remote Usability-Testing Tool', *Library Hi Tech*, 29 (3): 436–45.

Tomaksovic-Devey, D., Leiter, J. and Thompson, S. (1994) 'Organizational Survey Nonresponse', *Administrative Science Quarterly*, 39 (3): 439–57.

Tucker, B.P. and Parker, L.D. (2014) 'In our Ivory Towers? The Research–Practice Gap in Management Accounting', *Accounting and Business Research*, 44 (2): 104–43.

Van der Stede, W., Young, S.M. and Chen, C.X. (2005) 'Assessing the Quality of Evidence in Empirical Management Accounting Research: The Case of Survey Studies', *Accounting, Organizations and Society*, 30: 655–84.

Yin, R.K. (2009) *Case Study Research: Design and Methods*, 4th edn. Thousand Oaks, CA: SAGE.

Young, S.M. (1996) 'Survey Research in Management Accounting: A Critical Assessment', in A.J. Richardson (ed.), *Research Methods in Accounting: Issues and Debates*. Vancouver: The Canadian General Accountants Research Foundation. pp. 55–68.

Zimmerman, J.L. (2001) 'Conjectures Regarding Empirical Managerial Accounting Research', *Journal of Accounting and Economics*, 32 (1–3): 411–27.

TEN

Qualitative Methods

Chapter Contents

- Fieldwork
- Case study methods
- Mixed Methods Research
- The qualitative analysis protocol
- Grounded theory
- Verbal protocol analysis

We have seen from previous chapters how studies with large data sets make assumptions about the distributions of the data, and how they conduct specific procedures to eliminate 'outliers' because they are perceived to be problematic observations for modelling purposes. Now we do the opposite: far from being problematic, these outliers and anomalies provide opportunities, in fieldwork and case studies, for detailed observation. Because they are 'different', we have a source whose examination can yield rich, provocative and interesting findings, with the potential to help develop new theory. Rather than focusing on averages and distributions, they allow the focus to be shifted to specific events in specific contexts. Parker (2003) suggests that qualitative research in management accounting can create reality through its academic actors becoming involved at the 'organisational coal-face'. Such an involvement can reveal surprising, and often counter-intuitive, practices: for example, Smith (1994c) and Smith and Tucker (2013: 74) report on the abuse of backlog measurement systems by workers determined to wreck a reporting initiative; Smith and Graves (2002) and Smith and Tucker (2013: 205) provide evidence of manipulation of bonus plan schemes; Smith (2006) and Smith and Tucker (2013: 75) report the abuse of project evaluation methodologies to avoid scrutiny and to ensure the approval of 'pet' projects.

Parker (2003) and Ahrens (2008) suggest that the close-quarter engagement evident in qualitative research can offer a deeper understanding of management implementation issues, with the potential for the development of new theory, for example, with respect to management control issues associated with organisational change as in Hoque and Alam (1999), Andon et al. (2007) and Tuan Mat et al. (2011).

Qualitative data can be collected through a number of approaches, often described as field studies (Smith 2003, 2011) and further categorised as case studies, field studies or field experiments (Moll et al., 2006). Ferreira and Merchant (1992) do not distinguish between case studies and field studies, but if we wish to do so we might follow the guideline established by Lillis and Mundy (2005), who suggest that the case study implies a single unit of analysis, while the field study is considered to be broader and embraces a number of case studies. Yin (2013) distinguishes four types of case study: exploratory, descriptive, illustrative and explanatory. Field-based case study research is the most popular means of engagement apparent in the accounting literature, as evidenced by Merchant and Van der Stede (2006) and Parker (2012). Such field research usually incorporates mixed methods – archival, interview and direct observation – used together to develop a rich account of organisational processes. Qualitative data may be collected through documents, interviews or observations, but Jankowicz (2005) stresses that more serious attention should be paid to the non-verbal signals exhibited by interview respondents, which demonstrate any reluctance to participate in the research. While the *positivist* paradigm, and associated journals, emphasise the generation of findings which can be generalised across large populations, Merchant and Van der Stede (2006) identify the preferences of participants from small population studies for outcomes which are of direct use to them in solving specific problems. In these circumstances the differences between 'research' and 'consulting' can become blurred. Indeed, Baskerville and Wood-Harper (1996), in the context of action research, suggest that the closeness of the relationship between researchers and practitioners is such as to blur the boundaries between research and consulting.

Fieldwork

Over the past 25 years, accounting researchers have been urged to shift their study of the role and function of accounting to its natural contexts. This has been the case particularly in the management accounting literature, led by the seminal works of Hopwood (1983) and Kaplan (1983). While the call for fieldwork has been persistent, the penetration of this research into top-ranking journals, particularly in the USA, has been very limited (Foster and Young, 1997; Shields, 1997). Foster and Young (1997) argue that few studies meet the criteria of high-quality field research routinely applied in other disciplines. Similarly, Shields (1997: 10) attributes the lack of publication of case and field study research to several factors, with 'lack of knowledge about how to do good studies' leading the list. Kirk and Miller (1986), among others, emphasise the consideration of the validity and reliability of field studies, in particular:

- whether it presents a consistent interpretation of the data;
- whether the empirical observations justify the extent of the conceptual generalisations;
- whether rival explanations for the observations have been considered and/or eliminated; and
- the replicability of the findings; that is, whether different researchers in different time periods are likely to generate similar findings.

Internal validity is a problem because there are no opportunities to assign subjects randomly to treatment groups in the field, as we would under experimental conditions. This makes theory even more important to the process, because it forms the major means of eliminating competing explanations for different observations. Brownell (1995: 77) calls for attention to be given to the development of more systematic procedures for the assessment of internal and external validity and reliability in field studies. The nature of qualitative research, and the absence of structured survey questions, means that the data set will not include Likert-type multiple-items measures. Because traditional forms of reliability assessment are not possible, the demonstration of coherent and valid constructs presents a significant challenge for the researcher.

Chua (1996: 220) notes that typically, 'good' anthropological fieldwork requires 'a long stay in an alien place'. Such an approach is rarely adopted by accounting field researchers. Most field studies are cross-sectional rather than longitudinal (Ferreira and Merchant, 1992) and the latter is exceptional because extended in-depth access to commercial organisations is usually very difficult. Given that most studies will be associated with doctoral research, the availability of grant and/or scholarship support for a limited period means that onsite data collection for an extended period will be impracticable. Access of any kind will usually be opportunistic (e.g., see Buchanan et al., 1988) and may be subsequently denied (Young and Selto, 1993). Preston (1986), Chua and Degeling (1993) and Chua (1995) provide examples of longitudinal ethnographic studies in single organisations that facilitate the exploration of process issues; Merchant and Manzoni (1989) provide an example of a cross-sectional, multi-case design that may be potentially useful for theory testing.

Three distinct forms of field research can be distinguished, namely, complete participant, complete observer and participant–observer.

1. **Complete participant.** This type of research can take one of two forms:

    -   participant as observer: the observer's role as a researcher is concealed from the participant organisation (e.g., Rosenhahn, 1982, as a member of staff in a mental hospital); or
    -   observer as participant: where the observer is an existing member of the organisation and conducts research in that organisation (e.g., Ezzamel and Bourn, 1990).

2. **Complete observer.** The observer has no contact with the subjects being researched. Such an anthropological approach is almost unknown in the accounting literature. At the extreme (particularly when associated with ethnographic studies), involvement in the research process will be as a non-participating observer. However, unless it is covert, even observation at this level is likely to impact on the behaviour of individuals, and hence on research outcomes.

    So active involvement, rather than detached observation and measurement, is the norm in action research projects. Indeed, such involvement is facilitated by a researcher who has the practical expertise and theoretical knowledge to bring a new perspective to organisational issues. Brannick and Coghlan (2007) suggest that organisation-based research is best conducted by insiders, rather than by outside observers who lack detailed knowledge of the organisation.

The nature of the exercise requires a high level of trust and collaboration between researchers and management (non-researchers); the latter may resist any imposition of a structured research design, preferring action research that will result in outcomes of clear benefit to the organisation. For the internal participants, a feasible solution to a taxing problem will be the appropriate measure of success. They may not be interested in test-able hypotheses and causal methods, so reporting at two levels may be required: an internal report of a consulting nature, which will focus on problem-solving, and a research report which forms part of a dissertation, or which ultimately yields a refereed paper.

The ethnographic extreme has its origins in social anthropology, with the observation of tribes, and in natural science, with the observation of the behaviour of animal troops. A shared knowledge is used to account for patterns of behaviour and personal rela-tions, with potential implications for humans in business settings. Emphasis is on observation, but may be complemented with semi-structured interviews, though not active participation. A series of questions arises as to the manner in which ethno-graphic studies may be conducted. Consider them, for example, in terms of our wish to observe processes of an executive nature, perhaps at board level:

- Participant or non-participant observation?
- Overt or covert observation?
- Ethically defensible deception under covert conditions?
- Direct or indirect observation?
- The reliability of secondary data?

Of course, where sensitive issues are under discussion, we may have to settle for secondary data, or a sanitised version of events. Such material, for example, minutes of meetings, may well provide no detail of discussions or the contributions of individual participants, power structures or group dynamics.

Covert observation has the advantage of allowing manipulations (e.g., changes in behaviour or role) to be introduced, without their being attributed to the research pro-cess. It may also be impossible to conduct the research were the researcher to be so identified. However, Ditton (1977), reported in Bryman (2001: 93), amply illustrates the problems associated with covert operations. He was exploring fraudulent practices in a bakery, and was regularly forced to excuse himself to make notes on Bronco toilet paper. The time spent on toilet breaks eventually induced him to 'come out' regarding his covert research! Coffey (1999) provides an example of overt participation in his study within a UK accounting firm.

3. **Participant–observer.** The most common scenario, this is where the researchers inter-act with the members of the organisation in a collaborative venture. It is often termed 'action research'. The participation is usually active on both sides, and is more than either a consultancy project or an in-company problem-solving exercise. The research is

guided by theory in examining the change process, allowing the anticipation of conse-quences and outcomes. The process should have external validity in that it should pro-duce generalisations which have relevance to other organisations. However, we should be reminded here of the problems alluded to in Chapter 1 during our discussion of Heisenberg's Uncertainty Principle, in that the intrusion of the researcher, as participant–observer, may make it impossible to conduct measurement in an unbiased manner.

The research thus constitutes a planned intervention in the normal processes of an organisation, to observe the consequences, and measure and monitor how these differ from those expected from theory. Researcher intervention (either as observer or active participant) is an essential ingredient of the research design, as is the generation of results, which will be of interest to the host organisation and make a contribution to knowledge in the area. Although it may be possible to identify group membership and attempt to assign individuals, as we would in an experimental setting using either matching or randomisation, this would normally be avoided on the grounds that it would damage the research setting.

Scapens (2004) ranks researcher engagement at five levels depending on the level of participation and interaction:

1. outsider – relying on documentary (archival) sources only, with no direct engagement;
2. visitor – evidenced by repeated visits to the case study site over a period of time to conduct interviews and make observations;
3. facilitator – with direct involvement in the examination of issues – as would be common in **action research**;
4. participant – employed as a working member of an organisational group and able to observe events at close hand accordingly; and
5. actor – playing a leading role in organisational decision-making, where stage 4 would normally be a precursor for stage 5, and wherein both researchers would incorporate ethnographic/participant–observer roles.

Fieldwork and case studies provide the opportunity to demonstrate external validity by clos-ing the gap between theory and practice, as advanced by Kaplan (1998). But the interventionist (action research) type approach, so popular in the management literature, has been criticised in the accounting literature (e.g., Zimmerman, 2001) for having no underly-ing theory, and for adopting a 'consulting' approach to accounting research; the latter is widely frowned upon among academics. Healy and Perry (2000) argue that the quality of qualitative research should be judged on its own terms, so that different labels of evaluation and verification might be considered more appropriate. Golafshani (2003), among others, suggests terms like credibility, confirmability, trustworthiness, consistency, dependability, applicability and transferability. It is tempting to try to draw parallels between such labels and those closely associated with quantitative research (e.g., validity, reliability, significance etc.) but efforts to do so are likely to result in subjective claims of superiority/inferiority for the different approaches, as well as much semantic squabbling!

Kaplan has demonstrated significant contributions to practice with both activity-based costing (e.g., Cooper and Kaplan, 1992) and the balanced scorecard (e.g., Kaplan and Norton, 1993); such innovations may also yield significant contributions to theory, if they can be further developed in the manner suggested by Malmi and Granlund (2009). Pelto and Pelto (1978) suggest that qualitative approaches to accounting research are driven by ethnographic and field study fundamentals based in sociology and anthropology. Parker (2012) identifies three major characteristics that distinguish qualitative research from positivist quantitative research:

- recognition that accounting contributes to the construction of reality (e.g., Hines, 1988) rather than there being an independent objective reality of any kind;
- recognition that the data collection processes can inform theory, and vice versa (e.g., Ahrens and Chapman, 2006); and
- recognition that multiple theories can provide a richer understanding of processes and relationships (e.g., Brignall and Ballantine, 2004; Irvine and Gaffikin, 2006).

Zimmerman (2001) clearly illustrates the rift between the two schools of thought, blasting qualitative researchers for persisting with multi-theoretic approaches and failing to adopt the unifying economics-based approach of positivist accounting research. In accounting, qualitative approaches historically have been regarded as subservient to quantitative approaches, a perception which clearly still pervades the echelons of the top US journals! Qualitative approaches have only been deemed to be useful when identifying variables for subsequent quantitative analysis, or as supporting evidence for a statistical quantitative study. Outside of the US, attitudes towards qualitative research have changed markedly, so that it has become a widely accepted means of establishing exactly 'how' and 'why' account-ing change has been accomplished. Nowhere is this more apparent than in the field of management accounting.

Case study methods

Humphrey and Lee (2004, xxv) identify three classic worries among qualitative researchers with respect to case study projects:

- case studies are interesting, but they are not academic;
- case studies do not add to knowledge; and
- case studies are too hard to get published.

These same 'worries' might be applied to fieldwork generally, as well as to case studies. The literature in recent years has demonstrated that such work is 'academic'; indeed fieldwork and qualitative research can no longer be regarded as soft (see Yin, 1984, 2010, 2013), since they are, arguably, much more difficult to conduct well than are comparable quantitative studies. They have also indisputably added to 'knowledge' (e.g., Merchant and Van der Stede, 2006), though without the generalisation feasible in some quantitative research. But publication avenues do still remain problematic, as we have referred to above and in Chapter 13.

There is frequently much confusion over the terminology of fieldwork compared to case study research. The term 'case study' usually implies research confined to a single unit of analysis, which might be a single department, company, industry or even country. The scope of the case could still, therefore, be broad, but the 'single unit' focus means that it is much narrower than might be embraced by the term 'fieldwork', where the latter would encompass more general studies of social activity in the field. Ryan et al. (2002: 143) distinguish five categories of accounting case study:

1. **Descriptive** – where current practice is described in terms of the procedures adopted. The studies may seek to confer 'best-practice' or 'successful' labels to particular sites or companies (e.g., Peters and Waterman, 1982; Smith, 1994c).
2. **Illustrative** – where the researchers explore the implementation and outcomes associated with innovative practices (e.g., Dikolli and Smith, 1996; Kaplan, 1984; Kaplan and Norton, 1992).
3. **Experimental** – where the research concerns the conduct of an experiment in the field, whereby new treatments are applied to sub-units of the site. Examples of this type of research remain very rare in the accounting literature; the most famous and notorious example in related literature remains the Hawthorne studies (Mayo, 1933).
4. **Exploratory** – where the researchers conduct a preliminary investigation about how and why particular practices are adopted. Such research may be difficult to publish in itself, unless it makes a clear contribution to theory or method.
5. **Explanatory** – where research seeks to provide convincing explanations that justify practice choices and facilitate the development of theory. However, opportunities or attempts to generalise the findings are rare.

Yin (1984: 39) emphasises that case study sites must not be chosen because they are **representative** in some way, because researchers should not be concerned with producing statistical generalisations. Rather, he suggests that theoretical generalisations are more important. He compares case study research with experimental research, in that with the latter we start with a theory, devise an instrument to test the theory and then choose a representative sample of cases, which are to be subject to alternative experimental treatments. In case research, the case becomes the instrument through which we test the theory, thus the focus of the case must be on whether it can be used to test the extent to which existing theory provides good explanations. A 'representative' case may not be able to do this. Similarly, he suggests that it is impossible to assert how many cases should be included in a multi-case research design until the nature and scope of the cases has been determined. Selection of case study sites needs careful attention; they are rarely 'representative' in any form. Indeed Ryan et al. (2002: 151) suggest that a 'critical' case, or an 'extreme' case, would provide preferable selection options if interesting findings are to be generated.

Cooper and Morgan (2008), following Flyvbjerg (2001), suggest that the motive for the selection of cases falls into one of four alternative categories:

- **Extreme/deviant** – where the case is used to take advantage of a change in circumstances within an organisation. Berry et al. (1985) provide such an example, with their work on the National Coal Board during a period of intense change. Likewise, Lys and Vincent (1995) examine the processes and outcomes during a controversial acquisition.
- **Maximum variation** – where the case provides the opportunity to learn about one thing while varying another. Merchant and Manzoni (1989) provide just such an example by choosing company cases from several industries, and with different technology bases and growth rates. By examining the achievability of budget targets across all the cases they are able to provide new insights into the budget-setting process.
- **Critical** – where the case is deliberately selected to facilitate the potential for falsification of theory. Thus, Preston (1989) provides an example for an organisation implementing a sophisticated management control system, where before, nothing existed. The motives and benefits for the development of accounting ran counter to existing theory.
- **Paradigmatic** – where the case is selected to provide a specific contribution to theory. Tinker and Niemark (1987) do so by using a longitudinal study of General Motors to demonstrate the significance of the non-financial messages in the corporate annual report.

Importantly, this schema should be regarded as a general framework for the **prior** selection of case sites. The actual findings might suggest different, or overlapping, categorisation. Thus the **deviant** Lys and Vincent (1995) study provides **critical** outcomes in the form of falsification of theory; they suggest that the actions of the acquirer in their study, in selecting accounting methods to optimise earnings per share, are at odds with theory.

Case studies would normally collect data from multiple sources, including some or all of the following: documentary evidence, interview data, direct observation and participant observation. Merchant (1985) and Simons (1990) provide examples of studies that have incorporated data from multiple sources. The adoption of multiple methods might be termed 'triangulation' and offers the opportunity to access different sources both for a common research method (within-method triangulation) and with different methods (between-methods triangulation):

- within-method triangulation combines different researchers, different interviewers and different survey sites; and
- between-methods triangulation combines different results from, say, interviews, survey and archival data collection, and may include both quantitative and qualitative approaches.

It may be possible to offer alternative views of the same phenomenon through a process of 'triangulation', which may increase the validity and reliability of the research. Campbell and Fiske (1959) initiated the use of the term 'triangulation' and it has been extended to accounting research through the use of multiple research methods seeking to explain organisational behaviour, notably in the field of management accounting practice (e.g., Carpenter and Feroz, 2001). Hopper and Hoque (2006: 478) specify three forms of triangulation:

- **Theory triangulation** – through the use of different theoretical approaches to examine a single issue. They float the possibility of using rational choice models, a contingency approach, agency theory and human relations theory to investigate management accounting practice. Berry et al. (1991), Hoque and Hopper (1997), Carpenter and Feroz (2001) and Modell (2005) all provide examples of use of a triangulation approach in management accounting.
- **Data triangulation** – through the use of multiple data sources, quantitative and qualitative, providing data from a combination of interviews, field studies, surveys and archival sources (e.g., Lukka and Kasanen, 1995; Modell, 2005).
- **Investigator triangulation** – through the use of multiple independent researchers to collect the data. However, Lillis (2006: 467) warns of the potential dangers in over-estimating the benefits of such an approach.

Mixed methods research

Lillis (2008) and Malina et al. (2011) follow Rossman and Wilson (1984) in suggesting that the adoption of a mixed methods approach is often the best means of addressing a research question. Stronger research outcomes might result whether the quantitative or qualitative methods are used together or in sequence. Norreklit et al. (2007) suggest that such an approach might help to overcome misleading outcomes associated with either:

- quantitative methods using unrepresentative data, or missing key variables; or
- qualitative methods where interviews alone are inadequate.

However, the adoption of mixed methods for data collection may create difficulties: while the opportunity to examine formal accounting and control systems more deeply by addressing motivational and behavioural aspects (e.g., Drury and Tayles, 1995) is appealing, there are problems. Parker (2012: 60) identifies the chief among these as the perceived subservience of the qualitative methodology to a quantitative approach. Such a prejudicial misconception can have implications for the perceived value of a mixed methods approach, with potentially serious consequences:

- Single-discipline studies published in single-discipline journals receive favourable treatment from both university journal ranking systems and research funding agencies.
- Journal editors may be reluctant to accept qualitative papers, or will do so only with supporting quantitative evidence from triangulation. Yet there is no corresponding requirement for supporting qualitative evidence in quantitative papers!

Malina et al. (2011) and Parker (2012) recognise that alternative methods are addressing different questions – with qualitative methods seeking answers to 'how?' and 'why?' questions, while quantitative methods are focusing more on 'how often?' and 'how many?' questions, so that a mix of the two might be expected to yield empirical insights.

Lillis (1999) uses a semi-structured interview schedule in conjunction with a structured questionnaire to derive the benefits of quantitative and qualitative methods. But she notes that the semi-structured interview method that she uses is inevitably subject to the intrusive effects of interviewer bias, both during the interview and in the analysis of transcripts. Bias is potentially introduced in the coding and interpretive phases. The researcher ultimately decides how each sentence in the transcript will be coded and, more importantly, interprets the 'meaning' associated with selected sections of text in terms of the theoretical constructs. Consistent and valid coding and interpretation of transcript data are absolutely key to the reliability of this analysis. A means of reducing bias is to use multiple researchers in both the coding and interpretive phases. Ryan et al. (2002: 138) advance the use of sensitivity analysis where assumptions are being made, or where there are any doubts about choices. Thus, where measurement errors are suspected they emphasise the need to search for alternative means of measurement, perhaps through hold-out samples, to increase confidence in internal validity. The same principles apply to issues of external validity: if outcomes are to be generalised, differences associated with, for example, time period, industry and company size should be examined.

A fascinating account of changing perspectives towards mixed methods approaches is provided by Malina et al. (2011), who revealingly detail the choices and contradictions in a series of their papers (Malina and Selto, 2001; Malina and Selto, 2004; Malina et al., 2007) examining the cause and effect of the performance consequences of a balanced scorecard implementation. Their initial qualitative study (2001) detailed internal management tensions which threatened the successful implementation of the scorecard. The follow-up study (2004) revisited the interview data to conduct a quantitative analysis of performance attributes. The third paper (2007) adopted quantitative-econometric methods on key performance indicators to refute the supposed cause-and-effect relationships of the scorecard implementation assumed in the earlier papers. This sequential analysis of outcomes from mixed methods raised new questions about the firm's expanded commitment to a balanced scorecard methodology, shedding light on data inconsistencies. They concluded that, while the scorecard failed to demonstrate cause-and-effect performance improvements, it did provide an effective management control device.

Chua (1996: 227) emphasises that field research is not 'mere story telling', but rather an attempt to build a theory which leans heavily on existing theories and literature. However, Merchant (cited in Brownell, 1995: 150) suggests that in the context of field research that explores relationships between controls and management performance, 'there is no such thing as dependent and independent variables in the real world'.

Field study researchers do not have the equivalent of the Cronbach alpha, from survey research, nor do they have the control and treatment groups of laboratory experiments to demonstrate their attention to reliability and validity. Field research, by design, will never have the statistical basis for establishing construct validity that is common with other research methods. Critics and reviewers ask why focused field research should have construct validity requirements that are any less demanding than research addressing the same issues with different methods (e.g., a survey questionnaire). Arguably the concerns should be the same, but the issues are rarely so because fieldwork provides the opportunity to collect both richer and more complex data. The critical reader of research of all kinds should look for clear meanings of the constructs that describe the concepts under study.

Gibbert et al. (2008) provide an instructive discussion of the rigour of the case study process, noting the emphasis on external validity in existing studies, to the detriment of internal validity and construct validity.

The qualitative analysis protocol

Where the researcher and the researched interact there will be opportunities for bias. Silverman (1989) identifies two extreme forms of field-researcher bias: an unwillingness to collect and report quantitative data, and a tendency to convert all qualitative data into quantitative data. Mason (1994) emphasises that quantitative and qualitative data are complementary sources that should be combined to take advantage of the richness of the qualitative findings, and the potential rigour and increased credibility of the quantitative findings.

In addition to the potential interviewer-induced bias in the **collection** of qualitative data, the **analysis** of qualitative data is potentially subject to significant bias since it relies on interpretations and classifications imposed by the researcher. Qualitative data are also vulnerable because of the absence of established techniques for ensuring that data analysis is both complete and impartial. NUD*IST is helpful in this regard. It is a qualitative analysis package for coding raw interview transcripts, and it associates the sentences in the transcript with one or more predefined themes. Completeness should not therefore be a problem, but impartiality still is because the researcher will have already established the categories for search.

As detailed in Chapter 7 the use of a systematic analytical protocol such as that developed by Miles and Huberman (1994) enhances confidence in the impartiality of qualitative analysis because:

- it provides a chain of evidence from transcripts to the results of analysis;
- it ensures that all cases are used in the evaluation of data propositions, preventing interviewer-based elimination that may introduce unintended bias; and
- it provides an analytical framework within which hypotheses can be tested.

The field researcher attempts to use a small set of case data to illustrate and support more general theoretical arguments. However, irrespective of the research method used, the ability to make broad generalisations from a single study is necessarily limited. When evaluating the external validity of a field study, the results should be considered in the context of other studies that examine similar questions in different settings.

Jönsson and MacIntosh (1997) argue that ethnographic studies have been marginalised in the accounting literature by the focus on agency-based 'rational' accounting theory studies in the US, and 'critical' accounting theory studies in the UK. They express a preference for extensive field studies in actual companies, rather than approaches that are theory-laden but virtually free from empirics. Chua (1988) and Puxty (1993) provide extensive overviews of the then state of ethnographic research in accounting, and Jönsson and MacIntosh (1997) echo their view that ethnographic studies must be much more than 'good story telling'; they recognise that neutral studies are impossible and that appropriate regard for politics and theory should be shown. Merchant (2010) and Lukka (2010) acknowledge the dominance of the accounting literature (especially in the US) by quantitative economics-based account-ing research, a dominance which severely limits the scope for published qualitative research. Parker (2012: 68) refers to the condition as 'the monochromatic economic lens' that per-vades accounting research.

Silverman (1985) suggests a typology comprising three alternative approaches to ethno-graphic research:

- **Cognitive anthropology:** research that focuses on the individual's competence in com-municating within the culture under study (i.e., the way in which the actors are able to communicate and behave, thus making them acceptable to the rest of the group). Dent's (1991) study of the shift of British Rail's culture from an engineering one to a finance/accounting one provides an example of this approach in the accounting literature.
- **Symbolic interactionism:** research concerning the manner in which actors change the cul-ture of organisations with which they are involved. Preston's (1986) study of management information processing in a large plastics division, as a participant–observer, provides an example of this approach.
- **Ethnomethodology:** research which is less concerned with the communication and interaction approaches (above) and more concerned with the social behaviour of the actors involved and their interpretation of outcomes. Jönsson's (1982) study of budget-ary behaviour provides an example of this approach in the accounting literature.

Critical research, on the other hand (see Chapter 3 for more examples), focuses on power and class structures in interpreting meaning. Accounting systems are seen as a means of both achieving control and exploiting the workforce. Jönsson and MacIntosh (1997: 376) question the 'critical' approach in that its conclusions are always known in advance – 'the cart always comes before the horse'. The outcomes are always attributable to an exploitative capitalist system (see Ezzamel and Willmott, 1992). For example, Tinker's (1980: 147) study of financial accounting statements in Sierra Leone, which was able to conclude that 'accounting served to reinforce the institutionalised subordination of black wage labour over the entire period', had not necessitated a site visit or an ethnographic study.

We can enter into the field situation with very little theory to cling onto; the intention may be to develop theory as a result of the initial case findings. A number of alternative methods have been devised to accomplish this feat, including grounded theory (Glaser and Strauss, 1967), analytic induction (Denzin, 1970) and case study research (Bloor, 1978). Without attempting to argue over the superiority of alternative labels, the following common characteristics emerge:

- a definition of the phenomenon under investigation with initial expectations;
- a hypothetical explanation of the phenomenon;
- a sequential examination of cases to determine the extent to which they fit the hypothetical explanation;
- where variation is observed, a modification of the definition of the phenomenon, the case characteristics and reformulation of any hypotheses in light of the observations;
- an examination of a small number of incidences of the phenomenon (cases) to identify shared features and points of variance;
- speculation on the reason(s) for the continued observation of 'deviant' cases; and
- a continuation with the reformulation exercise for successive cases until a universal model can be established which fits a large number of observations.

Certain features of the participant–observer process can be identified that may be thought to constitute disadvantages, and to endanger the validity of the research outcomes and subsequent theoretical developments:

- closeness to unique events;
- limited opportunities to classify and generalise the data;
- the unrepresentativeness of the sample;
- the actual presence of the researcher, which may of itself distort observations;
- the treatment of unusual observations as typical;
- subjective personal observations which may have limited validity; and
- a host site which may block access to research subjects.

A number of common characteristics are apparent:

- the researcher's norms, values, code of ethics, assumptions;
- the researcher's impact on problem specification, research strategy and methodology;
- the political context within which the researcher operates;
- resource constraints which hamper the researcher; and
- contingencies and/or opportunities during the course of the research, particularly that of access to funding and host organisations.

Grounded theory

Grounded theory was identified in Chapter 3 as an increasingly popular method with accounting case researchers, though its acceptance by journal editors has been somewhat slower. While the theory itself was described earlier, its growing importance justifies separate treatment here of its characteristics and advantages.

Glaser and Strauss (1967: 3) argue that 'theory that inductively develops out of systematic empirical research is more likely to fit the data and thus is more likely to be useful, plausible and accessible'. Pure grounded theory analytical approaches are designed to manage and control the potential bias in building theory from empirical data, providing a method which is primarily non-quantitative and designed to find the latent or embedded meanings in data. In a pure grounded theory analysis, theory emerges during the analysis of data; the emergent theory is tested constantly against further theoretically sampled empirical data.

Grounded theory has been increasingly adopted as the preferred qualitative approach in accounting field study environments. However, the subsequent divergence of views between Glaser and Strauss has caused confusion over the meaning of the terms involved and their implications for acceptable procedures. As a result, alternative forms of 'grounded theory' have been developed:

- the basic Glaser and Strauss (1967) approach, embellished by Glaser (e.g., Glaser, 1992), which emphasises an individual approach and personal style; and
- the Strauss and Corbin (1990, 2008) approach, following Strauss (1987), which is much more structured and prescriptive, is arguably more acceptable to positivist researchers.

A number of other variants have also emerged (see Kools et al., 1996), most notably in the nursing discipline. The rigidity of the Strauss and Corbin (1990, 2008) approach was unacceptable to Glaser and other traditionalists because they appeared to be forcing the data into models which did not permit alternative interpretations. Even so, Gurd (2008) suggests that the basic principles of Strauss and Corbin are not being followed, even by researchers who profess to be doing so! All forms of grounded theory have been questioned by positivists on the basis of a lack of external validity, a factor which has contributed to a restriction in the number of journal editors to whom grounded theory approaches are acceptable.

Laughlin (1995) emphasises the importance of the 'researchers' in grounded theory studies in that they are fundamental to the discovery process and the validity of the research, which is dependent upon a shared meaning of events by both researcher and researched. Parker and Roffey (1997) stress the crucial role of language in grounded theory research as a significant discriminator relative to positivist studies. They too point to the crucial interplay between the researcher, the researched and the data in generating quality research with unique advantages.

Gurd (2008) observes the problems associated with 'labelling' in the reporting of grounded theory research, noting that papers that adopt grounded theory approaches, and report as such at the thesis, working paper and conference paper stages, frequently omit specific 'grounded theory' references when they are finally published. He notes the publication of Soin (1995) as an example. There are other examples, particularly in the management accounting literature, that appear from their content to be adopting grounded theory approaches, but do not admit as such explicitly. The interpretation must be that the confusion concerning what is 'really' grounded theory affords the opportunity for discrimination among journal referees and editors. Clearly it is safer for authors not to specify the adoption of a particular grounded theory approach for fear of generating opposition among referees. Doctoral supervisors must be particularly careful in their choice of external examiners to ensure that a common understanding of grounded theory terms exists between themselves and their candidates.

Verbal protocol analysis

Slovic (1969) provides the foundations for the use of verbal protocols as a method of data collection in judgement exercises. Subjects perform exercises in which they think aloud, detailing exactly what they are doing, in terms of information being used and the manner of its use. A tape recorder would normally be used during this exercise. The content of these verbal protocols provides the basis for the mapping of the decision process and problem-solving behaviour for each subject. The resultant flowchart will usually be complex, with numerous feedback loops, and will allow the development of conditional algorithms for decision-making. The accuracy of the resultant models can often be measured by comparing the model predictions with the actual subject outcomes, in a 'man vs. model of man' way. Verbal protocol analysis (VPA) has rarely been used in the accounting environment. It provides the opportunity for generating very rich data sets, but the resource involvement is great: only one subject at a time can be evaluated, and the researcher must monitor the conduct of the exercise and prompt the subject, where necessary, to ensure that he or she maintains a constant narrative throughout the decision process.

Larcker and Lessig (1983) use retrospective protocols of decisions, after the completion of an experimental task, to improve on regression models of investment decision-making, originally based on decision accuracy. Bouwman (1984) gives one of the earliest examples of the use of contemporaneous VPA in the accounting literature, when he compares the decision processes of expert and novice decision makers. Anderson (1985) and Harte and Koele (1995) provide evidence which suggests that contemporaneous verbal protocol analysis can give reliable information about pre-decision behaviour. Anderson (1988) presents a VPA of the examination of initial public offerings (IPOs) by financial analysts, with the focus on the search process, decision time, decision conclusions and the information items addressed.

Boys and Rutherford (1984) offer a fascinating example of the use of VPA, examining the use that investment analysts made of current cost accounting information in evaluating firm performance, when provided with both historic cost and current cost numbers. We may anticipate that this approach would confer benefits on investigations of the use of International Accounting Standard (IAS) information. More recently, Anderson and Potter (1998) suggest that regression analysis and verbal protocol analysis are complementary methods, as each contributes to model development in the analysis of decision-making behaviour. They develop a model of individual decision-making behaviour based on the outcomes of a VPA, but it should be noted that their very small sample size – which is a common problem in VPA – of only four individuals makes it difficult to generalise their outcomes.

In conclusion, where resources are available to employ more subjects, and to evaluate their deliberations in appropriate detail, VPA provides a powerful alternative means of exploring decision processes, and one that remains vastly underused.

Further reading

Cooper, D.J. and Morgan, W. (2008) 'Case Study Research in Accounting', *Accounting Horizons*, 22 (2): 158–78.

Gibbert, M., Ruigrock, W. and Wicki, B. (2008) 'What Passes as a Rigorous Case Study?', *Strategic Management Journal*, 29 (13): 1465–74.

Gurd, B.G. (2008) 'Remaining Consistent with Method? An Analysis of Grounded Theory Research in Accounting', *Qualitative Research in Accounting and Management*, 5 (2): 122–38.

Lillis, A. (1999) 'A Framework for the Analysis of Interview Data from Multiple Field Research', *Accounting and Finance*, 39 (1): 79–105.

Lillis, A. (2008) 'Qualitative Management Accounting Research: Rationale, Pitfalls and Potential', *Qualitative Research in Accounting and Management*, 5 (3): 239–46.

Lukka, K. (2010) 'The Roles and Effects of Paradigms in Accounting Research', *Management Accounting Research*, 18: 76–101.

Malina, M.A. and Selto, F.H. (2001) 'Communicating and Control Strategy: An Empirical Study of the Effectiveness of the Balanced Scorecard', *Journal of Management Accounting Research*, 13: 47–90.

Malina, M.A. and Selto, F.H. (2004) 'Choice and Change of Measures in Performance Measurement Models', *Management Accounting Research*, 15: 441–69.

Malina, M.A., Norreklit, H.S.O. and Selto, F.H. (2007) 'Relations Among Measures, Climate of Control and Performance Measurement Models', *Contemporary Accounting Research*, 24 (3): 935–82.

Malina, M.A., Norreklit, H.S.O. and Selto, F.H. (2011) 'Lessons Learned: Advantages and Disadvantages of Mixed Method Research', *Qualitative Research in Accounting and Management*, 8 (1): 59–71.

Malmi, T. and Granlund, M. (2009) 'In Search of Management Accounting Theory', *European Accounting Review*, 18 (3): 597–620.

Merchant, K. and Van der Stede, W. (2006) 'Field-based Research in Accounting: Accomplishments and Prospects', *Behavioral Research in Accounting*, 18: 117–34.

Miles, M.B. and Huberman, A.M. (1994) *Qualitative Data Analysis: An Expanded Sourcebook*. Thousand Oaks, CA: SAGE.

Norreklit, H., Norreklit, L. and Mitchell, F. (2007) 'Theoretical Conditions for Validity in Accounting Performance Measurement', in A. Neely (ed.), *Business Performance Measurement*. New York: Cambridge University Press.

Parker, L.D. (2003) 'Qualitative Research in Accounting and Management: The Emerging Agenda', *Journal of Accounting and Finance*, 2: 15–30.

Parker, L.D. (2012) 'Qualitative Management Accounting Research: Assessing Deliverables and Relevance', *Critical Perspectives on Accounting*, 23: 54–70.

Parker, L.D. and Roffey, B.H. (1997) 'Back to the Drawing Board: Revisiting Grounded Theory and the Everyday Accountant's Reality', *Accounting, Auditing and Accountability Journal*, 10 (2): 212–47.

Rossman, G.B. and Wilson, B.L. (1984) 'Numbers and Words: Combining Quantitative and Qualitative Methods in a Single Large-Scale Evaluation Study', *Evaluation Review*, 9 (5): 627–43.

Scapens, R.W. (2004) 'Doing Case Study Research', in C. Humphrey and B. Lee (eds), *The Real Life Guide to Accounting Research: A Behind-The-Scenes View of Using Qualitative Research Methods*. Amsterdam: Elsevier. pp. 257–79.

Smith, M. and Tucker, B. (2013) *Advanced Strategic Management Accounting: Theory and Practice*. Melbourne: Cengage.

Zimmerman, J.L. (2001) 'Conjectures Regarding Empirical Managerial Accounting Research', *Journal of Accounting and Economics*, 32 (1–3): 411–27.

ELEVEN

Archival Research

Chapter Contents

- Cross-section data
- Time-series data
- The validity trade-off in archival research
- Content analysis

We take a deliberately broad approach to the term 'archival' in this chapter, by embracing the sources used to generate research based on historical documents, texts, journal articles, corporate annual reports, company disclosures etc. The associated research approaches may therefore range from the fundamental analysis of accounting numbers, through to the content analysis of narratives and critical approaches to the development of accounting theory.

Searching for information can be a time-consuming and expensive exercise so it is important that researchers quickly develop the skills necessary to locate and use sources effectively. Such sources can usually be classified as **primary** (e.g., original research results published for the first time) or, more usually, **secondary** (e.g., information that has been disclosed by third parties – like that in corporate reports and press releases) and sometimes **tertiary** (e.g., for data which have been aggregated, categorised and/or reworked in databases). However, such a classification may not be clear-cut because a company annual report may be deemed a primary or secondary source depending on the identity of the user! Such sources can usually be accessed directly, or relevant references sought, through keyword and author searches of library catalogues, abstracts or internet databases. As we suggested in Chapter 1, a critical attitude should be adopted towards the research process, and this should apply just as much to accessing data sources as to subsequent stages. We need to be able to evaluate the suitability for purpose of the data set: Is it up to date? Is it from a reputable and authoritative source? Has it been gathered using reliable methods? Can we access the material in a timely and economic manner, given the constraints of our research budget? The latter is becoming increasingly problematical for extensive online databases, for without generous educational discounts many such sources would remain inaccessible to academic researchers.

Foster (1986) identifies a number of problems associated with data collection from secondary sources, in both cross-section and time-series studies.

Cross-section data

1. Data may exclude some current companies. This may be a particular problem if multiple databases are being used which do not overlap completely, so that some companies fall 'between the cracks'. In any case, small companies may not be included if there are size 'hurdles' specified for their inclusion. The same principles would apply to those companies which are not actively traded on stock markets. These conditions may also lead to the exclusion of private or foreign-owned companies. A common reason for such exclusions is the non-availability of the data. Particularly annoying in this respect is the absence of data for subsidiary companies where there is no requirement for them to report separately from the parent.
2. Data may exclude non-surviving firms. Merged, acquired and bankrupt firms will normally be omitted from current databases, necessitating searches from other sources if these are the subject of the research. Much past research in the failure prediction area has been criticised for suffering from a survivorship bias because, by definition, failed companies tend to be omitted from the analysis due to unavailable information.
3. Data may not be right up to date in that the most recent data may not have been incorporated. This is becoming less of an issue with more online and web-based databases operating either in a real-time mode or being capable of uploading information on a daily basis.
4. Data may be incomplete in that they omit some financial items. For example, earnings forecasts, or 'notes to the accounts', may not be there, necessitating the use of alternative sources.
5. There may be inconsistent classification of some financial items across firms. If the database comprises other than camera copies of original documents, then some assumptions are inevitable in order to produce systematic cross-company classifications. For example, where firms are permitted differences in reporting line items, there will be different levels of aggregation, which may only be separable with arbitrary decisions. Thus, one firm might include overhead expenses in 'costs of goods sold', while another might include overheads in expenses attributable to 'marketing, administrative and general'. Unreliable entries may thus result for items such as 'overhead' where disaggregation assumptions have to be made. These kinds of problems are exacerbated by non-synchronous reporting periods (resulting in large differences both within and between countries) and the non-uniformity of accounting methods, especially across industries, which makes comparisons difficult because different choices may still be consistent with accounting standard compliance.
6. There may be recording errors, necessitating checks against other comparable databases where feasible, and necessitating the use of simple internal validity checks.

For example, computing the mean and standard deviation of items allows all of those outside the range of two standard deviations, either side of the mean, to be identified and questioned. Similarly, simple comparisons of quick assets with current assets may reveal basic errors. Industry classification poses a particular problem here because there is no single, accepted definition of 'industry' and different databases may adopt alternative classifications. Although 'product group' or 'production process' would normally form the basis of classification, without reference to some external regulatory classification, problems may occur.

7. The nature of disclosure is expanding all the time, making it more and more difficult for researchers to be confident that they have captured the most reliable and comprehensive sources. In the financial reporting environment most studies still rely on the content of the corporate report, but increasingly newspaper sources are being used because they provide a more timely medium. Reuters Business Briefing (RBB) is probably the most detailed source of company news items available in the UK, though it is not widely used for academic purposes. The Financial Times Index (UK) and Wall Street Journal Index (USA) provide popular alternatives (see also www.bloomberg.com). Brookfield and Morris (1992) use the McCarthy Information fiches (now available on CD-ROM). Internet and e-mail disclosures represent additional, relatively untapped sources, potentially important because there is a wealth of evidence that companies are disclosing information through these means to investment analysts prior to its availability to the stock market. The use of e-mail content, however, remains relatively restricted because of the commercial and personal sensitivity of the disclosures. COMPUSTAT is prominent among the databases commonly used for the analysis of financial information. Accounting and market data, including multiple financial ratios, are readily available for most companies in the developed world for periods extending over 20 years. Friendly interfaces permit the researcher to examine single companies at a point in time, or multiple companies over many years, embracing many possible variables. (The latter example is often termed **panel data** and its analysis is examined in detail in Chapter 6).

With share price data of high validity now accessible through the CRSP/COMPUSTAT database, shareholder return studies have substantially replaced those using accounting returns. However, this has not been accomplished without some difficulty; Magenheim and Mueller (1988) identify the flaws that need to be eradicated when using shareholder gains to measure firm value.

Trimbath (2006) identifies the particular problems associated with adopting return on equity (ROE) as a measure of firm performance – notably where negative income and negative equity combine to indicate a **positive** ROE measure! She identifies similar problems when using debt/equity ratios in conditions of negative equity. Overcoming the problem may create more problems: Trimbath suggests that we may create serious sample bias if we simply treat cases of negative equity and/or negative income as outlier measures of ROE to be eliminated from the analysis – since the poorest performers will then all be considered outliers.

Trimbath (2006: 421) notes that 'we have demonstrated that there is no mathematical, statistical or econometric adjustment that makes return on equity a useable measure of firm performance. It simply should not be used in large sample econometric models.' However, she notes that, despite this evidence, there is editorial pressure in some accounting/finance journals to conform to precedent and use equity measures of performance.

Time-series data

1. Structural changes may have taken place in the company or the industry, making comparisons between time periods fraught with danger. Internally, these may be due to mergers, acquisitions or divestments; externally, they may be attributable to new government policy, deregulation, new products, new competitors or technological change.
2. Accounting method changes, particularly those associated with voluntary choices or switches, may make the financial numbers from successive periods difficult to reconcile. Where this constitutes deliberate obfuscation, it is a particular cause for concern.
3. Accounting classification issues may occasion different corporate interpretations being placed on particular items, perhaps again to cloud the communication issue. Thus, a firm may elect to consolidate the results of a subsidiary in one year, but not the next, even though there appears to have been no material change in circumstances between periods. Similarly, the flexibility in reporting the timing and amounts associated with accounting for 'extraordinary items' and 'goodwill write-downs' frequently necessitates adjustments being made in data if a comparative base is to be maintained.

Even if the research project being conducted would not normally be termed 'archival', the points above have implications for the use of any documentary materials to be used to support the other research methods addressed in earlier chapters:

1. Where the database is in the form of a mailing list to support survey research, failure to update it regularly will mean that the list both excludes some target persons and includes some who are either dead or have moved away. Such errors and omissions can cause both bias and irritation.
2. Where the database is a journal listing that forms the basis of our literature review, we have a number of potential problems. The journal may not be available online at all, and will be excluded from all databases; this still applies to many accounting journals which are published by individual universities rather than through professional publishers. Even where they are available, online selected journals may only appear in specific databases – we may need to access multiple databases to track down the required references. 'Old' papers may still not be readily available in an electronic form through most databases, although the databases are becoming more comprehensive in their coverage, with deep back-runs. If we need to access seminal works then they may be subject to restricted access, or we may still have to resort to a hardcopy print format

(see the literature search discussion in Chapter 3). Similarly, the most recent of papers may not be immediately available either; there is nothing quite so frustrating as having access to a title, and perhaps even the abstract, of a must-read paper only to realise that the whole paper will not be available for months. Beware, too, of the existence of the notion of a 'whole' paper because sometimes the online version will omit all the figures and references (fortunately this is becoming less of a problem with the pre-dominance of PDF files).

3. We have to beware of making unwarranted inferences from archival sources, especially where there is the danger that we may not be comparing like with like. Context differences may explain many of the apparent contradictions and inconsistencies in the findings of comparative pieces, making it imperative that we return to the original sources wherever possible. Indeed, Brownell (1995: 140) attributes many of the problems of accounting research to the fragmentation that means comparisons are difficult to make with confidence: namely, different studies using different methods and instruments in different locations.

The validity trade-off in archival research

An archival study will normally have more external validity than experimental or simulation approaches because of its reference to empirical data. But dangers will arise if our selection process (e.g., for company data) is flawed, so that it results in the generation of an unrepresentative sample. This situation will be exacerbated if we employ 'matching' procedures in the research design (typically matching on size and industry) because there will be no guarantees that the findings are not industry-specific, or that they may even be case-specific to the group of companies selected.

Libby (1981) suggests that econometric studies using archival data are essentially experimental in nature. They may be used to answer similar questions to those addressed by experimental studies, even though the opportunities for variable manipulation are limited. While laboratory experiments often manipulate treatments and infer causality, many archival studies search for association and systematic movement between variables of interest. Although an association, rather than causation, is being observed, internal validity concerns still exist. For example, Wallace (1991) specifies the internal validity problems associated with financial statement research, particularly those concerned with 'instrumentation' and 'history' – concerns which will also be relevant in other financial accounting fields.

With respect to instrumentation, Wallace suggests that there are always questions of what exactly constitutes an 'accounting change'. Technical details become critical in the instrumentation process. If different information sources are used or even different personnel to collect data from annual reports, measurement differences may arise which threaten the validity of outcomes. Similar problems of instrumentation arise in failure prediction research, since a variety of definitions of 'bankruptcy' have been used in past research. As Wallace observes, not only are there different types of bankruptcy, but there are questions as to how reorganisations, restructuring of debt and technical non-compliance with loan covenants are to be treated. If different definitions are being used in the source data or by fellow researchers then internal validity threats will arise. Houghton and Smith (1991) provide an excellent example of why researchers should be wary of comparing the findings of different studies if they are not prepared to check the detailed definitions employed. The definition of failure in their study included 'subject to stock exchange investigation' – a very wide definition, which is unlikely to coincide with that used in most other associated studies.

With respect to history effects, changes in bankruptcy law, reporting requirements and accounting policy over the period of interest would all affect the comparative findings from archival searches of company data. The absence of adequate controls for the impact of such changes is a cause for concern. The response of researchers is often to use a matched sample that tries to control for extraneous factors. But which factors do we match on? Another problem with this approach is that the selection process precludes any assessment of the importance of, say, size, industry or capital structure, where we have chosen to match on these factors. In addition, measurement issues mean that we are not sure we have matched correctly. For example, do we match size on assets or number of employees? If we select assets, just how close does the match have to be to be ruled acceptable – $1k, $10k, $100k, $1m, $10m? Such measurement issues may prove material.

Fogarty (2006) warns against over-reliance on publicly available databases, since there will be enormous pressures on researchers to find a 'scoop' publication when there will inevitably be many researchers using the same data and working on similar topics. He recommends the hand-collection of data for at least one variable in the study in order to provide a point of differentiation. This provides us with further opportunities for triangulation (in addition to those detailed in Chapter 10, particularly for management accounting): corporate governance research is one such opportunity. Most of the existing published research on corporate governance is based on archival data, but there is a limit to the number of proxy variables (and associated indices) that can be constructed when using secondary data, usually drawn from annual corporate disclosures. Thus, we have seen the emergence of survey-based studies seeking to elicit additional 'governance' information directly from corporate respondents. We still await the inevitable growth of field-based studies, which seek to observe how governance-based issues are dealt with in practice at board level, and how individual decision makers respond to organisational changes.

Content analysis

Content analysis allows us to make valid inferences from texts, and has been considered in detail in Chapter 7 as an analytical tool for qualitative data, in particular that sourced from interview transcripts.

But content analysis (e.g., Krippendorff, 2004) has traditionally been applied to the analysis of archival data, hence its inclusion here too. Typically, quantitative methods have been applied to archival data transcripts, usually through the measurement of key features – normally the number of occurrences of words, or the number of words relating to particular themes. These results can then be transformed into 'word-based' or 'theme-based' variables for subsequent statistical analysis. Much of this work has resembled a 'data mining' exercise, where theory has, at the least, been assigned a subordinate role. Thus, Smith and Taffler (2000) follow Krippendorff (1980) to develop simple variable definitions in their conduct of both form-oriented (word-based) and meaning-oriented (theme-based) analyses; the qualitative content of the archival narrative is transformed into quantitative variables for subsequent analysis with simple formulae. Jones and Shoemaker (1994) provide a general overview of empirical accounting narrative analytic studies, and note the focus on the corporate report, directors report and shareholders letters as narrative sources.

The ready availability of suitable narrative sources means that content analysis studies remain popular, and have been widely extended to studies in corporate social responsibility (e.g., Schreck, 2013; Gray et al., 2014). Many recent publications have also become concerned with the analysis of narratives that have moved beyond 'words' and 'themes' to address alternative stylistic features in corporate statements: Amernic and Craig (2006, 2008) rhetoric; Merkl-Davies and Brennan (2007) impression management; Jones and Smith (2014) understandability.

Further reading

Abrahamson, E. and Amir, E. (1996) 'The Information Content of the President's Letter to Shareholders', *Journal of Business Finance and Accounting*, 23 (8): 1157–82.

Amernic, J.H. and Craig, R. (2006) *CEO Speak: The Language of Corporate Leadership*. Montréal, Ithaca: McGill-Queens University Press.

Amernic, J.H. and Craig, R. (2008) 'A Privatization Success Story: Accounting and Narrative Expression over Time', *Accounting, Auditing and Accountability Journal*, 21 (8): 1085–115.

Beattie, V.A., McInnes, B. and Fearnley, S. (2004) 'A Methodology for Analyzing and Evaluating Narratives in Annual Reports: A Comprehensive Descriptive Profile and Metrics for Disclosure Quality Attributes', *Accounting Forum*, 28: 205–36.

Bowman, E.H. (1984) 'Content Analysis of Annual Reports for Corporate Strategy and Risk', *Interfaces*, 14, Jan–Feb: 61–71.

Brennan, N.M., Guillamon-Saorin, E. and Pierce, A. (2009) 'Impression Management: Developing and Illustrating a Scheme of Analysis for Narrative Disclosures – A Methodological Note', *Accounting, Auditing and Accountability Journal*, 22 (5): 789–832.

Foster, G. (1986) *Financial Statement Analysis*, 2nd edn. Englewood Cliffs, NJ: Prentice Hall.

Frazier, K.B., Ingram, R.W. and Tennyson, B.M. (1984) 'A Methodology for the Analysis of Narrative Accounting Disclosures', *Journal of Accounting Research*, 22 (1): 318–31.

Gray, R., Adams, C. and Owen, D. (2014) *Accountability, Social Responsibility and Sustainability: Accounting for Society and the Environment*. London: Pearson.

Holsti, O.R. (1969) *Content Analysis for the Social Sciences and Humanities*. Reading, MA: Addison-Wesley.

Jones, M.J. and Shoemaker, P.A. (1994) 'Accounting Narratives: A Review of Empirical Studies of Content and Readability', *Journal of Accounting Literature*, 13: 142–84.

Jones, M.J. and Smith, M. (2014) 'Traditional and Alternative Methods for Measuring the Understandability of Accounting Narratives', *Accounting, Auditing and Accountability Journal*, 27 (1): 183–208.

Krippendorff, K.H. (1980) *Content Analysis: An Introduction to its Methodology*. Beverley Hills, CA: SAGE.

Krippendorff, K.H. (2004) *Content Analysis: An Introduction to its Methodology*, 2nd edn. Thousand Oaks, CA: SAGE.

Maines, L.A. and Wahlen, J.M. (2006) 'The Nature of Accounting Information Reliability: Inferences from Archival and Experimental Research', *Accounting Horizons*, 20 (4): 399–425.

Merkl-Davies, D.M. and Brennan, N.M. (2007) 'Discretionary Disclosure Strategies in Corporate Narratives: Incremental Information or Impression Management', *Journal of Accounting Literature*, 26: 116–94.

Mosteller, F. and Wallace, D.L. (1963) 'Inference in an Authorship Problem', *Journal of the American Statistical Association*, 58: 275–309.

Schreck, P. (2013) 'Non-financial Disclosure and Analyst Forecast Accuracy: International Evidence on Corporate Social Responsibility Disclosure', *Social and Environmental Accountability Journal*, 33 (3): 180–81.

Smith, M. and Taffler, R.J. (2000) 'The Chairman's Statement: A Content Analysis of Discretionary Narrative Disclosures', *Accounting, Auditing and Accountability Journal*, 13 (5): 624–46.

Weber, R.P. (1990) *Basic Content Analysis*, 2nd edn. Newbury Park, CA: SAGE.

Supervision and Examination Processes

TWELVE

Chapter Contents

- The role of the supervisor
- Examiner profiles
- The examination process

Research supervision arrangements and examination processes differ quite significantly between countries, but whatever the environment it is important that the candidate has reasonable expectations as to the role of the supervisor(s), the level of guidance to be provided and the nature of the examination process. Thus, in the USA, a supervisory panel will be the norm and, following the completion of an extensive programme of structured coursework, the dissertation component will usually be shorter than those expected elsewhere. An oral examination of the dissertation will often be conducted in front of a large, potentially public, gathering.

In both the UK and Australia, a team of two supervisors is usually appointed, though one of these supervisors may adopt the 'principal' role. The second supervisor may be junior in both age and experience, and may be perceived by the candidate to be 'learning the ropes' in some way. In such circumstances it is desirable that the principal supervisor seeks to involve the second supervisor in all meetings and deliberations, to avoid his or her isolation, and to avoid the development of a one-on-one relationship with the principal supervisor, often at the instigation of the candidate. There may be little formal coursework other than studies of research methodology, and few, if any, assessment hurdles prior to completion of the dissertation/thesis. An oral defence of the thesis (*viva voce*) is the norm in the UK, a potentially fraught exchange in front of a small audience – two examiners (only one of whom is usually external to the university) and a non-participating supervisor. Travel costs to and from the *viva* examination frequently constrain the choice of examiner. This situation is magnified in countries like Australia, where the distances involved are so prodigious and the pool of potential examiners so shallow that overseas examiners regularly need to be sought. Consequently, it is more normal for there to be no *viva* there, though it remains an option in exceptional circumstances. Tinkler and Jackson (2002, 2004) discuss the content of the *viva* in detail and provide recommendations for student preparation.

We might anticipate an increasing use of video-conference technology and Skype in the future, to facilitate more *viva* examinations. As a trade-off, this scenario usually demands the employment of two (sometimes three) external examiners who report independently on the hard copy document. This arrangement has the advantage of making it possible to choose the best examiners possible worldwide, without the constraint of personal attendance. One downside is that there is no opportunity for oral evaluation of the candidate, another downside is that an opportunity is created for unethical collusion between overtly 'independent' examiners. Even though the latter are selected from different universities, usually in different countries, where very narrow subject specialisms are involved, the examiners may well be known to each other, may meet at conferences and might discuss a thesis that both are examining!

Whatever the arrangements, it is vital that candidates know what is expected of them, and how their supervisor(s) can help them to satisfy the examiners at the first attempt.

The role of the supervisor

The assignment of supervisor(s) to candidate may take place in a variety of ways. In the traditional model, a candidate will enrol with a specific supervisor attached, and with (at least) an outline research proposal in hand. The supervisor will usually have been given some say on the suitability of both candidate and project, and be prepared to modify the latter in order to satisfy the mutual objectives of the supervisor/candidate. Alternative arrangements include the acceptance of candidates on to an extensive structured programme, without either a supervisor being attached or a detailed research idea having already been developed. This second form has the advantage of facilitating the assignment of the most suitable supervisor to the candidate, but the disadvantage that the candidate may develop a proposal for which there is no suitable supervision available! However, a reality check during the structured programme should help to ensure that candidates do not pursue directions likely to pose insuperable supervision problems.

Where a candidate enters into a programme with specific grant or bursary funding already attached, then a specific project may already have been determined for which supervision is virtually self-selecting, being those academics who initiated the original project proposal.

Lack of supervisory capacity for doctoral study is a serious constraint for most accounting/business departments. There is usually no shortage of doctoral candidates requiring supervision, but incentives for supervisors to supervise are conspicuously absent. This is especially so for experienced supervisors, with a sustained record of on-time completions. Excess demand for the services of these individuals continues to mean that candidates have to be realistic in their expectations. For example, it is reasonable to anticipate that a supervisor will wish to supervise topics within their existing expertise, without the necessity of exploring new and complex literatures outside their normal sphere of activity. It is also reasonable to expect that they will wish to have the opportunity of publishing with the candidate, either during the period of candidature or after completion. A successful supervisor will usually have multiple candidates at different stages of the research process so that two or more candidates complete each year. But as well as excess demand there may be supply constraints in the form of arbitrary 'caps' implemented by the university to restrict the number of candidates attached to any one supervisor. These arrangements make it vital for candidates to sell themselves and their topics effectively, and to be prepared to be flexible in the structuring of their proposals, if they wish to be associated with the most successful supervisors.

Having said that, the 'most successful' supervisor may not be the 'best' choice in every case. The supervisory relationship is a very personal one, and one which will involve a great deal of detailed communication and close interpersonal relations. It helps if supervisor and candidate can get on with each other, and ideally develop a friendly working partnership which goes beyond a master–servant relationship. But all candidates and supervisors are different, making it difficult to dictate the behaviour of both parties. Unfortunately, in a minority of cases, this relationship can break down, often because of the intransigence of either or both. In my experience, problems are most likely to arise when the candidature is well advanced (often with less than one year to go before projected completion). By this time candidates should be confident; they should know their literature better than their supervisor – possibly better than anybody else in the world! At this time they may wish to pursue a direction tangential to the current one, and at variance with that agreed with the supervisor. The latter may be fearful that a new direction is risky and may lengthen the candidature outside a normal completion time. They may be unwilling to loosen the reins and back the new proposals, to the extent that working relationships become impossible. There are arguments on both sides of the divide, and the candidate's wish to innovate is part of his or her own personal development. However, he or she must be prepared to put a time limit on the new venture, so that he or she is prepared to come back into line if that is necessary to ensure timely completion. Where such compromises prove impossible, a change of supervisory arrangements will be necessary, but the candidate must recognise that the choice of alternatives may be limited. What is important is that there is a supervisor in place – even though he or she may not necessarily be a discipline expert – to guide the candidate through the final stages of structuring and writing the thesis prior to submission.

There are a number of distinct stages in the supervision process where the supervisor and candidate have particular responsibilities. There will inevitably be differences in the nature of responsibility for each, so Table 12.1, inspired by Moses (1985), provides a 12-stage checklist in the form of a 5-point Likert scale as a basis for discussion between the potential protagonists, so that some broad agreement can be reached.

Although we might reasonably anticipate that supervisors should select the first option in Table 12.1, many supervisors will themselves disagree on what their overall responsibilities are, so it is important that any supervisor/candidate pairing is clear from the outset on their mutual expectations.

Table 12.1 Expectations of supervisor and candidate

1	It is the supervisor's responsibility to select a research topic	1□ 2□ 3□ 4□ 5□	The candidate is responsible for selecting her/his own topic
2	It is the supervisor who decides which theoretical framework or methodology is most appropriate	1□ 2□ 3□ 4□ 5□	The candidate should decide which theoretical framework or methodology he/she wishes to use
3	The supervisor should develop an appropriate programme and timetable of research and study for the candidate	1□ 2□ 3□ 4□ 5□	The supervisor should leave the development of the programme of study to the candidate
4	The supervisor is responsible for ensuring that the candidate is introduced to the appropriate services and facilities of the school/faculty/university	1□ 2□ 3□ 4□ 5□	It is the candidate's responsibility to ensure that he/she is appropriately located and accommodated, and can access all relevant services and facilities for research
5	Supervisors should only accept candidates when they have specific knowledge of the chosen topic	1□ 2□ 3□ 4□ 5□	Supervisors should feel free to accept candidates, even if they do not have specific knowledge of their topics
6	A warm, supportive relationship between supervisor and candidate is important for successful candidature	1□ 2□ 3□ 4□ 5□	A personal, supportive relationship is inadvisable because it may obstruct objectivity for both candidate and supervisor during candidature
7	The supervisor should insist on regular meetings with the candidate	1□ 2□ 3□ 4□ 5□	The candidate should decide when he/she wants to meet with the supervisor
8	The supervisor should check regularly that the candidate is working consistently and on task	1□ 2□ 3□ 4□ 5□	The candidate should work independently and not have to account for how and where time is spent
9	The supervisor is responsible for providing emotional support and encouragement to the candidate	1□ 2□ 3□ 4□ 5□	Personal counselling and support are not the responsibility of the supervisor; the candidate should look elsewhere
10	The supervisor should insist on seeing all the drafts of work to ensure that the candidate is on the right track	1□ 2□ 3□ 4□ 5□	The candidate should submit drafts of work only when he/she wants constructive criticism from the supervisor
11	The supervisor should assist in the writing of the thesis if necessary	1□ 2□ 3□ 4□ 5□	The writing of the thesis should only ever be the candidate's work
12	The supervisor is responsible for decisions regarding the standard of the thesis	1□ 2□ 3□ 4□ 5□	The candidate is responsible for decisions concerning the standard of the thesis

The supervisor should be able to plan and manage the research process so that it produces interesting and innovative outcomes in a timely fashion. Although the candidate may generate the initial research idea, the supervisor must ensure that this topic will produce an 'acceptable' thesis in that it is neither too big (and impossible to complete on time without overwork or burn-out) nor so small that the examiners will not perceive it to make a sufficient contribution to knowledge. This can be a difficult compromise so many supervisors will overcompensate slightly to avoid the latter situation. It can cause conflict when candidates are anxious to complete and can point to much shorter PhD theses (especially US ones) for comparison. Supervisors must plan the whole research process to provide a structure and establish priorities to facilitate the development of a clear proposal within six months of candidature; such a process establishes expectations, but also imposes some discipline on the participants, which may also be the source of friction.

It is usual for the candidate to be enthusiastic about his or her project at the outset; lack of enthusiasm at this stage is a cause for concern and may suggest that the student will not stay the course and complete. Phillips and Pugh (1994), especially in their fourth chapter 'How not to get a PhD', provide an interesting and amusing guide as to what a candidate should not do if he or she seeks a timely doctoral completion! These issues are also addressed by Finn (2005) and Mullins and Kiley (2002). Supervisors must monitor levels of enthusiasm to ensure that motivation is preserved and progress is still being made. This can be a serious problem, particularly among part-time candidates, where the competing demands of 'work' mean that research progress becomes extremely slow or even non-existent. The specification of particular targets or milestones during the research process should help. Some candidates respond very well to deadlines. If these are associated with the submission of conference papers relating to work-in-progress, they can be particularly beneficial.

From the supervisor's perspective, the most problematical aspects are those to do with how much of themselves is in the thesis – the sort of considerations associated with points 1, 2, 7, 11 and 12 in Table 12.1 in particular – and these will often be closely associated with the differing skills of the candidate. Thus:

1 It helps if the candidate arrives with a well-developed research proposal because his or her motivation and commitment at the outset is usually greater. But candidates may have very sketchy ideas or be unable to prioritise issues in the literature satisfactorily at the beginning of their candidature. This will mean that supervisor input is great. Many candidates expect the supervisor to more or less specify the project; many supervisors will only countenance candidates in very narrow areas of research so that their projects are effectively supervisor-specified.

2 Some supervisors with narrow perspectives will work with a single methodology, so that theory and approach are effectively pre-selected. Others, myself included, see the development of theory and method as an essential part of the literature review process; an examination of prior relevant work is used to identify alternative theoretical justifications and different possible research methods.

7 The requirement for regular meetings between supervisor and candidate is eminently sensible, though it is not clear what constitutes 'regular' in this context. Some research regimes with well-developed quality assurance procedures will have strict reporting requirements for the regularity, duration and content of such meetings. However, the rapid improvements in information technology, and the equally rapid growth in candidates studying remotely and online, may make face-to-face meetings largely superfluous, especially for able and well-motivated candidates.

11 The intellectual property for the final dissertation manuscript rests with the candidates – the words chosen should be their own. However, some candidates, especially those for whom English is a second language, require a great deal of assistance in the editing of drafts, sometimes to such an extent that they resemble re-writes. It may be necessary to employ a professional editor to help the candidate prepare the final manuscript prior to submission, to ensure that it satisfies the minimum requirements of grammatical accuracy. If candidates are publishing and presenting their findings during their candidature, which is usually desirable, then the supervisor may well be the co-author on a number of papers that embrace the content of the dissertation. It would be unrealistic if the final version of the dissertation did not incorporate the majority of the edits and revisions necessary to generate publishable papers. In this case the final dissertation is the joint responsibility of candidate and supervisor.

12 The supervisor will normally be required to 'sign-off' candidates, that is, declaring that the work of their candidates is their own and deemed worthy of submission for examination purposes. It may be possible for the candidate to insist on submission without such an acknowledgement (e.g., where the working relationship has broken down irretrievably), but such action is inadvisable, being a significant source of subsequent failure at the examination stage of candidature. To make such a declaration the supervisor must have sighted the final drafts of the thesis, made appropriate recommendations for change and then sighted the final version to be submitted. Unfortunately, reference to some of the dissertations where I have been involved in the administration of the examination process suggests that this is not always the case. The supervisor should also be actively involved in the selection of external examiners (dealt with in more detail in the following section), by securing the collaboration of suitably qualified individuals. They may elicit the advice of candidates in this process, since their literature searches and conference attendance should have facilitated the identification of eminently qualified examiners. Some supervisors will want their candidates to know the identity of examiners well before the examination, not so that they can contact them (which is strictly forbidden and would disqualify the examiner), but so that they can ensure that they have appropriately cited relevant works published by the examiner. Indeed in some universities the involvement of the candidate in examiner selection is a mandatory part of the process.

The importance of the role of the supervisor in the research process cannot be underestimated. Excellent performance can bring great credit to both university and candidate.

Inadequate performance can cause a plethora of difficulties, which can result in slow progress, inappropriate choice of examiners, subsequent failure and potential legal ramifications. Research administrators have the vital task of providing supervisors with the freedom that exploits their gifts, while instituting an unobtrusive monitoring mechanism that protects the candidate's learning experience.

Examiner profiles

The supervisor will start the process of sourcing a suitable external examiner about three months prior to the expected submission date of the final thesis. Such a time lag is essential because it may be difficult to identify individuals who are both willing and capable of examining. This can be particularly problematic in areas like finance and banking, and for dissertations which span more than one discipline.

The external examiner will be an active researcher, currently supervising his or her own doctoral candidates, and with a healthy track record in the discipline area of the research project. These are fundamental requirements, and will usually be the minimum permissible qualifications for the examiner to be nominated to act in the first place. He or she will have published recently in areas within the scope of the dissertation, and this publication record will suggest that he or she is sympathetic to the research perspective adopted by the candidate. This is an important requirement, with which the supervisor should be well versed. Errors in this regard can produce enormous problems further down the track. For example, it may not be sufficient to identify a 'management accountant' as an examiner; the dissertation may be a qualitative, interpretivist piece while the selected examiner is an avowed positivist! Such a match would not be in the best interests of the candidate.

Given the expertise of the examiner in the area of research, it is highly likely that he or she will have published research close to the dissertation topic. It would be remiss, even rude, of the candidate not to have cited relevant work published by a potential examiner. In just the same way as we would not like to annoy unnecessarily a reviewer of a journal paper, then we should try not to irk an examiner through being unreasonably critical of his or her prior work. We must not forget that even examiners are typically sensitive academics, and they would prefer to see their work described as 'pioneering contributions' or 'seminal literature' in the area, even if the findings have subsequently been superseded. Ideally, examiner, supervisor and candidate will all have corresponding views of what constitutes good research.

In securing the collaboration of the external examiner, the supervisor must follow some of the sound principles of 'impression management' identified above in securing access to research sites. Flattery is often a key component of the initial approach adopted by the supervisor, since there is otherwise little motivation for the examiner to be involved. The financial inducements are usually negligible and, other than for inexperienced examiners, there is little professional kudos in being involved in the examination process – just a lot of work! It is important, therefore, that the dissertation topic is in an area of interest to the examiner, where the examiner has demonstrated his or her competence, and where he or she might be deemed something of an expert. A well-written abstract will help to 'sell' the dissertation topic to a potential examiner by demonstrating its importance and the contribution it will make. This is an important opportunity for candidates to sell themselves and their work to an examiner before the formal process commences. Good first impressions at this stage can be helpful. Unfortunately, most candidates write poor abstracts. They spend insufficient time on them and tend to try to cobble together pieces from elsewhere in the dissertation rather than write something original. Examiners will see through this and will not be impressed. Where an examiner has been identified as the best possible, it is worth making the effort to secure their cooperation.

The examination process

The formal evaluation process commences when the dissertation manuscript is delivered to the examiner. Impressions created in the first five minutes of perusal can be important to the examiner's ultimate opinion so it is important to take some care in this respect.

- Ideally, the dissertation should be a single volume, even where university regulations permit the submission of multiple volumes. Dissertations perceived as being too long give the impression that the supervisor may have exercised insufficient control over the progress of the research.
- The volume should be immaculately presented. It should be professionally bound in hard covers (even where regulations permit submission in cheaper, flimsy covers). The professional look does not cost much, and is well worth the impression it creates. Well-spaced gold lettering on both the cover and the spine add to this impression.
- The volume should be free of grammatical and spelling errors. Accurate editing and proofreading should ensure that this is so, making it doubly unfortunate that the front and contents pages of many theses contain glaring errors – even to the extent of spelling errors in the title! Tables, in particular, should be rigorously checked for both spelling and numerical errors, especially since routine proof-checking will normally entail 'reading around' the tables so that these are frequently overlooked in the checking process.
- The contents should be clearly and systematically organised. At the very least, the contents flagged at the front of the thesis should coincide with the subsequent contents in actuality – that is, the page numbers and chapter titles indicated should correspond. Frequent redrafting at the preparatory stage will mean that the pagination of contents will change frequently. The contents page is often one of the last to be revised and it must not be missed.
- The citations and references should correspond exactly. The match should mean that there is no citation unreferenced, and no reference that does not appear in the main body of the text. Errors here demonstrate a certain sloppiness in the revision process, and highlight the possibility that other mistakes will appear in the main text as well as the references.

Where the examiner is (by choice) only in receipt of an electronic version of the thesis, the candidate must take special care to ensure that the downloaded version of the file corresponds exactly with the hardcopy text.

The guidelines to examiners provided by university administrators vary very little in content. The words used may differ, but they normally ask the examiner to report in five specific areas:

- originality of research;
- critical insights conveyed;
- demonstration of a capacity to conduct independent research;
- contribution to knowledge; and
- publishability of the findings.

The examiner will recognise that the thesis is a result of the collaboration between supervisor and candidate, but that the thesis is properly the work of the latter. In criticising the thesis, the examiner is inevitably criticising both candidate and supervisor, this being particularly so where methodological flaws remain that we may reasonably have expected a competent supervisor to have corrected.

It is instructive to examine each of the five areas above in more detail, both to clarify expectations and identify potential difficulties.

- **Originality.** The idea must be new. While it will build on the existing literature, it will embrace innovations that are new to the literature. The research must be interesting and have implications for future research or business practice. The problem under investigation must be sufficiently important to be deemed worthwhile; that is, it must pass the 'so what?' test from an unconvinced reviewer.
- **Critical insight.** The literature review is both comprehensive and current, reflecting the outcomes of previous studies, extant theory and the empirical testing of theory. The literature review should be critical, rather than just descriptive, and should not ramble around aimlessly. It should be directed towards the development and justification of testable hypotheses. The review should be organised in a thematic manner to facilitate a critical approach and help in the identification of gaps and flaws in existing knowledge. As an examiner, all too often I read literature reviews with reference to little or nothing published in the last two years (apart from the occasional new textbook). The message is clear: the candidate completed the literature review chapter long ago and has not bothered to update it. Two areas of vulnerability often emerge here. First, in the development of theory, which is sometimes not taken seriously enough, though we know it has to be there. The ubiquitous 'agency theory' arises even though alternative competing theories are arguably more appropriate. Second, the jump from the literature to the hypotheses may be just too big to be adequately justified. In examining, I look for candidates to justify their choices, and to differentiate between alternative approaches with appropriate citations. For example, a recent doctoral candidate, reporting on the conduct

of a content analysis of narrative statements chose to sample 100-word segments, randomly from 30 narratives: but why only 30 narratives? Why only 100-word segments (when we have software support)? Why random selections, when the literature (e.g., Clatworthy and Jones, 2001, 2006) suggests that content will vary according to its position in the narrative? All of these decisions needed justification.

- **Independent capacity.** Candidates are in charge of the research project and must demonstrate that they are managing the process in a systematic, almost scientific, manner. Depending on the context of the study, the research design should ensure the internal and/or external validity of the research instrument. Failures in this regard are frequently apparent in two areas. First, candidates run out of steam around Chapter 6. All the hard work has been done, the data collected, the results analysed, but the candidates are so anxious to complete and submit that they do not do justice to their early work by skimping on the conclusions, recommendations, limitations and future research agenda. As an examiner, this is the most common criticism of the theses I evaluate. Second, the research problem and the literature do not appear to be driving the chosen method. Frequently, candidates have preconceived ideas of their preferred method (usually a survey) even before they have specified their research idea. This must be corrected in the dissertation so that the chosen method can be seen as superior to alternatives, follows naturally from the prior literature, and is consistent with the research question and hypotheses.
- **Contribution.** The study is more than just a replication. It is not the same research/ instrument in a different time, country or organisation. It must be more than this. Where it relies substantially on an existing body of work, there must still be some 'wrinkle' – some significant difference – which sets it apart from existing work. As a result, we get to know something worth knowing, something non-trivial, which will make a difference. Such differences might be recommendations for change in business practice, practical business applications, new models or new theoretical relationships. However, candidates should be realistic about the limitations of their studies, and try not to overstate the significance of their findings.
- **Publishability.** If the research is new, interesting and worthwhile, then the findings will be publishable somewhere. However, as detailed in the following chapter, the research approach may restrict the number and nature of potential target journals. A well-organised dissertation, with clearly labelled literatures and specific positive findings, will highlight publication opportunities and significantly facilitate the publication process. Where the study has clear implications for management practice, then the opportunities for publication in the professional and practitioner literatures will be increased. The thesis may make a contribution to our knowledge by demonstrating that no significant relationships exist (i.e., Null Hypotheses are accepted), and that empirical findings do not support theory; unfortunately such findings are very much more difficult to get published than those which report support for positive relationships.

Overall, examiners will be looking to make the minimum recommendation for change. They will usually not want the burden of re-examination unless they believe that major revisions must be made for a dissertation to meet an appropriate doctoral standard. The alternative examiner gradings will vary between countries, but will usually embrace the following categories:

- A – pass without further amendment.
- B – pass with only minor grammatical and editorial changes required.
- C – pass, subject to specified (minor) revisions having been made to the satisfaction of the supervisor and the university's conferring body.
- D – major revisions are required, with the revised manuscript returned to the examiner for re-evaluation within 12 months.
- E – fail, with the recommendation that a lesser award be made (e.g., of an MPhil in a PhD examination).
- F – outright fail, with no opportunity for re-submission.

Where a *viva* is part of the examination process, this provides an invaluable opportunity for candidates to mount a vigorous oral defence of their study, demonstrating that the work is all their own, that it has been conducted in a systematic manner and that they have a complete understanding of its intricacies. In Australia, where there is rarely a *viva* examination, problems can arise with multiple examiners and conflicting examiner opinions. But if appropriate examiners have been selected, the variance should not be great (i.e., no A and F grades to reconcile). For category D (major revisions), the nature of the required changes may vary greatly. It may mean only new literatures and major restructuring of the content – easily completed in three months. But if the examiner wants more data collection and analysis, this could be quite onerous, and for field studies may be very difficult to accomplish.

Most professional doctorates (e.g., Doctor of Business Administration, DBA) must satisfy very similar criteria at the examination stage. Although there are numerous DBA formats worldwide, with differing weightings attributable to the coursework and research components, the research dissertations must meet doctoral standards. They will usually be shorter than a corresponding PhD thesis (perhaps of the order of two-thirds' length) and must make a contribution to business practice, otherwise the examination criteria are very similar.

The dissertation examination may be seen as a preliminary stage in the publication process; many students will already have published during the period of their candidature. The time period between submission of the dissertation and knowledge of the final outcome of the examination process may be both lengthy and anxious. It is an ideal time to start dismantling the thesis in order to identify publishable papers. The findings of the doctoral study can then be conveyed to a wider audience of both practitioners and academics without delay.

Further reading

Finn, J.A. (2005) *Getting a PhD*. London: Routledge.

James, R. and Baldwin, G. (1999) *Eleven Practices of Effective Postgraduate Supervision*. Melbourne: School of Graduate Studies, University of Melbourne.

Moses, I. (1985) 'Supervising Postgraduates', Green Guide No. 3, *Higher Education Research and Development Society of Australia (HERDSA)*, Canberra.

Mullins, G. and Kiley, M. (2002) '"It's a PhD, not a Nobel Prize": How Experienced Examiners Assess Research Theses', *Studies in Higher Education*, 27 (4): 369–86.

Phillips, E.M and Pugh, D.S. (1994) *How To Get A PhD*, 2nd edn. Milton Keynes: Open University Press.

Tinkler, P. and Jackson, C. (2002) 'In the Dark? Preparing for the PhD Viva', *Quality Assurance in Education*, 10 (2): 86–97.

Tinkler, P. and Jackson, C. (2004) *The Doctoral Examination Process: A Handbook for Students, Examiners and Supervisors*. Maidenhead: Open University.

Turning Research into Publications

THIRTEEN

Chapter Contents

- Why publish?
- Where to publish?
- What to publish?
- How to publish?
- Co-authoring issues
- Concluding remarks

This chapter targets accounting researchers at the start of their publication careers, and academics who are either just starting to contemplate a research involvement, or who need their efforts kick-started after a period of non-productivity. Those enrolled for research degrees should be aiming to publish during their candidature, and should see publication in the practitioner and academic literatures as a means of promoting themselves and their research findings. This chapter aims to answer some basic research-related questions, like Why? Where? What? How? and Which? in a manner that at least reduces the frustrating 'trial and error' approach adopted by many inchoate researchers. The learning curve is still steep, but the gradient can be significantly reduced by observing some simple rules. The overall aim is to see more accounting students and academics conducting research, getting published, making contributions to the field and feeling the incredible buzz of seeing one's own work and name in print.

Why publish?

Research resources are spread extremely thinly around most accounting schools, especially outside the US. Many schools may have only a handful of active researchers, and they have the responsibility of conveying the research message to their fellow academics and doctoral candidates at a time when research output is assuming a greater prominence in all schools. The direct rewards from research involvement for both individual and academic department can be classified as:

- self-actualisation;
- increased appointment and promotion opportunities;
- improved tenure likelihood;
- enhancement of teaching through the research connection;
- possible remission from teaching/administration to conduct research;
- the opportunity to win research grants;
- increased availability of consultancy assignments;
- overseas travel to present papers at prestigious conferences;
- availability to provide postgraduate research supervision; and
- attraction of resources through national university funding mechanisms (such as the Excellence in Research initiative for Research in Australia (ERA) or the Research Assessment Exercise now (REF) in the UK).

These material gains may be less important than the personal pleasure accruing from research success – the pride in one's own publications and the almost addictive effect that initial success can have on the subsequent publication record.

Where to publish?

The avenues for publishing accounting pieces are extensive and ever-growing. Appendix 1 is far from comprehensive, but details the refereed journals in the accounting field (excluding tax and finance) recognised by the Australian Business Deans Council (ABDC) for 2017. The initial choice is likely to lie between:

- books;
- book chapters (including case studies);
- commissioned reports;
- refereed journal articles;
- professional journal articles; and
- conference papers.

The last of these is the easiest access point, and an almost essential precursor to the publication of a refereed journal article. Most established researchers will have started their publishing careers with conference papers and professional journal articles. However, the pros and cons of each are worth consideration in more depth.

Books

Writing a book is a tempting idea. The opportunity of appearing in print, bound between hard covers, is appealing – and there may even be royalties involved. In practice, think again. The chances of writing a bestseller are remote – there is rarely enough sex and violence in accounting to produce a blockbuster, though Goldratt and Cox (1989) provide an exception. Even so, books targeted at wider non-academic audiences, like Ian Griffiths (1986) and Terry Smith (1992), have been hugely successful. Books take longer to write and rarely generate the academic kudos that an equivalent number of top refereed journal articles would. Books tend to be all-consuming, leaving little time for other research (let alone teaching) for periods in excess of six months; the requirement to complement the text with online support in the form of websites, question banks and instructor guidelines have made academic book-writing even more burdensome! The review process may be as rigorous as for some refereed journals and the whole process can be very frustrating. In hindsight, many authors regret having embarked on ambitious book-writing projects, and prospective authors must not be blind to the work involved in constructing a standard undergraduate text aimed at a mass market (e.g., in management accounting a 'Horngren' for the US (Horngren et al., 2015), or a 'Drury' for the UK (Drury, 2012). A specialist text is much easier. Young academics may be tempted to write adaptations of successful UK and US texts for smaller markets (e.g., in Australia and New Zealand), but the dollar pay-off rarely justifies the time and energy devoted to reconstructing a tome and generating culturally appropriate support materials, at an important time in their careers. Having said that, at least one book, or major contribution to a book, like the successful competitive research grant application, contributes to the rounded résumé so sought by potential employees. However, it is probably not the best place to start; better to have a number of refereed and professional journal publications under one's belt before even contemplating writing a book.

Book chapters

These provide a much easier alternative, and embrace the contribution of case studies to an edited collection. However, you will still have to learn the art of compromise because the publisher will have at least one eye on the target market, while the editor must ensure that the whole volume conforms to a particular house style – usually his or her own! The result is that any contributor will be required to change the actual words and phrases they have chosen and be forced to add or delete paragraphs which they may believe to be unnecessary or essential, respectively. Many multi-author books are instigated in single university departments, but while all contributors are good friends at the outset, they frequently are not by the time the volume reaches the bookshops.

Commissioned reports

Once you have developed an area of recognised expertise, commonly associated with a doctoral research topic, opportunities will arise to produce (usually for money) commissioned research reports. The borderline between this activity and consulting is extremely blurred, especially if a niche of expertise is such that it results in a plethora of reports in a similar vein but slightly different environments (e.g., the same thing in different organisations, different industries, different countries etc.). However, many 'research streams' in the academic literature make certain individuals subject to the same criticisms. Reports of this nature are unlikely to carry a great deal of weight with academic peers, but they may foster valuable industrial networks, provide engagement opportunities and help to build a reputation within the profession.

Refereed journal articles

These are generally regarded as the pinnacle of achievement for an academic. Certainly for promotion and tenure purposes, the quantity and quality of your contributions to refereed journals will be important, if not paramount, to your success. Parker et al. (1998: 381) add weight to this perception with quotations from accounting professors responsible for academic recruitment. In assessing the relative importance of research, teaching, administration and community service in academic appointment and promotion, one interviewee reveals that: 'Publications is 101 per cent. Everything else is zero.'

The downside is that the better journals are difficult to get into – they reject something like 70% of pieces submitted (for *The Accounting Review* this figure is over 90%). The other, related, problem is the length of time it takes to get an article published in a refereed journal. To understand this delay, consider the nature of the reviewing process:

The relationship between author and referee(s) allows alternative forms of review process to emerge:

- open – they (referees) know who you (author) are *and* you know who they are;
- single-blind – they know who you are *but* you do not know who they are; or
- double-blind – referees and author(s) are anonymous to each other.

The best refereed journals use the double-blind method, but that does not totally remove the potential for reviewer bias because both topic area and writing style may reveal the identity of the author. It is also quite likely that the reviewer has already seen an earlier version of the paper, in conference paper or working paper form, a factor that the author should aim to exploit to his or her advantage.

The referees generally determine the publishability of the paper and they will report back (separately) to the editor, giving an opinion on the paper. This may take between three and six months, sometimes longer. The editor will make the initial decision as to whether the paper should be reviewed at all, or they may take advice from an associate editor in this regard. Where the referees disagree, the editor may resort to a third referee as an arbiter, extending the process by a further two to three months. When the response from the editor finally arrives it will come in one of the following alternative forms:

- Editorial rejection: returned as being unsuitable without recourse to referees. If the target journal is inappropriate, the editor may suggest an alternative which is more suitable. In the worst scenario, the editor may consider that the paper is so badly written it is unfit for refereeing.
- Rejection with referee reports: short referee reports are not good since they convey the message that there is no hope for the paper.
- Rejection but with rewrite suggestions: the referee reports are constructive in detailing the reworking that is needed to make the paper adequate. These revisions may be so excessive that they constitute a new paper (e.g., the redesign of an experiment or conducting a fresh sample), but at least they convey the promise that there is a paper in there somewhere, even though it may never be acceptable to this particular journal.
- Yes/but acceptance: the referees like the paper but have identified serious flaws which preclude its immediate acceptance. However, this should be treated as an 'accept', even if the corrections are extensive and time-consuming, because addressing them should guarantee success, as long as the journal editor remains consistent in his or her approach.
- Acceptance with minor revisions: the referees feel compelled to make some changes (this is part of their job after all), but they are so minor that they can often be completed by return of post. Success!
- Acceptance without revision: the referees recognise your genius and demand your publication!

The last event is extremely rare, and virtually unknown in the top journals. Several iterations of the reviewing process may take place (usually two or three) before the referees are finally satisfied. These iterations can prove a tortuous process, especially when the referees are looking to push the paper in seemingly opposite directions. Clear guidance from the editor as to their priorities is most helpful in such circumstances. Even after fully satisfying the referees, further iterations may be necessary to satisfy the editor. A year will normally have elapsed between submission of a paper and its acceptance, and appearance on the journal website; possibly another year will pass before it appears in print. On average, two years' work on researching the project and workshopping the paper will have been spent before its submission to the reviewing process. That is, four years in total between starting work on the paper and seeing your name in lights. It may be longer if one of the referees dies or changes his or her mind during the review process. Herein lies the major drawback of the refereed journal article – any one has a lengthy life cycle, making it essential that, as an author, you have several papers undergoing the review process simultaneously. It is not advisable to try to speed up the process by submitting the same paper to different journals at the same time. In fact, the better journals have a policy specifically prohibiting the acceptance of articles treated in this way.

The time lags in the refereeing and printing process usually go beyond that required to guarantee integrity of content, and most journal editors know it. They are conscious of the threats to relevance from lack of timeliness, but they have a difficult job when dealing with (usually) unpaid referees trying to fit an often demanding, but discretionary, activity into their busy schedules. Electronic submission and refereeing of papers for consideration and online publishing has helped to reduce some of these time lags, but some journals have been slow in adopting procedural changes.

Professional journal articles

All of the disadvantages of refereed articles are magically reversed when contemplating the professional journals:

- The articles do not take as long to write: more than a week's work spent on a professional piece might be considered excessive.
- The content does not have to be earth-shattering or even make an original contribution to the literature. It does have to be relevant and timely, and be able to make practitioners aware of issues they should know about, or may have forgotten.
- The review process is speedy: the editor may accept the piece without recourse to others, but often they will seek 'expert' opinion.
- Once accepted (and acceptance without revision is common) the article will usually be published within three months, providing that it can be accommodated within the back-log and the advertising pages. The more pressing the issues examined, the quicker the article appears in print.
- Feedback from readers will be quick (positive or negative) and is much more common than that associated with refereed journal articles.

Articles for professional journals are relatively easy to write and may be a direct consequence of teaching experiences. They can make active contributions to the professional development of accounting practitioners by bringing to their attention the results of relevant academic research, the potential for applying new methods or for applying old methods in new ways. For example, articles on Capital Asset Pricing Model, product life cycle and time-series analysis frequently appear in the professional literature because they have been written with respect to a particular issue and 'packaged' to say something new. They do not need to be academically rigorous and a shortage of citations is a distinct advantage. They do need to be brief, clear and concise. Catchy titles and acronyms are helpful too, giving the editor an ideal selling point. For academics who have published little or nothing, but have concentrated their efforts on teaching and assessment, this is the easiest means of penetrating the research genre. However, do be prepared to see versions of papers in professional journals that differ vastly from the ones that were actually submitted and accepted. Editors take the word 'editing' very seriously, and you can expect to see both the title changed and the content of 'your' paper abbreviated to fit the space requirements of the journal, often without reference back to the author. The 'dumbing down' of the content of practitioner journals in recent years is an unfortunate but unavoidable observation. Their magazine-like format, in which pieces on cars and holidays compete for space with technical issues, has a dual effect, which threatens the informing process:

- publishers are less willing to publish academic pieces, preferring shorter contributions from consultants; and
- academics are less willing to submit pieces to the practitioner literature because they perceive the medium to have been devalued.

The *Harvard Business Review* (*HBR*) is worthy of specific mention here, as a type of journal that really fits neither of the above descriptions for refereed or professional journals. This is especially appropriate given that it is a prestigious, highly cited journal that attracts contributions from the biggest names in academic accounting. The content, however, is rarely academically rigorous. The focus is on findings and the application of findings to practice, rather than on methodology or theoretical underpinning. The editorial process is very different from that for refereed journals too. Indeed, once it is convinced of the validity of an idea, the editorial team at *HBR* will work closely with the authors in the actual writing of the article to ensure that it reaches the target practitioner audience appropriately. Traditional accounting academics may accordingly begrudge the reputation that *HBR* has, but it remains a very useful citation to have in one's résumé.

Conference papers

The conference paper is rarely an end in itself in the accounting discipline, but may find itself in a published collection of conference proceedings. In other disciplines, notably marketing or information systems, published conference proceedings are more often the final resting place for a paper. The refereeing process for accounting conferences varies considerably, and this is reflected in the content that is considered acceptable: many conferences will review abstracts only, and make a decision on the acceptability of the whole paper based on preliminary evidence – at a stage when the paper itself may be in an early draft. Such conferences provide excellent vehicles for exposing preliminary findings. Where conference convenors wish to review the whole finished paper prior to deeming it acceptable for presentation, in a manner close to that for refereed journals, they seem much more inclined to accept polished papers, almost complete and ready for publication, on the grounds that internal and inter-university workshopping should have already been used to iron out flaws of construction and presentation. The proliferation of accounting conferences in recent years, where the organisers recognise that potential delegates must be presenting for their attendance to be funded, means that it is no longer difficult having a paper accepted for presentation at an international conference. Interestingly, Fogarty (2006) adopts a contrary position, based on US experience. He suggests that conference presentations are a waste of time (since few in the audience will even have read the paper) and that informed colleagues will not have the time to provide the necessary in-depth review of a draft paper. He recommends early submission of the paper to a journal provided the quality hurdle has been reached, so that the paper receives a 'revise and resubmit' response. As long as we do not get an outright 'reject' decision, he suggests that we will have established prior ownership of the topic in a highly competitive publication environment.

What to publish?

There are few restrictions on the topics for professional journals, or the manner in which they are written, as long as they comply with tight space restrictions. The same cannot be said of refereed academic journals, where the topics deemed appropriate and the approach deemed acceptable often seem to be unduly, even absurdly, constrained. These issues are explored in depth by Gray (1996).

Peat, Marwick and Mitchell's programme, *Research Opportunities in Auditing* (1976), identified a number of characteristics of research problems that need to be addressed for them to be attractive to the academic community:

- they should be interesting;
- they should be capable of scientific research, in terms of testable hypotheses and discernible outcomes;
- they should be rooted in knowledge and research methodologies which are easily attainable;
- data sets and sample information must exist to allow the development of theories and hypotheses;
- the problem should be sufficiently important to attract research funding; and
- the likely outcomes must be of a standard to justify publication in a refereed journal or another respected publication.

These points provide useful guidance, but in spotting a specific research question there is no substitute for reading the research literature. Keeping up with the current research literature across a wide span of interests is extremely time-consuming – some would argue impossible – if you are trying to **write** as well as **read**. There are shortcuts:

- make use of online alerting services, based on both journal title and key word, so that you are well informed of the contents of all relevant recently published journal articles;
- make use of online access to working paper series and conference proceedings, and of articles **in press**, so you can see what will appear in the journals at least a year in advance of appearance;
- read the 'abstract' of the paper – you may have no choice because that may be all that is available online;
- when full text or hard copy is readily available, begin by reading just the beginning and end of papers:

   o the 'abstract' and 'introduction' to see if the content and the approach are of interest; and
   o the 'conclusions' and 'limitations' to see what the paper has **not** done.

   These will frequently identify flaws in methodology that can be corrected by replication with 'a wrinkle' and opportunities for future research;

- read anthologies of the current state of research, which will identify those fields still to be explored or which have been researched inadequately;
- attend conferences to see what other people are working on – their ideas can often be adapted quite successfully without plagiarism.

In the accounting and finance areas the research topics can be grouped broadly as follows:

Analytical and non-empirical areas

- Formal, highly mathematical expositions based on the information economics and utility theory literature (e.g., in the *Journal of Accounting Research*).
- A return to fundamentals with a focus on 'measurement' or the 'value' of accounting information for decision-making.
- Critical theory research.

Focused empiricism

- A move away from narrow studies devoted to the 'information content' aspects of stock price reaction towards behavioural aspects, often in laboratory-type conditions.
- Applications in particular (under-researched) institutions, like insurance, healthcare, pensions and superannuation, the public sector and non-profit organisations, through survey-based or archival studies.

Socio-political structure

- Case-based development of systematic bodies of knowledge regarding accounting in complex situations.
- Unstructured, positive, exploratory, case-based investigations of actual practice and, for example, the impact of modern manufacturing technologies.
- Field-based experimental studies, which are still extremely rare in the literature.

Hypothetical deduction

- Survey-based statistical inference to appraise the effect on accounting systems of contingent variables.
- Impact of changes in accounting systems over time, relative to movements in competition and strategic direction.

All of these topics may be described by the NIRD acronym (i.e., new, interesting, reproducible and defensible), however, not **all** approaches are equally acceptable to **all** journals. Case study material, for example, is still difficult, though decreasingly so, to get published (perhaps because it fails the 'reproducible' test). It would therefore be a waste of time to send such a study to the *Journal of Accounting Research*, for example.

Similarly, in Chapter 3 we noted the difficulties that authors experience in publishing critical theory research in other than two or three of the top accounting journals. As noted in Chapter 9, Van der Stede et al. (2005) specify the four top-tier journals (*Contemporary Accounting Research*, *The Accounting Review*, *Journal of Accounting Research*, *Journal of Accounting and Economics*), which no longer appear to publish survey-based management accounting research studies. Reading the research literature involves 'researching the editors' so that you know what they have published and where, and the style and topics likely to be acceptable to them as editors. In this way journal submissions can be targeted towards journals that increase their likelihood of acceptance. Guthrie et al. (2002) and Merchant (2010) note that the top-rated accounting journals predominantly publish economics-based research and do not accept qualitative research. Fogarty (2006) notes the apparent bias in the editorial practices of top US journals, which appear to favour the outputs of the 'elite' US schools. Similarly, Humphrey (2008) notes that audit research is dominated by predictive empirical studies, many of them experimental, based in economics and statistics, to the neglect of issues concerning auditing practice.

Parker (2005), Humphrey (2005) and Armstrong (2008) are all critical of the neglect of qualitative initiatives to address accounting and auditing failures in the wake of the Enron debacle and the Global Financial Crisis. Lee (2004) had attributed such failures to academics' misguided focus on capital markets research – although such a focus might be a university requirement and is apparently also predominantly a requirement for top-tier publishing!

A paper is more likely to be accepted if it conforms to a standard structure that demonstrates the adoption of a systematic scientific approach. A paper would normally be developed through the five distinct stages detailed in Figure 2.2. These would be supported by an 'abstract' providing an overview of the paper. Many authors neglect the importance of this 'sixth' stage by using it as a receptacle for sentences and paragraphs used elsewhere in the main text. This is a big mistake. The abstract is the first thing the editor/reviewer reads and great care is necessary to ensure that it 'sells' the paper to the reader, while spelling out what it does and why it is important. It should be possible to identify the nature of the key results of the paper and the contribution it makes to the literature from the abstract and the initial pages of the introduction. If the abstract is poorly written and unexciting, the editor may read no further! The write-up of the five stages demands closer attention.

Research problem

The research question must be specified precisely, and in a manner which details the motivation for its study. It must be a problem worth studying. The importance of this section cannot be overstated; it provides the opportunity of 'selling' an idea and of setting out what the paper does clearly so that the key points are not buried in a mass of trivia. The paper must pass the 'so what?' test. (See also pages 19–21.)

Theory and literature review

The literature review must be current and fairly reflect both relevant theory and the outcomes of previous studies. It should provide a critique of earlier work, pinpointing flaws in the approach of others. Most importantly, it must not ramble about in an apparently undirected manner; it should be precise and link to the development of hypotheses. (See also pages 21–2.)

Hypotheses

Hypotheses must be driven by underpinning theory, and the latter should be sufficient to avoid making speculative leaps from theory to hypotheses. A single paper would not normally contain more than seven separate hypotheses – more than this and it starts to look like another paper. (See also pages 58–9.)

Research methodology

The method of investigation chosen should be consistent with both the research question and the hypotheses. The experimental design should ensure that the internal and external validity of the research instrument are, as far as possible, in the context of the study. The method of investigation should be justified (e.g., why a survey?) and must be structured in a scientific manner to demonstrate that it will test the question being researched. Any sampling method used should be described, justified and shown to be scientific in its selection. (See also pages 59–60.)

Results, conclusions and discussion

The empirical analysis should be appropriate to the chosen method and should be directed towards the measurement and testing of the hypotheses. The results should be clear, avoiding unnecessary mathematical complexity and 'mini-lectures' on the theory underpinning the application of standard tests. The author(s) should be realistic about the limitations of the study and not overstate the significance of its conclusions. Areas where the study might be extended and related research areas should be highlighted.

The paper should conclude with a set of references which exactly coincide with the contents (i.e., no citation is unreferenced and no reference is uncited). A checking technique used by many referees (including this author) to verify the care which authors take in completing their papers is to start their review by ensuring that the equation 'citations = references' balances. Lack of care by authors in this regard is a fair indication of their likely sloppiness and lack of attention to detail in other aspects of their paper. (See also pages 194–5.)

The whole paper should be interesting, readable and clear, reflecting the motivation of the author(s) to convey a message which they feel should be heard. A length of 25–30 pages, including appendices, is the norm, but both longer and shorter papers can be justified. If in doubt about including paragraphs, tables or appendices, then they should be omitted. The same applies to footnotes (or endnotes, depending on the journal), the number of which should be kept to a minimum. A check of the typical article in the target journal will quickly show the elements of house style and what editors are looking for. Make sure that articles submitted to journals for publication comply with that journal's editorial style in every respect – and particularly in the method of referencing. If you use the style of another journal, then you may send an unwitting message to the referee that this paper was originally destined elsewhere but has already been rejected by that journal! The use of the 'endnotes' software fortunately now makes the once time-consuming and tedious reformatting of references a simpler task.

How to publish?

There are many conflicting views on what constitutes an appropriate and ethical method of answering the 'publishing' question. They boil down to 'knowing your editor' and 'respecting' the views of referees. Some authors subscribe to the view that the submission of three-quarter finished papers to journals is justified by the fact that referees are bound to want to make changes (that is their job after all) and why not let them finish the paper for you? It is difficult to support this view. Apart from the ethics of the process, such practice will soon get you a bad reputation with both editors and reviewers. Generally, it is good practice to submit a polished piece to a journal, one which you would be happy to see published as it is, but which may still have some 'rough edges' that reviewers can further refine. A useful system would be:

- Write a rough first draft yourself.
- Edit the first draft with clarity, sense, structure and order of materials in mind, ensuring that spelling, grammar and references are perfect.
- Ask somebody else in the field, whose views you respect, to look critically at the paper and encourage his or her use of the red pen. Reading and altering the first drafts of others is an extremely time-consuming operation if done properly, so care should be taken to ensure that you, at least, have made a reasonable first attempt, and that you do not pepper the same colleague with too many first drafts per annum – not if you wish to retain their friendship and cooperation!
- Revise the paper with these views in mind. Some criticisms may be so fundamental as to necessitate a complete rethink/rewrite.
- 'Workshop' the paper at one or two other universities, to seek the views of a wider (possibly interdisciplinary) audience.
- Submit the paper to a respected conference in the field. This may be a regional, national or international conference, depending on timing.
- Further refine the paper based on these comments and submit this version to the target journal.

Truscott et al. (2010) observe that authors publishing mixed methods research may choose to send their quantitative and qualitative findings to different journals, to overcome potential problems with reviewers. In this context Malina et al. (2011) comment on their problems with 'blind' reviewers of opposing persuasions; they report details of a 'quantitative' reviewer asking for more tests before they would accept the refutation of causality, while the 'qualitative' reviewer wanted a more elaborate story to explain the findings!

Editors expect authors to adopt a systematic approach, so it is worth reminding them that this has been undertaken by making acknowledgements on the front page of the paper to individuals whose comments have been sought and to the participants of workshops, seminars and conferences where the paper has been read. A variation on this methodology that is frequently adopted in practice is to send a polished first draft of the paper to a member of the editorial board of the target journal for comment. Provided that this person's comments are then incorporated in the paper, the inclusion of his or her name on the front cover should elicit a positive reaction from the editor and may even induce them to use the same person as a formal reviewer.

In targeting the journal in the first place, check out the editor and members of the editorial board. What are their areas of strength? Have they published anything in the subject areas of your paper? This approach allows you to formulate a shortlist of likely referees (though journals will commonly also use *ad hoc* reviewers from beyond the editorial board too). It should also highlight pieces in the literature, which it would be prudent to cite, and those which it would be rude or even foolish to ignore.

When submitting the paper, write a brief accompanying letter to the editor, specifying clearly why you think theirs is is the appropriate journal to publish this paper, and the contribution that it makes to the current debate in the area.

When your paper has entered the reviewing process, be patient. Try not to call editors to check on the paper's progress as this is annoying and will soon get you a bad reputation. It is reasonable, though, to write a letter of enquiry or send an e-mail after a period of three or four months has elapsed without response. When the response arrives, it may indicate acceptance, although, more likely, rejection. However, a rejection is often not what it seems, as noted earlier. The initial reaction to rejection (of any description) and negative reviewer reports is usually swearing, and perhaps tears. This is normal, and an essential part of becoming a productive publisher is growing a hide thick enough to cope with repeated rejection. One immediate course of action, advocated by many, is to despatch the paper to the next-choice journal by return of post. This is rarely an optimum strategy, especially where it is highly likely that the **same** referee will be used by **different** journals – the narrower the topic area, the higher the probability of this happening. There is nothing that annoys a reviewer more than to be asked to referee a paper that he or she has already refereed and in which none of the previously recommended changes have been made. Such action can again cause damage to your long-term reputation as a researcher.

It is much better to consign the rejected article to a drawer, forget about it for a while and concentrate on another project. A sensible researcher will always have at least four projects running simultaneously, and all at different stages of the research process, in order to generate a continuous flow of output. Return to the rejected paper after a week or two and re-read the referee reports carefully. If the tenor of their remarks still causes a state of excitement and agitation, then re-consign the paper to the drawer for a little longer, at least until you have calmed down sufficiently for teeth to become ungritted. When the referee reports can be read in a relatively unemotional manner, note the thrust of their comments and re-read your paper to determine the extent to which they are justified. It is rare not to come away feeling 'the referee has a point there' in at least one or two instances. The referee reports can then be used positively and constructively in the rewrite of the paper:

- Specify the points made by each reviewer (usually two) separately and classify them as major (methodology, missing literature) and minor (labelling, positioning, footnotes) criticisms. Reviewers should normally be concerned with some common issues.
- Address each of the specified points. This does not necessarily mean agreeing with the reviewer on every point. If there are arguments for **not** making the suggested changes, then articulate them (reviewers **do** make statistical errors, and it is unlikely that they are as familiar with the current literature in a narrow specialist area as the author). It is possible that the reviewer has been quite unreasonable, and that you are tempted to request a referee change. Care should be taken in this regard, since by criticising a referee you are implicitly criticising the editor – since they were responsible for the initial selection.
- Do not attempt to make changes which are merely 'window dressing' – they fool nobody. Major criticisms will call for substantive reworks, possibly involving the results of new experiments or the adoption of improved testing procedures.

If all of the major criticisms can be addressed and/or corrected, then the revised article can be resubmitted to the same journal. If there are major gaps remaining, where the paper is still vulnerable, it may be better to target a lower-tier journal. Indeed, Fogarty (2006) views a 'reject' opinion as a 'revise and do not resubmit' decision. The paper must be changed and improved, and then directed towards a new target journal.

When resubmitting, the accompanying letter to the editor should thank the editorial team for their constructive remarks and identify the major changes made to improve the paper. Separate reports for each reviewer, detailing how each point has been addressed, and where in the revised paper changes to the text have been made, should be attached. The editor will normally return the resubmitted paper to the original reviewers, together with your comments on the points raised. They may be satisfied and recommend publication, or they may ask for more (on the same points) or identify different ones.

Reviewers may be obstinate or even hostile, or worse, they may change their minds. It is reasonable to make a fuss and/or ask for a different reviewer in such circumstances, but in my experience this is not normally helpful. Usually the editor has made the decision that **this** paper will not be published by **this** journal, and in such circumstances it is advisable to look elsewhere.

Co-authoring issues

A good curriculum vitae should have both sole-authored and co-authored papers, to demonstrate that you can both work on your own and as part of a team. Floyd et al. (1994) advocate the use of co-authorship both to enhance the quality of research and to increase the likelihood of the acceptance of the resulting papers for publication in top journals. Fleischman and Schuele (2009) identify a continuing trend in the relative proportion of co-authored articles appearing in accounting journals. From a personal perspective I always found sole-authored papers the easiest to write, but my 'best' papers (Smith and Taffler, 1995, 2000; So and Smith, 2009; Jones and Smith, 2014) have all been co-authored – partly because the questions posed by co-authors have often been more challenging than those of the reviewers.

In an empirical study Tucker et al. (2016) reported a number of specific advantages of working with co-authors:

- Added-value from co-authors with different but complementary skills – abilities in working on revisions and responding to reviewer comments; ability to produce first drafts or to act as a 'finisher' immediately prior to submission.
- The growing importance of team submissions in research grant applications, since funding bodies clearly treat projects addressed by skilled teams particularly favourably.
- Personal friendship is a key element in the co-authorship decision, and one that is part of the long-term collaborations which are so visible in the literature (e.g., Malmi and Granlund; Smith and Taffler; Ittner and Larcker; Parker and Guthrie, among many others).

However, co-authorship can provide a number of challenges, especially where the work styles of the contributors differ markedly. Poor time management, 'freeloading' and lack of commitment to the joint effort may signal the eventual failure of the collaboration – or at least ensure that there is no repeat of this particular collaboration. Academics will readily agree that you never really know a fellow academic until you have had the opportunity of trying to publish with them!

Concluding remarks

Appendix 1 illustrates the range of refereed publications available in the accounting area, distributed according to the ABDC (2017) listings in Australia. It provides 10 A* journals (8.1%); 20 A-rated journals (16.2%); 29 B-journals (23.4%) and 65 C-journals (52.3%). Such a categorisation follows similar efforts in the UK and New Zealand. Some academics (e.g., Beattie and Ryan, 1989; Hull and Wright, 1990; Brinn et al., 1996; Brown, 1996; Parker et al., 1998, Lowe and Lock, 2005; Kelly et al., 2009; Hussain, 2010) have addressed the quality issue and/or attempted scientific ranking methods for journal reputation.

Bonner et al. (2006) summarise the diversity of these rankings. There are always huge commonalities in these listings, but the anomalies can have significant implications for author behaviour. Northcott and Linacre (2010) detail the impact of the various research evaluation exercises and journal quality rankings on the perceived quality of outcomes and research behaviour. A number of other specified journals remain unranked, and 'predatory' journals, which seek submissions for a fee and with minimal refereeing, have been deliberately excluded. These rankings will be expected to change over time because some journals will significantly 'lift their game', while others will deteriorate in quality, both often as a result of a change in editor. In the short term, a C ranked journal editor might be starved of quality submissions, while the queues for review with A/A* journals will lengthen, along with the time to publication. This situation will be amplified for the editors of new journals, still subject to lowly rankings, or not ranked at all. Indeed concerns over ranking anomalies, and their potential impact, has persuaded many schools to abandon attempts to rank journals by quality in any formal manner.

For those seeking academic appointments or promotions, a combination of both refereed and professional journals is helpful, but with a clear emphasis on the refereed journals. In this way you can demonstrate an ability to relate to both the profession and fellow academics. Premier division publications will be particularly well regarded if they are representative of a stream of research productivity, while the résumé should include both sole-author and multiple-author publications to demonstrate that you can work alone and as part of a team. Junior academics might be persuaded to submit papers to top journals too soon in their careers, with negative implications for their motivation and retention; further, the influence of rankings alone may encourage submissions to less than totally appropriate outlets.

Journal rankings are based on reputation (driven by editor, editorial board etc.). But they do not necessarily reflect their usage by either academics or practitioners. Rowlinson et al. (2015) are critical of the RAE (now REF) journal ranking system in the UK for the distortion it causes in publication outcomes and the dysfunctional impact on the accounting research/teaching divide. Nevertheless, journal selection remains the most critical choice in the publication process, in order to ensure that we have a good 'match' of paper with the normal content of the journal. Rejected papers are not necessarily 'bad', they just do not accord with what that particular journal editor is looking for!

This chapter spells out the 'rules of the game' based on personal experience. If it facilitates one publication that would otherwise have gone unwritten, or inspires one new researcher, then it will have served its purpose.

Further reading

Ashton, D., Beattie, V.A., Broadbent, J., Brooks, C., Draper, P., Ezzamel, M., Gwilliam, D., Hodgkinson, R., Hoskin, K., Pope, P. and Stark, A. (2009) 'British Research in Accounting and Finance (2001–2007): The 2008 Research Assessment Exercise', *British Accounting Review*, 41: 199–207.

Brinn, T., Jones, M.J. and Pendlebury, M. (1996) 'UK Accountants' Perceptions of Research Journal Quality', *Accounting and Business Research*, 26 (3): 265–78.

Fogarty, T.J. (2006) 'Publishing in Academic Accounting: Practical Advice and Healthy Iconoclasm', in Z. Hoque (ed.), *Methodological Issues in Accounting Research: Theories and Methods*. London: Spiramus Press. pp. 515–34.

Lowe, A. and Locke, J. (2005) 'Perceptions of Journal Quality and Research Paradigm: Results of a Web-Based Survey of British Accounting Academics', *Accounting Organizations and Society*, 30 (1): 81–98.

Malina, M.A., Norreklit, H.S.O. and Selto, F.H. (2011) 'Lessons Learned: Advantages and Disadvantages of Mixed Method Research', *Qualitative Research in Accounting and Management*, 8 (1): 59–71.

Parker, L.D. (2012) 'Qualitative Management Accounting Research: Assessing Deliverables and Relevance', *Critical Perspectives on Accounting*, 23: 54–70.

Parker, L.D., Guthrie, J. and Gray, R. (1998) 'Accounting and Management Research: Passwords from the Gatekeepers', *Accounting, Auditing and Accountability Journal*, 11 (4): 371–402.

Rowlinson, M., Harvey, C., Kelly, A., Morris, H. and Todeva, E. (2015) 'Accounting for Research Quality: Research Audits and the Journal Rankings Debate', *Critical Perspectives on Accounting*, 26 (1): 2–22.

Truscott, D.M., Swars, S., Smith, S., Thornton-Reid, F., Zhao, Y., Dooley, C., Williams, B., Hart, I. and Matthews, M. (2010) 'A Cross-Disciplinary Examination of the Prevalence of Mixed-Methods in Educational Research: 1995–2005', *International Journal of Social Research Methodology*, 13 (4): 317–28.

Tucker, B.P., Parker, L.D. and Merchant, K.A. (2016) 'With A Little Help From Our Friends: An Empirical Investigation of Co-authoring in Accounting Research', *British Accounting Review*, 48 (2): 185–205.

Van der Stede, W., Young, S.M. and Chen, C.Z. (2005) 'Assessing the Quality of Evidence in Empirical Management Accounting Research: The Case of Survey Studies', *Accounting, Organizations and Society*, 30: 655–84.

Appendix 1

Journal Rankings (ABDC–2017)

A*

Accounting, Auditing and Accountability Journal
Accounting, Organizations and Society
Auditing: A Journal of Practice and Theory
Contemporary Accounting Research
Journal of Accounting and Economics
Journal of Accounting Research
Management Accounting Research
Review of Accounting Studies
The Accounting Review
The European Accounting Review

A

Abacus: A Journal of Accounting, Finance and Business Studies
Accounting and Business Research
Accounting and Finance
Accounting Horizons
Behavioral Research in Accounting
British Accounting Review
Critical Perspectives on Accounting
Financial Accountability and Management
Foundations and Trends in Accounting
International Journal of Accounting Information Systems
International Journal of Auditing
Issues in Accounting Education
Journal of Accounting and Public Policy

Journal of Accounting, Auditing and Finance
Journal of Accounting Literature
Journal of Business Finance and Accounting
Journal of Contemporary Accounting and Economics
Journal of International Accounting Research
Journal of Management Accounting Research
The International Journal of Accounting

B

Accounting and the Public Interest
Accounting Education: An International Journal
Accounting Forum
Accounting Historians Journal
Accounting History
Accounting History Review
Accounting in Europe
Accounting Research Journal
Advances in Accounting
Advances in Accounting Behavioral Research
Advances in Management Accounting
Asia-Pacific Journal of Accounting and Economics
Asian Review of Accounting
Australian Accounting Review
Current Issues in Auditing
International Journal of Accounting and Information Management
Journal of Accounting and Organizational Change
Journal of Accounting Education
Journal of Governmental and Nonprofit Accounting
Journal of Intellectual Capital
Journal of International Accounting, Auditing and Taxation
Journal of Public Budgeting, Accounting and Financial Management
Managerial Auditing Journal
Pacific Accounting Review
Qualitative Research in Accounting and Management
Research in Accounting Regulation
Research in Governmental and Non-Profit Accounting
Social and Environmental Accountability Journal
Sustainability Accounting, Management and Policy Journal

C

Academy of Accounting and Financial Studies Journal
Accountancy Business and the Public Interest
Accounting, Accountability and Performance
Accounting and Finance Research
Accounting and Taxation
Accounting Educators' Journal
Accounting Perspectives
Advances in Accounting Education: Teaching and Curriculum Innovations
Advances in Public Interest Accounting
African Journal of Accounting, Auditing and Finance
AIS Educator Journal
Art Law and Accounting Reporter
Asia Pacific Management Accounting Journal
Asian Academy of Management Journal of Accounting and Finance
Asian Journal of Accounting and Governance
Asian Journal of Business and Accounting
Asian Journal of Finance and Accounting
Australasian Accounting, Business and Finance Journal
Australasian Journal of Business and Behavioural Sciences
China Accounting Finance Review
China Journal of Accounting Research
Cost Management
Financial Reporting, Regulation and Governance
Global Perspectives on Accounting Education
IMA Educational Case Journal
Indonesian Management and Accounting Research
Internal Auditing
International Journal of Accounting and Finance
International Journal of Accounting and Financial Reporting
International Journal of Accounting, Auditing and Performance Evaluation
International Journal of Behavioural Accounting and Finance
International Journal of Business and Information
International Journal of Critical Accounting
International Journal of Economics and Accounting
International Journal of Government Auditing
International Journal of Managerial and Financial Accounting
Irish Accounting Review
Issues in Social and Environmental Accounting: An International Journal
Journal of Accountancy

Journal of Accounting and Management Information Systems
Journal of Accounting in Emerging Economies
Journal of Accounting, Business and Management
Journal of Accounting, Ethics and Public Policy
Journal of Applied Accounting Research
Journal of Applied Management Accounting Research
Journal of Applied Research in Accounting and Finance
Journal of Corporate Accounting and Finance
Journal of Emerging Technologies in Accounting
Journal of Financial Reporting and Accounting
Journal of Forensic and Investigative Accounting
Journal of Forensic Accounting: Auditing, Fraud and Taxation
Journal of Human Resource Costing and Accounting
Journal of Islamic Accounting and Business Research
Journal of the Asia-Pacific Centre for Environmental Accountability
Malaysian Accounting Review
Management Accounting Quarterly
Meditari Accountancy Research
Mustang Journal of Accounting and Finance
Petroleum Accounting and Financial Management Journal
Research in Accounting in Emerging Economies
Review of Accounting and Finance
The International Journal of Digital Accounting research
The Journal of Accounting Case Research
The Journal of Cost Analysis and Management
The Journal of Theoretical Accounting Research

Appendix 2

Sample Paper

This paper was originally published in *Managerial Auditing Journal*, Vol. 16, No. 1, 2001, pp. 40–9. It is reproduced here by kind permission of Emerald, UK.

Structure versus Judgement in the Audit Process: A Test of Kinney's Classification

Malcolm Smith*, Brenton Fiedler*, Bruce Brown* and Joanne Kestel**

*University of South Australia, **Murdoch University

Keywords

audit

judgement

creative accounting

Big 6

structure

accounting policy

Kinney Big 8

The authors acknowledge the helpful comments of Professors Keith Houghton, Gary Monroe and Brenda Porter, and those of delegates to BAA Conference, Manchester, April 1998.

Abstract

Sullivan (1984) suggests that the alternative audit approaches adopted by accounting firms be expressed in terms of 'structure' and 'judgement', with a division provided by the degree to which auditor judgement is replaced by structured quantitative algorithms. Cushing and Loebbecke (1986) attempt to operationalise this division by examining the guidance provided to practising auditors by their firms. Kinney (1986) extends this study by classifying accounting firms as 'structured', 'intermediate' or 'unstructured' in terms of their audit methodologies.

This study provides a test of Kinney's classification by examining the tolerance of accounting firms to accounting policy choices which have an income effect in their clients' financial statements. The paper argues that those firms with a structured audit approach will manage audit risk through a greater reliance on mechanistic procedures, resulting in a greater tolerance of income manipulation. The results are confirmatory for the period under study, but evidence is provided to suggest that audit firms have subsequently become less diversified in their approach.

1. Background

Organisational theory (e.g., Burns and Stalker, 1961; Mintzberg, 1979) has suggested the 'machine' and the 'organism' as analogies forming a basis for refined reasoning. In auditing, these analogies have been discussed in terms of the concepts of 'structure' and 'judgement' (Dirsmith and Haskins, 1991).

Auditing has variously been regarded as a well-structured and mechanistic process (e.g., Joyce and Libby, 1982) or as a judgemental process in which the audit is client dependent (e.g., Dirsmith and McAllister, 1982). Stringer (1981), among others, observes the trend towards increasing structure in auditing decision-making with the use of quantitative methods and well-documented procedures. Sullivan (1984) highlights the two camps into which auditors fall:

- those who favour structured quantitative algorithms over auditor judgement, and
- those who believe that such quantification is always unjustified because considerable professional judgement will always be required.

Cushing and Loebbecke (1986) explore this distinction with an empirical study of the guidance provided by accounting firms to their practising auditors. Their study of the policy manuals of twelve large public accounting firms revealed dramatic differences between firms in terms of the degree of 'structure' apparent in their audit methodologies, defining 'structure' as 'a systematic approach to auditing characterised by a prescribed, logical sequence of procedures, decisions and documentation steps, and by a comprehensive and integrated set of audit policies' (p. 32).

Cushing and Loebbecke noted that all firms placed a good deal of emphasis on pre-engagement planning and internal control questionnaires, but that beyond that they might be categorised as highly structured, semi-structured, partially structured and unstructured, with the extreme positions characterised by, respectively:

- quantification of audit risk; detailed comprehensive guidance; shift of audit decision-making from the auditor to the central firm, and
- no specification of the level of detail, integration or quantification.

Cushing and Loebbecke (1986) recommend that future research be directed towards identifying the differences in firms associated with structure and the consequent impact of alternative audit approaches. This recommendation provides a motivation for this study.

Kinney (1986) extends the work of Cushing and Loebbecke (1986), noting that the unstructured approach is associated with more judgement considerations being left in the hands of the field auditor. Kinney uses the results of an independent survey, together with those from the Cushing and Loebbecke study, to classify 22 auditing firms (the, then, 'Big 8' and 14 smaller firms) as follows:

structured – Deloitte, Haskins and Sells (DHS)
 – Peat, Marwick, Mitchell (PMM)
 – Touche Ross (TR)
 – two non-Big 8 firms

intermediate – Arthur Andersen (AA)
 – Arthur Young (AY)
 – Ernst & Whinney (EW)
 – three non-Big 8 firms

unstructured – Coopers & Lybrand (CL)
 – Price Waterhouse (PW)
 – nine non-Big 8 firms

It is this classification which forms the basis of the test conducted in this study. The degree of audit structure has been found to be associated with the financial disclosure patterns of clients. Morris and Nichols (1988) show that structured firms are more consistent in their treatment of accounting principle consistency exceptions; Williams and Dirsmith (1988) show that structured firms are more timely in their release of client financial statement disclosures. This study extends this area of research by examining the impact the degree of audit structure has in individual firms on the tolerance of income increasing/reducing accounting policy choices among client companies. This paper argues that audit structure impacts on such tolerance via perceptions of audit risk, the risk of incorrectly attesting that a client's financial statements are true and fair.

Dirsmith and Haskins (1991) note that audit risk as a planning construct is receiving increasing attention in the literature (e.g., Fellingham and Newman, 1985) and that high degrees of audit risk are associated with increased evidence gathering to support the audit opinion (e.g., Graham, 1985).

Contemporary auditing standards and the literature (e.g., Graham, 1985; Dirsmith and Haskins, 1991) recognise that internal control risk and inherent risk are interdependent and must be considered together in planning an audit so as to determine the desired detection risk. It has been suggested that audit structure may impact the assessment of inherent risk, whereby a more thorough evaluation of all the important quantitative variables will produce consistent auditor judgements (e.g., Joyce and Libby, 1982). Sullivan (1984) puts forward the opposing view, by suggesting that financial reporting requirements are too complex to be represented satisfactorily by quantitative measures alone, and that informed auditor judgement will always be required.

The response of audit firms to the ambiguity of approaches to inherent risk assessment suggests that 'audit firms which vary in terms of structure would orient differently to such an assessment' (Dirsmith and Haskins, 1991, p. 75). Dirsmith and Haskins conclude that researchers can usefully study auditing with reference to the public accounting firms' underlying root metaphors and world theories. Their study focused primarily on differences relevant to the assessment of audit risk using the 'mechanistic world' and 'organic world' hypotheses. The mechanistic world hypothesis sees auditing as a structured process that emphasises parts, priority relations within the parts, and the dominance of quantitative versus qualitative components of the audit judgement. Alternatively, the organic world hypothesis views auditing as a judgemental process emphasising holistic integration with more qualitative considerations forming part of the judgement process.

Dirsmith and Haskins postulate that:

> auditors' perceptions of inherent risk assessment, as well as the language they use to describe this assessment for specific clients, may be influenced by the world theory subscribed to their respective audit firms. (1991, p. 75)

Further, they state that mechanistic, structured audit firms would tend to discount their focus in audit areas that are qualitative in nature and less subject to analytic evaluation. Accordingly, such firms would be likely to focus on those parts of the audit that are 'relatively structured, programmable, concrete and familiar …'. Conversely, less structured firms are perceived to have a more balanced focus on both quantitative and qualitative forms of evidence.

These hypotheses confirm a nexus between structure of the firm and the attitude towards risk assessment. We perceive that auditors in structured firms place more reliance on their relative sophistication in, for example, outcomes of analytical review strategies (including analysis of quantitative non-financial indicators), sampling methodologies and greater strategic focus in the global audit approach. We perceive, therefore, that structured firms, while recognising the relative importance of assessment of both qualitative and quantitative risk factors in planning and conducting an audit, are able to reduce the emphasis on qualitative assessments due to their reliance on identifying risk factors using strategic quantitative analysis. It should be recognised that structured firms deploy substantial resources into technical divisions that produce high-quality generic research and technical data for use by audit field staff (e.g., industry statistics, generic qualitative industry risk assessments and pro-grammes, contemporary technical issue papers, circulars and so on). We perceive the availability of such data is significant in structured audit firms' assessment of the overall risk involved in a client. It is this reliance which leads to the proposition that structured firms may be more tolerant of accounting choices selected by audit clients for the purpose of income 'smoothing' or 'manipulation'. These firms have resources that impact their decision-making about the overall audit risk and ramifications of offering an inappropriate audit opinion. It is not suggested that the fundamental audit approach of structured firms is flawed, but the focus of structured firms seems to be more on the longer-term view of audit risk of client failure and short-term tolerance of income manipulation.[1]

In order to reach these same conclusions, it is contended that unstructured firms require a greater level of investigative qualitative assessment, and may be less tolerant of income manipulation by having access to more reliable qualitative data. Cushing and Loebbecke (1986) confirm a correlation between highly structured firms and reduced opportunities to apply professional judgement. We hypothesise that greater reliance on features of the audit firm structure (including detailed audit manuals, procedures and strategies) narrows the relative depth of qualitative assessment and broadens the toler-ance to income manipulation ('income smoothing') perceived by the firm as non-threatening to audit risk. This proposition is tested by exploring the degree to which the clients of Big 8 audit firms (classified according to Kinney, 1986) make accounting policy choices which impact on income. The circumstance not controlled by this experi-ment is the nature of the audit client portfolio, as certain audit firms attract clients that engage in certain accounting policy settings.

2. Research method

Annual reports of all 463 West Australian public companies were examined for financial years ending 1987 and 1988 to determine the incidence of accounting policy change. Those companies, numbering 96 in all, with no 1987 and/or 1988 accounts available, either because of incorporation post 30/6/87, failure prior to 30/6/88, or missing data, have necessarily been eliminated from the study. The financial years under study corre-sponded with the publication of Kinney's classification and provide an opportunity to investigate activities of Big 8 firms immediately prior to a series of mergers that reduced the numbers of the major companies.

---

[1] Here we follow developments in positive theories of accounting choice (e.g., Mian and Smith, 1990; Anderson and Zimmer, 1992a) suggesting that variation in accounting methods reflects the firm's demand for efficient contracting, is a function of differences in firm circumstances, and reflects the desire of firms not to make accounting changes which will reduce future operating profits.

A change in accounting policy from one financial year to the next was defined as a change in disclosed policy choice.[2] Although mandatory changes were identified, only the effects of discretionary changes were examined. These changes were determined by reference to the auditors' report and to the Notes to the Accounts (and in particular the note describing Significant Accounting Policies required by Australian Accounting Standard AASB 1001).

Every disclosed accounting change by the firms under observation was treated as an independent case, and data on all changes was collected, regardless of impact. After analysis, the changes were classified into five groups:

- change in response to a qualified audit report;
- mandatory changes in response to legislation and new/revised accounting standards;
- changes with indeterminate income effect (even though a clear balance sheet impact may be apparent);
- income increasing changes, including changes relating to normal and abnormal operations and changes which resulted in expenses being treated as extraordinary items even though they might reasonably have been included as normal/abnormal;
- income reducing changes resulting in reduced after-tax earnings.

Comparison of the independent assessments of accounting policy change made by the investigators resulted in substantial agreement of classification. A complete reclassification undertaken by the investigators at a three-month interval was substantially confirmatory, with only four per cent of changes being reclassified.

For all companies in the data set the following information was also collected:

- auditor (where a change of auditor had occurred over the period that observation was removed from the population);
- status (defined as 'failed', including 'failing', or 'non-failed');
- size, measured by total assets; and
- industry group.

The information was gathered to test the possible impact of these variables on the sample results. It was considered that the hypothesised results would be strengthened if the allowance of changes to accounting policies is not identifiably linked to auditor change, nor influenced by the financial condition, size or industry of the company being sampled.

---

[2] In so doing we follow Anderson and Zimmer (1992b, p. 58) in suggesting that 'accounting techniques are "independently" chosen each year, dependent on firm circumstances'.

3. Results

The analysis of the population of the 367 companies for which complete data was available revealed that 176 companies made accounting policy changes, resulting in a total of 278 changes, as follows:

Response to audit qualification	9
Mandatory change	109
Indeterminate income effect	52
Income increasing	79
Income reducing	29
	278

The accounting policy changes were distributed across companies in accordance with

Total accounting policy changes	No. of companies	Mandatory changes	No. of companies	Discretionary changes	No. of companies
0	191	0	276	0	249
1	105	1	73	1	77
2	48	2	18	2	32
3	17			3	8
4	4			4	1
5	2				
Total companies	367	Total companies	367	Total companies	367
Total changes	278	Total changes	109	Total changes	169

Figure 1

Of the nine companies with three or more discretionary accounting policy changes, seven were audited by Big 8 companies, five were from the extractive industry, only one was a 'large' company and four 'small' as designated in Figure 4. Of the 28 changes made, half were income increasing.

The detailed figures in Figure 2 enable a number of statistical evaluations to be made concerning the association of choice of auditor with the distribution of accounting policy changes. The tests described below in Figures 2a–2d are all based on data drawn from Figure 2.

The Big 8/non-Big 8 split is a significant factor in determining the incidence of accounting policy changes. Figure 2a gives $P < .002$ when all changes are considered, while Figure 2b yields $P < .01$ when mandatory changes are excluded.

AUDITOR	COMPANIES			ACCOUNTING POLICY CHANGES						TOTAL
	No. of companies	No changes	Policy changes	Mandatory	Response to AQ	Neutral	Income above line	Increasing Below line	Income reducing	
(DHS) DELOITTES	15	6	9	7	1	3	1	3	2	17
(PMH) PEAT MARWICK	18	9	9	3	0	3	2	3	2	13
(TR) TOUCHE ROSS	26	8	18	11	0	2	8	9	2	32
(AA) ARTHUR ANDERSEN	43	18	25	11	4	5	9	4	5	38
(AY) ARTHUR YOUNG	38	19	19	9	0	5	7	0	3	24
(EW) ERNST & WHINNEY	32	15	17	11	0	6	7	6	2	32
(CL) COOPERS & LYBRAND 25	13	12	11	1	2	1	0	1	16	
(PW) PRICE WATERHOUSE 18	9	9	8	0	4	0	0	1	13	
BIG '8'	215	97	118	71	6	30	35	25	18	185
NON-BIG '8'	152	94	58	38	3	22	8	11	11	93
TOTAL	367	191	176	109	9	52	43	36	29	278

Figure 2 Auditor impact on accounting policy change

Among Big 8 firms, the Kinney classification appears to have a bearing on accounting policy changes. In Figure 2c, the numbers of policy changes are indexed against the three levels I, II, III of the Kinney classification of Big 8 accounting firms. Although a general chi-squared test is not significant ($\chi^2. = 1.5$), when the natural ordering of the Kinney classification categories is considered, a test based on Kendall's tau, counting numbers of concordant and discordant pairs of observations, yields $z = -1.68$ and $P < .05$. For details of the Kendall tau test see Brown (1988), and for more on the general topic of testing contingency tables with ordered categories, see Best and Rayner (1996), Beh and Davey (1999), and references therein.

The conclusion in Figure 2c is strengthened considerably if mandatory accounting changes are excluded. Figure 2d has the details. Even a general test which ignores the ordering of the Kinney classification categories yields $\chi^2_2 = 7.84$, $P < .00$, while a Kendall tau test, which considers the ordered Kinney categories, gives $z = 2.295$, $P = .011$.

Further analysis can be carried out on the data in Figure 2 to investigate the association of 'income-changing events' with either the Big 8/non-Big 8 categorisation, or the Kinney classification of accounting firms. Because multiple 'income-changing events' (i.c.es) can be associated with single firms, a different form of statistical test is required.

However, a simple analysis results if the standard Poisson model is applied to the occurrence of i.c.es. Observed cell counts are realisations of independent Poisson random variables whose parameters are products of an underlying Poisson rate with the number of firms contributing to the count. Then, using the standard fact that the distribution of a collection of Poisson variables *conditional upon their sum* is just multinomial (or binomial for just two variables), the data structure reduces to testing a single row of observed counts against an expected pattern. For this situation, a goodness-of-fit test is standard.

For example, for the 'Big 8' versus 'non-Big 8' comparison, the data in Figure 2 yields:

	No changes made	Some changes made	Totals
'Big 8'	97	118	215
'Non-Big 8'	94	58	152
Totals	191	176	367

Figure 2a Incidence of policy changes and accounting firm classification

($\chi^2_1 = 9.98$, P $\leq$ .00.)

	No changes made	Some changes made	Totals
'Big 8'	97	47	144
'Non-Big 8'	94	20	114
Totals	191	67	258

Figure 2b Accounting firm classification and incidence of policy changes, excluding mandatory changes

($\chi^2_1 = 7.43$, P < .00.)

	Big 8	non-Big 8	Totals
Number of i.c.es	78	30	108
Number of accounting firms	215	152	367
Expected numbers	63.270	44.730	108

(Comparing 'observed' (78, 30) with 'expected' (63.27, 44.73) yields $\chi_1^2 = 8.27$, P = .00.)

Kinney classification	No changes made	Some changes made	Totals
I (DHS, PMH, TR)	23	36	59
II (AA, AY, EW)	52	61	113
III (CL, PW)	22	21	43
Totals	97	118	215

Figure 2c Incidence of policy changes and Kinney classification of Big 8 accounting firms

(Kendall tau test for ordered categories contingency tables gives z = 1.68, P < .05.)

Kinney classification	No changes made	Some changes made	Totals
I	23	15	38
ii	52	30	82
III	22	2	24
Totals	97	47	144

Figure 2d Incidence of policy changes and Kinney classification of Big 8 accounting firms, omitting mandatory changes

(Kendall tau test for ordered categories contingency tables gives z = 2.295, P = .011.)

Kinney classification	I	II	III	Totals
Number of i.c.es	32	43	3	78
Number of companies	59	113	43	215
Expected numbers	21.405	40.995	15.600	78

KINNEY CLASSIFICATION	INCOME INCREASING		INCOME REDUCING	TOTAL CHANGES	NO. OF COMPANIES
	ABOVE LINE	BELOW LINE			
GROUP 1	11	15	6	62	59
GROUP 2	23	10	10	94	113
GROUP 3	1	0	2	29	43
BIG '8'	35	25	18	185	215
NON-BIG '8'	8	11	11	93	152
TOTAL	43	36	29	278	367

Figure 3 Classification of income increasing/reducing changes 1986

The analysis of above the line and below the line changes does not take into account changes to the concept of extraordinary items since 1986; classification of changes as extraordinary items is now comparatively rare.

4. Discussion

The results clearly show that those audit firms classified as 'judgemental' in the Kinney (1986) categorisation are associated with far fewer client firms that report accounting policy choices, whether these increase or decrease reported income. Within the then Big 8, around whom this investigation has been conducted, Coopers & Lybrand and Price Waterhouse appear to be less tolerant of income manipulation through accounting policy choice than their fellow auditors. However, several other factors may be contributing to the observed outcomes of this study, and they are considered here.

A number of authors (e.g., Morse and Richardson, 1983) have suggested that size of company and industrial sector will impact on the incidence of income increasing accounting policies. Eichenseher and Danos (1981) note the specialisation of auditors in particular industries. It might, therefore, be that accounting policy changes are associated with company size or industry, rather than auditor. Figure 4 details the distribution of companies by size, across auditors and auditor groupings.

AUDITOR SIZE	SMALL (TA < $10m)	INTERMEDIATE	LARGE (TA > $60m)	TOTAL
Peat Marwick	11	4	3	18
Touche Ross	15	9	2	26
Deloittes	5	7	3	15
AUDITOR GP 1	31	20	8	59
Arthur Andersen	26	13	4	43
Arthur Young	15	13	10	38
Ernst & Whinney	16	14	2	32
AUDITOR GP 2	57	40	16	113
Coopers & Lybrand	10	7	8	25
Price Waterhouse	6	7	5	18
AUDITOR GP 3	16	14	13	43
TOTAL	104	74	37	215

Figure 4 Auditor and client size

There is some, though weak, evidence suggesting that across Big 8 auditors, an association exists between Kinney groupings and the size of client companies. While a conventional chi-squared test in Figure 4a is not significant, it can be noted that both classifications are ordinal (i.e., client size, and Kinney classification) and a Kendall tau test for association yields $z = 1.546$, $P = .06$. This P-value approaches significance, and raises the question that the Kinney classification may influence accounting policy changes indirectly through being associated with the sizes of client companies. However, this can have only a limited explanatory effect, because the strength of association throughout Figures 2a–2d is stronger than the association shown in Figure 4a.

Kinney classification	Size small	Size intermediate	Size large	Totals
I	31	20	8	59
II	57	40	16	113
III	16	14	13	43
Total	104	74	37	215

Figure 4a Auditor and client size totals

AUDITOR INDUSTRY GROUPING	Group 1	Group 2	Group 3	TOTAL
Research & Consultancy	7	11	2	20
Retail & Distribution	8	13	6	27
Manufacturing & Construction	5	16	1	22
Financial & Investment	10	16	10	36
Extractive	27	45	19	91
Leisure	2	6	2	10
Non-Bank Financial Institutions	0	6	3	9
TOTAL	59	113	43	215

Figure 5 Distribution of auditor across industry groupings

The distribution of companies across the Big 8 auditors in this sample does not appear to be influenced by industry grouping of client company; the data in Figure 5, after combining the small categories *Leisure* and *Non-Bank Financial Institutions* in order to produce expected values, yields $\chi^2_{10} = 10.77$ not significant.

Cravens, Flagg and Glover (1994) suggest that firms such as Price Waterhouse and Coopers & Lybrand have a client base which is associated with lower market risk, greater profitability and lower leverage ratios. It might, therefore, be that accounting policy changes are associated with companies and industries with inferior financial performance. The z-score measures of financial distress, due to Houghton and Smith (1991), and modelled specifically for the West Australian business environment, were used to compare financial performance across auditor and industry groupings. Figure 6 details differences in mean financial performance across the seven industry groupings.

The Non-Bank Financial Institutions and Extractive sectors are apparently the top performers, while the Financial & Investment sector exhibits the greatest financial distress. The data in Figure 6 can be used to construct an ANOVA to test for differences in z-scores of financial distress across industry groupings (see Figure 6a).

INDUSTRY GROUP	NO. OF COMPANIES	Z-SCORE	
		MEAN	S.D.
Research & Consultancy	20	0.730	2.279
Retail & Distribution	27	0.716	2.029
Manufacturing & Construction	22	0.202	2.721
Financial & Investment	36	−0.314	2.777
Extractive	91	0.724	1.728
Leisure	10	−0.019	1.508
Non-Bank F.I.	9	1.531	1.186
TOTAL	215	0.482	2.141

Figure 6 Industry grouping and financial performance

Source	df	SSQ	Analysis of variance Mean SQ	F
Sectors	6	44.947	7.49	1.66 (P > 0.1)
Error	208	938.103	4.51	
Total	214	983.050		

Figure 6a ANOVA to test for differences in financial distress across industry groupings

Thus there is no evidence suggesting that financial performance differs across the industry groupings represented. Also, variation in financial performance apparently does not extend across the Kinney auditor classification. Figure 7 details differences in mean financial performance across auditor and auditor grouping.

The data in Figure 7 can be used to construct an ANOVA to test for differences in mean z-scores of financial distress across the Kinney auditor groupings (see Figure 7a).

AUDITOR	NO. OF COMPANIES	Z-SCORE	
		MEAN	S.D.
Peat Marwick	18	0.784	1.590
Touche Ross	26	−0.130	1.349
Deloittes	15	0.749	1.156
AUDITOR GP 1	59	0.372	1.432
Arthur Andersen	43	−0.203	3.399
Arthur Young	38	0.018	1.746
Ernst & Whinney	32	0.790	1.621
AUDITOR GP 2	113	0.489	2.524
Coopers & Lybrand	25	0.784	1.935
Price Waterhouse	18	0.379	1.798
AUDITOR GP 3	43	0.615	1.868

Figure 7 Auditor and client financial performance

The ANOVA in Figure 7a is not significant. However, improved financial performance is apparent as we progress from Group 1, through Group 2, to Group 3; however, the variability in Group 2 makes the intra-group differences in z-scores so large relatively that the differences between the groups are not statistically different. On an individual auditor level, mean z-scores are highest for Arthur Young (Group 2), Coopers & Lybrand (Group 3) and Deloittes (Group 1) so there is no direct correspondence between the Kinney classification of audit structure and financial performance of client.

Analysis of variance				
Source	df	SSQ	Mean SQ	F
Between Auditor Groups	2	7.012	3.506	<1, not significant
Between Companies:				
within group 1	2	11.739	5.870	<1
within group 2	2	21.756	10.878	1.30, not significant
within group 3	1	1.717	1.717	<1
Error	206	931.487	4.522	

Figure 7a ANOVA to test for differences in mean levels of financial distress across the Kinney auditor classification

It might be argued that the outcomes of this research lack external validity, in that they are applicable only to Western Australia, and to a period in the late 1980s when the Big 8 still prevailed. Both issues are investigated below.

Smith (1998) re-evaluates the UK data reported by Smith (1992) to determine the link between auditor and twelve accounting manipulation techniques undertaken by the 208 largest quoted companies by market capitalisation. Smith (1998) identifies seven of these techniques to have a clear income effect, and explores the auditor connection for the 185 companies then associated with the Big 6 auditors. He notes that KPMG are associated with greater than average, and both Price Waterhouse and Coopers & Lybrand less than average, employment of pre-acquisition write-downs, and Price Waterhouse with less than average employment of extraordinary and exceptional items. Overall it is apparent that KPMG have significantly more manipulations than anticipated, and Coopers & Lybrand significantly fewer, but otherwise the direction of the auditor-effect is less clearly specified than in the findings of the present study. Certainly the 1992 UK data provides less support for the 1987 Kinney classification than the foregoing analysis.

Smith and Kestel (1999) conduct a time-series analysis of accounting policy changes over the period 1988–94 for the same West Australian companies that provide the data set for this study. However, only 49 companies survive independently across the whole period, and they make a relatively small number of policy changes (67 in all, but only 40 for the 'Big' group of auditors). The limited number of observations restrict the level of statistical analysis possible, but it is still clear that the auditor differences apparent in 1987 are not nearly so prominent across the subsequent period. The Group 3 (unstructured) auditors, Price Waterhouse and Coopers & Lybrand, had far fewer income reducing accounting policy changes than anticipated, but in other respects the three groupings are indistinguishable.

A number of studies have emphasised the importance of corporate image for the well-being of accounting firms. Scott and Van der Walt (1994) suggest that corporate image is the most important characteristic guiding firm selection by clients; Beattie and Fearnley (1995) find that 'reputation/quality' is their most important characteristic, Armstrong and Smith (1996) that professionalism is the most important aspect of service quality to the clients of Big 6 accountants. Image is therefore an important component of accounting/auditing firms in their pursuit of diversity and product differentiation. Moizer (1998) surveyed financial directors of UK companies in both 1987 and 1996 to develop a corporate personality for the big accounting firms. He looked at a number of phrases used to describe accounting firms, and employed a semantic differential to measure the degree to which directors associated with each description. The observed diversity among firms in 1987 (much of it attributable to the extreme perceptions associated with Arthur Andersen and Deloittes, Haskins and Sells), allowed firms to be clustered into a four-group structure based on corporate image:

Group A (CL, PW, KPMG); Group B (EW, AY); Group C (DHS, TR); Group D (AA)

This grouping closely corresponds with the Kinney classification of the same year.

The corresponding 1996 survey shows Arthur Andersen still to be perceived as the 'most different' firm from its competitors, but that much of the diversity has evaporated, so that a revised clustering is more appropriate:

Group A (CL, PW, KPMG); Group B (EY, D&T); Group C (AA)

The reduction in the diversity among the world's accounting firms 1987–96 in the Moizer study mirrors the findings from the studies of accounting policy changes above. The number of major players has fallen from eight to (currently) five, and at the same time the profiles of surviving firms have come together. All of the studies cluster (CL and PW) and (EW and AY) together, suggesting a closeness of corporate cultures which might facilitate successful merger.

5. Conclusions

The results from this study identify levels of accounting income policy change associated with auditor grouping in a similar manner to that identified by Kinney (1986) and Moizer (1998) for the corresponding time period. The closeness of operations of firms within the groups on a number of activities identified may help to explain the success, or otherwise, of subsequent merger activity among the, then, Big 8.

More recent empirical evidence suggests that the degree of diversification among the largest auditing firms has declined since the late 1980s with a more structured approach now being more widely adopted. However, differences between firms and the way in which they are perceived persist.

The findings of these studies may have implications for auditor choice, auditor switching and future merger activity among auditors, and warrant further research focusing on the activities of the Big 5 worldwide.

6. References

Anderson, D. and I. Zimmer (1992a) 'Reactions to Regulation of Accounting for Goodwill', *Accounting and Finance*, Vol. 32, No. 2, pp. 27–50.

Anderson, D. and I. Zimmer (1992b) 'Time Series Analysis of Accounting Policy Choice: Reply', *Accounting and Finance*, Vol. 32, No. 2, pp. 57–60.

Armstrong, R.W. and M. Smith (1996) 'Marketing Cues and Perceptions of Service Quality in the Selection of Accounting Firms', *Journal of Customer Service in Marketing and Management*, Vol. 2, No. 2, pp. 37–60.

Beattie, V.A. and S. Fearnley (1995) 'The Importance of Audit Firm Characteristics and the Drivers of Auditor Change in UK Listed Companies', *Accounting and Business Research*, Vol. 25, No. 100, Autumn, pp. 227–39.

Beh, E.J. and P.J. Davy (1999) 'Partitioning Pearson's Chi-squared Statistic for a Partially Ordered Three-way Contingency Table', *Australian and New Zealand Journal of Statistics*, Vol. 2, pp. 233–46.

Best, D.J. and J.C.W. Rayner (1996) 'Nonparametric Analysis for Doubly Ordered Two-way Contingency Tables', *Biometrics*, Vol. 52, pp. 1153–6.

Brown, B.M. (1988) 'Kendall's tau and Contingency Tables', *Australian Journal of Statistics*, Vol. 30, pp. 276–91.

Burns, T. and G.M. Stalker (1961) *The Management of Innovation*. London: Tavistock.

Cravens, K.S., J.C. Flagg and H.D. Glover (1994) 'A Comparison of Client Characteristics by Auditor Attributes: Implications for the Auditor Selection Process', *Managerial Auditing Journal*, Vol. 9, No. 3, pp. 27–36.

Cushing, B.E. and J.K. Loebbecke (1986) *Comparison of Audit Methodologies of Large Accounting Firms*, Studies in Accounting Research, No. 26, American Accounting Association, Sarasota, Florida.

Dirsmith, M.W. and M.E. Haskins (1991) 'Inherent Risk Assessment and Audit Firm Technology: A Contrast in World Theories', *Accounting Organizations and Society*, Vol. 16, No. 1, pp. 61–90.

Dirsmith, M.W. and J.P. McAllister (1982) 'The Organic vs. The Mechanistic Audit', *Journal of Accounting, Auditing and Finance*, Fall, pp. 60–74.

Eichenseher, J. and P. Danos (1981) 'The Analysis of Industry Specific Auditor Concentration: Towards an Explanatory Model', *The Accounting Review*, July, pp. 479–92.

Fellingham, J.C. and D.P. Newman (1985) 'Strategic Considerations in Auditing', *The Accounting Review*, October, pp. 634–50.

Graham, L.E. (1985) 'Audit Risk – Part III', *CPA Journal*, October, pp. 36–43.

Joyce, E.J. and R. Libby (1982) 'Behavioral Studies of Audit Decision Making', *Journal of Accounting Literature*, Spring, pp. 103–21.

Houghton, K.A. and M. Smith (1991) 'Loan Risk and the Anticipation of Corporate Distress: West Australian Evidence', in K. Davis and I. Harper (eds), *Risk Management in Financial Institutions*. Sydney, NSW: Allen & Unwin, pp. 61–74.

Kinney, W. (1984) 'Discussants' Response to an Analysis of the Audit Framework Focusing on Inherent Risk and the Role of Statistical Sampling in Compliance Testing', in H.F. Stettler and N.A. Ford (eds), *Auditing Symposium VII*. University of Kansas, pp. 127–32.

Kinney, W. (1986) 'Audit Technology and Preferences for Auditing Standards', *Journal of Accounting and Economics*, Vol. 8, No. 1, pp. 73–89.

Mian, S.L. and C.W. Smith (1990) 'Incentives for Unconsolidated Financial Reporting', *Journal of Accounting and Economics*, Vol. 12, pp. 141–71.

Mintzberg, H. (1979) *The Structuring of Organizations*. Englewood Cliffs, NJ: Prentice Hall.

Moizer, P. (1998) 'The Corporate Images of the 1996 Big Six and the 1987 Big Eight', *Conference of the European Accounting Association*, Antwerp, April.

Morris, M. and W. Nichols (1988) 'Consistency Exceptions: Materiality Judgements and Audit Firm Structure', *The Accounting Review*, April, pp. 237–54.

Morse, D. and G. Richardson (1983) 'The LIFO/FIFO Decision', *Journal of Accounting Research*, Vol. 21, Spring, pp. 106–27.

Scott, D.R. and N.T. Van der Walt (1994) 'Choice Criteria in the Selection of International Accounting Firms', *European Journal of Marketing*, Vol. 29, No. 1, pp. 27–39.

Smith, M. (1998) 'Creative Accounting: The Auditor Effect', *Managerial Auditing Journal*, Vol. 13, No. 3, pp. 155–8.

Smith, M. and J. Kestel (1999) 'A Time-Series Analysis of Accounting Policy Changes: West Australian Evidence', *School of Accounting Seminar Series*, University of South Australia.

Smith, T. (1992) *Accounting for Growth*. London: Century Business.

Stringer, K.W. (1981) 'Future Directions in Auditing Research', *The Auditor's Report*, Summer, pp. 3–4.

Sullivan, J.D. (1984) 'The Case for the Unstructured Audit Approach', in H.F. Stettler and N.A. Ford (eds), *Auditing Symposium VII*. University of Kansas.

Williams, D.D. and M.W. Dirsmith (1988) 'The Effects of Audit Technology on Auditor Efficiency: Auditing and the Timelines of Client Earnings Announcements', *Accounting Organizations and Society*, Vol. 13, No. 5, pp. 487–508.

References

Abdel-Khalik, A.R. and Ajinkya, B.B. (1979) *Empirical Research in Accounting: A Methodological Viewpoint*, American Accounting Association, Accounting Education Series, 4. Sarasota FL.

Abdolmohammadi, M. and Wright, A. (1987) 'An Examination of the Effects of Experience and Task Complexity on Audit Judgments', *The Accounting Review*, January: 1–13.

Abernethy, M.A., Chua, W.F., Luckett, P.F. and Selto, F.H. (1999) 'Research in Managerial Accounting: Learning from Others' Experiences', *Accounting and Finance*, 39 (1): 1–27.

Abernethy, M.A., Horne, M., Lillis, A.M., Malina, M.A. and Selto, F.H. (2005) 'A Multi-method Approach to Building Causal Performance Maps from Expert Knowledge', *Management Accounting Research*, 16 (2): 135–55.

Abrahamson, E. and Amir, E. (1996) 'The Information Content of the President's Letter to Shareholders', *Journal of Business Finance and Accounting*, 23 (8): 1157–82.

Abrahamson, E. and Park, C. (1994) 'Concealment of Negative Organizational Outcomes: An Agency Theory Perspective', *Academy of Management Journal*, 37 (5): 1302–34.

Aerts, W. (2005) 'Picking up the Pieces: Impression Management in the Retrospective Attributional Framing of Accounting Outcomes', *Accounting, Organizations and Society*, 30 (6): 493–517.

Agarwal, V. and Taffler, R.J. (2007) 'Twenty-five Years of the Taffler Z-score Model: Does It Really Have Predictive Value?', *Accounting and Business Research*, 37 (4): 285–97.

Agnew, N.M. and Pike, S.W. (1994) *The Science Game: An Introduction to Research in the Social Sciences*, 6th edn. Englewood Cliffs, NJ: Prentice Hall.

Ahrens, T. (2008) 'Overcoming the Subjective–Objective Divide in Interpretive Management Accounting Research', *Accounting, Organizations and Society*, 33: 292–7.

Ahrens, T. and Chapman, C. (2006) 'Doing Qualitative Field Research in Management Accounting: Positioning Data to Contribute to Theory', *Accounting, Organizations and Society*, 31 (8): 819–41.

Ahrens, T. and Dent, J.F. (1998) 'Accounting and Organizations: Realizing the Richness of Field Research', *Journal of Management Accounting Research*, 10: 1–39.

Aiken, M. and Hage, J. (1968) 'Organizational Interdependence and Intra-organizational Structure', *American Sociological Review*, December: 912–30.

Alcouffe, S., Berland, N. and Levant, Y. (2008) 'Actor-networks and the Diffusion of Managerial Accounting Innovations: A Comparative Study', *Management Accounting Research*, 19 (1): 1–17.

Aljifri, K. and Hussainey, K. (2007) 'The Determinants of Forward-Looking Information in Annual Reports of UAE Companies', *Managerial Auditing Journal*, 21 (5): 476–96.

Allison, P.D. (2009) *Fixed Effects Regression Models*. California: SAGE Publications.

Altman, E.I. (1968) 'Financial Ratios, Discriminant Analysis and the Prediction of Corporate Bankruptcy', *Journal of Finance*, 23 (4): 580–609.

Altman, E.I. (1993) *Corporate Financial Distress and Bankruptcy: A Complete Guide to Predicting and Avoiding Distress and Profiting from Bankruptcy*, 2nd edn. New York: Wiley.

Altman, E.I., Haldeman, R. and Narayanan, P. (1977) 'Zeta Analysis: A New Model to Identify Bankruptcy Risk of Corporations', *Journal of Banking and Finance*, 1 (1): 29–54.

Altman, E.I., Marco, G. and Varetto, F. (1994) 'Corporate Distress Diagnosis: Comparisons using Linear Discriminant Analysis and Neural Networks (the Italian Experience)', *Journal of Banking and Finance*, 18 (3): 505–29.

Amernic, J.H. and Craig, R. (2006) *CEO Speak: The Language of Corporate Leadership*. Montréal, Ithaca: McGill-Queens University Press.

Amernic, J.H. and Craig, R. (2008) 'A Privatization Success Story: Accounting and Narrative Expression over Time', *Accounting, Auditing and Accountability Journal*, 21 (8): 1085–115.

Anderson, M.J. (1985) 'Some Evidence on the Effect of Verbalization on Process: A Methodological Note', *Journal of Accounting Research*, 23: 843–53.

Anderson, M.J. (1988) 'A Comparative Analysis of Information Search and Evaluation Behavior of Professional and Non-professional Financial Analysts', *Accounting, Organizations and Society*, 13 (5): 431–46.

Anderson, M.J. and Potter, G.S (1998) 'On the Use of Regression and Verbal Protocol Analysis in Modeling Analysts' Behavior in an Unstructured Task Environment: A Methodological Note', *Accounting, Organizations and Society*, 23 (5/6): 435–50.

Anderson, T.W. and Rubin, H. (1949) 'Estimation of the Parameters of a Single Equation in a Complete System of Stochastic Equations', *Annals of Mathematics and Statistics*, 20: 46–63.

Andon, P., Baxter, J. and Chua, W.F. (2007) 'Accounting Change as Relational Drifting: A Field Study of Experiments with Performance Measurement', *Management Accounting Research*, 18: 273–308.

Andrews, F.M. (1984) 'Construct Validity and Error Components of Survey Methods: A Structural Modelling Approach', *Public Opinion Quarterly*, 48: 409–42.

Ansari, S. and Bell, J. (1991) 'Symbolism, Collectivism and Rationality in Organizational Control', *Accounting, Auditing and Accountability Journal*, 4 (2): 4–27.

Ansari, S. and Euske, K.J. (1987) 'Rational, Rationalizing and Reifying Uses of Accounting Data in Organizations', *Accounting Organizations and Society*, 12 (6): 549–70.

Argenti, J. (1993) *Your Organization. What Is It For?* London: McGraw Hill.

Argyris, C. (1952) *The Impact of Budgets on People*. Ithaca, NY: Controllership Foundation Inc., Cornell University.

Armstrong, P. (1987) 'The Rise of Accounting Controls in British Capitalist Enterprises', *Accounting, Organizations and Society*, 12 (5): 415–36.

Armstrong, P. (2008) 'Calling Out For More: Comment on the Future of Interpretive Accounting Research', *Critical Perspectives on Accounting*, 19 (6): 867–79.

Arrington, C.E. and Francis, J.R. (1989) 'Letting the Chat out of the Bag: Deconstruction, Privilege and Accounting research', *Accounting, Organizations and Society*, 14 (1/2): 1–28.

Arrington, C.E. and Puxty, A.G. (1991) 'Accounting, Interests and Rationality: A Communicative Relation', *Critical Perspectives on Accounting*, 2 (1): 31–58.

Ashton, R.H. (1974) 'An Experimental Study of Internal Control Judgments', *Journal of Accounting Research*, Spring: 143–57.

Ashton, R.H. (1983) *Research in Audit Decision-Making: Rationale, Evidence and Implications*. Vancouver: The Canadian General Accountants Research Foundation.

Ashton, R.H. and Ashton, A.H. (eds) (1995) *Judgment and Decision-Making Research in Accounting and Auditing*. New York: Cambridge University Press.

Ashton, R.H. and Kramer, S.S. (1980) 'Students as Surrogates in Behavioral Accounting Research: Some Evidence', *Journal of Accounting Research*, 18: 1–15.

Askarany, D. and Smith, M. (2008) 'The Diffusion of Management Accounting Innovation: A Longitudinal Study of PACIA', *Managerial Auditing Journal*, 23 (9): 900–916.

Assal, H. and Keon, J. (1982) 'Nonsampling vs. Sampling Error in Survey Research', *Journal of Marketing*, 46, Spring: 114–23.

Atkinson, A.A. and Shaffir, W. (1998) 'Standards for Field Research in Management Accounting', *Journal of Management Accounting Research*, 10: 41–67.

Baddeley, M.C. and Barrowclough, D.V. (2009) *Running Regressions: A Practical Guide to Quantitative Research in Economics, Finance and Development Studies*. New York: Cambridge University Press.

Bai, C.E., Liu, Q.L., Lu, J., Song, F.M. and Zhang, J.X. (2004) 'Corporate Governance and Market Valuation in China', *Journal of Comparative Economics*, 32 (4): 599–616.

Bai, J. and Kao, C. (2006) 'On the estimation and inference of a panel co-integration model with cross-sectional dependence', in B. Baltagi (ed.) *Contributions to Economic Analysis*. New York: John Wiley & Sons Inc., 3–30.

Baiman, S. (1982) 'Agency Research in Managerial Accounting: A Survey', *Journal of Accounting Literature*, 1: 154–213.

Baiman, S. (1990) 'Agency Research in Management Accounting: A Second Look', *Accounting, Organizations and Society*, 15 (4): 341–71.

Baines, A. and Langfield-Smith, K. (2003) 'Antecedents to Management Accounting Change: A Structural Equation Approach', *Accounting, Organizations and Society*, 28 (6): 675–98.

Baker, C.R. and Bettner, M.S. (1997) 'Interpretive and Critical Research in Accounting: A Commentary on its Absence from Mainstream Accounting Research', *Critical Perspectives on Accounting*, 18 (4): 293–310.

Ball, R. and Brown, P. (1968) 'An Empirical Evaluation of Accounting Income Numbers', *Journal of Accounting Research*, 6: 159–78.

Ball, R. and Brown, P. (2014) 'Ball and Brown (1968): A Retrospective', *The Accounting Review*, 89 (1): 1–26.

Baltagi, B.H. (ed.) (2005) *Econometric Analysis of Panel Data*. Chichester: John Wiley.

Bandura, A. (1977) *Social Learning Theory*. Englewood Cliffs, NJ: Prentice Hall.

Barrett, M., Cooper, D.J. and Jamal, K. (2005) 'Globalisation and the Co-ordinating of Work in a Global Audit', *Accounting, Organizations and Society*, 25 (2): 1–24.

Barrow, J.C. (1977) 'The Variables of Leadership: A Review and Conceptual Framework', *Academy of Management Review*, 2 (2): 231–51.

Baruch, Y. (1999) 'Response Rates in Academic Studies – A Comparative Analysis', *Human Relations*, 52 (4): 421–38.

Baskerville, R.L. and Wood-Harper, A.T. (1996) 'A Critical Perspective on Action Research as a Method for Information Systems Research', *Journal of Information Technology*, 11: 235–46.

Bauman, M.P. (1996) 'A Review of Fundamental Analysis Research in Accounting', *Journal of Accounting Literature*, 15: 1–33.

Bayne, C.K., Beauchamp, J.J., Kane, V.E. and McCabe, G.P. (1983) 'Assessment of Fisher and Logistic Linear and Quadratic Discriminant Models', *Computational Statistics and Data Analysis*, 1: 257–73.

Beattie, V.A. and Ryan, R.J. (1989) 'Performance Indices and Related Measures of Journal Reputation in Accounting', *British Accounting Review*, 21: 267–78.

Beattie, V.A. and Thomson, S. (2007) 'Lifting the Lid on the Use of Content Analysis to Investigate Intellectual Capital Disclosures in Corporate Annual Reports', *Accounting Forum*, 31 (2): 129–63.

Beattie, V.A., McInnes, B. and Fearnley, S. (2004) 'A Methodology for Analyzing and Evaluating Narratives in Annual Reports: A Comprehensive Descriptive Profile and Metrics for Disclosure Quality Attributes', *Accounting Forum*, 28: 205–36.

Beaver, W.H. (1966) 'Financial Ratios as Predictors of Failure', *Empirical Research in Accounting* (supplement to *Journal of Accounting Research*): 71–111.

Becker, S. and Green, D. (1962) 'Budgeting and Employee Behaviour', *The Journal of Business*, October: 392–402.

Bedford, N.M. (1965) *Income Determination Theory: An Accounting Framework*. London: Addison-Wesley.

Bem, D.J. (1972) 'Self-Perception Theory', in L. Berkowitz (ed.), *Advances in Experimental Social Psychology*, 6: 1–62.

Beneish, M.D. (1997) Detecting GAAP Violation: Implications for Assessing Earnings Management Among Firms with Extreme Financial Performance', *Journal of Accounting and Public Policy*, 16 (3): 271–309.

Beneish, M.D. (1999) 'The Detection of Earnings Management', *Financial Analysts Journal*, 5 (5): 24–36.

Bennett, R. (1991) 'How is Research Carried Out?', in N.C. Smith and P. Dainty (eds), *The Management Research Handbook*. London: Routledge.

Berelson, B. (1952) *Content Analysis in Communication Research*. London: Free Press.

Berry, A.J., Capps, T., Cooper, D., Ferguson, P., Hopper, T. and Lowe, E.A. (1985) 'Management Control in an Area of the NCB: Rationales of Accounting in a Public Enterprise', *Accounting, Organizations and Society*, 10 (1): 3–28.

Berry, A.J., Laughton, E. and Otley, D.T. (1991) 'Control in a Financial Services Company (RIF): A Case Study', *Management Accounting Research*, 2 (2): 109–39.

Bettman, J.R. and Weitz, B.A. (1983) 'Attributions in the Boardroom: Causal Reasoning in Corporate Annual Reports', *Administrative Science Quarterly*, 28: 165–83.

Birnberg, J. Shields, M. and Young, S. (1990) 'The Case For Multiple Methods in Empirical Research in Management Accounting (With an Illustration from Budget Setting)', *Journal of Management Accounting Research*, 2: 33–66.

Birnberg, J.G., Turopolec, L. and Young, S.M. (1983) 'The Organizational Context of Accounting', *Accounting, Organizations and Society*, 8 (2/3): 111–29.

Bisbe, J., Batista-Fouget, J. and Chenhall, R.H. (2007) 'Defining Management Accounting Constructs: A Methodological Note on the Risks of Conceptual Misspecification', *Accounting Organizations and Society*, 32 (7): 789–820.

Black, B.S., Jang, H. and Kim, W. (2006) 'Does Corporate Governance Predict Firms' Market Values? Evidence from Korea', *Journal of Law, Economics and Organization*, 22 (2): 366–413.

Black, F. and Scholes, M. (1973) 'The Pricing of Options and Corporate Liabilities', *Journal of Political Economy*, 81: 637–54.

Blau, P.M. (1964) *Exchange and Power in Social Life*. New York: Wiley.

Bloomfield, R. and O'Hara, M. (1999) 'Market Transparency: Who Wins and Who loses?' *Review of Financial Studies*, 12: 5–35.

Bloor, M. (1978) 'On the Analysis of Observational Data: A Discussion of the Worth and Uses of Inductive Techniques and Respondent Validation', *Sociology*, 12: 542–54.

Blum, M. (1974) 'Failing Company Discriminant Analysis', *Journal of Accounting Research*: 1–25.

Bollen, K.A. and Long, J.S. (1993) 'Introduction', in K.A. Bollen and J.S. Long (eds), *Testing Structural Equation Models*. Newbury Park, CA: SAGE. pp. 1–9.

Bonner, S.E. and Sprinkle, G.B. (2002) 'The Effects of Monetary Incentives on Effort and Task Performance: Theories, Evidence and a Framework for Research', *Accounting, Organizations and Society*, 27 (4/5): 303–45.

Bonner, S.E., Hesford, J.W., Van der Stede, W.A. and Young, S.M. (2006) 'The Most Influential Journals in Academic Accounting', *Accounting Organizations and Society*, 31 (7): 663–85.

Bouwman, M.J. (1984) 'Expert Versus Novice Decision Making in Accounting: A Summary', *Accounting, Organizations and Society*, 9 (3): 325–27.

Bowman, E.H. (1984) 'Content Analysis of Annual Reports for Corporate Strategy and Risk', *Interfaces*, 14, Jan–Feb: 61–71.

Boys, P.G. and Rutherford, B.A. (1984) 'The Use of Accounting Information by Institutional Investors', in B. Carsberg and M. Page (eds), *Current Cost Accounting: The Benefits and the Costs*, Vol. 2. London: Prentice Hall. pp. 103–27.

Brannick, T. and Coghlan, D. (2007) 'In Defence of Being Native: The Case for Insider Academic Research', *Organisational Research Methods*, 10 (1): 59–74.

Brennan, N.M., Guillamon-Saorin, E. and Pierce, A. (2009) 'Impression Management: Developing and Illustrating a Scheme of Analysis for Narrative Disclosures – A Methodological Note', *Accounting, Auditing and Accountability Journal*, 22 (5): 789–832.

Briers, M. and Hirst, M. (1990) 'The Role of Budgetary Information in Performance Evaluation', *The Accounting Review*, 15 (4): 373–98.

Brignall, S. and Ballantine, J. (2004) 'Strategic Enterprise Management Systems: New Directions for Research', *Management Accounting Research*, 15: 225–40.

Brinn, T, Jones, M.J. and Pendlebury, M. (1996) 'UK Accountants' Perceptions of Research Journal Quality', *Accounting and Business Research*, 26 (3): 265–78.

Broadbent, J. (1998) 'The Gendered Nature of "Accounting Logic": Pointers to an Accounting that Encompasses Multiple Values', *Critical Perspectives on Accounting*, 9 (3): 267–97.

Broadbent, J., Laughlin, R. and Read, S. (1991) 'Recent Financial and Administrative Changes in the NHS: A Critical Theory Analysis', *Critical Perspectives on Accounting*, 2 (1): 1–29.

Brookfield, D. and Morris, R. (1992) 'The Market Impact of UK Company News Announcements', *Journal of Business Finance and Accounting*, 9 (4): 585–602.

Brown, B.M. (1988) 'Kendall's-*tau* and Contingency Tables', *Australian Journal of Statistics*, 30: 276–91.

Brown, C.E. and Solomon, I. (1993) 'An Experimental Investigation of Explanations for Outcome Effects on Appraisals of Capital Budgeting Decisions', *Contemporary Accounting Research*, 10 (1): 83–111.

Brown, D.A., Booth, P. J. and Giacobbe, F. (2004) 'Technological and Organisational Influences, on the Adoption of Activity-based Costing in Australia', *Accounting and Finance*, 44 (3): 329–56.

Brown, L.D. (1996) 'Influential Accounting Articles, Individuals, PhD Granting Institutions and Faculties: A Citation Analysis', *Accounting Organizations and Society*, 21 (7/8): 723–54.

Brownell, P. (1981) 'Participation in Budgeting, Locus of Control and Organizational Effectiveness', *The Accounting Review*, 56 (4): 844–60.

Brownell, P. (1982) 'The Role of Accounting Data in Performance Evaluation, Budgetary Participation, and Organizational Effectiveness', *Journal of Accounting Research*, Spring: 12–27.

Brownell, P. (1995) *Research Methods in Management Accounting*. Melbourne: Coopers & Lybrand.

Bryer, R.A. (1999) 'Marx and Accounting', *Critical Perspectives on Accounting*, 10 (5): 683–709.

Bryman, A. (2001) *Social Research Methods*. Oxford: Oxford University Press.

Buchanan, D., Boddy, D. and McCalman, L. (1988) 'Getting In, Getting On and Getting Out', in A. Bryman (ed.), *Doing Research in Organizations*. London: Routledge. pp. 53–67.

Burgstahler, D. and Eames, J. (2003) 'Earnings Management to Avoid Earnings Decreases and Losses: Are Analysts Fooled?', *Contemporary Accounting Research*, 20 (2): 253–94.

Burns, J. and Scapens, R.W. (2000) 'Conceptualizing Management Accounting Change: An Institutional Framework', *Management Accounting Research*, 11 (1): 3–25.

Burns, R.P. and Burns, R. (2008) *Business Research Methods and Statistics Using SPSS*. London: SAGE.

Burns, T. and Stalker, G.M. (1961) *The Management of Innovation*. London: Tavistock.

Byrne, B.M. (2001) *Structural Equation Modelling with AMOS: Basic Concepts, Applications and Programming*. Mahwah, NJ: Lawrence Erlbaum.

Callon, M. (1986) 'The Sociology of an Actor-Network: The Case of the Electric Vehicle', in M. Callon, J. Law and A. Rip (eds), *Mapping the Dynamics of Science and Technology*. London: MacMillan. pp. 19–34.

Campbell, D.T. (1965) 'Ethocentric and other altruistic moves', in D. Levine (ed.) *Symposium on Motivation*. Lincoln, NB: University of Nebraska Press. pp. 283–311.

Campbell, D. (2003) 'Intra- and Intersectoral Effects in Environmental Disclosures: Evidence for Legitimacy Theory?', *Business Strategy and the Environment*, 12 (6): 357–71.

Campbell, D. (2006) 'Protocol Analysis', in Z. Hoque (ed.), *Methodological Issues in Accounting Research: Theories and Methods*. London: Spiramus Press. pp. 399–409.

Campbell, D.T. and Fiske, D.W. (1959) 'Convergent and Discriminant Validation by the Multitrait Multimethod Matrix', *Psychological Bulletin*, 56: 81–105.

Campbell, D.T. and Stanley, J. (1963) *Experimental and Quasi-Experimental Designs for Research*. Chicago, IL: Rand-McNally.

Campbell, J.E. (1984) 'An Application of Protocol Analysis to the 'Little GAAP' Controversy', *Accounting, Organizations and Society*, 9 (3/4): 329–42.

Canning, J.B. (1929) *The Economics of Accountancy: A Critical Analysis of Accounting Theory*. New York: Ronald Press.

Carpenter, V.L. and Feroz, E.H. (2001) 'Institutional Theory and Accounting Rule Choice: An Analysis of Four US State Governments' Decision to Adopt Generally Accepted Accounting Principles', *Accounting, Organizations and Society*, 26: 565–96.

Carruthers, B.G. and Espeland, W. (1991) 'Accounting For Rationality: Double-Entry Bookkeeping and the Rhetoric of Economic Rationality', *The American Journal of Sociology*, 1: 31–69.

Casey, C.J. (1980) 'Variation in Accounting Information Overload: The Effect on Loan Officers' Predictions of Bankruptcy', *The Accounting Review*, 55 (1): 36–49.

Chapman, C.S. (1997) 'Reflections on a Contingent View of Accounting', *Accounting Organizations and Society*, 22 (2): 189–205.

Chapman, C.S. (1998) 'Accountants in Organizational Networks', *Accounting, Organizations and Society*, 23 (8): 737–66.

Chen, J., Patten, D.M. and Roberts, R.W. (2008) 'Corporate Charitable Contributions: A Corporate Social Performance or Legitimacy Strategy?' *Journal of Business Ethics*, 82 (1): 131–44.

Cheng, M., Luckett, P.F. and Schulz, A.K.-D. (2003) 'The Effects of Cognitive Style Diversity on Decision Making Dyads: An Empirical Analysis in the Context of a Complex Task', *Behavioral Research in Accounting*, 15: 13–36.

Cheng, M.-T. (2012) 'The Joint Effect of Budgetary Participation and Broad-Scope Management Accounting Systems on Management Performance', *Asian Review of Accounting*, 20 (3): 184–97.

Chenhall, R.H. (2003) 'Management Control Systems Design Within Its Organizational Context: Findings from Contingency-Based Research and Directions for the Future', *Accounting Organizations and Society*, 28 (2/3): 127–68.

Chenhall, R.H. (2005) 'Integrative Strategic Performance Measurement Systems: Strategy, Strategic Alignment of Manufacturing, Learning and Organizational Performance', *Accounting Organizations and Society*, 30 (5): 395–422.

Chenhall, R. and Chapman, C. (2006) 'Theorising and Testing Fit in Contingency Research on Management Control Systems', in Z. Hoque (ed.), *Methodological Issues in Accounting Research: Methods and Theories*. London: Spiramus Press. pp. 35–54.

Chenhall, R.H. and Langfield-Smith, K. (1998) 'The Relationship Between Strategic Priorities, Management Techniques and Management Accounting: An Empirical Investigation Using a Systems Approach', *Accounting Organizations and Society*, 23 (3): 243–64.

Chua, W.F. (1988) 'Interpretive Sociology and Management Accounting Research – A Critical Review', *Accounting, Auditing and Accountability Journal*, 1 (2): 59–79.

Chua, W.F. (1995) 'Experts, Networks, and Inscriptions in the Fabrication of Accounting Images: A Story of the Representation of Three Public Hospitals', *Accounting, Organizations and Society*, 20 (2/3): 111–45.

Chua, W.F. (1996) 'Issues in Substantive Areas of Research: Field Research in Accounting', in A.J. Richardson (ed.), *Research Methods in Accounting: Issues and Debates*. Vancouver: The Canadian General Accountants Research Foundation. pp. 209–28.

Chua, W.F. and Degeling, P. (1993) 'Interrogating an Accounting-Based Intervention on Three Axes: Instrumental, Moral and Aesthetic', *Accounting, Organizations and Society*, 18 (4): 291–318.

Checkland, P. (1981) *Systems Thinking, Systems Practice*. Chichester: Wiley.

Chong, V.K. and Chong, K.M. (1997) 'Strategic Choices, Environmental Uncertainty and SBU Performance: A Note on the Intervening Role of Managerial Accounting Systems', *Accounting and Business Research*, 27: 268–76.

Chong, V.K. and Johnson, D.M. (2007) 'Testing a Model of the Antecedents and Consequences of Budgetary Participation on Job Performance', *Accounting and Business Research*, 37 (1): 3–16.

Christensen, L.B. (1994) *Experimental Methodology*, 6th edn. Boston, MA: Allyn & Bacon.

Clapham, S.E. and Schwenk, C.R. (1991) 'Self-serving Attributions, Managerial Cognition and Company Performance', *Strategic Management Journal*, 12: 219–29.

Clatworthy, M. and Jones, M.J. (2001) 'The Effect of Thematic Structure on the Variability of Annual Report Readability', *Accounting, Auditing and Accountability Journal*, 14 (3): 311–26.

Clatworthy, M. and Jones, M.J. (2006) 'Differential Patterns of Textual Characteristics and Company Performance in the Chairman's Statement', *Accounting, Auditing and Accountability Journal*, 19 (4): 493–511.

Clor-Proell, S.M. (2009) 'The Effects of Expected and Actual Accounting Choices on Judgments and Decisions', *The Accounting Review*, 84 (5): 1465–93.

Coad, A.F. and Glyptis, L.G. (2014) 'Structuration: A Position-Practice Perspective and an Illustrative Study', *Critical Perspectives on Accounting*, 25 (2): 142–61.

Coffey, A. (1999) *The Ethnographic Self: Fieldwork under the Representation of Reality*. London: SAGE.

Cohen, J.R., Krishnamoorthy, K. and Wright, A.M. (2008) 'Form Versus Substance: The Implications for Auditing Practice and Research of Alternative Perspectives on Corporate Governance', *Auditing: A Journal of Practice and Theory*, 27 (2): 181–98.

Cole, C.J. and Jones, C.L. (2005) 'Management Discussion and Analysis: A Review and Implications for Future Research', *Journal of Accounting Literature*, 24: 135–74.

Collier, P.M. (2001) 'The Power of Accounting: A Field Study of Local Financial Management in a Police Force', *Management Accounting Research*, 12 (4): 465–86.

Collins, F., Lowensohn, S.H., McCallum, M.H. and Newmark, R.I. (1995) 'The Relationship between Budgetary Management Style and Organizational Commitment in a Not-for-Profit Organization', *Behavioral Research in Accounting*, 7: 65–79.

Colombo, R. (2000) 'A Model for Diagnosing and Reducing Nonresponse Bias', *Journal of Advertising Research*, 40 (1/2): 85–93.

Conrad, L. (2014) 'Reflections on the Application of and Potential for Structuration Theory in Accounting Research', *Critical Perspectives on Accounting*, 25 (2): 128–34.

Cook, T.D. and Campbell, D.T. (1979) *Quasi-Experimentation: Design and Analysis of Issues for Field Settings*. Boston, MA: Houghton Mifflin.

Cooper, D.C. and Emory, C.W. (1995) *Business Research Methods*. New York: Irwin.

Cooper, D.J. and Morgan, W. (2008) 'Case Study Research in Accounting', *Accounting Horizons*, 22 (2): 158–78.

Cooper, D.J. and Scherer, M. (1984) 'The Value of Corporate Accounting Reports: Arguments for a Political Economy of Accounting', *Accounting, Organizations and Society*, 9 (3/4): 207–32.

Cooper, R. and Kaplan, R.S. (1992) 'Profit Priorities From Activity-Based Costing', *Harvard Business Review*, 70, May–June: 130–35.

Coppage, R.E. and Baxendale, S. (2001) 'A Synergistic Approach to an Accounting Educator's Primary responsibilities', *Accounting Education: An International Journal*, 10 (3): 239–46.

Covaleski, M.A. and Dirsmith, M.W. (1990) 'Dialectic Tension, Double Reflexivity and the Everyday Accounting Researcher: On Using Qualitative Methods', *Accounting, Organizations and Society*, 15 (6): 543–73.

Covaleski, M.A., Dirsmith, M.W. and Michelman, J.E. (1993) 'An Institutional Theory Perspective on the DRG Framework, Case-Mix Accounting Systems and Healthcare Organizations', *Accounting Organizations and Society*, 18 (1): 65–80.

Covaleski, M.A., Evans III, J.H., Luft, J.L. and Shields, M.D. (2003) 'Budgeting Research: Three Theoretical Perspectives and Criteria For Selective Integration', *Journal of Management Accounting Research*, 15: 3–49.

Crichton, M. (1995) *The Lost World*. New York: Arrow Books.

Cushing, B.E. and Loebekke, J.K. (1986) 'Comparison of Audit Methodologies of Large Accounting Firms', Studies in Accounting Research No. 26, American Accounting Association, Sarasota, FL.

Cyert, R.M. and March, J.G. (1963) *A Behavioural Theory of the Firm*. Englewood Cliffs, NJ: Prentice Hall.

D'Aveni, R.A. and MacMillan, A.C. (1990) 'Crisis and Content of Managerial Communications: A Study of the Focus of Attention of Top Managers in Surviving and Failing Companies', *Administrative Science Quarterly*, 35: 634–57.

Davila, T. (2000) 'An Empirical Study on the Drivers of Management Control Systems' Design in New Product Development', *Accounting Organizations and Society*, 25 (4/5): 383–409.

Dechow, P.M. and Dichev, I. (2002) 'The Quality of Accruals and Earnings: The Role of Accrual Estimation Error', *The Accounting Review*, 77: 35–59.

Dechow, P.M., Hutton, A., Kim, J. and Sloan, R. (2012) 'Detecting Earnings Management: A New Approach', *Journal of Accounting Research* 50: 275–334.

Dechow, P.M., Sloan, R.G. and Sweeney, A.P. (1995) 'Detecting Earnings Management', *The Accounting Review*, 70 (2): 193–225.

Deegan, C. (2006) 'Legitimacy Theory', in Z. Hoque (ed.), *Methodological Issues in Accounting Research: Theories and Methods*. London: Spiramus Press. pp. 161–81.

Deegan, C., Rankin, M. and Tobin, J. (2002) 'An Examination of the Corporate Social and Environmental Disclosures of BHP From 1983–1997', *Accounting Auditing and Accountability Journal*, 17 (4): 312–43.

Defond, M. and Jiambalvo, J. (1994) 'Debt Covenant Violation and Manipulation of Accruals', *Journal of Accounting and Economics*, 17 (1–2): 145–76.

Deming, W.E. (1986) *Out of the Crisis: Quality, Productivity and Competitive Position*. Cambridge: Cambridge University Press.

Demski, J.S. and Feltham, G.A. (1976) *Cost determination: A Conceptual Approach*. Ames, IA: Iowa State University Press.

Dent, J. (1991) 'Accounting and Organizational Cultures: A Field Study of the Emergence of a New Organizational Reality', *Accounting, Organizations and Society*, 16 (8): 705–32.

Denzin, N.K. (1970) *The Research Act in Sociology*. London: Butterworth.

De Sanctis, G. and Poole, M.S. (1994) 'Capturing the Complexity in Advanced Technology Use: Adaptive Structuration Theory', *Organization Science*, 5 (2): 121–47.

Diamond, S.S. (2000) 'Reference Guide on Survey Research', in *Reference Manual on Scientific Evidence*, 2nd edn. Washington, DC: The Federal Justice Center. pp. 229–76.

Dikolli, S. and Smith, M. (1996) 'Implementing ABC: An Australian Feasibility Study', *Australian Accounting Review*, 6 (2): 45–55.

Dillard, J.F. (1991) 'Accounting as a Critical Social Science', *Accounting, Auditing and Accountability Journal*, 4 (1): 8–28.

Dillman, D.A. (1978) *Mail and Telephone Surveys: The Total Design Method*. New York: John Wiley.

Dillman, D.A. (2007) *Mail Internet Surveys: The Tailored Design Method*, 2nd edn. Hoboken, NJ: Wiley.

DiMaggio, P.J. and Powell, W.W. (1983) 'The Iron Cage Revisited: Institutional Isomorphism and Collective Rationality in Organizational Fields', *American Sociological Review*, 48 (2): 147–60.

Dirsmith, M.W. and Haskins, M.E. (1991) 'Inherent Risk Assessment and Audit Firm Technology: A Contrast in World Theories', *Accounting, Organizations and Society*, 16 (1): 61–90.

Ditton, J. (1977) *Part-time Crime: An Ethnography of Fiddling and Pilferage*. London: MacMillan.

Djajadikerta, H.G., Mat Roni, S. and Trireksani, T. (2015) 'Dysfunctional Information System Behaviours Are Not All Created the Same: Challenges to the Generalizability of Security-based Research', *Information Management*, 52 (8): 1012–24.

Donaldson, T. and Preston, L.E. (1995) 'The Stakeholder Theory of the Corporation: Concepts, Evidence and Implications', *Academy of Management Review*, 20: 65–91.

Dooley, D. (1995) *Social Research Methods*. Englewood Cliffs, NJ: Prentice Hall.

Dowd, K. (2004) 'Qualitative Dimensions in Finance and Risk Management Research', in C. Humphrey and B. Lee (eds), *The Real Life Guide to Accounting Research*. London: Elsevier. pp. 509–24.

Drury, C. (2012) *Management and Cost Accounting*, 8th edn. London: Cengage Learning.

Drury, C. and Tayles, M.E. (1995) 'Issues Arising from Surveys of Management Accounting Practice', *Management Accounting Research*, 6: 267–80.

Dunk, A.S. (1993) 'The Effect of Budget Emphasis and Information Asymmetry on the Relation between Budgetary Participation and Slack', *The Accounting Review*, 68 (2): 400–10.

Dunk, A.S. (1995) 'The Joint Effect of Participative Budgeting and Managerial Interest in Innovation on Departmental Performance', *Scandinavian Journal of Management*, 11 (1): 75–85.

Dunk, A.S. and Nouri, H. (1998) 'Antecedents of Budgetary Slack: A Literature Review and Synthesis', *Journal of Accounting Literature*, 17: 72–96.

Dunlap, A.J. (1996) *Mean Business*. Singapore: Butterworth-Heinemann Asia.

Dwyer, P.D. and Roberts, R.W. (2004) 'The Contemporary Gender Agenda of the US Public Accounting Profession: Embracing Feminism or Maintaining Empire?' *Critical Perspectives on Accounting*, 15 (1): 159–77.

Easterby-Smith, M., Thorpe, R. and Jackson, P.R. (2008) *Management Research*, 3rd edn. London: SAGE.

Edwards, R.S. (1938) 'The Nature and Measurement of Income', *The Accountant*, 99: 22–6.

Edwards, S.P., Roberts, I., Clarke, M., Di Giuseppe, C., Prataps, S., Wentz, R. and Kwan, I. (2002) 'Increasing Response Rates to Postal Questionnaires: Systematic Review', *British Medical Journal*, 324, May: 1183–91.

Eisenbeis, R.A. (1977) 'Pitfalls in the Application of Discriminant Analysis in Business, Finance and Economics', *Journal of Finance*, 22 (3): 875–90.

Eisenhardt, K. (1989) 'Building Theories from Case Study Research', *The Academy of Management Review*, 14 (4): 532–50.

Eisenhardt, K. (1991) 'Better Stories and Better Constructs: The Case For Rigor and Comparative Logic', *Academy of Management Review*, 16 (3): 620–27.

Elliott, W.B., Jackson, K.E. and Peecher, M.E. (2014) 'The Unintended Effect of Corporate Social Responsibility Performance on Investors' Estimates of Fundamental Value', *The Accounting Review*, 89 (1): 275–302.

Englund, H. and Gerdin, J. (2014) 'Structuration Theory in Accounting Research: Applications and Applicability', *Critical Perspectives on Accounting*, 25 (2): 162–80.

Ericsson, K.A. and Simon, H.A. (1980) 'Verbal Reports as Data', *Psychological Review*, 87 (3): 215–51.

Ericsson, K.A. and Simon, H.A. (1993) *Protocol Analysis: Verbal Reports as Data*. Cambridge, MA: The MIT Press.

Ezzamel, M. and Bourn, M. (1990) 'The Roles of Accounting Information Systems in an Organization Experiencing Financial Crisis', *Accounting, Organizations and Society*, 15 (5): 399–424.

Ezzamel, M. and Willmott, H. (1992) 'Accounting and Trust: Some Implications for Management Control', in T. Polesie and I.L. Johansson (eds), *Responsibility and Accounting: The Organizational Regulations of Boundary Conditions*. Lund: Studentlitteratur.

Fama, E.F. (1970) 'Efficient Capital Markets: A Review of Theory and Empirical Work', *Journal of Finance*, 25: 383–417.

Ferreira, L.D. and Merchant, K.A. (1992) 'Field Research in Management Accounting and Control: A Review and Evaluation', *Accounting, Auditing and Accountability Journal*, 5 (4): 3–34.

Ferris, K.R. (1977) 'A Test of the Expectancy Theory of Motivation in an Accounting Environment', *The Accounting Review*, July: 604–15.

Festinger, L. (1957) *A Theory of Cognitive Dissonance*. Stanford, CA: Stanford University Press.

Fielding, N.G. and Lee, R.M. (1998) *Using Computers in Qualitative Research*. London: SAGE.

Finn, J.A. (2005) *Getting a PhD*. London: Routledge.

Fleischman, R.K. and Schuele, K. (2009) 'Co-Authorship in Accounting History: Advantages and Pitfalls', *Accounting, Business and Financial History*, 19 (3): 287–303.

Floyd, S.W., Schroeder, D.M. and Finn, D.M. (1994) '"Only if I'm the First Author": Conflict Over Credit in Management Scholarship', *The Academy of Management Journal*, 37 (3): 734–47.

Flyvbjerg, B. (2001) *Making Social Science Matter*. Cambridge: Cambridge University Press.

Fogarty, T.J. (2006) 'Publishing in Academic Accounting: Practical Advice and Healthy Iconoclasm', in Z. Hoque (ed.), *Methodological Issues in Accounting Research: Theories and Methods*. London: Spiramus Press. pp. 515–34.

Fogarty, T.J., Singh, J., Rhoads, G.K. and Moore, R.K. (2000) 'Antecedents and Consequences of Burnout in Accounting: Beyond the Role Stress Model', *Behavioral Research in Accounting*, 12: 31–69.

Foster, G. (1986) *Financial Statement Analysis*, 2nd edn. Englewood Cliffs, NJ: Prentice Hall.

Foster, G. and Young, S.M. (1997) 'Frontiers of Management Accounting Research', *Journal of Management Accounting Research*, 9: 63–77.

Frazier, K.B., Ingram, R.W. and Tennyson, B.M. (1984) 'A Methodology for the Analysis of Narrative Accounting Disclosures', *Journal of Accounting Research*, 22 (1): 318–31.

Freeman, R.E. (1984) *Strategic Management: A Stakeholder Approach*. Boston, MA: Pitman.

Friedman, A.O. and Lyne, S.R. (2001) 'The Beancounter Stereotype: Towards a General Model of Stereotype Generation', *Critical Perspectives on Accounting*, 12: 423–51.

Friedman, M. (1953) 'The Methodology of Positive Economics', in *Essays in Positive Economics*. Chicago, IL: University of Chicago Press.

Friedman, M. (1970) 'The Social Responsibility of Business is to Increase its Profits', *New York Times Magazine* 13 September.

Frydman, H.E., Altman, E.I. and Kao, D.L. (1985) 'Introducing Recursive Partitioning for Financial Classification: The Case of Financial Distress', *Journal of Finance*, 40 (1): 269–91.

Gallhofer, S. (1998) 'The Silences of Mainstream Feminist Accounting Research', *Critical Perspectives on Accounting*, 9 (3): 355–75.

Gerakos, J. (2012) 'Discussion of Detecting Earnings Management: A New Approach', *Journal of Accounting Research* 50: 335–47.

Gerdin, J. and Greve, J. (2004) 'Forms of Contingency Fit in Managerial Accounting Research – A Critical Review', *Accounting Organizations and Society*, 29 (3/4): 303–26.

Gerdin, J. and Greve, J. (2008) 'The Appropriateness of Statistical Methods for Testing Contingency Hypotheses in Management Accounting Research', *Accounting, Organizations and Society*, 33 (7/8): 995–1009.

Gibbert, M., Ruigrok, W. and Wicki, B. (2008) 'What Passes as a Rigorous Case Study?' *Strategic Management Journal*, 29 (13): 1465–74.

Gibbins, M. (1992) 'Deception: A Tricky Issue for Behavioral Research in Accounting and Auditing', *Auditing: A Journal of Theory and Practice*, Fall: 113–26.

Gibbins, M. and Salterio, S. (1996) 'Experimental Accounting Research: Current Methodological Issues and Debates', in A.J. Richardson (ed.), *Research Methods in Accounting: Issues and Debates*. Vancouver: The Canadian General Accountants Research Foundation. pp. 9–24.

Gibbins, M., Richardson, A. and Waterhouse, J. (1990) 'The Management of Corporate Financial Disclosure: Opportunism, Ritualism, Policies and Processes', *Journal of Accounting Research*, 28 (1): 121–43.

Giddens, A. (1984) *The Constitution of Society: Introduction to the Theory of Structuration*. Berkeley, CA: University of California Press.

Giddens, A. (1991) *Modernity and Self-Identity*. Cambridge: Polity.

Gill, J. and Johnson, P. (1997) *Research Methods for Managers*, 2nd edn. London: SAGE.

Gill, J. and Johnson, P. (2002) *Research Methods for Managers*, 3rd edn. London: SAGE.

Gill, J. and Johnson, P. (2010) *Research Methods for Managers*, 4th edn. London: SAGE.

Glaser, B.G. (1978) *Advances in the Methodology of Grounded Theory: Theoretical Sensitivity*. Mill Valley, CA: The Sociology Press.

Glaser, B.G. (1992) *Basics of Grounded Theory Analysis*. Mill Valley, CA: The Sociology Press.

Glaser, B.G. and Strauss, A.L. (1967) *The Discovery of Grounded Theory: Strategies for Qualitative Research*. New York: Aldine Publishing.

Goddard, A. (2004) 'Budgetary Practices and Accountability Habitus – A Grounded Theory', *Accounting, Auditing and Accountability Journal*, 17 (4): 543–77.

Golafshani, N. (2003) 'Understanding Reliability and Validity in Qualitative Research', *The Qualitative Report*, 8 (4): 597–607.

Goldratt, E.M. and Cox, J. (1989) *The Goal*. Aldershot: Gower.

Gordon, M.J. (1964) 'Postulates, Principles and Research in Accounting', *The Accounting Review*, 39: 251–63.

Graham, J.R., Harvey, C.R. and Rajgopal, S. (2005) 'The Economic Implications of Corporate Financial Reporting', *Journal of Accounting and Economics*, 40 (1–3): 3–73.

Gramling, A.A. and Stone, D.N. (2001) 'Audit Firm Industry Expertise: A Review and Synthesis of the Archival literature', *Journal of Accounting Literature*, 20: 1–29.

Gray, R. (1996) *'Some Personal Reflections on Publication, Journal 'Quality' and Journal Ranking in the Academic Accounting Community'*, University of Dundee Discussion Paper, Dundee.

Gray, R., Adams, C. and Owen, D. (2014) *Accountability, Social Responsibility and Sustainability: Accounting for Society and the Environment*. London: Pearson.

Gray, R., Dey, C., Owen, D., Evans, R. and Zadek, S. (1997) 'Struggling with the Praxis of Social Accounting: Stakeholders, Accountability, Audits and Procedures', *Accounting, Auditing and Accountability Journal*, 10 (3): 325–64.

Gray, R., Owen, D. and Maunders, K. (1988) 'Corporate Social Reporting: Emerging Trends in Accountability and the Social Contract', *Accounting, Auditing and Accountability Journal*, 1 (1): 6–20.

Grey, C. (1996) 'On Being a Professional in a "Big Six" Firm', *Accounting, Organizations and Society*, 23 (5/6): 569–87.

Griffith, E.E., Hammersley, J.S. and Kadous, K. (2015) 'Audits of Complex Estimates as Verification of Management Numbers: How Institutional Pressures Shape Practice', *Contemporary Accounting Research*, 32 (3): 833–63.

Griffiths, I. (1986) *Creative Accounting: How to Make Your Profits What you Want Them to Be*. London: Firethorn Press.

Guilding, C., Cravens, K.S. and Tayles, M. (2000) 'An International Comparison of Strategic Management Accounting Practices', *Management Accounting Research*, 11 (1): 113–35.

Gummerson, E. (2007) 'Case Study Research and Network Theory: Birds of a Feather', *Qualitative Research in Organizations and Management*, 2 (3): 226–48.

Gurd, B.G. (2008) 'Remaining Consistent with Method? An Analysis of Grounded Theory Research in Accounting', *Qualitative Research in Accounting and Management*, 5 (2): 122–38.

Guthrie, J., Gray, R. and Parker, L.D. (2002) 'Rites of Passage and the Self-Immolation of Academic Accounting Labour: An Essay Exploring Exclusivity Versus Mutuality in Accounting Scholarship', *Accounting Forum*, 26 (1): 1–30.

Hair, J.F., Anderson, R.E., Tatham, R.L. and Black, W.C. (1995) *Multivariate Data Analysis with Readings*, 4th edn. Upper Saddle River, NJ: Prentice Hall.

Hair, J.F., Black, W.C., Babin, B.J., Anderson, R.E. and Tatham, R.L. (2006) *Multivariate Data Analysis*, 6th edn. Upper Saddle River, NJ: Prentice Hall.

Hair, J.F., Ringle, C.M. and Sarstedt, M. (2011) 'PLS-SEM: Indeed a Silver Bullet', *Journal of Marketing Theory and Practice*, 19 (2): 139–51.

Hair, J.F., Sarstedt, M., Hopkins, L. and Kuppelweiser, V.G. (2014) 'Partial Least Squares Structural Equation Modelling (PLS-SEM)', *European Business Review*, 26 (2): 106–121.

Hamer, M. (1983) 'Failure Prediction: Sensitivity of Classification Accuracy to Alternative Statistical Methods and Variable Sets', *Journal of Accounting and Public Policy*, 2: 289–307.

Hamilton, D.L. and Troiler, T.K. (1986) 'Stereotypes and Stereotyping: An Overview of the Cognitive Approach', in J.F. Dovidio and S.L. Gaertner (ed.), *Prejudice, Discrimination and Racism*. Orlando, FL: Academic Press. pp. 127–58.

Hammersley, M. and Atkinson, P. (1983) *Ethnography: Principles in Practice*. London: Tavistock.

Hammond, T. (1997) 'Culture and Gender in Accounting Research: Going Beyond Mynatt et al.', *Critical Perspectives on Accounting*, 8 (6): 685–92.

Hammond, T. and Oakes, L. (1992) 'Some Feminisms and their Implications for Accounting Practice', *Accounting, Auditing and Accountability Journal*, 3 (3): 52–70.

Han, J. (2013) 'A Literature Synthesis of Experimental Studies on Management Earning Guidance', *Journal of Accounting Literature*, 31 (1): 31–48.

Harte, J.M. and Koele, P. (1995) 'A Comparison of Different Methods for the Elicitation of Attribute Weights: Structural Modeling, Process Tracing and Self Reports', *Organizational Behavior and Human Decision Processes*, 64: 49–64.

Hartmann, F.G.H. and Moers, F. (1999) 'Testing Contingency Hypotheses in Budgetary Research: An Evaluation of the Use of Moderated Regression Analysis', *Accounting, Organizations and Society*, 24 (4): 291–315.

Hartmann, L. (2000) 'Ethics in Business Research: Some Issues', Adelaide: University of South Australia Working Paper Series.

Harvey-Jones, J. (1992) *Troubleshooter 2*. London: BBC Books.

Harvey-Jones, J. and Massey, A. (1990) *Troubleshooter*. London: BBC Books.

Hawking, S. (1998) *A Brief History of Time*. London: Bantam Press.

Healy, M. and Perry, C. (2000) 'Comprehensive Criteria to Judge Validity and Reliability of Qualitative Research within the Realism Paradigm', *Qualitative Market Research*, 3 (3): 118–26.

Healy, P.M. (1985) 'The Effect of Bonus Schemes on Accounting Decisions', *Journal of Accounting and Economics*, April: 85–107.

Heiman, V. (1990) 'Auditors' Assessments of the Likelihood of Error Explanations in Analytical Review', *The Accounting Review*, 65 (4): 875–90.

Henri, J.-F. (2007) 'A Quantitative Assessment of the Reporting of Structural Equation Modeling Information: The Case of Management Accounting Research', *Journal of Accounting Literature*, 26: 76–115.

Hepworth, S.R. (1953) 'Smoothing Periodic Income', *The Accounting Review*, 28 (1): 32–9.

Herzberg, F. (1966) *Work and the Nature of Man*. Cleveland, OH: World Publishing Co.

Hines, R. (1988) 'Financial Accounting: In Communicating Reality We Construct Reality', *Accounting, Organizations and Society*, 13 (3): 251–61.

Hines, R. (1992) 'Accounting: Filling the Negative Space', *Accounting, Organizations and Society*, 17 (3/4): 313–41.

Hirst, M.K. (1983) 'Reliance on Accounting Performance Measures, Task Uncertainty, and Dysfunctional Behavior: Some Extensions', *Journal of Accounting Research*, 21 (4): 595–605.

Höglund, H. (2012) 'Detecting Earnings Management With Neural Networks', *Expert Systems with Applications*, 39 (10): 9564–70.

Holsti, O.R. (1969) *Content Analysis for the Social Sciences and Humanities*. Reading, MA: Addison-Wesley.

Homans, G.C. (1961) *Social Behavior. Its Elementary Forms*. New York: Harcourt-Brace Jovanovich.

Hopper, T. and Hoque, Z. (2006) 'Triangulation Approaches to Accounting Research', in Z. Hoque (ed.), *Methodological Issues in Accounting Research: Theories and Methods*. London: Spiramus Press. pp. 477–86.

Hopper, T., Storey, J. and Willmott, H. (1987) 'Accounting for Accounting: Towards the Development of a Dialectical View', *Accounting, Organizations and Society*, 12: 437–56.

Hopwood, A.G. (1974) *Accounting and Human Behaviour*. London: Accountancy Age.

Hopwood, A.G. (1983) 'On Trying to Study Accounting in the Contexts in Which it Operates', *Accounting, Organizations and Society*, 8 (2/3): 287–305.

Hopwood, A.G. (1987) 'The Archaeology of Accounting Systems', *Accounting, Organizations and Society*, 12 (3): 207–34.

Hoque, Z. (2006) *Methodological Issues in Accounting Research: Theories and Methods*. London: Spiramus Press.

Hoque, Z. and Alam, M. (1999) 'TQM Adoption, Institutionalisation and Changes in Management Accounting Systems: A Case Study', *Accounting and Business Research*, 29 (3): 199–210.

Hoque, Z. and Hopper, T. (1997) 'Political and Industrial Relations Turbulence, Competition and Budgeting in the Nationalized Jute Mills of Bangladesh', *Accounting and Business Research*, 2: 125–44.

Horngren, C.T., Datar, S.M. and Rajan, M.V. (2015) *Cost Accounting: A Managerial Emphasis*, 15th edn. Upper Saddle River, NJ: Pearson.

Houghton, K.A. (1987) 'The Development of Meaning in Accounting: An Inter Temporal Study', *Accounting and Finance*, 27 (2): 25–40.

Houghton, K.A. (1988) 'The Measurement of Meaning in Accounting: A Critical Analysis of the Principal Evidence', *Accounting, Organizations and Society*, 13 (3): 263–80.

Houghton, K.A. and Smith, M. (1991) 'Loan Risk and the Anticipation of Corporate Distress: West Australian Evidence', in K. Davis and I. Harper (eds), *Risk Management in Financial Institutions*. Sydney: Allen & Unwin.

House, R.J. (1970) 'Scientific Investigation in Management', *Management International Review*, 4/5 (10): 139–50.

Howard, K. and Sharp, J.A. (1983) *The Management of a Student Research Project*. Aldershot: Gower.

Hoyos, R.E.D. and Sarafidis, V. (2006) 'Testing for Cross-Sectional Dependence in Panel-Data Models', *The Stata Journal*, 6 (4): 482–96.

Hronsky, J.J.F. and Houghton, K.A. (2001) 'The Meaning of a Defined Accounting Concept: Regulatory Changes and the Effect on Auditor Decision Making', *Accounting, Organizations and Society*, 26 (2): 123–39.

Hsiao, C. (2003) *Analysis of Panel Data*. Cambridge: Cambridge University Press.

Hsiao, C. (2007) 'Panel Data Analysis – Advantages and Challenges', *Test*, 16 (1): 1–22.

Hull, R.P. and Wright, F.B. (1990) 'Faculty Perceptions of Journal Quality: An Update', *Accounting Horizons*, 4 (1): 77–80.

Hult, G.T.M., Ketchen, D., Cui, A.S., Prudhomme, A.M., Seggie, S.H., Stanko, M.A., Xu, A.S. and Cavuseil, S.T. (2006) 'An Assessment of the Use of Structural Equation Modelling in International Business Research', in *Research Methodology in Strategy and Management*, 3: 385–415.

Humphrey, C. (2005) 'In the Aftermath of Crisis: Reflections on the Principles, Values and Significance of Academic Inquiry in Accounting', *European Accounting Review*, 14 (2): 341–51.

Humphrey, C. (2008) 'Auditing Research: A Review Across the Disciplinary Divide', *Accounting, Auditing and Accountability Journal*, 21 (2): 170–203.

Humphrey, C. and Lee, B. (2004) *The Real Life Guide to Accounting Research*. London: Elsevier.

Hussain, S. (2010) 'Accounting Journals and the ABS Quality Rankings', *British Accounting Review*, 42 (1): 1–16.

Hutchison, P.D., Fleischman, G.M. and Johnson, D.W. (1998) 'E-mail versus Mail Surveys: A Comparative Study', *The Review of Accounting Information Systems*, 2 (3): 43–56.

Inanga, E.L. and Schneider, W.B. (2005) 'The Failure of Accounting Research to Improve Accounting Practice: A Problem of Theory and Lack of Communication', *Critical Perspectives on Accounting*, 16 (3): 227–48.

Ingram, R.W. and Frazier, K.B. (1980) 'Environmental Performance and Corporate Disclosure', *Journal of Accounting Research*, 18 (2): 614–22.

Ingram, R.W. and Frazier, K.B. (1983) 'Narrative Disclosures in Annual Reports', *Journal of Business Research*, 11: 49–60.

Irvine, H. and Gaffikin, M. (2006) 'Getting In, Getting On and Getting Out: Reflections on a Qualitative Research Project', *Accounting, Auditing & Accountability Journal*, 19 (1): 115–45.

Ittner, C. and Larcker, D. (2001) 'Assessing Empirical Research in Managerial Accounting: A Value-based Management Perspective', *Journal of Accounting and Economics*, 32 (1–3): 349–410.

Ittner, C.D. and Larcker, D.F. (2002) 'Empirical Management Accounting Research: Are We Just Describing Management Consulting Practice?', *European Accounting Review*, 11 (4): 787–94.

Ittner, C.D. Larcker, D.P. and Meyer, M.W. (2003) 'Subjectivity and the Weighting of Performance Measures: Evidence from the Balanced Scorecard', *The Accounting Review*, 78 (2): 725–58.

Ittner, C., Larcker, D.F. and Rajan, M.V. (1997) 'The Choice of Performance Measures in Annual Bonus Contracts', *The Accounting Review*, 72: 231–55.

Ittner, C., Larcker, D. and Randall, T. (2003) 'Performance Implications of Strategic Performance Measurement in Financial Services Firms', *Accounting Organizations and Society*, 28 (7/8): 715–41.

Jack, L. and Kholeif, A. (2007) 'Introducing Strong Structuration Theory for Informing Qualitative Case Studies in Organization, Management and Accounting Research', *Qualitative Research in Organizations and Management*, 2 (3): 208–25.

Jager, P.D. (2008) 'Panel Data Techniques and Accounting Research', *Meditari Accountancy Research*, 16 (2): 53–68.

Jankowicz, A.D. (2005) *Business Research Projects*. London: Thomson.

Jaworski, B.J. and Young, S.M. 'Dysfunctional Behaviour and Management Control: An Empirical Study of Marketing Managers', *Accounting, Organizations and Society*, 17 (1): 17–35.

Jayazeri, M. and Cuthbert, P. (2004) 'Research in Management Accounting: What needs to be researched?', British Accounting Association Annual Conference, April, York.

Jensen, M.C. and Meckling, W.H. (1976) 'Theory of the Firm: Managerial Behavior, Agency Costs and Ownership Structure', *Journal of Financial Economics*, 3: 305–60.

Johannson, I.-L. and Baldvinsdottir, G. (2003) 'Accounting for Trust: Some Empirical Evidence', *Management Accounting Research*, 14 (3): 219–34.

Jones, J. (1991) 'Earnings Management During Import Relief Investigations', *Journal of Accounting Research*, 29 (2): 193–228.

Jones, M.J. and Shoemaker, P.A. (1994) 'Accounting Narratives: A Review of Empirical Studies of Content and Readability', *Journal of Accounting Literature*, 13: 142–84.

Jones, M.J. and Smith, M. (2014) 'Traditional and Alternative Methods of Measuring the Understand-ability of Accounting Narratives', *Accounting, Auditing and Accountability*, 27 (1): 183–208.

Jones, T.C. and Dugdale, D. (1994) 'Academic and Practitioner Reality: The Case of Investment Appraisal', *British Accounting Review*, 26: 3–25.

Jones, T.C. and Dugdale, D.A. (2002) 'The ABC Bandwagon and the Juggernaut of Modernity', *Accounting, Organizations and Society*, 27 (1/2): 121–63.

Jönsson, S. (1982) 'Budgetary Behavior in Local Government – A Case Study over Three Years', *Accounting, Organizations and Society*, 7 (3): 287–304.

Jönsson, S. and MacIntosh, N.B. (1997) 'Cats, Rats and Ears: Making the Case for Ethnographic Accounting Research', *Accounting, Organizations and Society*, 22 (3/4): 367–86.

Jöreskog, K.G. (1969) 'A General Approach to Confirmatory Maximum Likelihood Factor Analysis', *Psychometrica*, 34: 183–202.

Joyce, E.J. and Biddle, G.C. (1981) 'Anchoring and Adjustment in Probabilistic Inference in Auditing', *Journal of Accounting Research*, 19 (1): 120–45.

Kahneman, D. and Tversky, A. (1972) 'Subjective Probability: A Judgment of Representativeness', *Cognitive Psychology*, July: 430–54.

Kaplan, R.S. (1983) 'Measuring Manufacturing Performance: A New Challenge for Managerial Accounting Research', *The Accounting Review*, 58 (4): 686–705.

Kaplan, R.S. (1984) 'The Evolution of Management Accounting', *The Accounting Review*, 58 (4): 390–418.

Kaplan, R.S. (1998) 'Innovation Action Research: Creating New Management Accounting Theory and Practice', *Journal of Management Accounting Research*, 10: 89–118.

Kaplan, R.S. and Norton, D.P. (1992) 'The Balanced Scorecard: Measures that Drive Performance', *Harvard Business Review*, 70, Jan–Feb: 61–74.

Kaplan, R.S. and Norton, D.P. (1993) 'Putting the Balanced Scorecard to Work', *Harvard Business Review*, 71, Sept–Oct: 134–47.

Kaplan, R.S. and Norton, D.P. (2004) 'Strategy Maps', *Strategic Finance*, March: 27–35.

Kelle, U. (1995) *Computer-Aided Qualitative Data Analysis: Theory, Methods and Practice*. London: SAGE.

Kelley, H.H. (1972) 'Attribution in Social Interaction', in E. Jones (ed.), *Attribution: Perceiving the Causes of Behavior*. Morristown, NJ: General Learning Press.

Kelly, A., Morris, H., Rowlinson, M. and Harvey, C. (2009) *ABS Academic Journal Quality Guide*. London: Association of Business Schools.

Kelly, M. and Alam, M. (2008) 'Management Accounting and the Stakeholder Value model', *Journal of Applied Management Accounting Research*, 6 (1): 75–86.

Kelly-Newton, L. (1980) 'A Sociological Investigation of the USA Mandate for Replacement Cost Disclosures', *Accounting, Organizations and Society*, 5 (3): 311–21.

Kent, P. and Ung, K. (2003) 'Voluntary Disclosure of Forward-Looking Earnings Information in Australia', *Australian Journal of Management*, 28 (3): 273–85.

Khlif, H. and Chalmers, K. (2015) 'A Review of Meta-Analytic Research in Accounting', *Journal of Accounting Literature*, 35: 1–27.

Kidder, L.H. and Judd, C.L. (1986) *Research Methods in Social Relations*. London: Holt, Rinehart & Winston.

Kighir, A., Omar, N. and Norhayati M. (2014) 'Earnings Management Detection Modelling: A Methodological Review', *World Journal of Social Sciences*, 4 (1): 18–32.

Kinney, W. (1986) 'Audit Technology and Preferences for Auditing Standards', *Journal of Accounting and Economics*, 48 (1): 73–89.

Kirk, J. and Miller, M.L. (1986) *Reliability and Validity in Qualitative Research*. Newbury Park, CA: SAGE.

Kline, R.B. (1998) *Principles and Practice of Structural Equation Modeling*. New York: Guilford Press.

Koh, H.C. (1991) 'Model Predictions and Auditor Assessments of Going Concern Status', *Accounting and Business Research*, 21 (4): 331–8.

Kolb, D.A., Rubin, I.M. and McIntyre, J.M. (1979) *Organisational Psychology: An Experimental Approach*. London: Prentice Hall.

Kools, S., McCarthy, M., Durham, R. and Robrecht, L. (1996) 'Diminishing Analysis: Broadening the Conception of Grounded Theory', *Qualitative Health Research*, 6 (3): 312–30.

Krippendorff, K.H. (1980) *Content Analysis: An Introduction to its Methodology*. Beverley Hills, CA: SAGE.

Krippendorff, K.H. (2004) *Content Analysis: An Introduction to its Methodology*, 2nd edn. Thousand Oaks, CA: SAGE.

Krumweide, K.R. (1998) 'The Implementation Stages of Activity-based Costing and the Impact of Contextual and Organizational Factors', *Journal of Management Accounting Research*, 10: 239–77.

Kuhn, T.S. (1970) *The Structure of Scientific Revolutions*, 2nd edn. Chicago, IL: University of Chicago Press.

Lachenbruch, P.A. (1967) 'An Almost Unbiased Method of Obtaining Confidence Intervals for the Probability of Misclassification in Discriminant Analysis', *Biometrics*, 23 (4): 639–45.

Lang, M.H. and Lundholm, R.J. (1996) 'Corporate Disclosure Policy and Analyst Behavior', *Accounting Review*, 71: 467–92.

Lang, M.H., Lins, K.V. and Miller, D.P. (2003) 'ADRs, Analysts and Accuracy: Does Cross Listing in the United States Improve a Firm's Information Environment and Increase Market Value?', *Journal of Accounting Research*, 41 (2): 317–45.

Langfield-Smith, K. (1997) 'Management Control Systems and Strategy: A Critical Review', *Accounting, Organizations and Society*, 22 (2): 207–32.

Lapsley, I. (2004) 'Making Sense of Interactions in an Investigation of Organisational Practices and Processes', in C. Humphrey and B. Lee (eds), *The Real Life Guide to Accounting Research*. London: Elsevier. pp. 175–90.

Larcker, D.F. and Lessig, V.P. (1983) 'An Examination of the Linear and Retrospective Process Tracing Approaches to Judgment Modeling', *The Accounting Review*, 58: 58–77.

Laswell, H.D. (1948) 'The Structure and Function of Communications in Society', in L. Bryson (ed.), *The Communication of Ideas*. New York: Harper & Row.

Latour, B. (1986) 'The Powers of Association: Power Action and Belief. A New Sociology of Knowledge?', in J. Law (ed.), *Sociological Review Monograph 32*. London: Routledge. pp. 264–80.

Laughlin, R.C. (1987) 'Accounting Systems in Organizational Contexts: A Case for Critical Theory', *Accounting, Organizations and Society*, 12 (5): 479–502.

Laughlin, R.C. (1995) 'Empirical Research in Accounting: Alternative Approaches and a Case for Middle-range Thinking', *Accounting, Auditing and Accountability Journal*, 8 (1): 63–87.

Laughlin, R.C. (1999) 'Critical Accounting: Nature, Progress and Prognosis', *Accounting, Auditing and Accountability Journal*, 12 (1): 73–8.

Lawler, E. (1973) *Motivation in Organizations*. Monterey, CA: Brodis/Cole.

Leake, J. (2009) 'Climate Change Data Dumped', *The Sunday Times*, 29 November.

LeClere, M.J. (2000) 'The Occurrence and Timing of Events: Survival Analysis Applied to the Study of Financial Distress', *Journal of Accounting Literature*, 19: 158–89.

Lee, N. and Lings, I. (2008) *Doing Business Research: A Guide to Theory and Practice*. London: SAGE.

Lee, T.A. (2004) 'Accounting and Auditing research in the United States', in C. Humphrey and B. Lee (eds), *The Real Life Guide to Accounting Research*. London: Elsevier. pp. 57–62.

Lehman, G. (1999) 'Disclosing New Worlds: Social and Environmental Accounting', *Accounting, Organizations and Society*, 24 (3): 217–41.

Lehmann, C.M., Norman, D.S. and Kerr, D.S. (2009) 'Goal Orientation, Knowledge Encapsulation, Experience and Personality Factors in Accounting Research', *The Journal of Theoretical Accounting Research*, 4 (2): 37–59.

Lennox, C. (1999) 'Identifying Failing Companies: A Re-evaluation of the Logit, Probit and DA Approaches', *Journal of Economics and Business*, 51: 347–64.

Le Quesne, L. (1983) *The Bodyline Controversy*. London: Unwin.

Libby, R. (1981) *Accounting and Human Information Processing: Theory and Applications*. Englewood Cliffs, NJ: Prentice Hall.

Libby, R. and Frederick, D. (1990) 'Expertise and Ability to Explain Audit Findings', *Journal of Accounting Research*, 28 (2): 348–67.

Libby, R. and Lipe, M. (1992) 'Incentive Effects and the Cognitive Processes Involved in Accounting Judgments', *Journal of Accounting Research*, 30 (2): 249–73.

Libby, R. and Luft, J. (1993) 'Determinants of Judgment Performance in Accounting Settings: Ability, Knowledge, Motivation and Environment', *Accounting, Organizations and Society*, 18 (5): 425–50.

Libby, R., Bloomfield, R. and Nelson, M.W. (2002) 'Experimental Research in Financial Accounting', *Accounting Organizations and Society*, 27: 775–810.

Lightbody, M. (2000) 'Storing and Shielding: Financial Management Behavior in a Church Organization', *Accounting, Auditing and Accountability Journal*, 13 (2): 156–74.

Lillis, A.M. (1999) 'A Framework for the Analysis of Interview Data from Multiple Field Research', *Accounting and Finance*, 39 (1): 79–105.

Lillis, A.M. (2006) 'Reliability and Validity in Field Study Research', in Z. Hoque (ed.), *Methodological Issues in Accounting Research: Theories and Methods*. London: Spiramus Press. pp. 461–75.

Lillis, A.M. (2008) 'Qualitative Management Accounting Research: Rationale, Pitfalls and Potential', *Qualitative Research in Accounting and Management*, 15 (3): 239–46.

Lillis, A.M. and Mundy, J. (2005) 'Cross-Sectional Field Studies in Management Accounting Research – Closing the Gap Between Surveys and Case Studies', *Journal of Management Accounting Research*, 17: 119–41.

Liou, D.K. and Smith, M. (2007) 'Financial Distress and Corporate Turnaround: A Review of the Literature and Agenda for Research', *Journal of Accounting, Accountability and Performance*, 13 (1): 76–116.

Littleton, A.C. (1933) *Accounting Evolution to 1900*. New York: American Institute Publishing.

Lo, A.W. (1986) 'Logit versus Discriminant Analysis', *Journal of Econometrics*, 31: 151–78.

Locke, A.E (1968) 'Toward a Theory of Task Motivation and Incentives', *Organizational Behaviour and Human Performance*, 3: 157–69.

Lowe, A. and Locke, J. (2005) 'Perceptions of Journal Quality and Research Paradigm: Results of a Web-Based Survey of British Accounting Academics', *Accounting Organizations and Society*, 30 (1): 81–98.

Lowe, E.A. and Shaw, R.W. (1968) 'An Analysis of Managerial Biasing: Evidence of a Company's Budgeting Process', *Journal of Management Studies*, October: 304–15.

Luft. J. and Shields, M.D. (2003) 'Mapping Management Accounting: Graphics and Guidelines for Theory Consistent Empirical Research', *Accounting Organizations and Society*, 28 (2/3): 169–249.

Luft, J.L. and Shields, M.D. (2014) 'Subjectivity in Developing and Validating Causal Explanations in Positivist Accounting Research', *Accounting, Organizations and Society*, 39 (7): 550–8.

Lukka, K. (2007) 'Management Accounting Change and Stability: Loosely Coupled Rules and Routines in Action', *Management Accounting Research*, 18: 76–101.

Lukka, K. (2010) 'The Roles and Effects of Paradigms in Accounting Research', *Management Accounting Research*, 21: 110–15.

Lukka, K. and Kasanen, E. (1995) 'The Problem of Generalizability: Anecdotes and Evidence in Accounting Research', *Accounting, Auditing and Accountability Journal*, 8 (5): 71–90.

Lye, J., Perera, H. and Rahman, A. (2005) 'The Evolution of Accruals-Based Crown (Government) Financial Statements in New Zealand', *Accounting, Auditing and Accountability Journal*, 18 (6): 784–815.

Lye, J., Perera, H. and Rahman, A. (2006) 'Grounded Theory: A Theory Discovery Method for Accounting Research', in Z. Hoque (ed.), *Methodological Issues in Accounting Research: Theories and Methods*. London: Spiramus Press. pp. 129–60.

Lynn, J. and Jay, A. (1987) *Yes, Prime Minister*. London: BBC Books.

Lys, T. and Vincent, L. (1995) 'An Analysis of Value Destruction in AT & T's Acquisition of NCR', *Journal of Financial Economics*, 39: 353–78.

MacDonald, A.P. Jr (1970) 'Revised Scale for Ambiguity Tolerance, Reliability and Validity', *Psychological Reports*, 26: 791–98.

MacIntosh, N.B. (1994) *Management Accounting and Control Systems: An Organizational and Behavioral Approach*. New York: John Wiley.

MacIntosh, N.B. and Scapens, R.W. (1990) 'Structuration Theory in Management Accounting', *Accounting, Organizations and Society*, 15 (5): 455–77.

MacKay, D.B. and Villareal, A. (1987) 'Performance Differences in the Use of Graphic and Tabular Displays of Multivariate Data', *Decision Science*, 18 (4): 535–46.

McClelland, D.C. (1967) *The Achieving Society*. New York: Free Press.

McConnell, D., Haslem, J.A. and Gibson, V.R. (1986) 'The President's Letter to Stockholders: A New Look', *Financial Analysts Journal*, Sept/Oct: 66–70.

McGowan, S., Lehman, G. and Smith, M. (2000) 'Stakeholder Accountability and Corporate Environmental Perspectives', *Journal of Accounting, Accountability and Performance*, 6 (2): 63–88.

McLeay, S. (1986) 'Student's t and the Distribution of Financial Ratios', *Journal of Business, Finance and Accounting*, 13 (2): 209–22.

McLeay, S. and Omar, A. (2000) 'The Sensitivity of Prediction Models to the Non-Normality of Bounded and Unbounded Financial Ratios', *British Accounting Review*, 58 (2): 228–46.

Magenheim, E.B. and Mueller, D.C. (1988) 'Are Acquiring-Firm Shareholders Better off After an Acquisition?' in J.C. Coffee Jr, L. Lowenstein and S. Rose-Ackerman (eds), *Knights, Raiders and Targets: The Impact of Hostile Takeovers*. New York: Oxford University Press. pp. 171–93.

Magilke, M.J., Mayhew, B.W. and Pike, J. (2009) 'Are Independent Audit-Committee Members Objective?: Experimental Evidence', *The Accounting Review*, 84 (6): 1959–82.

Magness, V. (2008) 'Who are the Stakeholders Now? An Empirical Examination of the Mitchell, Agle and Wood Theory of Stakeholder Salience', *Journal of Business Ethics*, 83 (2): 177–92.

Mahoney, T.A., Jerdee, T.H. and Carroll, S.J. (1963) *Development of Managerial Performance: A Research Approach*. Cincinnati, OH: South-West Publishing.

Maines, L.A. and Wahlen, J.M. (2006) 'The Nature of Accounting Information Reliability: Inferences from Archival and Experimental Research', *Accounting Horizons*, 20 (4): 399–425.

Major, M. and Hopper, T. (2007) 'Extending Institutional Analysis through Theoretical Triangulation: Regulation and Activity-Based Costing in Portuguese Telecommunications', *European Accounting Review*, 16 (1): 59–97.

Malina, M. and Selto, F. (2001) 'Communicating and Controlling Strategy: An Empirical Study of the Balanced Scorecard', *Journal of Management Accounting Research*, 13: 47–90.

Malina, M.A. and Selto, F.H. (2004) 'Choice and Change of Measures in Performance Measurement Models', *Management Accounting Research* 15(4): 441–469.

Malina, M.A, Norreklit, H.S.O and Selto, F.H. (2007) 'Relations Among Measures, Climate of Control and Performance Measurement Models', *Contemporary Accounting Research*, 24 (3): 935–82.

Malina, M.A., Norreklit, H.S.O. and Selto, F.H. (2011) 'Lessons Learned: Advantages and Disadvantages of Mixed Methods Research', *Quantitative Research in Accounting and Management*, 8 (1): 59–71.

Malmi, T. and Granlund, M. (2009) 'In Search of Management Accounting Theory', *European Accounting Review*, 18 (3): 597–620.

Malsch, B. and Salterio, S.E. (2016) 'Doing Good Field Research: Assessing the Quality of Audit Field Research', *Auditing: A Journal of Practice and Theory*, 35 (1): 1–22.

Marginson, D.E.W. and Ogden, S.G. (2005) 'Coping With Ambiguity through the Budget: The Positive Effects of Budgetary Targets on Managers' Budgeting Behaviours', *Accounting, Organizations and Society*, 30 (5): 435–6.

Markowitz, H. (1952) 'Portfolio Selection', *The Journal of Finance*, March: 77–91.

Maruyama, G.M. (1998) *Basics of Structural Equation Modeling*. Thousand Oaks, CA: SAGE.

Maslow, A.H. (1954) *Motivation and Personality*. New York: Harper & Row.

Mason, J. (1994) 'Linking Qualitative and Quantitative Data Analysis', in A. Bryman and R.G. Burgess (eds), *Analysing Qualitative Data*. London: Routledge.

Mayo, E. (1933) *The Human Problems of Industrial Civilisation*. New York: MacMillan.

Merchant, K. (1985) 'Organizational Controls and Discretionary Program Decision Making: A Field Study', *Accounting, Organizations and Society*, 10 (1): 67–85.

Merchant, K.A. (2010) 'Paradigms in Accounting Research: A View From North America', *Management Accounting Research*, 21: 116–20.

Merchant, K. and Manzoni, J.-F. (1989) 'The Achievability of Budget Targets in Profit Centers: A Field Study', *The Accounting Review*, 64 (3): 539–58.

Merchant, K. and Van der Stede, W. (2006) 'Field-Based Research in Accounting: Accomplishments and Prospects', *Behavioral Research in Accounting*, 18: 117–34.

Merkl-Davies, D.M. and Brennan, N.M. (2007) 'Discretionary Disclosure Strategies in Corporate Narratives: Incremental Information or Impression Management', *Journal of Accounting Literature*, 26: 116–94.

Mia, L. (1989) 'The Impact of Participation in Budgeting and Job Difficulty on Managerial Performance and Work Motivation', *Accounting, Organizations and Society*, 14 (4): 347–57.

Milani, K.W. (1975) 'The Relationship of Participation in Budget Setting to Industrial Supervisor Performance and Attitudes: A Field Study', *The Accounting Review*, April: 274–84.

Miles, M.B. and Huberman, A.M. (1994) *Qualitative Data Analysis: An Expanded Sourcebook*. Thousand Oaks, CA: SAGE.

Modell, S. (2005) 'Triangulation Between Case Study and Survey Methods in Management Accounting Research: An Assessment of Validity Implications', *Management Accounting Research*, 16: 231–54.

Modigliani, F. and Miller, M.H. (1958) 'The Cost of Capital, Corporation Finance and the Theory of Investment', *American Economic Review*, 48: 261–97.

Moizer, P. (1998) 'The Corporate Images of the 1996 Big Six and the 1987 Big Eight', Conference of the European Accounting Association, April, Antwerp.

Moll, J. Major, M. and Hoque, Z. (2006) 'The Qualitative Research Tradition', in Z. Hoque (ed.), *Methodological Issues in Accounting Research: Theories and Methods*. London: Spiramus Press. pp. 375–98.

Moore, D.l. and Tarnai, J. (2002) 'Evaluating Nonresponse Errors in Mail Surveys', in R.M. Groves, D.A. Dillman, J.L. Eltinge and R.J.A. Little (eds), *Survey Nonresponse*. New York: Wiley. pp. 197–211.

Morgan, S.J. and Symon, G. (2004) 'Electronic Interviews in Organizational Research', in C. Cassell and G. Symon (eds), *Essential Guide to Qualitative Methods in Organizational Research*. London: SAGE. pp. 3–33.

Moses, I. (1985) 'Supervising Postgraduates', Green Guide No. 3, *Higher Education Research and Development Society of Australia (HERDSA)*, Canberra.

Mosteller, F. and Wallace, D.L. (1963) 'Inference in an Authorship Problem', *Journal of the American Statistical Association*, 58: 275–309.

Muhr, T. (1992) *ATLAS/ti User Manual Beta Version 0.94c*. Berlin: Berlin Technival University.

Mullins, G. and Kiley, M. (2002) '"It's a PhD, not a Nobel Prize": how experienced examiners assess research theses', *Studies in Higher Education*, 27 (4): 369–86.

Myers, C.S. (1924) *Industrial Psychology in Great Britain*. London: Jonathon Cape.

Myers, S. (1977) 'Determinants of Corporate Borrowing', *Journal of Financial Economics*, 5 (2): 147–75.

Nazari, J., Kline, T. and Herremans, I. (2006) 'Conducting Survey Research in Management Accounting', in Z. Hoque (ed.), *Methodological Issues in Accounting Research: Theories and Methods*. London: Spiramus Press. pp. 427–59.

Nelson, R.R. and Winter, S.G. (1982) *An Evolutionary Theory of Economic Change*. Cambridge, MA: Belknap Press, Harvard University.

Newell, A. and Simon, H.A. (1972) *Human Problem Solving*. Englewood Cliffs, NJ: Prentice Hall.

NHMRC (National Health and Medical Research Council, Australia) (2000) 'Australian Health Ethics Committee', www.health.gov.au/nhmrc/inside/part3c.htm (accessed 12 November 2002).

Nisbett, R. and Ross, L. (1980) *Human Inference: Strategies and Shortcomings of Social Judgment*. Englewood Cliffs, NJ: Prentice Hall.

Norreklit, H., Norreklit, L. and Mitchell, F. (2007) 'Theoretical Conditions For Validity in Accounting Performance Measurement', in A. Neely (ed.), *Business Performance Measurement*. Cambridge, NY: Cambridge University Press.

Northcott, D. and Linacre, S. (2010) 'Producing Spaces For Academic Discourse: The Impact of Research Assessment Exercises and Journal Quality Rankings', *Australian Accounting Review*, 20 (1): 63–79.

Nunnally, J. (1978) *Psychometric Theory*. New York: McGraw-Hill.

Oakes, L.S. and Hammond, T.A. (1995) 'Biting the Epistemological Hand: Feminist Perspectives on Science and their Implications for Accounting Research', *Critical Perspectives on Accounting*, 6 (1): 49–75.

O'Donovan, G. (2002) 'Environmental Disclosures in the Annual Report: Extending the Applicability and Predictive Power of Legitimacy Theory', *Accounting, Auditing and Accountability Journal*, 15 (3): 344–71.

Ohlson, J.S. (1980) Financial Ratios and the Probabilistic Prediction of Bankruptcy', *Journal of Accounting Research*, 18 (1): 109–31.

Onsi, M. (1973) 'Factor Analysis of Behavioral Variables Affecting Budgetary Slack', *The Accounting Review*, 48 (3): 535–48.

Osgood, C.E. and Walker, E.G. (1959) 'Motivation and Language Behavior: A Content Analysis of Suicide Notes', *Journal of Abnormal and Social Psychology*, 59: 58–67.

Osgood, C.E., Suci, G.J. and Tannenbaum, P.H. (1957) *The Measurement of Meaning*. Urbana, IL: University of Illinois Press.

Otley, D.T. (1978) 'Budget Use and Managerial Performance', *Journal of Accounting Research*, 16: 122–49.

Otley, D.T. (1980) 'The Contingency Theory of Management Accounting: Achievement and Prognosis', *Accounting, Organizations and Society*, 5 (4): 423–8.

Otley, D.T. (1984) 'Management Accounting and Organization Theory', in R.W. Scapens, D.T. Otley and R.J. Lister (eds), *Management Accounting, Organisation Theory and Capital Budgeting*. London: MacMillan.

Otley, D.T. (2001) 'Extending the Boundaries of Management Accounting Research: The Role of Case Study Methods', *British Accounting Review*, 33: 243–61.

Ouchi, W.G. (1977) 'A Conceptual Framework for the Design of Organizational Control Mechanisms', *Management Science*, 25 (9): 833–48.

Owens, D.L., Swift, T.A., Humphrey, C. and Bowerman, M. (2000) 'The New Social Audits: Accountability, Managerial Capture or the Agenda of Social Champions?' *European Accounting Review*, 9 (1): 81–98.

Parker, L.D. (1992) 'Questionnaires and Mail Surveys', School of Commerce Working Paper, Adelaide: Flinders University of South Australia.

Parker, L.D. (2001) 'Reactive Planning in a Christian Bureaucracy', *Management Accounting Research*, 12: 321–56.

Parker, L.D. (2002) 'Budgetary Incrementalism in a Christian Bureaucracy', *Management Accounting Research*, 13: 71–100.

Parker, L.D. (2003) 'Qualitative Research in Accounting and Management: The Emerging Agenda', *Journal of Accounting and Finance*, 2: 15–30.

Parker, L.D. (2005) 'Corporate Governance Crisis Down Under: Post-Enron Accounting Education and Research Inertia', *European Accounting Review*, 14 (2): 383–94.

Parker, L.D. (2008) 'The Interview Method', Qualitative Research Colloquium, *Centre for Accounting, Governance and Sustainability*, Adelaide: University of South Australia, July.

Parker, L.D. (2012) 'Qualitative Management Accounting Research: Assessing Deliverables and Relevance', *Critical Perspectives on Accounting*, 23: 54–70.

Parker, L.D. and Roffey, B.H. (1997) 'Back to the Drawing Board: Revisiting Grounded Theory and the Everyday Accountant's reality', *Accounting, Auditing and Accountability Journal*, 10 (2): 212–47.

Parker, L.D., Guthrie, J. and Gray, R. (1998) 'Accounting and Management Research: Passwords from the Gatekeepers', *Accounting, Auditing and Accountability Journal*, 11 (4): 371–402.

Paton, W. and Littleton, A.C. (1940) *An Introduction to Corporate Accounting Standards*, American Accounting Association Monograph, No. 3, New York.

Patten, D.M. (1992) 'Intra-Industry Environmental Disclosures in Response to the Alaskan Oil Spill: A Note On Legitimacy', *Accounting, Organizations and Society*, 15 (5): 471–5.

Patton, M.Q. (2002) *Qualitative Research and Evaluation Methods*. Thousand Oaks, CA: SAGE.

Peat, Marwick and Mitchell (1976) *Research Opportunities in Auditing*. New York: Peat, Marwick Mitchell & Co.

Pedhazur, E.J. (1982) *Regression in Behavioral Research: Explanation and Prediction*, 2nd edn. New York: Holt, Rhinehart and Winston.

Pelto, P. J. and Pelto, G.H. (1978) *Anthropological Research: The Structure of Inquiry*. Cambridge: Cambridge University Press.

Perrow, C. (1970) *Organizational Analysis: A Sociological View*. Belmont, CA: Wadsworth.

Perrow, C. (1972) *Complex Organizations: A Critical Essay*. Glenview, IL: Scott, Foreman & Co.

Pesaran, H.M. (2003) 'Estimation and Inference in Large Heterogeneous Panels with Cross Section Dependence', *Cambridge Working Papers in Economics*, Faculty of Economics, University of Cambridge.

Peters, T.J. and Waterman, R.H. (1982) *In Search of Excellence: Lessons from America's Best-run Companies*. New York: Harper & Row.

Phillips, E.M and Pugh, D.S. (1994) *How to Get a PhD*, 2nd edn. Milton Keynes: Open University Press.

Popper, K.R. (1959) *The Logic of Scientific Discovery*. London: Hutchinson.

Porter, M.E. (1980) *Competitive Strategy; Techniques for Analyzing Industries and Competitors*. New York: Free Press.

Porter, M.E. (1985) *Competitive Advantage: Creating and Sustaining Superior Performance*. New York: Free Press.

Power, M. and Gendron, Y. (2015) 'Qualitative Research in Auditing: A Methodological Roadmap', *Auditing: A Journal of Practice and Theory*, 34 (2): 147–65.

Power, M. and Laughlin, R.C. (1996) 'Habermas, Law and Accounting', *Accounting, Organizations and Society*, 21 (5): 441–65.

Power, M., Laughlin, R.C. and Cooper, D.J. (2003) 'Accounting and Critical Theory', in M. Alvesson and H. Wilmott (eds), *Studying Management Critically*. London: SAGE. pp. 132–56.

Preston, A.M. (1986) 'Interactions and Arrangements in the Process of Informing', *Accounting, Organizations and Society*, 11 (6): 521–40.

Preston, A.M. (1989) 'The Taxman Cometh: Some Observations on the Interrelationship Between Accounting and Inland Revenue Practice', *Accounting, Organizations and Society*, 15 (5/6): 389–413.

Preston, A., Chua, W.F. and Neu, D. (1997) 'The Diagnostic-related Group Prospective Payment System and the Problem of Government Rationing of Health Care to the Elderly', *Accounting, Organizations and Society*, 22 (2): 147–64.

Preston, A., Cooper, D.J. and Coombs, R.W. (1992) 'Fabricating Budgets: A Study of the Production of Management Budgeting in the National Health Service', *Accounting, Organizations and Society*, 17 (6): 561–93.

Rahaman, A.S. and Lawrence, S. (2001) 'Public Sector Accounting and Financial Management in a Developing Country Organizational Context: A Three-Dimensional View', *Accounting Forum*, 25 (2): 189–210.

Rapkin, D.P. and Braaten, D. (2009) 'Conceptualising Hegemonic Legitimacy', *Review of International Studies*, 35 (1): 113–49.

Rawls, J. (1971) *A Theory of Justice*. Cambridge, MA: Harvard University Press.

Richards, T., Richards, L., McGalliard, J. and Sharrock, B. (1992) *NUD*IST 2.3 Users Manual*. Australia: Replee Pty, La Trobe University.

Robbins, S.P. (1995) *Organizational Behavior: Concepts, Controversies and Applications*. Englewood Cliffs, NJ: Prentice Hall.

Roberts, E.S. (1999) 'In Defence of the Survey Method: An Illustration from a Study of User Information Satisfaction', *Accounting and Finance*, 39 (1): 53–78.

Roberts, J. (2014) 'Testing the Limits of Structuration Theory in Accounting Research', *Critical Perspectives on Accounting*, 25 (2): 135–41.

Robinson, G. (2004) *I'll Show Them Whose Boss: The Six Secrets of Highly Successful Management*. London: BBC Active.

Rockness, H.O. (1977) 'Expectancy Theory in a Budgetary Setting: An Experimental Examination', *The Accounting Review*, October: 893–903.

Roethlisberger, F.J. and Dickson, W.J. (1939) *Management and the Worker*. Cambridge, MA: Harvard University Press.

Rogers, E.M. (1995) *Diffusion of Innovation*. New York: Free Press.

Rogers, E.M. (2003) *Diffusion of Innovation*, 5th edn. New York: Free Press.

Ronen, J. and Livingstone, J.L. (1974) 'An Expectancy Approach to the Motivational Impacts of Budgets', *The Accounting Review*, October: 671–85.

Rosenhahn, D.L. (1982) 'On Being Sane in Insane Places', in M.Bulmer (ed.), *Social Research Ethics: An Examination of the Merits of Covert Participation Observation*. London: MacMillan. pp. 42–56.

Rosenthal, R. (1966) *Experimenter Effects in Behavioral Research*. New York: Appleton Century Crofts.

Roslender, R. (2006) 'Critical Theory', in Z. Hoque (ed.), *Methodolological Issues in Accounting Research: Theories and Methods*. London: Spiramus Press. pp. 247–70.

Ross, S.A. (1977) 'The Determination of Financial Structure – The Incentive Signaling Approach', *Bell Journal of Economics*, 8 (1): 23–40.

Rossman, G.B. and Wilson, B.L. (1984) 'Numbers and Words: Combining Quantitative and Qualitative Methods in a Single Large-Scale Evaluation Study', *Evaluation Review*, 9 (5): 627–43.

Rowlinson, M., Harvey, C., Kelly, A., Morris, H. and Todeva, E. (2015) 'Accounting For Research Quality: Research Audits and the Journal Rankings Debate', *Critical Perspectives on Accounting*, 26 (1): 2–22.

Roychowdhury, S. (2006) 'Earnings Management Through Real Activities Manipulation', *Journal of Accounting and Economics*, 42 (3): 335–70.

Ryan, R., Scapens, R.W. and Theobald, M. (2002) *Research Method and Methodology in Finance and Accounting*, 2nd edn. London: Thomson.

Salancik, G.R. and Meindl, J.R. (1984) 'Corporate Attributions as Strategic Illusions of Management Control', *Administrative Science Quarterly*, 29: 238–54.

Sandelowski, M. (1986) 'The Problem of Rigor in Qualitative Research', *Advances in Nursing Science*, April: 27–37.

Sapsford, R. (2000) *Survey Research*, 2nd edn. London: SAGE.

Saravanamuthu, K. (2013) 'Enhancing Stakeholder Interaction Through Environmental Risk Accounts', *Critical Perspectives on Accounting*, 24 (6): 410–37.

Saunders, M., Lewis, P. and Thornhill, A. (2009) *Research Methods for Business Students*, 5th edn. London: Prentice Hall.

Scapens, R.W. (1990) 'Researching Managing Accounting Practice: The Role of Case Study Methods', *British Accounting Review*, 22 (3): 259–81.

Scapens, R.W. (2004) 'Doing Case Study Research', in C. Humphrey and B. Lee (eds), *The Real Life Guide to Accounting Research: A Behind-The-Scenes View of Using Qualitative Research Methods*. Amsterdam: Elsevier. pp. 257–79.

Scapens, R.W. and Jazayeri, M. (2003) 'ERP Systems and Management Accounting Change: Opportunities or Impacts? A Research Note', *European Accounting Review*, 12 (1): 201–33.

Scapens, R.W. and Roberts, J. (1993) 'Accounting and Control: A Case Study of Resistance to Accounting and Change', *Management Accounting Research*, 4 (1): 1–32.

Schepanski, A., Tubbs, R.M. and Grimlund, R.A. (1992) 'Within-subjects and Between-subjects Designs in Behavioral Accounting Research: An Examination of Some Issues of Concern', *Journal of Accounting Literature*, 11: 121–50.

Schreck, P. (2013) 'Non-financial Disclosure and Analyst Forecast Accuracy: International Evidence on Corporate Social Responsibility Disclosure', *Social and Environmental Accountability*, 33 (3): 180–81.

Schulz, A.K.-D. (1999) 'Experimental Research Method in a Management Accounting Context', *Accounting and Finance*, 39 (1): 29–52.

Schumacker, R.E. and Lomax, R.G. (1996) *A Beginner's Guide to Structural Equation Modeling*. Mahwah, NJ: Lawrence Erlbaum.

Scott, J. (1981) 'The Probability of Bankruptcy: A Comparison of Empirical Predictions and Theoretical Models', *Journal of Banking and Finance*, September: 317–44.

Searcy, D.L. and Mentzer, J.T. (2003) 'A Framework for Conducting and Evaluating Research', *Journal of Accounting Literature*, 22: 130–67.

Shan, Y.G. and McIver, R.P. (2011). 'Corporate Governance Mechanisms and Financial Performance in China: Panel Data Evidence on Listed Non-Financial Companies', *Asia Pacific Business Review*, 17 (3): 301–24.

Sharpe, W. (1964) 'Capital Asset Prices: A Theory of Market Equilibrium under Conditions of Risk', *Journal of Finance*, 19: 425–42.

Shields, J.F. and Shields, M.D. (1998) 'Antecedents of Participative Budgeting', *Accounting, Organizations and Society*, 23 (1): 49–76.

Shields, M.D. (1997) Research in Management Accounting by North Americans in the 1990s', *Journal of Management Accounting Research*, 9: 3–62.

Shumway, T. (2001) 'Forecasting Bankruptcy More Accurately: A Simple Hazard Model', *Journal of Business*, 74 (1): 101–23.

Sikka, P. (2001) 'Regulation of Accountancy and the Power of Capital', *Critical Perspectives on Accounting*, 12 (2): 199–211.

Sikka, P. and Willmott, H. (1997) 'Practising Critical Accounting', *Critical Perspectives on Accounting*, 8 (1/2): 149–65.

Silverman, D. (1985) *Qualitative Methodology and Sociology*. Aldershot: Gower.

Silverman, D. (1989) 'Telling Convincing Stories: A Plan for Cautious Positivism in Case Studies', in B. Glassner and T.D. Moreno (eds), *The Qualitative-Quantitative Distinction in Social Sciences*. London: Kluwer Academic.

Silverman, D. (2005) *Doing Qualitative Research: A Practical Handbook*. London: SAGE.

Simnett, R. and Trotman, K.T. (1992) 'Identification of Key Financial Ratios for Going Concern Decisions', *Charter*, April: 39–41.

Simon, H.A. (1959) Theories of Decision Making in Economics and Behavioral Science', *American Economic Review*, 49: 253–83.

Simon, H.A. (1976) 'From Substantive to Procedural Rationality', in S. Latsis (ed.), *Method and Appraisal in Economics*. Cambridge: Cambridge University Press.

Simons, R. (1987) 'Accounting Control Systems and Business Strategy: An Empirical Analysis', *Accounting, Organizations and Society*, 12 (4): 357–74.

Simons, R. (1990) 'The Role of Management Control Systems in Creating Competitive Advantage: New Perspectives', *Accounting, Organizations and Society*, 15 (1/2): 127–43.

Simsek, Z. and Veiga, J.F. (2001) 'A Primer on Internet Organizational Surveys', *Organizational Research Methods*, 3 (4): 218–35.

Slovic, P. (1969) 'Analyzing the Expert Judge: A Descriptive Study of a Stockbroker's Decision Processes', *Journal of Applied Psychology*, 53 (4): 255–63.

Smith, D. and Langfield-Smith, K. (2004) Structural Equation Modeling in Management Accounting Research', *Journal of Accounting Literature*, 23: 49–86.

Smith, K.J., Everly, G.S. and Johns, T.R. (1993) 'The Role of Stress Arousal in the Dynamics of the Stressor-to-Illness Process among Accountants', *Contemporary Accounting Research*, 9, Spring: 432–49.

Smith, M. (1992) 'Quantification of the Trade-off Between the Desirable Characteristics of Accounting Disclosures', Conference of the Accounting Association of Australia and New Zealand, Palmerston, New Zealand, July.

Smith, M. (1993) 'The Effect of Heuristics on Accounting Decision Making', *Accounting Research Journal*, Spring: 38–47.

Smith, M. (1994a) 'Improving Management Accounting Reporting Practices: A Total Quality Management Approach (Part 1), *Journal of Cost Management*, 7 (4): 50–57.

Smith, M. (1994b) 'Improving Management Accounting Reporting Practices: A Total Quality Management Approach (Part 2), *Journal of Cost Management*, 8 (1): 49–56.

Smith, M. (1994c) 'Benchmarking in Practice: Some Australian Evidence', *Managerial Auditing Journal*, 9 (3): 19–22.

Smith, M. (1996) 'Qualitative Characteristics in Accounting Disclosures: A Desirability Trade-off', *Managerial Auditing Journal*, 11 (3): 11–16.

Smith, M. (1997) *Strategic Management Accounting: Issues and Cases*, 2nd edn. London: Butterworth.

Smith, M. (1998a) 'Creative Accounting: The Auditor Effect', *Managerial Auditing Journal*, 13 (3): 155–8.

Smith, M. (1998b) 'Conflicting Messages in Annual Reports', *Accountability and Performance*, 4 (2): 43–60.

Smith, M. (2003) *Research Methods in Accounting*. London: SAGE.

Smith, M. (2005) *Performance Measurement and Management*. London: SAGE.

Smith, M. (2006) 'Alumina PLC: Post-audit of Capital Investment Expenditure', *Accounting Education: An International Journal*, 15 (2): 217–26.

Smith, M. (2011) *Research Methods in Accounting*, 2nd edn. London: SAGE.

Smith, M. and Briggs, S.P. (1999) 'From Bean Counter to Action Hero: Changing the Image of the Accountant', *Management Accounting*, 77 (1): 28–30.

Smith, M. and Chang, C. (2009) 'The Impact of Customer Related Strategies on Shareholder Value: Evidence from Taiwan', *Asian Review of Accounting*, 17 (3): 247–68.

Smith, M. and Chang, C. (2009) 'Measuring the Efficiency of Customer Related Strategies: A Review of the Literature and Agenda for Research', *Journal of Accounting, Accountability and Performance*, 15 (2): 71–103.

Smith, M. and Graves, C. (2002) 'Cunningham Construction: Bonus Schemes and Participant Behaviour', *Journal of Accounting Case Research*, 7 (1): 1–6.

Smith, M. and Graves, C. (2005) 'Corporate Turnaround and Financial Distress', *Managerial Auditing Journal*, 20 (3): 304–20.

Smith, M. and Gurd, B.G. (2000) *Accounting Organisations and Society*. Sydney: Prentice Hall.

Smith, M. and Kestel, J.M. (1999) 'A Time Series Analysis of Accounting Policy Changes: West Australian Evidence', School of Accounting Seminar Series, University of South Australia, Adelaide.

Smith, M. and Taffler, R.J. (1992) 'The Chairman's Statement and Financial Performance', *Accounting and Finance*, 32 (2): 75–90.

Smith, M. and Taffler, R.J. (1995) 'The Incremental Effect of Narrative Accounting Information in Corporate Annual Reports', *Journal of Business Finance and Accounting*, 22 (8): 1195–210.

Smith, M. and Taffler, R.J. (1996) 'Improving the Communication of Accounting Information through Cartoon Graphics', *Accounting, Auditing and Accountability Journal*, 9 (2): 70–87.

Smith, M. and Taffler, R.J. (2000) 'The Chairman's Statement: A Content Analysis of Discretionary Narrative Disclosures', *Accounting, Auditing and Accountability Journal*, 13 (5): 624–46.

Smith, M. and Tucker, B. (2013) *Advanced Strategic Management Accounting: Theory and Practice*, Melbourne: Cengage.

Smith, M., Fiedler, B., Brown, B. and Kestel, J. (2001) 'Structure Versus Judgement in the Audit Process: A Test of Kinney's Classification', *Managerial Auditing Journal*, 16 (1): 40–49.

Smith, T. (1992) *Accounting for Growth: Stripping the Camouflage from Company Accounts*. London: Random House.

So, S. and Smith, M. (2002) 'Colour Graphics and Task Complexity in Multivariate Decision Making', *Accounting, Auditing and Accountability Journal*, 15 (4): 565–93.

So, S. and Smith, M. (2004) 'Multivariate Decision Accuracy and the Presentation of Accounting Information', *Accounting Forum*, 28 (3): 283–306.

So, S. and Smith, M. (2009) 'Value Relevance of IAS27 (2003) Revisions Presentation of Non-controlling Interests: Evidence from Hong Kong', *Journal of International Financial Management Accounting*, 20 (2): 166–198.

Sobel, D. (1995) *Longitude*. London: Fourth Estate.

Soin, K. (1995) 'Management Control in the Financial Services Sector', in A.J. Berry, P. Broadbent and D.T. Otley (eds), *Management Control – Theories, Issues and Practices*. Basingstoke: MacMillan. pp. 283–98.

Soin, K., Seal, W. and Cullen, J. (2002) 'ABC and Organizational Change: An Institutional Perspective', *Management Accounting Research*, 13: 249–71.

Southwood, K.E. (1978) 'Substantive Theory and Statistical Interactions: Five Models', *American Journal of Sociology*, 83 (5): 1154–230.

Spence, M. (1973) 'Job Market Signaling', *Quarterly Journal of Economics*, 87 (3): 355–74.

Spicer, B.H. and Ballew, V. (1983) 'Management Accounting Systems and the Economics of Internal Organization', *Accounting, Organizations and Society*, 8 (1): 73–96.

Staw, B.M. (1984) 'Organizational Behavior: A Review and Reformulation of the Field's Outcome Variables', in M.R. Rosenzweig and L.W. Porter (eds), *Annual Review of Psychology*, 35: 627–66.

Staw, B.M., McKechnie, P. I. and Puffer, S.M. (1983) 'The Justification of Organizational Performance', *Administrative Science Quarterly*, 28 (4): 582–600.

Stock, D. and Watson, C.J. (1984) 'Human Judgment Accuracy, Multidimensional Graphics and Humans versus Models', *Journal of Accounting Research*, 22: 192–206.

Stone, P.J. and Hunt, E.B. (1963) 'Computer Approach to Content Analysis using the General Inquirer System', in E.C. Johnson (ed.), *Conference Proceedings of the American Federation of Information Processing Societies* (Baltimore, MD), Montvale, NJ, AFIPS. pp. 241–56.

Strauss, A. (1987) *Qualitative Analysis for Social Scientists*. New York: Cambridge University Press.

Strauss, A. and Corbin, J. (1990) *Basics of Qualitative Research: Grounded Theory Procedures and Techniques*. Newbury Park, CA: SAGE.

Strauss, A. and Corbin, J. (1998) *Basics of Qualitative Research: Techniques and Procedures for Developing Grounded Theory*. Thousand Oaks, CA: SAGE.

Strauss, A. and Corbin, J. (2008) *Basics of Qualitative Research*, 3rd edn. Thousand Oaks, CA: SAGE.

Stringer, C. (2007) 'Empirical Performance Management Research: Observations From AOS and MAR', *Qualitative Research in Accounting and Management*, 4 (2): 92–114.

Stuart, I, Shin, Y.-C., Cram, D.P. and Karan, V. (2013) 'Review of Choice-Based Matched and Other Stratified Sample Studies in Auditing Research', *Journal of Accounting Literature*, 32 (1): 88–113.

Subramaniam, N. (2006) 'Agency Theory and Accounting Research: An Overview of Some Conceptual and Empirical Issues', in Z. Hoque (ed.), *Methodological Issues in Accounting Research: Methods and Theories*. London: Spiramus Press. pp. 55–82.

Sullivan, J.D. (1984) 'The Case for the Unstructured Audit Approach', in H.F. Stettler and N.A. Ford (eds), *Auditing Symposium VII*. Kansas City, KS: University of Kansas.

Svenson, O. (1979) 'Process Descriptions of Decision Making', *Organisational Behaviour and Human Performance*, 23: 86–112.

Swales, G.S. (1988) 'Another Look at the President's Letter to Stockholders', *Financial Analysts Journal*, March–April: 71–3.

Symonds, E. (2011) 'A Practical Application of Surveymonkey as a Remote Usability-Testing Tool', *Library Hi Tech*, 29 (3): 436–45.

Tabachnick, B.G. and Fidell, L.S. (2001) *Using Multivariate Statistics*. Boston, MA: Alyn and Bacon.

Taffler, R.J. (1983) 'The Assessment of Company Solvency and Performance Using a Statistical Model: A Comparative UK-based Study', *Accounting and Business Research*, 15 (5): 295–308.

Taffler, R.J. (1995) 'The Use of the Z-score Approach in Practice', Working Paper No. 95/1, Centre for Empirical Research in Finance and Accounting, City University, London.

Tajfel, H. and Turner, J. (1985) 'The Social Identity Theory of Intergroup Behavior', in S. Worchel and W. Austin (eds), *Psychology of Inter Group Relations*. Chicago, IL: Nelson-Hall.

Tennyson, B.M., Ingram, R.W. and Dugan, M.T. (1990) 'Assessing the Information Content of Narrative Disclosures in Explaining Bankruptcy', *Journal of Business Finance and Accounting*, 17 (3): 390–410.

Thompson, J.D. (1969) *Organizations in Action*. New York: McGraw-Hill.

Tinker, A.M. (1980) 'Towards a Political Economy of Accounting: An Empirical illustration of the Cambridge Controversies', *Accounting, Organizations and Society*, 5 (1): 147–60.

Tinker, A.M. (1985) *Paper Prophets: A Social Critique of Accounting*. London: Holt, Rinehart and Winston.

Tinker, A.M. and Niemark, M.D. (1987) 'The Role of Annual Reports in Gender and Class Contradictions at General Motors: 1917–1976', *Accounting, Organizations and Society*, 12 (1): 71–88.

Tinker, A.M., Lehman, C. and Niemark, M. (1991) 'Falling Down the Hole in the Middle of the Road: Political Quietism in Corporate Social Reporting', *Accounting, Auditing and Accountability Journal*, 4 (2): 28–54.

Tinkler, P. and Jackson, C. (2002) 'In the Dark? Preparing for the PhD Viva', *Quality Assurance in Education*, 10 (2): 86–97.

Tinkler, P. and Jackson, C. (2004) *The Doctoral Examination Process: A Handbook for Students, Examiners and Supervisors*. Maidenhead: Open University.

Tomaksovic-Devey, D., Leiter, J. and Thompson, S. (1994) 'Organizational Survey Nonresponse', *Administrative Science Quarterly*, 39 (3): 439–57.

Tomkins, C. and Groves, R. (1983) 'The Everyday Accountant and Researching his Reality', *Accounting Organizations and Society*, 8 (4): 361–74.

Trimbath, S. (2006) 'Financial Ratios in Quantitative data Analysis: A Practical Guide', in Z. Hoque (ed.), *Methodological Issues in Accounting Research: Theories and Methods*. London: Spiramus Press. pp. 411–25.

Trotman, K.T. (1996) *Research Methods for Judgment and Decision-Making Studies in Auditing.* Melbourne: Coopers & Lybrand.

Trotman, K.T. and Wright, W.F. (1996) 'Recency effects, Task Complexity, Decision Mode and Task Specific Experience', *Behavioral Research in Accounting*, 8: 175–98.

Trubik, E. and Smith, M. (2000) 'Developing a Model of Customer Defection in the Australian Banking Industry', *Managerial Auditing Journal*, 15 (5): 199–208.

Truscott, D.M., Swars, S., Smith, S., Thornton-Reid, F., Zhao, Y., Dooley, C., Williams, B., Hart, I. and Matthews, M. (2010) 'A Cross-Disciplinary Examination of the Prevalence of Mixed Methods in Educational Research: 1995–2005', *International Journal of Social Research Methodology*, 13 (4): 317–28.

Tuan Mat, T.Z., Smith, M. and Djajadikerta, H. (2011) 'Management Accounting and Organizational Change: An Exploratory Study in Malaysia', *Journal of Applied Management Accounting Research*, 9 (2): 51–80.

Tucker, B.P. and Lowe, A. (2014) 'Practitioners are from Mars; Academics are from Venus? An investigation of the research-practice gap in management accounting', *Accounting, Auditing and Accountability Journal* 27 (3): 394–425

Tucker, B.P. and Parker, L.D. (2014) 'In Our Ivory Towers? The Research–Practice Gap in Management Accounting', *Accounting and Business Research*, 44 (2): 104–43.

Tucker, B.P., Parker, L.D. and Merchant, K.A. (2016) 'With a Little Help from Our Friends: An Empirical Investigation of Co-Authoring in Accounting Research', *British Accounting Review*, 48 (2): 185–205.

Tversky, A. and Kahneman, D. (1973) 'Availability: A Heuristic for Judging Frequency and Probability', *Cognitive Psychology*, 5 (2): 677–95.

Van der Laan, G., Van Ees, H. and Van Wittesloostuijn, A. (2008) 'Corporate Social and Financial Performance: An Extended Stakeholder Theory and Empirical Test with Accounting Measures', *Journal of Business Ethics*, 79 (3): 299–310.

Van der Stede, W., Young, S.M. and Chen, C.X. (2005) 'Assessing the Quality of Evidence in Empirical Management Accounting Research: The Case of Survey Studies', *Accounting, Organizations and Society*, (30) 5: 655–84.

Vroom, V.H. (1964) *Work and Motivation.* New York: Jossey-Bass.

Vroom, V.H. and Yetton, P.W. (1973) *Leadership and Decision Making.* Pittsburgh, PA: University of Pittsburgh Press.

Walker, M. and Tsalta, A. (2001) *Corporate Financial Disclosure and Analyst Forecasting Activity: Preliminary Evidence for the UK.* London: Certified Accountants Educational Trust.

Wallace, W.A. (1991) *Accounting Research Methods: Do Facts Speak for Themselves?* Holmwood, IL: Irwin.

Watson, J.D. (1968) *The Double Helix.* New York: Penguin Books.

Watts, T. and McNair, C.J. (2008) 'Trigger Points: Enhancing Generic Skills in Accounting Education Through Changes to Teaching Practice', *Australasian Accounting Business and Finance Journal*, 2 (2): 34–51.

Watts, R. and Zimmerman, J.L. (1978) 'Towards a Positive Theory of the Determination of Accounting Standards', *The Accounting Review*, 53: 112–33.

Watts, R. and Zimmerman, J.L. (1986) *Positive Accounting Theory.* Englewood Cliffs, NJ: Prentice Hall.

Watts, R.L. and Zimmerman, J.L. (1990) 'Positive Accounting Theory: A Ten Year Perspective', *The Accounting Review*: 131–56.

Weber, R.P. (1985) *Basic Content Analysis.* Beverley Hills, CA: SAGE.

Weber, R.P. (1990) *Basic Content Analysis*, 2nd edn. Newbury Park, CA: SAGE.

Weber, S.J. and Cooke, T.D. (1972) 'Subject Effects in Laboratory Research: An Examination of Subject Roles, Demand Characteristics and Valid Inference', *Psychological Bulletin*, 77 (4): 273–95.

Welsh, E.M. (2002) 'Dealing with Data: Using NVivo in the Qualitative Data Analysis Process', *Forum Qualitative Social Research*, 3 (2): 26–8.

Wilcox, J. (1971) 'A Simple Theory of Financial Ratios as Predictors of Failure', *Journal of Accounting Research*, 9 (2): 389–95.

Williamson, O. (1975) *Markets and Hierarchies: Analysis and Anti-Trust implications. A Study in the Economics of Internal Organisation*. New York: Free Press.

Williamson, O.E. (1979) 'Transaction-Cost Economics: The Governance of Contractual Relations', *Journal of Law and Economics*, October: 233–61.

Williamson, O. (1985) *The Economic Institutions of Capitalism: Firms, Markets, Relational Contracting*. New York: Free Press.

Willmott, H. (2008) 'Listening, Interpreting, Commending: A Commentary on the Future of Interpretive Accounting Research', *Critical Perspectives on Accounting*, 19 (6): 920–5.

Wold, H. (1985) 'Partial Least Squares', in S. Kotz and N.L. Johnson (eds), *Encyclopedia of Statistical Sciences*, Vol. 6. New York: Wiley. pp. 581–91.

Woodward, J. (1965) *Industrial Organization: Theory and Practice*. Oxford: Oxford University Press.

Wooldridge, J.M. (2002). *Economic Analysis of Cross Section and Panel Data*. London: The MIT Press.

Wooldridge, J.M. (ed.) (2009) *Introductory Econometrics: A Modern Approach*, 4th edn. Mason, OH: South-Western Cengage Learning.

Xia, D.L. and Zhu, S. (2009) 'Corporate Governance and Accounting Conservatism in China', *China Journal of Accounting Research*, 2 (2), 81–107.

Yin, R.K. (1984) *Case Study Research: Design and Methods*. Beverley Hills, CA: SAGE.

Yin, R.K. (2010) *Case Study Research: Design and Methods*, 4th edn. Thousand Oaks, CA: SAGE.

Yin, R.K. (2013) *Case Study Research: Design and Methods*, 5th edn. Thousand Oaks, CA: SAGE.

Yoon, Y. and Swales, G. (1991) 'Predicting Stock Market Performance: A Neural Network Approach', *Proceedings of the IEEE 24th Annual international Conference of Systems Science* (January), IEEE Computer Society Press, Hawaii. pp. 156–62.

Young, S.M. (1996) 'Survey Research in Management Accounting: A Critical Assessment', in A.J. Richardson (ed.), *Research Methods in Accounting: Issues and Debates*, Vancouver: The Canadian General Accountants Research Foundation. pp. 55–68.

Young, S.M. and Selto, F.H. (1993) 'Explaining Cross-sectional Workgroup Performance Differences in a JIT Facility: A Critical Appraisal of a Field-based Study', *Journal of Management Accounting Research*, 5: 300–26.

Zavgren, C.V. (1985) 'Assessing the Vulnerability of Failure of American Industrial Firms: A Logistic Analysis', *Journal of Business Finance and Accounting*, 12 (1): 19–45.

Zimmerman, J.L. (2001) 'Conjectures Regarding Empirical Managerial Accounting Research', *Journal of Accounting and Economics*, 32 (1–3): 411–27.

Zmijewski, M.E. (1984) 'Methodological Issues Related to the Estimation of Financial Distress Prediction Models', *Journal of Accounting Research* (Supplement), 22: 59–86.

Index

Abdel-Khalik, A.R., 20, 40, 127
Abdolmohammadi, M., 128
Abernethy, M., 9, 120, 121
abnormal performance index, 6
Abrahamson, E., 123
absenteeism, 158
abstracts, 19, 20, 194, 205, 207, 208
Accounting and Business Research (journal), 52
Accounting, Auditing and Accountability Journal
    (journal), 47, 52
Accounting & Finance (journal), 9, 47
Accounting Organizations and Society (journal), 8, 19,
    47, 144, 160
The Accounting Review (journal), 8, 20, 47, 52, 79, 144,
    202, 208
accounting change, 20, 182, 206
accounting narratives, 112, 120, 123, 124, 185
accounting policy change, 12, 183
accounting research
    critical approach to, 7–13
    theory and, 1–7
accounting stereotypes, 43
action research, 34, 69, 163–165
actor-network theory, 40, 42, 44, 162, 167, 173
activity based costing, 51, 167
adaptive structuration theory, 40
Adelberg, A.H., 52
Aerts, W., 125
agency theory, 6, 39, 40, 42–43, 129, 195
Agarwal, V., 2, 112
Agnew, N.M., 64–66
Ahrens, T., 19, 121, 162, 167
Aiken, M., 146
Ajinkya, B.B., 40, 127
Alam, M., 43–44, 162
Alcouffe, S., 44
Aljifri, K., 8
Allison, P.D., 98, 99, 109, 110
Altman, E.I., 2, 43, 77, 101, 112
Amernic, J.H., 124, 185
Amir, E., 123
AMOS (software), 97, 106

analysis of variance (ANOVA), 75, 103–104, 115,
    133, 138
analytic induction, 174
Anderson, M.J., 125, 176
Anderson, T.W., 96, 105
Andon, P., 162
Andrews, F.M., 155
anonymity, 159
Ansari, S., 42
appendices, 210
Appleby, Sir Humphrey, 6
archival research
    content analysis and, 185
    cross-section data and, 163, 179–182
    informed consent and, 59, 61
    regression-type methods of analysis and, 65–66
    sources and, 12, 31, 122, 179–185
    time-series data and, 180–181
    validity and, 181–183
Argenti, J., 41
Argyris, C., 48
Aristotle, 44
Armstrong, P., 47, 208
Arrington, C.E., 4, 46–47
Arthur Andersen, 13
Ashton, A.H., 19
Ashton, R.H., 19, 96, 125, 128, 129
Askarany, D., 144, 146
Assal, H., 156
Atkinson, A.A., 121
Atkinson, P., 67
ATLAS/ti (software), 120
attribution theory, 46
audit judgement, 40, 122, 128, 208
Australian Business Deans Council (ABDC), 200, 213,
    215–218
autocorrelation errors, 109

backlog measures, 162
Baddeley, M.C., 98, 109
Baiman, S., 42, 43
Baines, A., 97, 106

Baker, C.R., 18, 46
balanced scorecard, 51, 167, 171
Baldvinsdottir, G., 42
Ball, R., 6, 42, 45
Ballantine, J., 167
Baltagi, B.H., 97, 98, 108, 110, 111
Bandura, A., 43
bankruptcy prediction, 2, 123, 183–184
Barrett, M., 74
Barrow, J.C., 48
Barrowclough, D.V., 98, 109
Baruch, Y., 129, 144
Baskerville, R.L., 163
battery length, 155–156
Bauman, M.P., 19
Baxendale, S., 69
Bayne, C.K., 113
Beattie, V.A., 124, 213
Beaver, W.H., 43
Becker, S., 48
Bedford, N.M., 41–42
Behavioral Research in Accounting (journal),
    144, 160
behavioural accounting research, 40
Bell, J., 42
Bem, D.J., 43
Beneish, M.D., 77
Bennett, R., 2
Berelson, B., 122
Berry, A.J., 44, 46, 169, 170
Bettman, J.R., 123
Bettner, M.S., 18, 46
between-methods triangulation, 169
between-subjects factorial design, 131
Biddle, G.C., 43, 131
Big Bang Theory, 2
Birnberg, J.G. 49, 158
Bisbe, J., 48, 129
Black, F., 43
Black, B.S., 108
Blau, P.C., 44
Bloomfield, R., 60
Bloor, M., 174
The Bodyline Controversy (Le Quesne), 26
Bollen, K.A., 95, 106
Bonner, S.E., 130, 214
bonus-plan schemes, 162
bottlenecks, 33
bounded rationality, 41
Bourn, M., 164
Bouwman, M.J., 125, 176
Bowman, E.H., 123
Boys, P.G., 176
Braaten, D., 44

Bradman, Don, 25–28
Bragg, Sir Lawrence., 24–25
Brannick, T., 164
Brennan, N.M., 124, 185
Briers, M., 50
Briggs, S.P., 43
Brignall, S., 167
Brinn, T., 213
Broadbent, J., 46
Brookfield, D., 181
Brown, B.M., 12, 85, 220
Brown, C.E., 132
Brown, D.A., 144
Brown, L.D., 213
Brown, P., 6, 40, 42
Brownell, P.
    on theory, 1, 19, 171, 183
    on archival research, 183
    on budgetary participation, 37–39, 49
    on experimental research, 128, 132, 135, 136
    on fieldwork, 164
    on survey research, 143, 144, 160
    on validity, 135–138
Bryer, R.A., 47
Bryman, A., 149, 165
Buchanan, D., 164
budgetary control, 49, 50
budgetary participation, 39, 45, 135, 145
Burgstahler, D. 77
Burns, J., 42, 48
business innovation, 22
Byrne, B.M., 106

Callon, M., 44
Campbell, D.T., 44, 131, 136, 169
Campbell, J.E., 125
Canning, J.B., 42
capital markets research, 208
capital structure, 43, 204
Carpenter, V.L., 170
Carruthers, B.G., 42
carry-over effects, 133
case study research, 73–74, 160, 163, 167, 172, 174
Casey, C.J., 136
categorical scales (itemised scales), 76
causal links, 7, 22, 127
Chain, Ernst, 44
Chalmers, K. 19
Chang, C., 19, 107
Chapman, C., 19, 48, 158, 167
Chargaff, Ernst, 26
Checkland, P., 18
Chen, J., 44
Cheng, M., 105, 137

Chenhall, R.H., 48
chi-square test, 13, 75, 82, 85, 100
choice of method, 10, 72
Chong, K.M., 96, 106
Chong, V.K., 43, 96, 106
Christensen, L.B., 138
Chua, W.F., 149, 164, 171, 173
Church of Latterday Saints, 31
Clapham, S.E., 123
Clatworthy, M., 196
climate change, 80
Clor-Proell, S.M., 45
co-authorship, 69, 213
Coad, A.F., 46
coding, 49, 120–121, 122, 149, 153, 158, 171
coefficient of correlation, 75, 86
Coffey, A., 165
Coghlan, D., 164
cognitive anthropology, 173
cognitive dissonance theory, 45
cognitive psychology, 43
cognitive style, 134
Cohen, J.R., 51
Cole, C.J., 19
Collier, P.M., 46
Collins, F., 97, 106
Colombo, R., 144, 155
comparative scales, 76, 155
COMPUSTAT, 181
concepts, 38
conceptual frameworks, 23–24, 42, 119
conceptual schema, 23
conceptual specification, 49
conditional relationships, 131
conference papers, 200, 205, 207
confidentiality, 59, 159
conflicting messages, 45
conflict theory, 44
confounding variables, 132
Connole, H., 5
Conrad, L., 46
construct validity
    definition of, 37–40
    experimental research and, 135–136, 145
    field research and, 172
    overview, 58–59
    qualitative research and, 121
constructs, 38
consulting, 163, 166, 202, 205
Contemporary Accounting Research (journal), 47,
    144, 208
content analysis, 107, 120–121, 122–125, 184–185, 196
contingency theory, 40, 48, 50, 105
control groups, 127, 131, 133, 139, 140

convenience sampling, 130
Cooke, T.D., 130, 136, 140
Cooper, D.C., 84, 98
Cooper, D.J., 47, 169
Cooper, R., 167
Coppage, R.E., 69
Corbin, J., 49, 50, 175
corporate failure theory, 43, 123
corporate governance research, 184, 185
correlation coefficients, 75, 86, 156
counterbalancing, 133
Courtis, J., 52
Covaleski, M.A., 42, 49
covert observation, 141, 164–165
covert research, 67, 165
Cox, J., 201
Craig, R., 124, 185
Cramer's V, 75, 91, 94
creative accounting, 77
Crichton, Michael, 7
Crick, Francis, 24–25
cricket, 26–28
critical case studies, 173
critical-feminist research, 47
critical-interpretive research, 47
critical-Marxist research, 47
Critical Perspectives on Accounting and Accounting
    (journal), 47
critical-radical research, 47
critical research, 4, 8, 173
critical theory, 46–47, 206, 208
critique of research, 9
Cronbach's Alpha Coefficient, 39, 101, 154, 157, 171
cross-section data, 108, 146, 180–182
cross-sectional dependence test, 99
cross-tabulations, 85–87
cultural issues, 70
Cushing, B.E., 12
customer defection, 115
Cuthbert, P., 40
CVP analysis, 41
Cyert, R.M., 41

data collection
    data management and, 78–80, 119
    measurement issues and, 79
    in qualitative research, 17, 78–79
    research methods and, 73–75
    sample selection and, 74
    survey research and, 151–154
data display, 119
data interpretation, 119
data management, 78–79, 119
data mining, 12, 119

data reduction, 119
data transformation, 74
data triangulation, 31, 170
database software, 77, 179, 181
D'Aveni, R.A., 123
Datar, S.M., 201
Davila, T., 48
De Sanctis, G., 46
deception, 130
Dechow, P.M., 77
decision theory, 43
decision-making heuristics, 20, 140, 176
deductive reasoning, 2, 3, 21–23, 119
Deegan, C., 44
Defond, M., 77
Degeling, P., 47, 164
degrees of freedom, 83
Deming, W.E., 49
Demski, J.S., 42, 129
Dent, J.F., 121, 173
Denzin, N.K., 174
descriptive case studies, 170
descriptive statistics, 7, 80–84
deviant case studies, 169
Diamond, S.S., 146, 156
Dichev, I., 77
Dickson, W.J., 139
DICTION software, 120
diffusion of innovation, 22, 46
DiMaggio, P.J., 46
differences in sample means, 80–89
Dikolli, S., 168
Dillard, J., 46
Dillman, D.A., 145, 152–153
Dirsmith, M.W., 12
discourse analysis, 121, 124
discretionary accruals, 77
discriminant analysis, 98, 99–101, 111–113
dissertations, 187–195
Ditton, J., 165
Djajidikerta, H.G., 107
DBA, 197
DNA, 25–26, 80
doctoral supervision, 176, 187
Donaldson, T., 41
Dooley, D., 63
double-blind reviews, 202, 211
The Double Helix (Watson), 25
Dowd, K., 8
Drury, C., 170, 201
Dugdale, D., 42, 51
dummy variables, 110
Dunk, A.S., 19, 56, 105
Dunlap, A.J., 41

Durbin-Watson statistic, 102
Dwyer, P.D., 47
dysfunctional behaviour, 50

Eames, J., 77
earnings management, 77
Easterby-Smith, M., 53
ecological validity, 138
econometrics, 171
economics, 41–43, 129, 167, 208
editorial process, 203–206
Edwards, R.S., 41
Edwards, S.P., 36
Efficient Markets Hypothesis (EMH), 7
Eisenbeis, R.A., 114
Eisenhardt, K., 121
electronic interviews, 159
Elliott, W.B., 135
email surveys, 143, 147, 159
Emory, C.W., 84, 98
Engels, Frederick, 44
Englund, H., 46
Enron, 208
environmental disclosures, 123
Ericsson, K.A., 125
Ernst & Young, 13
Espeland, W., 42
ethical guidelines, 69, 130
ethics quiz, 64–66. See also research ethics
ethnographic studies, 125, 167
ethnomethodology, 125, 173
European Accounting Review (journal), 47
Euske, K.J., 42
examiners and examination process, 187–197
expectancy theory, 45
experiential learning cycle, 22,
experimental case studies, 163
experimental research
    guidelines for, 127–141
    problem statement and, 127–128
    research design and, 73, 127–133, 141
    theory and context in, 127, 129–131
    validity and, 127, 136, 140
    See also quasi-experimental research
explanatory case studies, 163
exploratory case studies, 163
external validity
    archival research and, 181–183
    definition of, 39–40
    experimental research and, 132, 138, 164
    grounded theory and, 174
    overview, 59–60
    qualitative research and, 121, 172
    quasi-experimental research and, 139

extreme case studies, 163
Ezzamel, M., 46, 164

factorial design, 131–134
failure prediction models, 12, 43, 57, 112, 114, 138, 183–184
Fama, E.F., 43
family tree research, 31–32
Federalist papers, 122
Feltham, G.A., 42, 129
feminist-interpretive research, 47
Feroz, E.H., 170
Ferreira, L.D., 49, 163, 164
Ferris, K.R., 46
Festinger, L., 45
Fidell, L.S., 154
Fiedler, B., 85, 220
field studies, 32, 73, 119–121, 138, 160, 163, 164. *See also* case study research
Fielding, N.G., 120
fieldwork, 171–175
finance, 42–43
financial distress, 114
Financial Times Index (UK), 181
Finn, J.A., 190
firm-specific effects, 109
Fiske, D.W., 169
fixed effects model, 98, 109
Flamsteed, John, 30
Fleischman, R.K., 213
Fleming, Alexander, 44
Florey, Howard, 44
Floyd, S.W., 213
Flyvbjerg, B., 169
focus groups, 147
Fogarty, T. J., 96, 106, 120, 184, 205, 208, 212
form-oriented content analysis, 123, 124, 185
Foster, G., 19, 161, 163, 180
Foucauldian Theory, 40
Francis, J.R., 4
Franklin, Rosalind, 25
Frazier, K.B., 123
Frederick, D., 129
Freeman, R.E., 43
Friedman, A.O., 43
Friedman, M., 41
Frydman, H.E., 113

Gaffikin, M., 167
Galilei, Galileo, 30
Gantt charts, 16
Gendron, Y., 5
generalisability, 121, 138
Gerakos, J., 77

Gerdin, J., 19, 46, 48
Gibbert, M., 172
Gibbins, M., 49, 67, 127
Giddens, A., 45
Gill, J., 20, 159
Glaser, B.G., 49, 50 174, 175
global financial crisis, 208
Glyptis, L.G., 46
goal-setting theory, 43
Goddard, A., 50
Golafshani, N., 166
Goldratt, E.M., 201
Gordon, M.J., 77
Graham, J.R., 77
Gramling, A.A., 19
Granlund, M., 1, 50–51, 167, 213
graphic scales (linear scales), 76
Graves, C., 114, 162
Gray, R., 41, 185, 206
Green, D., 48
Greve, J., 19, 48
Grey, C., 67
Griffiths, E.E., 46
Griffiths, T., 77
Griffiths, I., 201
grounded theory, 3, 23, 49–50, 119, 121, 174–176
group dynamics, 48
Groves, R., 40
Guilding, C., 146
Gummerson, E., 44
Gurd, B.G., 19, 175, 176
Guthrie, J., 208, 213

Habermasian Theory, 40, 46
Hage, J., 146
Hair, J.F., 105, 107, 110
Halpin, A.W., 146
Hamer, M., 113
Hamilton, D.L., 43
Hammersley, M., 67
Hammond, T., 47
Han, J., 53
Harris, Sir Henry, 44
Harrison, John, 29–30
Harte, J.M., 176
Hartmann, F.G.H., 8, 19, 48, 56, 70, 95, 105
Hartmann, L., 69–70
Harvard Business Review (journal), 205
Harvey-Jones, J., 34
Haskins, M.E., 12
Hausman specification test, 99, 110
Hawking, S., 2, 7
Hawthorne Experiments, 32, 139–140, 168

Healy, M., 166
Healy, P.M., 3
Heatley, Norman, 44
Heiman, V., 131
Heisenberg's Uncertainty Principle, 6–7, 166
Henri, J-F., 19
Hepworth, S.R., 77
Herzberg, F., 45
heterogeneity bias, 109
heteroskedasticity, 96, 101, 110
heuristics, 43, 129, 140
hidden messages, 122
high-risk projects, 20
Hines, R., 3, 47, 167
Hirst, M., 49, 50
Hobbes, Thomas, 44
Höglund, H., 77
hold-out samples, 113, 171
Holsti, O.R., 122
Holy Grail, 32–34
Homans, G., 44
homoskedasticity, 96, 101, 110
Hopper, T., 42, 152, 152–163
Hopwood, A.G., 3, 47, 49, 163
Hoque, Z., 41,163, 170
Houghton, K.A., 11, 12, 158, 184
House, R.J., 17
Howard, K., 15
Hoyers, R.E.D., 110
Hronsky, J.J.F., 158
Hsiao, C., 108
Huberman, A.M., 120, 172
Hull, R.P., 213
Hult, G.T.M., 96, 105
human relations theory, 49
Humphrey, C., 167, 208
Hunt, E.B., 122
Hussain, S., 213
Hussainey, K., 8
Hutchison, P.D., 143, 147
Huygens, Christiaan, 29
hypotheses, 38, 58–59, 74, 129

illustrative case studies, 168
impression management, 67, 124, 185, 193
Inanga, E. L., 50
incentive signalling theory, 43
incentives, 129–130
income determination, 41
income increasing policies, 77
inductive reasoning, 2–3, 23, 119
information economics theories, 42
information overload, 140
informed consent, 67, 68–70, 159

Ingram, R.W., 123
innovation diffusion, 22
institutional theory, 41, 46
instrumentation, 135, 136, 137, 144, 145, 183
inter-coder reliability, 121, 124
interaction terms, 104, 132, 138
intellectual property, 192
internal validity
    definition of, 39–40
    experimental research and, 121, 136
    fieldwork and, 164, 183
    overview, 59–60
    quasi-experimental research and, 139–140
    survey research and, 143
internet surveys, 143, 160
interpretive research, 4–5, 47
interval scales, 75
intervening variables, 55, 139
interview methods, 120–122, 147, 157, 163, 171
investigator triangulation, 170
Irvine, H., 167
itemised scales (categorical scales), 76, 154
Ittner, C., 48, 50, 51, 107, 158, 213

Jack, L., 46
Jackson, C., 188
Jager, P. D., 98, 109, 110
Jankowicz, A.D., 163
Jardine, D.R., 28
Jaworski, B.J., 97, 106
Jay, A., 5–6
Jazayeri, M., 40, 42
Jensen, M.C., 43
Jiambalvo, J., 77
job performance, 50
Johannson. I.-L., 42
Johnson, D.M., 43
Johnson, P., 20, 159
Jones, C.L., 19
Jones, M.J., 19, 52, 123, 185, 196
Jones, J., 77
Jones, T.C., 42, 51
Jönsson, S., 46, 173
Jöreskog, K.G., 96, 105
Journal of Accounting, Accountability and Performance (journal), 19
Journal of Accounting and Economics (journal), 144, 208
Journal of Accounting Literature (journal), 18, 46
Journal of Accounting Research (journal), 144, 206, 208
Journal of Management Accounting Research (journal), 144, 160
journal rankings, 214, 215–218

journals
  grounded theory and, 174
  professional journals, 204, 214
  refereed journals, 8–10, 47, 52, 144, 182, 202,
    206–208
  survey research and, 143, 209
Joyce, E.J., 43, 131
Judd, C.L., 75

Kahneman, D., 32, 43, 129
Kaplan, R.S., 51, 163, 166, 167, 168
Kasanen, E., 170
Kelle, U., 120
Kelly, A., 213
Kelly, M., 43–44
Kelley, H.H., 45
Kelly-Newton, L., 123
Kendall's tau, 13
Kent, P., 8
Keon, J., 156
Kestel, J.M., 12, 85, 220
keyword searches, 79, 120, 124
Khlif, H., 19
Kholeif, A., 46
Kidder, L.H., 75
Kighir, A., 78
Kiley, M., 190
Kinney, W., 12, 220
Kirk, J., 163
Kline, R.B., 105
Knopf, J.W., 53
Koele, P., 176
Koh, H.C., 105
Kolb, D.A., 22
Kools, S., 175
Kramer, S.S., 125, 128
Krippendorff, K.H., 123, 124, 184, 185
Krumweide, K.R., 155
Kruskal–Wallis test, 76, 82, 96–97
Kuhn, T.S., 5

labour process theory, 44, 46
Lachenbruch, P.A., 102, 113
Lang, M.H., 8, 55
Langfield-Smith, K., 19, 48, 96–97, 106, 108
Lapsley, I., 20, 67
Larcker, D.F., 48, 50–51, 158, 176, 213
Larwood, Harold, 28
Laswell, H., 122
latent variables, 39, 101, 105, 107, 122
Latour, B., 44
Lauer, T.W., 125
Laughlin, R.C., 46, 47, 175
Lawler, E., 45

Lawrence, S., 42
LBDQ (leader behaviour description questionnaire),
  146
Le Quesne, L., 26
leader–participation model, 48
learning theory, 129, 132
LeClere, M.J., 103, 114
Leake, J., 80
Lee, B., 167
Lee, N., 54
Lee, R.M., 120
Lee, T.A., 18, 208
legitimacy theory, 44
Lehman, G., 47
Lehmann, C.M., 43
Lennox, C., 114
Lessig, V.P., 176
Libby, R., 19, 129, 131, 183
Lightbody, M., 50
Likert scales, 75, 76, 147, 149, 154, 164, 189
Lillis, A.M., 121, 122, 158, 163, 170, 171
Linacre, S., 143, 147, 214
linear discriminant analysis (LDA), 99–101, 111–113
linear programming, 41
linear scales (graphic scales), 76, 105
Lings, I., 54
Lipe, M., 129
LISREL (Linear Structural Equations Model for
  Latent Variables), 89, 97, 106
literature reviews, 20, 21, 52–54, 183, 191
Littleton, A.C., 40
Livingstone, J.L., 45
Lo, A.W., 113
Locke, A.E, 43
Loebekke, J.K., 12
logistic (LOGIT) regressions, 102–104, 112, 113–116
Lomax, R.G., 105
Long, J.S., 95, 106
longitude, 27–29
Longitude (Sobel), 29
longitudinal studies, 140, 146, 164
The Lost World (book/film), 7
Lowe, A., 213
Lowe, E.A., 46, 157
Luft, J., 19, 48, 51, 55, 129
Lukka, K., 41, 170, 173
Lundholm, R.J., 8, 55
Lye, J., 50
Lyne, S.R., 43
Lynn, J., 5–6
Lys, T., 80, 152, 169

MacDonald, A.P. Jr, 145
MacIntosh, N.B., 44, 46, 173

MacKay, D.B., 128
MacMillan, A.C., 123
Magenheim, E.B., 181
Magilke, M.J., 135
Magness, V., 43
Mahoney, T.A., 145
mail surveys, 143–146, 151–152, 182
Maines, L.A., 135
Major, M., 42, 163
Malina, M., 121, 158, 170, 171
Malmi, T., 1, 50–51, 167, 213
Malsch, B., 5, 47, 51, 119
management accounting change, 40, 129, 163, 170
management control systems (MCS), 48
managerial risk, 123
Mann–Whitney U-test, 75–76, 82, 89–91
Manzoni, J-F., 121, 164, 169
March, J.G., 41
Marginson, D.E.W., 158
market efficiency, 43
market forces theory, 50
Markowitz, H., 42
Maruyama, G.M., 95, 106
Marx, Karl, 44, 46
Maskelyne, Nevil, 30
Maslow, A.H., 45
Mason, J., 172
Massey, A., 34
matching, 133, 139, 184
maturation effects, 133, 136
Mayo, E., 32, 139, 168
maximum likelihood measures, 105
McCarthy Information, 181
McClelland, D.C., 45
McConnell, D., 123
McGowan, S., 19
McIver, R.P., 108
McNair, C.J., 45
McLeay, S. 74, 114
mean-deviation methods, 110
meaning-oriented content analysis, 122, 124, 185
measurement, 22–23, 75–78, 158, 206
measurement error, 155
measures of association,75, 84–85, 91, 156
Meckling, W.H., 43
mediating variables, 55, 139
Meindl, J.R., 123
Mentzer, J.T., 19
Merchant, K.
    on case study research, 160, 164, 169
    on fieldwork, 163
    on grounded theory, 49, 121, 173
    on LBDQ, 146
    on publication, 208

Merchant, K. cont.
    on qualitative research, 168
    on survey research, 1, 153, 158, 164, 171
Merkl-Davies, D.M., 124, 185
Meyer, M.W., 50–51
Mia, L., 45, 56
microeconomic theory, 40
Milani, K.W., 38–39, 135, 145
Miles, M.B., 120, 172
Miller, M.H., 43
Miller, M.L., 163
misspecification errors, 58–59, 109, 170
mixed methods, 68, 163, 170
Modell, S., 170
modelling relationships, 54–58
moderated regression analysis (MRA), 56, 98, 104
moderating variables, 56
Modigliani, F., 43
Moers, F., 8, 19, 48, 56, 70, 95, 105
Moizer, P., 12, 13
Moll, J., 163
Moore, D.L., 155
Morgan, S.J., 159
Morgan, W., 169
Morris, R., 181
Moses, I., 189–190
Mosteller, F., 122
motivation, 9, 45
Mueller, D.C., 181
Muhr, T., 120
Mullins, G., 190
multiple-item scales, 76
multiple methods, 120–121, 158, 163, 167, 170
multicollinearity, 96, 101, 108
multivariate models, 98–116
multivariate analysis of variance (MANOVA), 98, 104, 115
Mundy, J., 163
Myers, C.S., 140
Myers, S., 43

narrative data, 52, 79, 112, 120, 123, 124, 185, 196
National Health and Medical Research Council (Australia), 64
Nazari, J., 147, 160
Nelson, R.R., 41
neo-classical theory, 41
neural networks, 78
Newell, A., 125
Newton, Sir Isaac, 3, 29
Niemark, M.D., 4, 47, 169
NIRD (new, interesting, replicable, defendable), 20, 206
Nisbett, R., 32
nominal scales, 75

non-linear models, 77
non-normality, 77
non-parametric statistics, 74, 76, 83, 89–98
non-response bias, 144, 146, 153–156, 158
non-response error, 156
non-sampling error, 156
non-verbal signals, 163
normative theory, 40
Norreklit, H., 170
Northcott, D., 143, 147, 214
Norton, D.P., 51, 167, 168
Nouri, H., 19
NUD*IST (software), 79, 120, 172
Nunnally, J., 135
NVivo (software), 120

Oakes, L., 47
objective measurement, 3, 146
objectives, 19, 20
observation, 120
O'Donovan, G., 44
O'Hara, M., 60
Ogden, S.G., 158
Ohlson, J.S., 103, 112, 114
Omar, A., 74
omitted variables, 109, 170
online publication, 204, 206
online surveys, 132
Onsi, M., 158
option pricing model, 43
oral defence, 187–197
ordinal scales, 75, 76, 138
ordinary least squares (OLS), 77, 98–103, 111
organisation theory, 40, 48
organisational behaviour, 45–48, 170
Osgood, C.E., 76, 122
Otley, D.T., 48, 49, 105, 122
Ouchi, W.G., 48
Owens, D.L., 41

paired-case t-test, 88
panel data, 97–98, 108–111, 181
paradigm shift, 6, 163
parametric statistics, 74, 83–88
Park, C., 123
Parker, L.D., 148, 171
    on accounting research, 3
    on case study research, 162
    on grounded theory, 50, 175
    on interview process, 159
    on publication, 18, 173, 202, 208, 213
    on qualitative research, 160, 163, 167, 170
    on research-practice gap, 145
    on theory, 40, 46

partial least squares (PLS), 39, 48, 96, 105–108
participant observer field research, 125, 164–166, 174
path analysis, 98, 106–107
Paton, W., 40
Patten, D.M., 44
Patton, M.Q., 119
Pauling, Linus, 25
Peacock, E., 125
Pearson correlation coefficient (r), 75, 91–92, 100
Peat, Marwick & Mitchell, 206
Pedhazur, E.J., 106
Pelto, G.H., 167
Pelto, P.J., 167
penicillin, 44, 80
Perrow, C., 48
Perry, C., 166
Pesaran, H.M., 99, 110
Peters, T.J., 168
PhD theses, 187–194
Phi, 75
Phillips, E.M, 190
Pike, S.W., 64–66
pilot testing, 130, 135–175, 147, 150–151, 156
Plato, 44
PLS (partial least squares), 39, 48, 96, 105–108
political economy, 46
Poole, M.S., 46
Popper, K.R., 7, 23
population validity, 138
Porter, M.E., 50
portfolio risk, 42
positivist approach, 4–5, 17–18, 40, 163, 167
Potter, G.S, 125, 176
Powell, W.W., 46
Power, M., 5, 46, 47
pre-test/post-test control group design, 131
predatory journals, 214
Preston, A.M., 164, 169, 173
Preston, L.E., 41
primary sources, 179
probabilistic (PROBIT) regressions, 102–104, 113–116
process improvement, 35
production bottlenecks, 33
production economics, 40
professional doctorates, 197
professional journals, 191, 200, 204
propaganda, 124
protocol analysis, 111–112
proxy variables, 39, 133, 134, 155, 184
psychology, 43–44, 129
publication
    avenues for, 199–204
    co-authorship and, 69–70, 213

publication *cont.*
  dissertations and, 213
  ethical guidelines for, 69–70, 208–209
  material gains from, 200–201
  topics and contents of papers and, 204–205
  See also journal rankings; journals
publication credit, 66
publishability, 144, 151, 163, 167, 170, 173, 176, 192, 195–196
Pugh, D.S., 190
Puxty, A.G., 46–47, 173

qualitative research
  case study research, 79–81, 162–168, 184
  characteristics of, 164–168
  content analysis, 122
  data analysis in, 119, 172
  data collection in, 31, 40, 79–81
  fieldwork, 162–168
  grounded theory, 23, 49–50, 107, 174
  validity and, 119
  verbal protocol analysis, 172
quality assurance, 192
quality rankings, 214, 215–218
quantitative data analysis
  analysis of variance (ANOVA), 75, 103–104, 115, 133, 138
  descriptive statistics, 82–86
  differences in sample means, 78–79, 86–92
  measures of association, 82, 84–85, 91–95
  multivariate model building, 119–121, 184
quasi-experimental research, 139–142, 168

radical-feminist research, 47
radical research, 47
radical structuralist tradition, 44
Rahaman, A.S., 42
Rajan, M.V., 201
Randall, T., 48
random effects model, 99, 1109, 110–112
random sampling, 67, 137
randomisation, 133, 139
Rapkin, D.P., 44
ratio scales, 76
Rational Choice Theory, 42
Rawls, J., 44
realistic conflict theory, 44
refereed journals, 8–10, 47, 52, 79, 144, 200, 202–203, 188–192, 193–196
references, 195, 209
regression analysis, 98–100, 108–111
reliability, 38, 58–59, 121, 124, 156, 163
repeated measures, 133
replication, 20, 163, 196, 206

research ethics
  deception and, 25, 130
  ethics quiz and, 64–66
  guidelines for, 63, 68–70
  informed consent and, 65, 66–67, 159
  introduction to, 63
  publication and, 68–69, 208–209
research methods, 18, 20, 72–74. *See also specific methods*
Research Opportunities in Auditing (Peat, Marwick & Mitchell), 206
research participants
  incentives and, 130, 137, 167
  professionals as, 131
research problems, 9, 208
research proposals, 19–21, 191
research sequence, 14–17
research topics, 17–19
response error, 139–140
response rates, 144, 149, 153, 155
return on equity, 181–182
Reuters Business Briefing (RBB), 181
review monographs, 19
rival explanations, 2, 7–8, 121, 143, 163, 195
Robbins, S.P., 45
Roberts, E.S., 148
Roberts, J., 41, 45, 46
Roberts, R.W., 47
Robinson, G., 35
Rockness, H.O., 45
Roethlisberger, F.J., 139
Roffey, B.H., 175
Rogers, E.M., 22, 46
Ronen, J., 45
Rosenhahn, D.L., 164
Rosenthal, R., 140
Roslender, R., 46
Ross, L., 32
Ross, S.A., 43
Rossman, G.B., 170
Rowlinson, M., 214
Roychowdhury, S., 77
Rubin, H., 96, 105
Rutherford, B.A., 176
Ryan, R., 40, 168, 171, 213

Salancik, G.R., 123
Salterio, S., 5, 47, 51, 119, 127
sample selection, 10, 74, 149
sample size, 74, 154
sampling, 74, 145, 181
Sandelowski, M., 49
Sapsford, R., 155
Sarafidis, V., 110

Saravanamuthu, K., 41
SAS (statistical software), 147
Saunders, M., 80, 160
Scapens, R.W., 40, 41, 45, 46, 121, 167
Schepanski, A., 130, 133
Scherer, M., 47
Scheule, K., 213
Schneider, W.B., 50
Scholes, M., 43
Schreck, P., 185
Schulz, A.K-D., 134
Schumacker, R.E., 105
Schwenk, C.R., 123
Scott, J., 43
Searcy, D.L., 19
secondary sources, 165, 179, 184
selection bias, 137
self-reported performance, 146
self-perception theory, 43
Selto, F.H., 20, 121, 158, 164, 171
semantic differential, 76
SEM (structural equation modelling) 39, 48, 95–97,
    105–108
semi-structured interviews, 158, 160
sensitivity analysis, 120, 154, 171
Shaffir, W., 121
Shan, Y.G., 108
shareholder theory, 41
Sharp, J.A., 15
Sharpe, W., 42
Shaw, R.W., 157
Shields, J.F., 49, 101
Shields, M.D., 48, 49, 51, 55, 101, 158, 163
Shoemaker, P.A., 19, 123, 185
Shumway, T., 103, 114
Sign test, 82, 89
signalling theory, 38, 54
significance tests, 84
Sikka, P., 47
Silverman, D., 119, 172, 173
Simnett, R., 102, 113
Simon, H.A., 41–42, 125
Simons, R., 48, 169
Simsek, Z., 159
single-blind refereeing, 202, 211
single-item scales, 76
Skype, 143, 148, 188
Slovic, P., 176
Smith, D., 96–97, 106, 108
Smith, K.J., 97
Smith, M.
    analysis of paper by, 10–12
    on archival research, 185
    on content analysis, 124, 185
    on deception, 67, 130

Smith, M. *cont.*
    on experimental research, 45, 130, 134
    on informed consent, 67
    on linear discriminant analysis, 101, 112, 114, 184
    on qualitative research, 162
    on quasi-experimental research, 140
    on regression analysis, 93
    on signalling theory, 38
    on survey research, 144, 146, 160
    on validity, 184
Smith, Terry, 12, 201
So, S., 138, 213
Sobel, D., 28–29
social exchange theory, 44
social identity theory, 44
social learning theory, 43
sociology, 38–39, 43–44, 167
software
    data management and, 78–79, 210
    electronic interviews and, 159
    qualitative research and, 106, 172
    survey research and, 147
Soin, K., 42, 176
Solomon, I., 132
Southwood, K.E., 105
So What? test, 208
Spearman coefficient ('rho'), 75, 91, 92–93
Spence, M., 38, 43
Split-Half Reliability Coefficient, 156
spreadsheet software, 78, 153
Sprinkle, G.B., 130
SPSS (statistical software), 78, 102, 147, 153
stakeholder theory, 41, 43
Stanley, J., 131
STATA (statistical software), 97, 99, 108, 110
statistical packages, 70, 108, 120, 147, 153. *See also*
    AMOS (software); STATA (statistical software)
Staw, B.M., 50, 123
Steady State Theory, 2
Stock, D., 128
Stone, D.N., 19
Stone, P.J., 122
Stone-Geisser test, 108
strategic management accounting, 34–35
strategy development, 26
Strauss, A., 49, 50, 174, 175
Stringer, C., 41
structural equation modelling (SEM), 39, 48, 95–97,
    105–108
structuration theory, 45
structured interviews, 157–158
Stuart, I., 53
student surrogates, 128, 130, 137
Subramaniam, N., 42
suicide notes, 122

Sullivan, J.D., 12
supervision, 176, 187–192
survey research
   data collection and, 143–150
   design and planning issues in, 73, 143–145
   informed consent and, 68
   interview methods and, 157–159
   journals and, 144, 208
   mail surveys, 143–147
   measurement error and, 150–151
   pilot testing and, 147, 150–151, 156
SurveyMonkey, 147
Svenson, O., 140
Swales, G.S., 123
symbolic interactionism, 173
Symon, G., 159
Symonds, E., 147
systematic sampling, 74, 149
systems theory, 40

Tabachnick, B.G., 154
Taffler, R.J.
   on archival research, 185
   on content analysis, 124, 185
   on deception, 130
   on discriminant analysis, 43, 112, 124
   on experimental research, 45, 122, 130
   on failure prediction, 2, 57, 112
   on informed consent, 67
   on linear discriminant analysis, 101
   on quasi-experimental research, 140
   on signalling theory, 38
Tajfel, H., 44
Tarnai, J., 155
task complexity, 129
Tayles, M., 170
telephone interviews, 143, 159
temporal validity, 138
Tennyson, B.M., 123
tertiary sources, 179
Test–Retest Reliability Coefficient, 156
theme-based content analysis, 185
theoretical framework, 9
theoretical saturation, 74
theoretical sensitivity, 49
theory
   accounting research and, 1–7
   definition of, 37
   development of, 23–25, 191, 209
   disconfirmation, 7, 169
   laden-observation, 3
   research proposals and, 20
   sources of, 37–40
   as testable explanation, 6–7
theory triangulation, 167, 169, 170

theses, 187–194
Thompson, J.D., 48
time-series data, 108, 180–182, 204
Tinker, A.M., 4, 46, 169, 173
Tinkler, P., 188
tolerance of ambiguity, 134, 145
Tomaksovic-Devey, D., 155
Tomkins, C., 40
topic selection, 20
Total Design Method (TDM), 153–154
Total Quality Management (TQM), 49
triangulation, 31, 120, 169–170, 184
Trimbath, S., 181, 182
Troiler, T.K., 43
Trotman, K.T.
   on discriminant analysis, 102, 113
   on experimental research, 131, 132, 134, 138
   on informed consent, 67
The Troubleshooter, (television series) 34
Trubik, E., 114
Truscott, D.M., 211
Tsalta, A., 8, 55
Tuanmat Z., 162
Tucker, B.P., 33, 40, 44, 46, 74, 145, 148,
   162, 213
Turner, J., 44
Tuskegee Syphilis study, 33, 63
Tversky, A., 32, 43, 129
Two-stage techniques, 105
Type I/ Type II errors, 113, 115

uncertainty principle, 6–7, 166
understandability, 185
Ung, K., 8
unstructured interviews, 160
utility maximization, 36

validity
   archival research and, 183–185
   definition of, 38–39
   experimental research and, 135–138
   overview, 59
   qualitative research and, 121–122, 163
   quasi-experimental research and, 139–142
   survey research and, 154
   See also construct validity; external validity;
      internal validity
Van der Laan, G., 44
Van der Stede, W.
   on case study research, 163
   on survey research, 10, 144, 146, 147, 151, 154,
      168, 208
variables, 38, 54–58
Veiga, J.F., 159
verbal protocol analysis (VPA), 176

Villarreal, A. 128
Vincent, L., 80, 169
viva voce, 187–197
voluntary disclosure, 8, 54
Vroom, V. H., 45, 48

Wahlen, J.M., 135
Walker, E.G., 122
Walker, M., 8, 55
Wall Street Journal Index (USA), 181
Wallace, D.L., 122, 183
Wallace, W.A., 184
Waterman, R.H., 168
Watson, C.J., 128
Watson, J.D., 24–25
Watts, R.L., 6, 39, 41–43, 45
Wave Theory of Light, 3
web-based surveys, 143
Weber, R.P., 122, 123, 124
Weber, S.J., 130, 140
Welsh, E.M., 120
Weitz, B.A., 123
Wilkins, Maurice, 24–25
Williamson, O.E., 41–42
Willmott, H., 46, 47
Wilson, B.L., 170
window-dressing, 212

winsorising data, 74
Winter, S.G., 41
within-method triangulation, 169
Wold, H., 107
Wood-Harper, A.T., 163
Woodward, J., 48
Wooldridge, J.M., 98, 99, 109, 110–111
word-based content analysis, 122, 185
workshopping papers, 203, 205, 210
work study, 125
Wright, A., 128
Wright, F.B., 213
Wright, W.F., 134

Xia, D.L., 108

Yes Minister (television series), 5–6
Yetton, P.W., 48
Yin, R.K., 163, 168
Yoon, H., 123
Young, S.M., 10, 20, 97, 106, 143–145, 146, 158, 163, 164

Zavgren, C.V., 112
Zhu, S., 108
Zimmerman, J.L., 6, 39, 41–43, 144, 166, 167
Zmijewski, M.E., 114